THE SHI'ITES OF LEBANON

Middle East Studies Beyond Dominant Paradigms
Peter Gran, *Series Editor*

THE SHI'ITES
OF LEBANON

Modernism, Communism,
and Hizbullah's Islamists

RULA JURDI ABISAAB
AND MALEK ABISAAB

Syracuse University Press

First Paperback Edition 2017

17   18   19   20   21   22   6   5   4   3   2   1

∞ The paper used in this publication meets the minimum requirements
of the American National Standard for Information Sciences—Permanence
of Paper for Printed Library Materials, ANSI Z39.48-1992.

For a listing of books published and distributed by Syracuse University Press,
visit www.SyracuseUniversityPress.syr.edu.

ISBN: 978-0-8156-3509-3 (paperback)   978-0-8156-3372-3 (cloth)   978-0-8156-5301-1 (e-book)

Library of Congress has cataloged the hardcover edition as follows:

Abisaab, Rula Jurdi.

The Shi`ites of Lebanon : modernism, communism, and Hizbullah's Islamists /
Rula Jurdi Abisaab and Malek Abisaab. — First edition.

pages cm. — (Middle East studies beyond dominant paradigms)
Includes bibliographical references and index.

ISBN 978-0-8156-3372-3 (cloth : alkaline paper) — ISBN 978-0-8156-5301-1 (ebook)

1. Shiites—Lebanon—Politics and government.   2. Shiites—Lebanon—Social conditions.
3. Islam and politics—Lebanon—History.   4. Hizballah (Lebanon)—History.   5. Lebanon—
Politics and government.   6. Communism—Lebanon—History.   7. Social change—Lebanon—
History.   I. Abisaab, Malek Hassan.   II. Title.   III. Title: Shiites of Lebanon.

DS80.55.S54A25 2014

303.4095692—dc23   2014031582

Manufactured in the United States of America

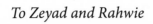

To Zeyad and Rahwie

RULA JURDI ABISAAB is an associate professor at the Institute of Islamic Studies, McGill University. Her research has followed two trajectories: First: The Shi'ite juristic tradition and its historical transformation from the late medieval period to the late seventeenth century. Her previous research focused on religion and power in Safavid Iran, exploring questions of orthodoxy, heresy and the *'ulama*'s legal authority. She also examined the interface of the *shari'a* (Islamic law) with Sufism and heterodoxy. This research was presented in her book *Converting Persia: Religion and Power in Safavid Iran* (2004) and in several articles such as "The Shi'ite 'ulama, the madrasas, and Educational Reform in the Late Ottoman Period, *Ottoman Studies* 36 (2010): 155–83. She is currently preparing another monograph on early *akhbari* (traditionist) thought delineating the discursive intellectual shifts and sociopolitical conditions leading to the refutation of the *usuliyya* (rationalism). Second: Clerical leadership in modern Shi'ite society; Marxism and postcolonial Shi'ite thinkers. Her previous research in these areas is reflected in "Lebanese Shi'ites and the *Marja'iyya*: Polemic in the late 20th Century" (2009), and "Deconstructing the Modular and the Authentic: Husayn Muroeh's Early Islamic History" (2008).

MALEK ABISAAB is an associate professor of history at McGill University, Montreal, Canada, where he teaches courses dealing with the social and political transformation of the Middle East and women in Islamic societies, exploring new conceptual tools and comparative frameworks for discussing gender, labor, and the nation-state in the Middle East. He authored *Militant Women of a Fragile Nation* (Syracuse University Press, 2010); "Shi'ite Peasants and a New Nation in Colonial Lebanon: The *Intifada* (Uprising) of Bint Jubayl, 1936," *Comparative Studies of South Asia, Africa and the Middle East* (November 2009); "Orientalism and Historiography of Arab Women and Work," *Journal of Women of the Middle East and the Islamic World* (HWWA) (Fall 2009); "Contesting Space: Gendered Discourse and Labor among Lebanese Women," in *Geographies of Muslim Women*, ed. Ghazi Falah and Caroline Nagel (New York: Guilford Publications, 2005), 249–74; and "'Unruly'" Workingwomen: Contesting French Colonialism and the National State in Lebanon, 1940-1946," *Journal of Women's History* 16, no. 3 (2004): 55–82; and "Warmed or Burnt by Fire? The Lebanese Maronite Church navigates French Colonial Policies, 1935," *Arab Studies Quarterly* 35, no. 3 (Fall 2013).

Contents

Illustrations

Map

Chart

Acknowledgments

This book synthesizes our research on the intellectual, sociopolitical, and economic history of Lebanon for over a decade. It also builds upon a series of panels and conference papers on Lebanese Shiʿite society, Marxism, and Islamism. Rifaʿat Abou El-Hajj and Peter Gran shaped in no small way the theoretical and conceptual features of these panels.

We are grateful to Juan Cole for proposing to us that we write this book. In addition to him, Wael Hallaq, Peter Gran, Roschanack Shaery, Laila Parsons, Tracey Boisseau, Kirk Hoppe, and Karen Flynn all read parts of this work at various stages in its development offering valuable comments and suggestions. They are not responsible, however, for any errors or shortcomings.

The research trips we took to Lebanon from 2005 until 2009 were supported by McGill University's Start-Up Fund, Internal SSHRC and Research Incentive Funds, and by a grant from the Social Sciences and Humanities Research Council (SSHRC) in Canada. Our archival research and fieldwork in Lebanon was greatly facilitated by the expertise and assistance of Fahd Abisaab, Faris Abisaab, Ghazi Abisaab, Rabiʿ Abisaab, Tareq Abisaab, Walid Abisaab, ʿAbd al-Halim Fadlallah, Dr. ʿAli Fayyad, Rita Hamdan, Fadi Hammoud, Nazih Hamzeh, ʿImad Hashisho, Dr. Bashir ʿIsmat, Amer al-Jurdi, Anis al-Jurdi, Fadi al-Jurdi, Hiba al-Jurdi, ʿIsam al-Jurdi, Janan al-Jurdi, Dr. Bassel Nazha, Dr. Nada Saab, Habib Sadiq, and Dr. Jamal Wakim.

Our appreciations go to Mary Selden Evans and Deanna McCay, the editors at Syracuse University Press, for their distinct professionalism. We deeply thank Annie M. Barva, Karen Flynn, and Jessica LeTourneur Bax for editing our work.

xi

During the writing of this book we lost our mothers, a sister, and a brother in Lebanon. We thank our families and friends for offering us their warm support and encouragement throughout these painful periods. To Michelle Hartman, Wael Hallaq, Charry Karamanoukian, Setrag Manoukian, Laila Parsons, Jamil and Sally Ragep, and Rob Wisnovsky, we owe the unique intellectual environment that enriched our thoughts and lives. We are grateful to the staff and librarians at the Islamic Studies Library at McGill for their help and support. Last but not least, our two sons, Zeyad and Rahwie, managed through their wit and humor to pull us away from our computers when necessary and kept us stimulated as we completed the book. To them, we offer this work and our love.

Prologue

Landscapes of Shiʿite Protest

In 1920, the regions of Jabal ʿAmil (the South) and the Biqaʿ were annexed to Grand Liban, the nation-state carved out of Greater Syria by European colonialists following the disintegration of the Ottoman Empire. Faced with a strong Shiʿite resistance to the annexation, the French mandatory authorities instigated a separate administration for the South, which exercised political surveillance, regulated local and parliamentary elections, and imposed strict economic sanctions and tax penalties.[1] With the imposition of the tobacco monopoly in 1935, the Régie Co-Intéressée Libanaise des Tabacs et Tombac, another phase of peasant and elite resistance to French colonial policies unfolded in the South. Following the clashes between the French and the peasants during the 1936 revolt, more notables and landed dignitaries conceded to the French what they had asked for—namely, forsaking unity with Syria and joining the nation-state of Grand Liban. Meanwhile, the Shiʿite nationalist elite, who supported Grand Liban, tried to redress the marginal representation of the Shiʿites in Parliament and state offices.

The modern state of Grand Liban inscribed sectarian difference in Lebanese citizenry at the same time as it established secular administrative organs and legal procedures critical to the function of modern states. This arrangement fostered recurrent struggles among the Lebanese over decision making, political representation, and economic resources. The French officials and Libanist (Lebanese nationalist) politicians ironically justified sectarian inequalities by recourse to liberal democracy itself—the assurance of Christian freedom and security in a vast Arab-Muslim expanse. The French sugarcoated these inequalities by embellishing the newly found freedoms of the Shi'ites in Grand Liban and the dignity they had been denied under the Sunnite Ottomans. They were referring to freedom of religious worship and permission to administer the shari'a (Islamic law) on the basis of the *Ja'fari madhhab* (school of law). This claim carried the deception of half a truth. Most of the social and economic domains regulated traditionally by the shari'a were paradoxically no longer applicable to the Lebanese state in 1920 because they contradicted its secular foundations and impeded European colonial policies. Family and inheritance laws were the only areas that survived elimination. These laws were codified in a manner that accommodated the state's modern judicial structure and in the case of Lebanon its sectarian divisions. True, the Shi'ite communities in French Syria and Lebanon explored new features of religious worship, but the implementation of the shari'a faced serious hurdles. The jurists hardly considered the institutionalization of the *Ja'fari* courts a triumph for Shi'ism. These courts became a platform for fitting partial aspects of the shari'a into the secular-sectarian framework of the state. A segment of the Shi'ite nationalist elite justified the new polity, but most of the peasants, religious scholars, and intellectuals fluctuated between accommodation to it, ambivalence toward it, and protest against it.

The political struggles in Grand Liban carried ideological, sectarian, regional, and class overtones. They encompassed the integrity of the Islamic legal tradition and Shi'ite religious culture. Orientalist perceptions of Islam and colonial representations of Muslims had found resonance among the Libanists, in particular the Maronite clerical and entrepreneurial elites who played a leading role in legitimizing the emerging polity. Christian Libanists stressed their affinity with Europe and their own "civilizing" role and hence the "modernizing" agency in Grand Liban. Muslim scholars and intellectuals, anxious to ascertain their legitimate place in the Lebanese nation-state, advocated "religious reform" and embellished the "modern" features of their traditions. Indeed, "modernism" encompassed varied ideas, texts, and movements, which received local interpretation. The social-intellectual scene was not divided between the modernists and the traditionists as it is typically presented in Lebanese and Western scholarship. Rather, it was shared by different groups of modernists, each proposing a course of modern "reform" with a range of secular-religious features. This was a time when distinct historical processes had valorized secular modernism, processes starting in the Ottoman period and culminating with European colonial rule and the formation of nation-states.

The approaches that the Shi'ite Iraqi jurists took toward colonial rule and modernism had significant implications for Syrian Lebanese *talaba* (seminary students) who traveled for study at Najaf's *hawza* (seminary). The senior jurists faced unprecedented challenges in ascertaining the relevance of the seminary and the shari'a to the modern believer. Husayn Muroeh, a Lebanese student aspiring to become a jurist, complained about the *hawza*'s eschewal of secular fields of knowledge and its reserve toward the political struggles of the day. From the moment when Muroeh became receptive to modernist Communist ideas until his expulsion from the *hawza* on accusations of heresy, the relationship of knowledge to power was considerably altered for a generation of Syrian Lebanese *talaba*. The Communists, as Peter Gran has argued, did not view secular knowledge and secularism merely as a "tactic." They instead considered them the stepping stone for a modern culture, which "meant fighting Europe but adopting the principles found in Europe, on which science and social science could proceed."[2] The need to modernize, Muroeh suggested, could be resolved by drawing upon the resources of Islamic tradition itself, selecting elements of Western modernity that best resolved local problems.

Najaf and Baghdad provided creative urban milieus for discussing Western modernism and secular ideas. From these milieus, Marxist thought and communism found their way into the houses of the Shi'ite *'ulama* and intellectuals. Three sons of the Lebanese *marja' al-taqlid* (religious-legal exemplar) Sayyid Muhsin al-Amin—Hashim, 'Abd al-Muttalib, and Ja'far—expressed Marxist inclinations. The southerners would say that Hashim had gone to Najaf in pursuit of clerical training only to emerge as "a first rate ideologue" in Marxism.[3] Years later, after clashing with the secretary general of the Syrian Lebanese Communist Party, Hashim declared that "[Muslim] clerics drove me to the path of Marxism and those who brought me back to religion and Islam were the Communists themselves."[4] Communist ideals and local religious culture were intertwined in many Shi'ites' experiences. Aside from defending private religion and the confinement of the shari'a in public legislation, many Communist thinkers turned to Islamic scientific and philosophical traditions to "find" models for "modern progress." To be sure, Marxism in Lebanon and Iraq, far from leading to the demise of religious sensibilities, encouraged new ways of approaching religion and the Islamic tradition, which is not the same as "using" religious symbolisms to promote secular organization of society.

During the 1950s, the curious phrase "Shi'i-Shuyu'i" (a Shi'ite, thus a Communist) became a popular watchword among Arab nationalists such as the Ba'thists and the Nasserites in Iraq and Lebanon. It treated communism as a Shi'ite phenomenon. It also alleged that Shi'ites, unlike Sunnites, were hostile to Arab culture and nationalism.[5] Perhaps the phrase also pertained to the Arab Communist support for the United Nations (UN) decision to partition Palestine into an Arab and an Israeli state in the 1940s. In the end, the term *Communist* evoked a culture of social and political protest associated with the Shi'ites. When Shaykh Muhammad Jawad Mughniyya, a distinguished Lebanese jurist, echoed leftist concerns during his attacks on the landed elites and deputies, he earned the label *al-shaykh al-ahmar* (the red cleric). He commented that it "was fashionable in the 1950s" to accuse anyone who supported "social justice" of communism.[6]

The depiction of Shi'ite Communists as anti-Arab ran parallel to the denunciation of them by Najaf's jurists as atheists beyond the pale of Islam. Communist atheism, however, appeared among very few intellectuals. The real threat to Najaf, however, came from secularism and economic reform pertaining to what Faleh A. Jabar calls "sheikhly landlordism," and hence to existing patterns of land ownership.[7] Deeply unsettling to clerical leaders was not the absence of "religion" among the Communists but the new associations they drew between secular socialist ideals, on the one hand, and Shi'ite belief and ritual, on the other. Throughout the 1950s, the Communists became a force to be reckoned with in Najaf's community.[8] We get a glimpse of this reality from Shaykh Hani Fahs, a Lebanese cleric living in Najaf at the time. He recalls that in an underground periodical issued by two students at the seminary, the image of Che Guevara loomed on the cover, along with the words "alive in every bullet."[9] Similar features appear also in Karbala', a city defined by the shrines of its martyred Imam Husayn, and his half-brother al-'Abbas. In a famous poem titled "Where Is My Right?" Muhammad Salih, a Communist sympathizer from the prominent family of Bahr al-'Ulum, denounced clerical impiety and greed. He challenged the view that class divisions (*nizam al-tabaqat*) are God given and accused affluent jurists of exploiting Shi'ite peasants and workers.

> You have interpreted the book of God in a corrupt manner
> And took religion as a snare to hunt with it
>
> . . .
>
> How can the majority continue to watch this mockery?
> The people toil without wage to serve a few persons . . .

The conflict between the powerful jurists and the Communists took a new turn after 'Abd al-Karim Qasim seized power in 1958, supported by the nationalists and the Communists. An organized clerical movement emerged in Najaf and Karbala' spearheaded by the highest *marja'*, Sayyid Muhsin al-Hakim. It mobilized the *'ulama* and seminary students against communism and the regime's secularization policies in economic, educational, and, more importantly, legal domains. In 1960, a year before Sayyid al-Hakim became the sole surviving *marja'*, he elevated communism to a heretical theology whose advocates needed to be physically removed from society.

The conflict between Najaf's clerical leadership and the Communists left its imprint on the early Lebanese Islamists who studied in Najaf or were part of the transnational clerical arenas tying Iran, Iraq, and Lebanon. The most prominent of these Islamists were Muhammad Husayn Fadlallah (d. 2010), and two of the founders of Hizbullah (the Party of God)—Shaykh Subhi al-Tufayli and Sayyid Hasan Nasrallah. Through the adversarial but dialectical relation with the Communists, Islamist ideologues adapted certain elements of Marxism and Third Worldist concepts. Fadlallah's expression "harakiyyat al-waqi'" (perpetual transformation of reality) through jihad (holy war) against an unjust power was inspired by Marx's discussion of the "radical negation of social reality" affected by the proletariat.[10] In Fadlallah's discourse, however, reality is transformed

spiritually rather than materially.[11] Alternatively, a number of leftist think-
ers were moving in the direction of Islamism. The last statement of the
Maoist Shi'ite thinker from Baghdad Hadi al-'Alawi before he died was:
"The future will be on the side of the Islamic civilization not the West."[12]

In Lebanon, the Shi'ites were facing distinct challenges. Land shortage
and the failure of state policies contributed to rural disintegration in the
Biqa' and the South during the 1950s. Foreign capitalists controlled investment initiatives, preventing some of the credits and resources from being
reinvested in public sectors of the economy. Agrarian subsistence patterns
were eroding, and migration to the city intensified. Meanwhile, resources
of expatriate communities, urbanization, and expansion in public education contributed to upward social mobility and a shift in class boundaries.
Political activism was evident among a new generation of urbanized and
educated Shi'ites. From the mid- to the late 1960s, a series of economic
setbacks and political crises led to intense labor strikes and anti-state protests. Tens of thousands of Shi'ites lent their numbers to these strikes and
protests, expressing diverse secular ideas associated with the Syrian Social
Nationalist Party (Al-Hizb al-suri al-qawmi al-ijtima'i), the Party of Arab
Socialist Action (Hizb al-'amal al-ishtiraki al-'arabi), the Ba'th Party (Hizb
al-ba'th), the Organization of Socialist Lebanon (Munazzamat Lubnan
al-ishtiraki), the Organization of Communist Action (Munazzamat al-
'amal al-shuyu'i), and the Lebanese Communist Party (Al-Hizb al-shuyu'i
al-lubnani). The 1960s was also a time of reconciliation between Arab
nationalism and Marxism, both of which attracted Shi'ite activists. About
his own experience in the Organization of Socialist Lebanon, the poet and
intellectual 'Abbas Baydun reflects, "It was an undefined Marxism, manifested in the Organization of Socialist Lebanon. The founders were former
members and intellectuals of the Socialist Ba'th party, the ethereal party
for the Shi'ite intellectuals in the 1950s. Despite their urge to validate
Marxism, socially and nationally—to fit it to the Lebanese context—the
members of the Organization continued to long for a populist Arabism."[13]

The growth of the Palestinian resistance movement in the South and
episodic Israeli raids against it had significant consequences for the Shi'ites.
Many joined militant organizations and civil forums that denounced state
neglect and economic discrimination. To be sure, Palestinian statelessness

resonated with experiences of Shi'ite impoverishment and political marginality. It is probably this state of mind or sentiment that caught the attention of Sayyid Musa al-Sadr, a popular Shi'ite cleric, who commented that the Shi'ites must be persuaded that they were not "stateless" like the Palestinians.[14] Shi'ite radicalism, Sayyid Musa's followers would argue, hindered the bourgeoisie's efforts to bargain for a greater share in decision making, resources, and sectarian representation. Sayyid Musa spoke on behalf of the sect, urging the state to resolve the Shi'ites' grievances in order to win their loyalty. He gradually emerged into a national leader, appropriating the Libanist discourse to secure sectarian "gains" for the Shi'ites. He suggested that sectarianism could be reconstructed as a form of pluralism, a "balance" of sects, leading to national modernity. But a rude awakening loomed in 1970 when he found that his trust in the illusive principle of sectarian "equity" and his intent on resolving Shi'ite grievances through state channels was futile. He did not, however, forfeit the idea that the Shi'ites must own modern citizenry, with or without state support. Addressing families in Ba'labak and al-Hirmil tangled in fierce disputes, he announced: "Even if the state had abandoned you due to fear or collapsed due to ethical hypocrisy and bankruptcy in vision, how could you desert yourselves, your happiness, your honor, your humanity, and your citizenry?"[15] If the state has failed to acknowledge the sectarian demands of the Shi'ites, Sayyid Musa seemed to be saying, the Shi'ites should still achieve "happiness" as "self-governing" agents and citizens of a national community.[16]

As Sayyid Musa's relationship to the state deteriorated, he came to benefit from a Shi'ite culture of dissent and leftist protest, which he had earlier criticized. In what became a landmark in Shi'ite history, he spearheaded a national strike against the government on May 26, 1970, that gave birth to the *mahrumin* (dispossessed) movement.[17] A few years later the tobacco growers marched in protest from Nabatiyya in the South to the Arab University in Beirut.[18] The mounting crisis brought the convening of a National Congress for Tobacco Growers in April 1974, which demanded, among other things, job security, health insurance, creation of a syndicate, and government protection for the tobacco production.[19] Despite Sayyid Musa's magnetism, he was hardly the cause for a Shi'ite "awakening."

The Shi'ites were already in the middle of a maelstrom, confronting the state and exhibiting tremendous dynamism in labor protests, nationalist organizations, and leftist civil arenas.[20] What Sayyid Musa brought to the scene was a candid sectarian delineation of Shi'ite grievances.

The Communists who experienced these events describe a different scene. They note that Sayyid Musa hoped to weaken the Shi'ite left in order negotiate with the state's new sectarian "rights" for the Shi'ite bourgeoisie. They denied that state reform was possible without dismantling its sectarian foundations. Sectarianism and the economic arrangements tied to it, they suggested, were responsible for episodic civil crises.[21] Mahdi 'Amil, an eminent Shi'ite Communist, distinguished this form of modern sectarianism from premodern communal affiliations. Enshrined in the Lebanese National Pact of 1943, sectarianism became an expression of the hegemony of one Lebanese sect (the Maronite Christian) over other sect—in particular, Muslim ones. Replacing one sectarian domination by another, 'Amil reflected, would not remedy the problem of inequality or instability. Rather, the sectarian system as a whole had to be eliminated.[22]

If Sayyid Musa had argued that the Biqa'i Shi'ites needed to be saved from civil "lethargy," then he wanted the southerners to dissociate themselves from the secular programs as well as from the Communists' and the secular nationalists' (Syrian and Arab) ideas. He hoped to "remove the Left's exclusive custody of Shi'ite activism, and prevent it from investing in a project that destroys the state."[23] But certain leftist sensibilities, demands for economic and political reform, and discontent with state sectarianism had been enunciated by sundry Shi'ite groups and figures, not the least of whom was Shaykh Muhammad Jawad Mughniyya. The latter, troubled by the atheistic implications of Soviet communism, admitted nonetheless that Marxist concepts of justice and socialist ethics were competing with Islam's tacit "moral economy." When common Shi'ites described the early defender of Imam 'Ali—Abu Dharr al-Ghifari—as a pristine "socialist," Mughniyya protested that Abu Dharr's sense of justice was "Qur'anic Muhammadan," neither Communist nor capitalist.[24]

After the disappearance of Sayyid Musa in 1978, the paramilitary organization that he had established, the Lebanese Resistance Detachments (Afwaj al-muqawama al-lubnaniyya, AMAL), emerged into a major political party. Under the leadership of Nabih Berri, AMAL succeeded in securing some state funds for building roads and schools in several rural towns. Despite AMAL's entrenched sectarianism, it adhered to certain features of secularity, including the privatization of religion. Inside and outside AMAL, however, Islamist leanings had been growing inspired by the Islamic Revolution in Iran, and the Islamist movements in Najaf and Karbala'. These leanings took definite form at the time of Israel's second invasion of Lebanon in 1982 and its occupation of the entire South. The invasion gave new meanings to Karbala in the collective imagination, and an association was soon drawn between the tragedy of Imam Husayn, the Palestinian crisis, and the Israeli occupation. The resistance to the occupation conjured up Islamist notions of martyrdom and sacrifice.

Prior to the 1982 Israeli invasion, AMAL was bent on weakening the Communists in the South and Beirut with the support of Syria. After the invasion, it faced a formidable contender—Hizbullah, an Islamist party with a major Shi'ite base and with better organization and resources than the Communists. Hizbullah's leaders considered Israel the principal cause of injustice committed against Muslims today. They declared also that neither diplomacy nor peaceful negotiations with Israel and the United States had succeeded in altering this reality. Under these circumstances, a defensive war or jihad would be the only means for self-liberation. Before the rise of Hizbullah, Fadlallah had been publicizing the "modernist" features of revolutionary Islam among his students and followers in Beirut. Revolutionary Islam confronts an imperious global system (*nizam al-istikbar al-'alami*), achieves self-liberation through militancy, and renews the shari'a through tools of rational inference. Despite their differences, Hizbullah's and Fadlallah's Islamists were united in their advocacy of public Islam and jihadi resistance to Israel. The "resisting society" (*al-mujtama' al-muqawim*), as they saw it, receives God's benediction through proper worship and perseverance against injustice. Reminded of the steadfastness of *ahl al-bayt* (the house of the Prophet) in the face of death, Nasrallah maintained: "We are used to death, and our dignity is derived from the martyrdom God grants us."[25] Without the history of political conflicts, socioeconomic grievances, and the displacements caused by the Israeli occupation, it is difficult to conceive of the local threads that wove Hizbullah's Islamism and its *muqawama* (resistance). A sharp critic of Hizbullah, Sayyid Muhammad Hasan al-Amin, the Shi'ite judge in Sidon, tied the *muqawama* directly to the state's crisis. Popular devotion to Nasrallah, he boldly noted, must be blamed on the state's failings and fragility.[26] To address the emerging questions of national identity and loyalty, activists such as Nasrallah turned to the Iraqi and Iranian milieus, exploring Islam's "revolutionary capacity." At this juncture, a new rhetoric against the Communists and secularists at large, with distinct polemics and tropes, traversed Shi'ite transnational spaces. The hostilities between the Islamists and the Communists, for one, became part of small-town and family conflicts. The former gradually dominated the scene in the South, the Biqa', and Beirut only to face accusations of cultural Iranization and the promotion of Iran's interests in the region. When asked by a journalist whether the Shi'ites as a whole were facing "an identity crisis, given their divided loyalty between Iran, Syria, and Lebanon," Fadlallah remonstrated,

> Why is this question posed to the Shi'ites? There are Christian sects that do not know whether they are loyal to the United States, France, or Israel. There are also Muslim sects that do not know whether they are loyal to Egypt, Iraq, Syria, or Saudi Arabia. Why is there an insistence on giving the Muslim Shi'ite sect these political labels that accord it a marginal place in the countries of the region and strip it of its autonomy, its indigenous character, and [its] political position in Lebanon. The Muslim Shi'ite sect is more Lebanese than any other sect that constitutes Lebanon. The [Shi'ites] had lived in Lebanon before the time that those people(s) claimed to be [the true] Lebanese.[27]

Disputes over cultural "identity" and national "loyalty" are a pervasive feature of sectarian politics in Lebanon. There is hardly a sect in Lebanon that has not been accused of promoting "non-Lebanese" interests at some point in time. Hizbullah and Fadlallah's followers' local roots and patriotism are unmistakable. Saying this, however, is not the same as saying that the Islamists' worldview coheres with modern constructs of nationalism or that their relationship to the nation-state is definite or strong.

An Islamist network of medical, economic, and educational organizations had sprung up as the militant resistance in the South reaped its first fruits of success in the 1990s. During Hizbullah's early stages of development, members were drawn mostly from the working class. As the Islamists achieved a reputable public image, undercut AMAL's interests, and achieved parliamentary representation, a segment of the bourgeoisie lent its weight to Hizbullah's movement. These developments in turn paved the way for Hizbullah's domination of the Shi'ites.

The Islamists' entry into the Lebanese public sphere was marked by a challenge to leftist and Western liberal notions of "secularity." Islamist civil arenas were shaped by a semiautonomous culture of piety—namely, a call for commanding right and forbidding wrong, "al-amr bi-al-ma'ruf wa-al-nahi 'an al-munkar," that flourished in suburban Beirut, the South, and the Biqa'. The Islamists contributed to the pluralistic features of civil society, which remained visible until 2004–2005, when effective domination of the Shi'ites was achieved through the unity between Hizbullah and Amal. Hizbullah's (and Amal's) recourse to armed intervention in 2008 in order to shield the *muqawama* impaired the democratic forces regulating civil society. The preoccupation with the *muqawama* also dissipated whatever interest Hizbullah's leaders had in economic and political reform and hence their ability to create lasting ties to diverse voluntary associations and heterogeneous civil arenas.

Theoretical Framework

The 1979 Islamic Revolution in Iran has had a profound effect on the writing of the history of modern Shi'ite societies, which has been increasingly tied to cultural frameworks such as the rebirth of religion, the clash between Islam and Western "civilization," and the failure of modern reform in Islamic society. Local history involving an understanding of long-term political processes, socioeconomic conditions, relations to the nation-state, and colonialism rarely figure in the accounts on Arab Shi'ite Islamists—in particular, the Lebanese. Our study stresses the importance of communal and revolutionary ideology to the reshaping of the political sphere in Lebanon. The stories we tell in this book weave together the local picture and transnational political forces as well as the profound interactions they entail. Contemporary historians have largely neglected the Islamists' approaches to religious modernism and communism. Worse, there is little attempt to account for the secular processes and ideas shaping the modernists, the Communists, and the Islamists and for their overlap with religious sensibilities. To explore these processes and overlays between the secular and the religious, we revisit sectarianism, the Lebanese state, and the Shiʻites' varied relations to the state. The book delineates the central features of Islamist civil arenas—in particular, the renewal of the shariʻa. In this section, we present the book's main theoretical questions and arguments.

The Shiʻites and the Lebanese Nation-State

The religious modernists', Communists', and Islamists' engagement with the state in its secular-sectarian facets constitute the most significant aspect of the Shiʻites' history in Lebanon. The 1926 Lebanese Constitution, which signaled the formation of the state of Grand Liban under the French Mandate (1920–46), reflected the aspirations of the entrepreneurial elite toward mercantilist urbanity following Western civic and legal models. The state now possessed the secular legal organs and political-administrative bureaus known to modern nation-states. With the demise of the Ottoman caliphate and emphasis on secularization, the shariʻa administered by the jurists ceased to be the basis of legal regulation in Syria and Lebanon. Only family law was preserved or, rather, reformed and turned into a body of codified laws administered by state-appointed clerics and bureaucrats.

The uppermost state functions devolved to the Christian elites, in particular the Maronites. The architects of the constitution extolled the traditional "virtues" of Grand Liban's diverse "communities," but they also feared that "parochial" customs would threaten national unity and urban development.[28] The national vision fashioned by the constitution was one of a liberal polity open to Western initiatives and investments. Liberalism was translated into a service-based economy that developed around banking and tourism. The laissez-faire program attracted financial capital, but it did not turn capital to productive investments in the main economic sectors.[29] Cultural liberalism embellished Lebanon's modernism, "openness" to the West, and the need to "reform" religious (in particular, Muslim) institutions and traditions. A number of Christian thinkers and entrepreneurs justified and defended these ideas, presenting "Libanism," or Lebanese nationalism, as a "civilizing" sentiment in the Arab-Islamic region. The "adventurous" Maronites were considered the natural leaders of Lebanon's liberal economy and ideal agents of modern "progress."

Libanism, French colonial logic, and the communalist model of Mount Lebanon set the stage for state sectarianism in Grand Liban. As the sectarian rubric became hegemonic, the resistance that some nationalist leaders expressed toward it slowly receded. Governance was to be "shared" among the diverse communities of Grand Liban, yet with the underlying assumption that the Maronites were entitled to certain rights and privileges. The presidency was reserved for a Maronite and carried significant power over other state bureaus. Along with the Maronite elite, a group of Muslim leaders—namely, Sunnite, Druze, and Shi'ite—held distinct posts and functions within the state and Parliament.[30] Influential sectarian thinkers laid claims to particular ethnic or cultural origins and challenged the claims of rivaling sects in order to legitimize their drive for domination.[31] Within a sect, powerful families or clusters of families sharing a perceived ancestry or culture were expected to compete for political sway and resources.[32] Sectarianism also authorized gender inequalities, which diverted attention away from class and suppressed its role as an organizing principle of social and political life.[33] In this respect, Peter Gran suggested that male workers and peasants whose interests were undermined by the sectarian system nonetheless participated in its production and justification. Their accommodation of sectarianism, he noted, derived to a large extent from the higher public status and legal power that it accords to men over women.[34] Suad Joseph added that sectarianism extended a legal status to men's kin "obligations and duties" toward women, fostering distinct types of control over women's labor and sexuality.[35] In addition, a range of social services, political opportunities, religious identities, and economic resources are mediated through sectarian channels.

The relation between Lebanese sectarianism and civil crisis has received much scholarly attention. Ussama Makdisi's study of the Maronite and Druze communities of Mount Lebanon in the nineteenth century illustrates the complex links between sectarianism, modernity, and violence.[36] Gran in turn argued that although violence is evident in nonsectarian political systems, it "may become a necessity" in sectarian ones, which face recurrent crises of law and order.[37] The "supergrouping" based on the state's incorporation of its dominant elements is volatile and faces constant threats. Against this view, a few studies denied any fundamental link between sectarianism and violence. Michael Young attributed the "liberal openings" and "liberal diversity" in Lebanon to sectarianism rather than and more properly to a weak state.[38] Max Weiss in turn considered the range of civil adjustments to sectarianism an exercise in modern citizenry.[39] Sectarianism, he claimed, was a "malleable product" that made colonial and Libanist interests compatible with Shi'ite politics.[40] Shi'ite civil actors benefited from the sectarian system and used their "agency" to enhance their bargaining power with the Lebanese state. The Shi'ites' sectarian status, as such, led to their religious-legal autonomy. This view assumes that the Shi'ites continued to experience the same religious-legal realities under Grand Liban and ignores the shifts caused by the rise of the modern nation-state in the 1920s. Under the modern state, large sections of the shari'a were abandoned and the rest was replaced by a set of codified family and inheritance laws. In other words, at the moment when the Ja'fari *madhhab* acquired full legal recognition in Grand Liban, some of its core features became irrelevant to the modern state. The connection between its juristic apparatus and its positive law did not extend beyond family law. In stressing the benefits of sectarianism, Weiss set up a straw man exaggerating the religious-legal "autonomy" of the Shi'ites and the improvement in their "communal status" since the Ottoman period.[41] This improvement was a consequence of the establishment of the modern state and its politicolegal procedures found elsewhere in the Middle East, not the outcome of sectarianism per se.[42] Freedom of religious belief and ritual were evident in Syria and Iraq as well even though their states did not inscribe sectarianism.

Despite the force of institutionalized sectarianism and its normative patterns described earlier, in looking at the case in Lebanon one is faced with a range of sensibilities, ideas, and activities that do not cohere with sectarianism or that interfere with its practice. Some studies have extended an independent role to sectarianism in organizing civil society and determining the public actions of Lebanese citizens.[43] In contrast, our book brings to light occasions of overlap between sectarian, class, and gender issues. At the same time, it notes how the anticolonial struggle, economic grievances, and social inequities destabilize sectarianism. The book also departs from much of the Western scholarship on Lebanon that gives the secular and the secularists generic descriptions or assigns them peripheral roles in shaping the public and private worlds of the Lebanese. This study stresses the pervasiveness of particular secular ideas and processes in Lebanese society and their complex interface with sectarianism and religion. The Lebanese state used secular procedures to organize areas such as the economy, education, dispensation of justice, and the army. Clerical leaders were compelled to fit areas of the sacred law to the state's judicial framework and turn them into legal codes. Among Muslims, the shari'a was trimmed down to the personal-status laws pertaining to marriage, divorce, child custody, and inheritance.[44] Today, the Islamists' public demand for preserving, if not developing, these laws reveals the way in which religion and sectarianism have coalesced in the spheres of sociolegal and economic activity.

The Shi'ite Left: Traditions of the Sacred and the Secular

In Iraq and Lebanon after World War I, numerous Shi'ites turned to communism to resolve problems of poverty, rural disintegration, colonial rule, and political marginalization. Soviet communism represented an alternative model of social and economic development to that of capitalist Europe, which was closely associated with colonialism in the Middle East and North Africa.[45] The book revisits the assumption widely held by Arab and Western scholars alike that Shi'ite clerical leaders and Islamists became mobilized in Iraq and Lebanon against the spread of Communist atheism (*ilhad*) and the erosion of faith and religiosity. The growth of communism in Shi'ite locales known for their religious-legal scholarship and devotional traditions have pushed us to ask new questions about the relationship of local communism to public/political Islam. In Najaf and Karbala', several Communists were schooled at Shi'ite madrasas and seminaries, partaking in the local religious culture, including the ritual processions of 'Ashura', commemorating the martyrdom of Imam Husayn (d. 680), his family members, and his companions.[46] Liturgical recitals for *ahl al-bayt*, devotional literature, martyrological poetry, as well as pilgrimage to the shrines of al-Husayn and his half-brother al-'Abbas were pivotal to the formation of Shi'ite moral belief and religious worldview. The Communists' engagement with such activities allows us to explore not only their religious experiences, but also the way in which these experiences tied with secular sensibilities.[47] The Communists' secular notions of justice seemed to have stimulated religious conceptions of sacrifice and redemption offered by the Karbala' event.[48] At the same time, honoring the martyrdom of al-Husayn provided new spaces for secular action against class inequities, colonial policies, and state repression.[49] Local communism also presented a secularized framework for Shi'ite messianism, or achieving justice on earth, marked by the fulfillment of human material needs and spiritual realization. As the worshippers lamented the usurpation of Imam 'Ali's rights, they helped bestow spiritual merit on secular action against oppressive political powers. The leftists evidently drew versatile associations between the secular organization of society and a religious culture centered on the hero martyr of *ahl al-bayt*, Imam Husayn. Thus, not all the Communist intellectuals who aspired to "modernize" Islam or "rationalize" Islamic tradition turned to Western models. A number of them located faith and spirituality in Islamic mystical and philosophical traditions, but not in the shari'a.

The view that the secular is simply "the nonreligious" faces many challenges, as does the assumption that public Islam is a "return" to faith or, in the case of Iraqi and Lebanese Shi'ites, a reaction to atheism and disenchantment in a modern world that chased God and the spirits out.[50] To be sure, Shi'ite collective rituals involving prayer and sacrifice continued with rigor through the modern period, transforming the person as well as her or his relations to the supernatural. The modern landscape in Iraq and Lebanon offered unexpected patterns of spirituality and religious experience. As a consequence, the source of anxiety for Islamist clerics and thinkers appeared to lie not in the absence of faith or religiosity, but in the particular form each had taken under the modern state. God's Law or the shari'a, the Islamists insisted, is the cornerstone of faith. In comparison, the Communists critiqued the shari'a, on which the nomocentric traditions of Islam are based, and rejected clerical authority.[51] In the second half of the twentieth century, although a few clerics were sympathetic to the political and economic demands of the Communists, the latter's insistence on privatizing the shari'a threatened the clerical community and the function of the seminaries in Shi'ite society. Iraqi and Lebanese Islamist leaders tried to recenter the public enactment of the shari'a as the kernel of Islamic belief and identity. They came to argue that state secularization, having originated and developed in the West, is alien to Islamic society and a cause of cultural displacement. The Islamists insisted that one has to live by the shari'a in its full sociolegal dimension in order to realize the true life of a Muslim.

Secularism (covering various forms of privatized religion) and anti-clericalism appear, then, to be the main forces provoking the mobilization of a group of powerful jurists against the Communists and the rise of Islamist movements in Iraq and Lebanon. The issuance of the secular statutes of the 1959 Code of Personal Status under the government of 'Abd al-Karim Qasim enhanced this mobilization.[52] The Communists praised the code as a milestone in the process of building a national democratic government devoid of sectarian-ethnic and gendered discrimination. Tied to secularism and no less significant was the fear of economic reform, in particular the redistribution of land owned by large landholders who contributed to the seminary and supported powerful jurists' financial interests.

Public Religion and Civil Society

Another area of investigation in this book is public religion and its place in Lebanese civil society. A few ideas have expressed Arab and Iranian Shi'ites' aspirations in the late twentieth century, as has public religion (and political Islam), and perhaps no contemporary Islamist movement in the Middle East has mustered as much popular enthusiasm and dissension as Hizbullah in Lebanon. Hizbullah's founders maintained that Islam, as a body of religious beliefs and legal edicts, is not only the source of individual guidance, but also the sociopolitical and economic foundation of modern society. As advocates of public religion, the Islamists whom this book refers to as Hizbullah's members and the followers of Muhammad Husayn Fadlallah, rejected the separation between the shari'a and the organization of modern society. Meanwhile, they defeated Israeli occupation in South Lebanon in 2000 and continued to confront a local system of domination put into effect by Israel and defended by the United States. They notably made the assertion that Islam is resourceful against the political and cultural hegemony of the West and promoted a particular engagement with modernity. *Al-mujtama' al-muqawim*, the resisting society, the Islamists argue, liberates itself from physical occupation (Israel) and cultural occupation (the West) and lives by a modern active faith known through the shari'a. The terms *West* and *Western* refer here not to an identifiable geographical or cultural entity, but rather to the hegemonic truisms about the West and the rest, grounded in Western colonial domination, and to imperial American intrusions (sustained by a constellation of countries around the globe) into societies and ideas.

In some ways, the Lebanese Islamists have tried to intervene in the Hegelian telos—one of the hallmarks of Western modernity—that the history of humanity is a "progress" that reaches final fulfillment, a process in which reason has a sovereign status.[53] Having challenged the absolute idealism of Hegelian thought, twentieth-century Western thinkers nonetheless renewed Hegel's view of the inherent superiority of Western "civilization" (standing for the monarchy in Prussia and projected onto the wider canvas of European cultures) set apart from other "civilizations," such as the Asian and the African.[54] Through attributes of "individuality"[55] and "universality," discussed at length by Hegel, Europe (and the West at large) achieves the shift to secular modernism. Islam, in Hegel's view, embodied particular cultural traits that became stagnant and lost their relevance to the modern world.[56] This presumption resonates with current Western accounts of Islam—in particular, those studies that utilize "civilization" (with inherent cultural qualities) as a unit of analysis and others that present Islamism as a sign of "failure" to achieve "modern progress," the latter having become intertwined with Western liberal democracy.[57] In its epistemic framework, if not in its particular postulates, the Hegelian model appears as a reference point in a range of Lebanese liberal and Marxist discussions about the nation, civil society, renewal of Arab-Islamic tradition, and relations to Western modernism.[58] Nor have the Islamists themselves escaped the narrative of history as a "progress" or to that matter the division of peoples into "civilizations," in their case privileging the "Islamic" over others.[59] Yet they juxtapose their own notion of progress against Eurocentric trajectories of modernism. They locate "progress" in the sociolegal *ijtihadi* (based on rational inference) renewal of sacred laws governing all aspects of human activity. Rather than being a "rational process," "progress" in Islam is bound by God's will and a faith that shapes the believer's relationship to the natural and social worlds. The Islamist discourse as such rejects the Hegelian declaration that "free subjectivity" is the "essence of true morality" and attempts instead to fashion subjectivity through legal-moral obligations and rituals of worship.[60]

New readings of "civil society" and the "public sphere" have unearthed a spectrum of public spheres in both Western and Islamic societies alike.[61] A central criticism proffered by these readings is the inadequacy of Weberian conceptions of civil society as one formed by secularized voluntary associations seeking individual autonomy from the state.[62] These studies equally questioned the presence of an "Islamic" civil society based on Hegelian conceptions of the role that the Western nation-state plays in arranging civil society and the necessity of "individuality." To inhabit a modern world, humans, Hegel insisted, must have the "freedom of subjectivity, the principle that all the essential factors present in the intellectual whole are now coming into their right in the course of their development."[63] For Hegel, individuals are truly free when they fully identify with their nation. In other words, civil society mirrors and confirms the freedom attained through the nation.[64] Utilizing this framework, several twentieth-century Lebanese scholars insisted that a Western-style secular state is essential for the production of civil society.[65] Prior to the 1990s, most liberal and leftist writers denied the existence of a civil society (*mujtamaʿ*

madani) in Lebanon, contrasting it to kin-based, religious, and sect-based associations. A few scholars, however, came to argue that the contours of civil society had emerged in the 1960s and 1970s, shaped by secularized arenas and voluntary associations.[66] They continued to utilize, however, Weberian criteria for civil society, identifying it solely with voluntary secular formations falling outside the state.[67] Notable among those who questioned these approaches was Wajih Kawtharani, a Lebanese thinker who considered the term *communal society* (*mujtama' ahli*) more accurate in describing Lebanese society.[68] He argued that traditional Arab-Islamic society was the site of civil formations, many of them lying outside the state, including political sects, merchants, guilds, and Sufi orders, as well as arenas defined by tribal and ethnic ties.[69] Kawtharani has recently revisited the question of civil society in connection to the domination of a single party or single political sect, noting the hegemony of the *ahli* over the *madani*.[70] The distinction he makes between the two, however, is not always discernible.

A body of Western literature on contemporary Islamic society indicated that individualism is not essential to the emergence and function of the public sphere.[71] Some studies revisited Jürgen Habermas's conception of the public sphere as a bourgeois entity shaped primarily by the Enlightenment tradition. Habermas restated Hegel's view of the principal role that subjectivity plays in producing modernity, but he was equally aware of the risk that subjectivity poses to democracy—hence, his emphasis on communicative reasoning. Habermas viewed communicative reasoning and rational argumentation as the lynchpin of civil society.[72] Based on this model, neither conflict nor religious sensibilities are seen as integral to the public sphere. In contrast, the Lebanese case reveals that discord and coercion were as much a part of the Islamists' access to the public sphere as was communicative reasoning and negotiation of difference.[73] This book joins a number of scholars in considering conflict and a degree of coercion integral to civil society. In the case of Lebanon, the conflict created by the Islamists' entry into the public sphere enhanced the sphere's pluralistic constitution. Democratic elements of this sphere, however, were imperiled by the coalescence of the major Shi'ite-based parties Hizbullah and AMAL by 2004–2005 and by their recourse to armed intervention to protect the resistance in the South. Sectarian conflicts played no small role in accentuating the subsequent civil crisis in Lebanon during the first decade of the twenty-first century.

Public Religion and the Nation-State

The scholarship on the Lebanese Islamists in general and on Hizbullah in particular seems to be polarized between a majority of studies presenting Islamism as a failure to modernize and a few others confirming its modernist constitution.[74] Those who insist on the Islamists' modernness, in particular Lara Deeb, have provided impressive ethnographic material and sociological analysis against views of their "traditionalism." These studies, however, do not problematize modern constructs of rationality and history and tend to recenter the narrative of progress.[75] The Lebanese Islamists undoubtedly have a profound engagement with modernity and advance their localized experiences of it. Yet they also harbor antimodern and postmodern sensibilities that reflect the dialectic of adaptation and conflict. Talal Asad's insights into relations between public Islam and the modern state seem highly useful in this context.[76] Asad focuses attention on the way a discursive religion inhabits a public sphere and alters the relation between the believer, on the one hand, and the state and secularism, on the other. Because secularism is a core feature of the nation-state, Asad maintains, public-political religion is not easily reconciled with modernism.[77] To be sure, Hizbullah's modernist project carries incongruent elements and expresses unresolved tensions toward the nation-state, a central element of the modern landscape.[78] Of particular consequence for the Islamists' relationship to the state is their tendency to apply the shari'a in various domains of public life. Wael Hallaq has recently made new assertions about the epistemic break between the modern rubric of the nation-state and the organic matrix of the shari'a.[79] As a body of moral principles shaped into legal norms, the shari'a seeks to make the believer accountable to a sovereign God, not a sovereign state. Reorganizing the shari'a to fit the state's legal structure, Hallaq declares, would dismantle the former's matrix entirely, bringing forth a state that is "Islamic" in appearance only. Although our study is not concerned with the nature or reality of an Islamic state in Lebanon, Hallaq and Asad's arguments help illuminate the question of whether Islamist sensibilities cohere with nationalism and the modern state. This study, then, starts with the local environment of Fadlallah's and Hizbullah's "resisting society" beginning in the 1980s and its links to developments in the Middle East and the world order. Through the Lebanese Islamists' understanding of public religion and militancy, one learns about those discourses, collective articulations, and textures that are unique to them in this period. One also learns about those regional and international historical processes that make their movement comparable to others in several world societies.

Division of Chapters

This book is divided into eight chapters. Chapter 1 sheds light on peasant life and political leadership in Jabal 'Amil (the South) and the Biqa' on the eve of French colonial rule. It illuminates the cross-class alliances involving social bandits, peasants, and members of the elite that marked the Shi'ite countryside's anticolonial struggles. It explores French colonial discourse about Muslim "backwardness," which resonated with Libanist arguments about the Christians' "civilizing" role in Grand Liban. The chapter also discusses the way in which British colonialism in Palestine and Zionist militancy in the South have shaped Shi'ite political experiences since the late 1920s.

Chapter 2 draws attention to urgent peasant demands and to Shi'ite ambiguity surrounding the acceptance of Grand Liban as a national homeland. The peasants and a section of the notables and provincial leaders were in open revolt against the French in 1936. The second part of the chapter sheds light on intellectual changes shaped by these confrontations and by European domination in general. It explores the approaches that the Shi'ite 'ulama and intellectuals took toward educational modernism and religious reform. It throws light on a particular group of modernists, the Marxist seminary students and intellectuals of the South, showing how they legitimized certain adaptations of Western modernism through an emphasis on Islam's long-standing rationalist and scientific traditions.

Chapter 3 delineates the socioeconomic and political reasons for communism's appeal to southern seminary students and peasants. It highlights also the Communists' local interpretation of Marxism as well as the association that leftist Shi'ites drew between religious culture and Communist revolutionary ideals. Emancipatory features of communism found an affinity with Imam Husayn's pursuit of justice and reinforced a Shi'ite utopian restorative order. Through the biographical accounts of two Shi'ite Communists, Sayyid Ja'far Muhsin al-Amin and Husayn Muroeh, the chapter gives the reader a lively picture of the concerns and aspirations of religious modernists and Marxists at the time.

Chapter 4 examines the conflict between the Shi'ite Communists and Islamic jurists in Iraq during the 1960s, which was critical in shaping the thought of the early Lebanese Islamists. It revisits the Communists' secular programs and their engagement with local religious culture and nonlegalistic Islamic traditions. It also investigates the historical forces that gave rise to the clerical movement led by the *marja'* Sayyid Muhsin al-Hakim and the discourse of Communist "atheism." Islamist adaptations of modernism and the dialectical confrontation with communism are reflected in the writings of Muhammad Baqir al-Sadr on Islamic economics and social justice. A small group of Baqir al-Sadr's students set up early Islamist organizations in Lebanon and advocated a range of ideas on public Islam, modernism, and power.

Chapter 5 explores the socioeconomic and political experiences of the Lebanese Shi'ites in the South and the Biqa' from the late 1950s to the 1970s. It captures processes of rural disintegration and political marginalization as well as the displacement of tens of thousands of Shi'ites because of Israeli attacks on the South. Seeking solutions to these problems, many Shi'ites turned to secular nationalist and leftist organizations, particularly the Lebanese Communist Party and the Communist Action Organization. The chapter also revisits the clash of the charismatic cleric Sayyid Musa al-Sadr with the Communists and his attempt to facilitate Shi'ite conformity to the state. The establishment of the Supreme Islamic Shi'ite Council (Al-Majlis al-Islami al-Shi'i al-A'la) is reassessed in the light of the relationship between sectarianism and the state's secular apparatus.

Chapter 6 discusses Hizbullah's grassroots movement and the spread of public Islam (Shi'ite) in Lebanon during the 1980 and 1990s. It explores the links that the Islamists drew between liberating the South from Israeli occupation, minimizing economic grievances, and inspiring public piety. It stresses the role of transnational arenas and seminary circles in shaping the Lebanese Islamists' ideas, assessing the conflict with the Communists and the latter's declining role in the *muqawama*. Finally, the chapter's main themes are elucidated through a biographical portrait of Hizbullah's current leader, Sayyid Hasan Nasrallah.

Chapter 7 examines the Islamists' entry into the Lebanese public sphere, the coercive measures they took, and the sensibilities and discourses they communicated. It highlights the role of their charitable, economic, and educational organizations in shaping an Islamist subject. It also explores the *muqawama* not merely as a militant activity, but also as a societal experience unmonitored by the state. Ideals of piety, self-reliance, and sacrifice drew the ethical boundaries of the "resisting society." The chapter looks more closely at the connection between men's self-sacrifice and women's rituals of prayer and purity.

The last chapter highlights the main features of Hizbullah's modernist Islam—namely, legal renewal through *ijtihad* (legal inference using rationalist methods) and liberation through jihad. It also investigates the tensions and disparate elements of Hizbullah's modernism manifested through its approach to the nation-state. The chapter highlights the "transactions" that Hizbullah made with the Lebanese state and the shifts in its position on sectarianism and the constitution, as reflected in its second manifesto (2009). The chapter ends with a portrait of Muhammad Husayn Fadlallah, an eminent jurist who popularized new ideas about Islamism, modernity, and the world order.

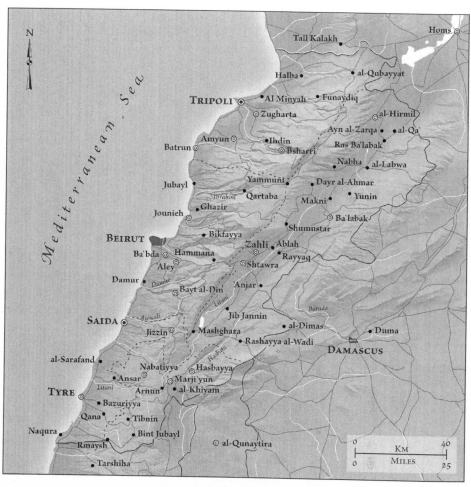

1. Modern-day Lebanon

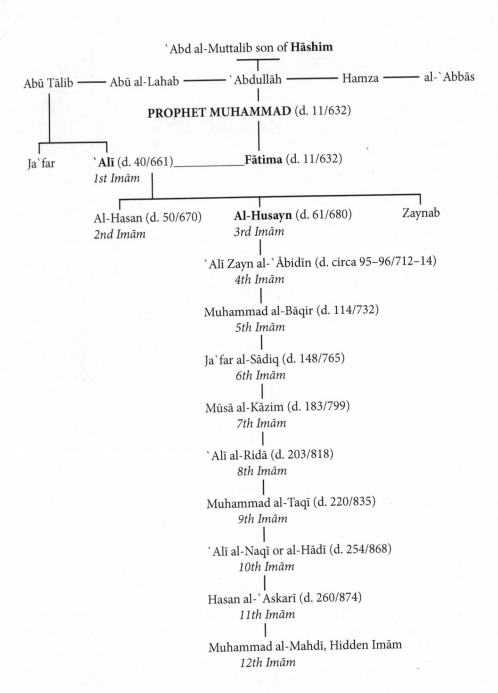

`Abd al-Muttalib son of **Hāshim**

Abū Tālib —— Abū al-Lahab —— `Abdullāh —— Hamza —— al-`Abbās

PROPHET MUHAMMAD (d. 11/632)

Ja`far — **`Alī** (d. 40/661)_____**Fātima** (d. 11/632)
1st Imām

Al-Hasan (d. 50/670)   **Al-Husayn** (d. 61/680)   Zaynab
2nd Imām   *3rd Imām*

`Alī Zayn al-`Ābidīn (d. circa 95–96/712–14)
4th Imām

Muhammad al-Bāqir (d. 114/732)
5th Imām

Ja`far al-Sādiq (d. 148/765)
6th Imām

Mūsā al-Kāzim (d. 183/799)
7th Imām

`Alī al-Ridā (d. 203/818)
8th Imām

Muhammad al-Taqī (d. 220/835)
9th Imām

`Alī al-Naqī or al-Hādī (d. 254/868)
10th Imām

Hasan al-`Askarī (d. 260/874)
11th Imām

Muhammad al-Mahdī, Hidden Imām
12th Imām

1. The Twelve Imams Descending from `Ali and Fatima

THE SHI'ITES OF LEBANON

1

The Shi'ites and Grand Liban

The social processes that shaped the ideas of Shi'ite nationalists, Marxists, and religious modernists in Lebanon during the first half of the twentieth century were inextricably tied to European colonial remapping of Greater Syria and the formation of the Lebanese nation-state.[1] For this reason, we start our history with the creation of Grand Liban in 1920 following the European powers' dismemberment of the Ottoman Empire in 1918. The French and British colonizers divided Greater Syria into the following states: Iraq, Syria, Alexandretta, Grand Liban, Palestine, and Transjordan. The two major Shi'ite regions of Grand Liban were Ba'labak and al-Hirmil in the Biqa' and the South (known earlier as Jabal 'Amil).[2] (See map 1.) This chapter highlights the Shi'ites' socioeconomic conditions at the eve of French rule and lays emphasis on the South where major confrontations with the French unfolded and where the Palestinian crisis was directly felt a few years later.

In this chapter, the French administration of the South is distinguished from its counterparts in Grand Liban, where it is formally depicted as "Mount Lebanon." It appears in the South as a distinct form of colonial rule involving direct supervision, the imposition of exclusive taxes and economic restrictions, and intervention in parliamentary elections. Southern Shi'ite peasants and a section of the provincial leaders and notables refused to join Grand Liban, insisting on being united with Syria under the Arab crown prince, Faysal (d. 1933), the son of Sharif Husayn of Mecca. This chapter illuminates these developments, focusing on Shi'ite banditry and peasant revolts against the French in 1919–20. It highlights the southern elites' support of the bandits and later condemnation of their anarchism. It also draws attention to the presentation of the Shi'ites in French colonial discourse. As the French pacified the Shi'ite regions, their reports embellished the southern Shi'ites' provinciality, economic retardation, and isolation. The religious and entrepreneurial Maronite elites articulated the connection between colonial discourse and Libanism (Lebanese nationalism).[3] Despite resistance from Maronite leftists and Syrian nationalists, these elites stressed their ties to French culture, its "civilizing" mission, and their own role in modernizing Grand Liban.

The last section of this chapter depicts the Shi'ites' links to Syrian and Palestinian cities, noting the interruption that colonization brought to the flow of peoples, goods, and traditions between these cities, on the one hand, and the Biqa' and the South, on the other. This chapter highlights the role of European colonialism and Zionism in shaping the southern Shi'ites' political experiences and struggles during the 1930s.

Most studies of Grand Liban have grouped the Shi'ites under one cohesive sectarian entity, overlooking ways in which social class, regional background, and power relations have undermined or accentuated their sectarian affiliation. Despite the institutionalization of sectarianism in Grand Liban at the hands of the French and the Lebanese nationalist elites, sectarian identity was neither cohesive nor well defined. Sectarianism was also fitted to a secular apparatus of governance shaped by modern civil laws (rather than religious laws), producing overall a sectarian-secular structure. Moreover, sectarianism, though hegemonic, did not govern the Shi'ites' public civil performances. A close examination of banditry and peasant revolts illustrates this point and reveals the Shi'ites' diverse class interests and national positions.

Twelver Shi'ism: An Overview

An overview of the origins of Twelver Shi'ism illuminates aspects of Shi'ite belief, ritual, and messianic expectations as well as the legal-political theory discussed in this book. The Twelver Shi'ites (hereafter referred to simply as the Shi'ites) hold that spiritual and temporal authority originated in Imam 'Ali b. Abi Talib (d. 661), the cousin of Prophet Muhammad (d. 632) and his legitimate successor. The early Shi'ites believed that the Qur'an and the tradition (hadith) that preserves the Prophet's words and actions explicitly state the superior spiritual rank and political privileges of Imam 'Ali and his progeny through Fatima, the Prophet's daughter. For Shi'ites, Imam 'Ali is the first of twelve Imams or infallible religious guides chosen by God to ensure the accurate interpretation of the scriptures and Muhammad's statements found in the tradition. This form of moral and political authority is transmitted to Imam 'Ali's twelve descendants from Fatima—the designated Imams—the last being Muhammad al-Mahdi, who went into occultation in 873–74. In classical Shi'ite thought, all forms of government are illegitimate until the return of the Mahdi, who is expected to rise against tyranny and establish a just social order.[4]

For thirty years after the Prophet's death, three of his companions in turn became caliphs: Abu Bakr (d. 634), 'Umar (d. 644), and 'Uthman (d. 656). These caliphs came to represent the so-called consensus of the commercial and military elites of Meccan and Medinan societies.[5] The dominant majority that established this consensus came to be known as the Sunnite Muslims. The latter acknowledged the special rank Imam 'Ali occupied in early Islam on the basis of his piety and steadfastness in defending Islam but disagreed with Imam 'Ali's partisans on the nature of succession and leadership in Islamic society. The Sunnites argued that Imam 'Ali's claims to the caliphate rested, first, on controversial statements made by the Prophet and, second, on hereditary rule (through the house of the Prophet) that violated the consensus of the Muslim community and the Prophet's exemplary actions.[6] The Sunnites also insisted that the Prophet did not leave a clear will designating Imam 'Ali as the caliph after him. They argued that the successor to the Prophet should be chosen by election among the leading companions and supporters of the Prophet. The partisans of Imam 'Ali, the Shi'a, challenged the Sunnites' claim to have followed the "Sunna" (the right path) and considered their consensus void because it did not include Imam 'Ali's opinions and those of his descendants from Fatima. The Shi'a also argued that 'Umar and 'Uthman promulgated Islam in ways contrary to the Qur'an and to the Prophet's statements, basing their legal rulings on conjecture and discretionary opinion.

From its nascent phase, Shi'ism embodied popular political protest, messianic expectations, as well as a legal vision for the organization of Muslims' daily affairs. Protest movements appear to have crystallized in

Kufa, an Iraqi garrison city, in the late seventh century, expressing Shi'ite struggle against the Umayyad caliphate (660–750). The Kufans called upon Imam Husayn (d. 680), son of 'Ali, to rise against the Umayyads and take his rightful post as caliph.[7] A group of Kufans, "the Penitents," went on a death march in 684 seeking atonement for failing to assist Husayn in his uprising and for leaving him to face death along with seventy-two members of his family and supporters at the hands of the Umayyad caliph Yazid b. Mu'awiya (r. 683–84).[8] Husayn's death fell on the tenth day of the Islamic month of Muharram, 680, in Karbala', Iraq, west of the Euphrates. In modern times, rituals marking this event, called "Muharram" or "'Ashura'," embody central features of Shi'ite piety, protest, and self-sacrifice.[9] Imam Husayn emerged in medieval Arab and Persian history as the "prince of martyrs" who died protesting the injustices of a corrupt ruler and who struggled to restore the caliphate to its rightful candidates—the progeny of 'Ali and Fatima—who alone possessed knowledge, piety, and divinely guided leadership. We must point out, however, that other Imams who succeeded Husayn, such as Imams Muhammad al-Baqir (d. 735) and Ja'far al-Sadiq (d. 765), avoided a confrontation with the rulers and rebellion.[10] Shi'ite groups expressed propensity for protest as well as acquiescence with the rulers depending on their conditions at a given time in history.[11]

A distinct legal perspective and a heterogeneous philosophical tradition also were part and parcel of Shi'ite intellectual life in the medieval period. Even though the Imams were the original sources for legal thought and ethos, the Shi'ite scholars affected developments in Shi'ite law and jurisprudence. Many of these developments reflected the social interests, experiences, and outlook of the Shi'ite learned elites, be they in Iraqi cities of Kufa, Basra, and Baghdad or in the Persian cities Qom and Rayy. The scholarly elites in the ninth century were, for the most part, disgruntled by internal disagreements over Imami succession, the appeal of messianism, and the popular tendency to deify the Imams. Nonetheless, the confusion caused by the death of the eleventh Imam, Hasan al-'Askari (d. 873) and the absence of a clear successor forced the scholars to rehabilitate some of the same popular messianic precepts they had rejected earlier. Shi'ite doctrine has insisted that God, being just and compassionate, does not leave the earth for one moment without an Imam to guide believers. Leading scholars thus declared that the twelfth Imam, Muhammad al-Mahdi, al-'Askari's son, to be the last Imam, but that he remains invisible on earth as long as there is injustice and corruption. By accepting the concept of the "return" of the last invisible Imam, the Shi'ite scholars accommodated new eschatological traditions, but, more important, they ensured their own continued leadership over a critical mass of Shi'ite believers.[12] This form of clerical leadership that is neither a state nor an institutional appointment involved a fluid negotiation of ideas and practices between various sectors of Shi'ite society.

The Shi'ites of the Biqa'

The Biqa' region, with its two areas, Ba'labak and al-Hirmil, featured clusters of peasant families that traced their lineage to a common tribe. These families cultivated ties of kinship, social alliances, and intermarriage. Members of each cluster endorsed the informal authority of a senior leader or "chief" from among its wealthier and more influential families. Clear class distinctions existed within these clusters. The vast lands that a senior leader owned seemed in practice to be shared, though unequally, by members of this cluster.[13] Owing to this collective sense of access to the land and its produce, poor peasants warded off fears of destitution and felt thankful to the chief as both a family figure and a landowner. This system differed significantly from the societal arrangements in the South, where peasants worked largely on lands owned by families unrelated to them. Biqa'i peasants had mixed feelings of inferiority and filial loyalty toward their blood-related propertied chief. It is for this reason—and not owing to a seminomadic or pastoral life pattern—that the Biqa'i Shi'ites came to be perceived as organized into tribes ('asha'ir).

The Shi'ites did not form a majority in the Biqa' as they did in the South. The Catholics were the largest religious group in the region. Their chiefs and religious dignitaries controlled the city of Zahle, the commercial hub of the Biqa'.[14] The Hamadas and the Haydars were the most influential Shi'ite families in the Biqa' during the nineteenth century. The first resided in al-Hirmil as a major landholder, but it also owned property in Mount Lebanon (see map 1).[15] In the 1920s, the Hamadas coalesced with

Maronite feudal leaders in support of French colonial plans and rejected unity with Syria under Faysal.[16] Shi'ite advocates of Arab nationalism hoped Faysal would establish independent rule in the eastern Arab lands that the Ottoman Empire had lost. They envisaged a regional nationalism with Syria at its center. The Maronite provincial leaders and entrepreneurs, however, believed that their interests were better served through Grand Liban than Greater Syria.[17] They hoped to exert greater influence over domestic affairs and enjoy more autonomy away from the commitments of Muslim-Arab countries in the region.

The Haydar family resided in Ba'labak, which was larger in size and population than al-Hirmil.[18] Ba'labak and al-Hirmil had a few 'ulama who cultivated religious learning up until the modern period.[19] Yet in the first half of the twentieth century, the South was the center of religious leadership and legal expertise. The Shi'ite literati in the Biqa' seemed more inclined toward literature, poetry, and journalism.

Peasant Life in the South

The increase in the creation of private property under the Ottomans in the eighteenth century allowed the elites to exploit further the peasants who were now deprived of "the means of production and reproduction."[20] The land reforms that the Ottomans introduced in the mid–nineteenth century were not effective in altering the peasants' conditions. Tarif Khalidi argues, however, that during World War I the South's agricultural produce demanded by the Ottoman army was inaccurately assessed, leaving the peasants and the tax collectors with more than the allotted amount of tax revenue.[21] He suggests that the 'Amilis benefited from this system of taxation and improved their social conditions. Yet we would argue that the underassessment of crops was not particularly helpful for peasants, who struggled with taxes, forced military conscription, hunger, and epidemics during the war. The Ottomans levied an 'ushr (or miri) tax that was one-tenth of the value of agricultural production.[22] It was the state's share of peasant production from all cereals and fruits, such as figs and grapes, as well as from olive oil and bee production.[23] Several chiefs competed over tax-farming (iltizam) privileges from the Ottoman state that specified, before the start of each agricultural season, the duration of a tax-farming assignment. In order to avoid loss of profit, a few landed chiefs and Ottoman-appointed officials divided the one-tenth tax of all villages among themselves, irrespective of who was given the tax-farming assignment in a particular year. Each of the landed chiefs then had a portion in the tax-farmed village areas. A landed chief would exempt influential men from the tax, fixed at one-tenth (*'ushr* or *miri* tithes) of production and paid in kind. He could also bribe them with money to cover up the abusive acts of the agents who collected the *'ushr* for him and their illegal extraction of money from the villagers for themselves.[24]

In the mid–nineteenth century, another phase of Ottoman administrative and rural reform began. The Ottomans tried to collect taxes more effectively and reverse the debilitating impact of the tax-farming system on the peasants. They also aimed to decrease the autonomy and arbitrary practices of tax-farming officers and large landowners. The Ottomans encouraged peasant ownership of land and invited peasants to register fixed areas of lands in their names. Yet Ottoman land reforms faced many hurdles because peasants had to come up with registration fees for the land and pay taxes on it. Some evaded registering these lands in their names or sold them for a cheap price to the tax-farming officers or large landowners.[25] More important, many tried to escape military conscription by giving up their land rights in return for an official declaration that they were dead or had immigrated.[26] The obstacles posed by the mountainous areas of Jabal 'Amil, widespread dependence on traditional means of transportation, and shortage of capital limited the development of the agrarian economy. The 'Amilis partook in an array of craftwork, and women featured prominently in the cottage industry in the region.[27] Industrial ventures were rare, and only a few small manufactures of cigarettes had emerged in Bint Jubayl.[28] An outcome of late Ottoman rule in Jabal 'Amil was the decline in some provincial leaders and notables' profits.

'Amili peasants were of unequal economic standing. Some barely scraped by with a small amount of land and a few sheep, whereas others were able to sell a small surplus of agricultural products in the market. There also were the "free" (*falatiyya*) peasants without any land or animals who occupied the lowest rank of 'Amili rural society.[29] Images of peasant life can be gleaned from a few sources. The view in 1916 from Ottoman Jibsheet, a 'Amili town, is one of panic and poverty for peasants and craft workers, many of whom starved or were executed for leaving their posts in the Ottoman army.[30] Defectors were forced at times to lease themselves to a powerful leader or notable, working in his fields or house for little or no money under the threats of being turned over to the authorities. Other defectors paid a monthly tax, divided between a leader and the police, in return for immunity. [31] Those who could not pay were given to the army, which punished them by death or sent them to combat zones. Many families did not register their newborn boys at the government's bureau out of fear they would be conscripted into the army when they reached adulthood or forced to pay a tax.[32] Among the abuses suffered by the 'Amilis at the hands of Ottoman officials was the *balsa*, a tax imposed on the people for the benefit of the notables and the village mayors. The army punished those who did not pay the *balsa* by breaking into their homes and destroying their winter staples.[33] When caught by Ottoman soldiers, a defector faced certain death. Out of despair, the sisters and mothers of a few defectors pleaded with a notable to intercede on their behalf. A number of these notables took advantage of the women in return for bribing Ottoman soldiers to release the women's loved ones.[34] In Shaqra', people shouted the coded words "a wolf's sacraments" to alert defectors that the police had arrived so they could hide. It did not take long before the secret expression reached the police, who tightened their grip on army defectors.[35]

Money was scarce, and barter continued in some parts of Jabal 'Amil.[36] During World War I, staples dwindled, and the 'Amilis were hit by famine and epidemics such as cholera and "the yellow fever."[37] Many died, and others took refuge in tents in the prairies out of fear of contagion from other villagers.[38] Those who died found few people willing to bury them. Swarms of locusts invaded the farms, devouring tree fruits and both green and dry crops, forcing villagers to boil acorn or grind it like flour. Wheat, barley, and lentils disappeared from the markets. Peasant children who did not die were emaciated from hunger. When the French occupied Syria, the poor health conditions in Jabal 'Amil were further augmented by filthy water wells that supported mosquitoes carrying malaria.[39] French officers, however, considered the high rate of childhood mortality an outcome of the Muslims' "characteristic" refusal of "medical care." It is unclear what the French reports meant by "medical care" or whether Muslim rejection of it was tied to suspicion of the French. As far as the sources show, the high mortality rate among children resulted from the effects of poverty, disease, and famine during the war that stripped the region of its hygienic benefits.[40]

The Southern 'Ulama, Provincial Leaders, and Notables

In the early twentieth century, 'Amili society witnessed greater stratification and intraelite divisions.[41] Provincial leaders (zu'ama) were landed rural chiefs who competed among themselves for Ottoman favors and political sway. Among the well-known provincial leaders were the As'ads (family of al-As'ad). The latter dominated 'Amili politics and divided tax-farming revenues on peasant landholdings among themselves. A new upper social stratum known as the "notables" (wujaha') that had been forming during the nineteenth century came to compete for power with the landed chiefs.[42] The notables derived their status from a combination of financial and commercial activities as well as education.[43] At times, the two strata overlapped and were referred to together as the afandiyya.[44] Khalidi explains that the wujaha' comprised the small urban grain merchants who became multazims or acquired property and civil servants following the promulgation of the 1858 Ottoman land reform.[45] As mentioned earlier, the law was not beneficial to peasants; it did not yield any direct ownership of land or a stable source of livelihood because of the taxes, commissions, and fees they had to pay to intermediary chiefs and civil servants on that land. Meanwhile, the law fostered the development of a network of "financial and judicial bureaucrats" appointed by the Ottomans to oversee the implementation of the laws. This social stratum of intermediary administrative servicemen to the Ottomans in the municipal districts of Sidon, Tyre, and Marji'yun enjoyed relative prosperity and power.[46] French colonization, however, jeopardized the intermediaries' economic base and social position. Jabal 'Amil, now the South of Grand Liban also became heavily taxed under the French, unlike the city of Beirut, which put additional pressure on the notables. Among these notables

were the 'Usayran, al-Khalil, and al-Zayn families.[47] In the early twentieth century, intermarriage between the notables and the *'ulama* (religious
scholars) brought together a mercantilist culture and a tradition of religious learning.

The *'ulama* came from landed well-to-do families such as the Sharaf
al-Din, al-Amin, and Mughniyya, as well as from modest ones such as
the Muroeh and Sadiq.[48] Sayyid 'Abd al-Husayn Sharaf al-Din (d. 1957)
who was the *marja' al-taqlid*—or highest religious authority—of his era
was wealthy and influential.[49] Sayyid Muhsin al-Amin (d. 1952), another
exemplar, had sufficient means through family land and the religious
endowments of his school, al-Muhsiniyya, in Damascus, Syria.[50] Exemplars were chosen from among Shi'ite mujtahids or jurists who received
certification at the seminary in Najaf, Iraq. A mujtahid had the authoritative knowledge to derive Shi'ite law and renew legal rulings using the
methods of the rationalist (*usuli*) school of jurisprudence.

In Ottoman administrative dictum and theory, Syrian Shi'ites were
considered a legitimate Muslim sect on a par with their Sunnite counterparts. As such, they were expected to mediate their needs and resolve their
grievances through Sunnite legal courts. Until the mid–nineteenth century, Shi'ite *'ulama* were not permitted to adjudicate in Ottoman courts
on the basis of the Ja'fari school of law. Shi'ite muftis (jurists who could
derive rulings in one or more areas of the law) applied Sunnite Hanafi
law, the official legal school endorsed by the Ottomans. Some *'ulama*
who disregarded this legal framework or supported the Ottomans' foes,
the Safavids, as well as those who lost local patronage, faced accusations
of heresy.[51] One leading Shi'ite jurist was executed in the early Ottoman
period for practicing Shi'ite *ijtihad* and thus challenging Sunnite legal
orthodoxy.[52] Ottoman bureaucrats seem to have associated this jurist
with anti-Sunnite rituals in the Safavid empire.[53] At the time, the Ottomans permitted Shi'ite rituals marking the birth of the Mahdi or visita-
tion (referred to as "pilgrimage" or *hajj*) to the shrines in al-'Atabat (Najaf,
Karbala', al-Kazimayn, Samarra') and other holy sites in Syria.

In the late Ottoman period, important changes in the conditions of
the Shi'ite *'ulama* occurred. The Ottomans declared the Ja'fari *madhhab*
licit. Shi'ite scholars received appointments as judges in Burj al-Barajina

in Beirut, as well as in Sidon, Tyre, Marji'yun, al-Nabatiyya, and Ba'labak and al-Hirmil.[54] This development aimed to organize sociolegal relations with the Ottomans on a new basis.[55] The judges' functions were restricted to marriage and divorce; the implementation of Shi'ite dissimulation (*taqiyya*), inheritance (*mawarith*), wills (*wasaya*); and the administration of religious endowments and possessions pertaining to children under the legal age (*wilayat al-awqaf wa-al-qasirin*). The Ottoman rulers, however, required the judges to ensure that Shi'ites refrain from religious activities involving the defamation of Sunnite figures and emblems. The Ottomans also permitted the observance of 'Ashura' as long as it did not involve the cursing of the companions of the Prophet or rulers revered by Sunnite Muslims.[56]

A number of '*ulama* owned land and relied on community contributions.[57] They occasionally received *khums* (one-fifth of the value of several items including gold, pearls, and commercial profit) from believers, but it was not a systematic or substantive source of support for them or their students. The Shi'ite '*ulama* had relative juridical autonomy and arbitrated a large number of civil cases in accordance with the Ja'fari school of law.[58] Some enjoyed independence from the provincial leaders and notables through their posts as muftis and judges. The muftis in particular obtained social visibility and became an important link between the locals and the Ottomans. The mufti received the *kharaj* land revenues of seven villages, which amounted to 100 *dunum* (or ten hectares) for each village.[59] These lands were registered in the personal name of the Shi'ite mufti. Sayyid 'Ali al-Amin was able through such a post to revive the madrasa (school) in Shaqra' believed to have trained 400 students in the legal sciences.[60] The Syrian Shi'ite madrasas drew intellectual links to other centers of Shi'ite and Sunnite learning in Syria, Iraq, Iran, India, and Mecca.

From Ottoman Rule to French Colonial Arrangements

In comparison to their Druze (Muslim) and Maronite counterparts in Mount Lebanon, the Shi'ite provincial leaders experienced a decisive setback during the late eighteenth century. The increasing autonomy of the Druze emirates in Mount Lebanon under the Ottomans was achieved precisely through the elimination of the Shi'ite Hamadas and Harfush emirates, Stefan Winter argues.[61] These Shi'ite emirates had been established in the sixteenth century when the Ottoman state gave Shi'ite leaders, who enjoyed local power and organizational capabilities, cash tax-farming contracts in Mount Lebanon and Ba'labak.[62] In this same period, the Shi'ite merchants had made limited investments in the silk industry.

In 1860, the Ottomans tried to resolve civil strife caused by a clash between the feudal leaders of the Druze and the Maronites in the region of Mount Lebanon. Under pressure from European powers in 1861, the Ottomans established a system of self-rule (the *mutasarrifiyya*) in Mount Lebanon, later called "Petit Liban," which recognized the increasing power and economic weight of the Maronites.[63] On the one hand, self-rule aimed to organize relations between the Druze and the Maronites, but on the other it secured the political stability necessary for the growth of French capitalist investments in the silk industry of Mount Lebanon. Under Petit Liban, the French and the Maronites cultivated political as well as cultural ties that laid the groundwork for a new hegemonic colonial system—namely, Grand Liban. The Maronites became the "single most important beneficiary of the French missionary schools, hospitals, and dispensaries" and enjoyed unprecedented financial and political backing from the French government.[64] Jabal 'Amil, Mount Lebanon's adjacent neighbor, experienced a more restrictive form of Ottoman rule through the As'ad landed chiefs, who wielded greater control over peasant affairs than had their predecessors.[65] European investments in Shi'ite regions were meager when Mount Lebanon rose to prominence with its silk industry and Beirut did so with its commercial and transportation industries. In the 1850s and the 1860s, Beirut became a flourishing city with the largest port on the Syrian coast,[66] largely owing to a major increase in foreign trade, development of local industries, and Beirut's political stability. Meanwhile, the French had been investing in commerce, railways, and port facilities.[67] They also were competing with the British over resources and strategic locations in Greater Syria.

Following the partition of the Ottoman Empire by the French and British in 1918, Prince Faysal, the son of Sharif Husayn of Mecca, proceeded to establish his monarchical rule in Syria. Sharif Husayn, a descendant of the house of the Prophet, ruled the Hijaz in Arabia and presided over the affairs of the sacred cities of Mecca and Medina. Once promising Husayn and his son independent rule, the European powers reneged in 1920 and dismantled the young Arab kingdom in Syria. The French nurtured the formation of Grand Liban as a separate geographical-national entity and ruled it through a mandate from 1920 until 1946. The French Mandate referred to indirect rule wherein French resources were installed in military defense as opposed to economic, educational, or medical development.[68] Under the French, Mount Lebanon lost its semiautonomous status, which it had enjoyed in the late Ottoman period. For instance, it was free of tobacco monopolistic regulations for several years and enjoyed a "free-enterprise system," which attracted many investors.[69] However, it lost this system, too, after 1935. The South received harsher treatment. Its colonial administration dominated economic and political affairs, using systematic surveillance and police coercion.

The French tried to appease Shi'ite leaders and notables by offering them a handful of political and administrative posts. They expected the Shi'ites to consider them more "lenient" rulers than the Sunnite Ottomans, arguing that they had brought the Shi'ites freedom of religious worship and management of legal and social affairs.[70] With respect to religious rituals, this argument seemed valid. On a few occasions, however, late Ottoman officials allowed the Shi'ites to observe 'Ashura'. In one instance, Beirut's *vali* (provincial governor) allowed Iranian residents in Jabal 'Amil to hold 'Ashura' and perform the Passion Play, which openly condemns Sunnite companions of the Prophet for the tragedy that befell the Shi'ites.[71] The Ottomans had already put Shi'ite religious courts in function and made them independent from their Sunnite counterparts in the late nineteenth century, so on January 27, 1926, when the French authorized the establishment of Shi'ites courts, they were simply reinforcing an earlier Ottoman arrangement.[72] Disaffected peasants and religious intellectuals, however, were not convinced that obtaining the freedom in observing 'Ashura' should make them loyal to Grand Liban. In fact, many preferred to join Syria with its Sunnite majority than belong to Grand Liban.

Banditry, the National Elites, and Unity with Syria

In 1918, when French troops landed on the coasts of Greater Syria, they encountered thousands living under strenuous conditions. People were still suffering from the economic effects and trauma of the famine that had occurred in the previous four years during World War I.[73] Some hoped that the French would help the economy prosper by offering jobs for those in distress. These hopes soon vanished with the spread of the great world depression in the late 1920s. When the Ottoman Empire collapsed, Faysal declared an Arab government in Damascus and attempted to incorporate other parts of Greater Syria under his rule. Meanwhile, the French anticipated a full confrontation with the Shi'ites and tried to quell the peasants' growing desires to remain part of Syria.[74] The incoming Allied armies—namely, those of the French and British—quickly dismantled the administrative councils established on behalf of the Arab government in Damascus. The Maronite clergy and leading businessmen hoped for a Lebanese polity protected by the French and completely separate from Syria that could safeguard their political and economic privileges.[75] The Maronite peasantry, however, expressed at different junctures views at variance with its religious and secular leaderships. It shared the grievances of Shi'ite tobacco peasants and workers and protested in unison with them against the colonial designs of the French.[76]

In April 1920,[77] when it became clear that all hopes for independent Arab rule under Faysal had dissolved, Shi'ite hostility toward the French peaked. Several Haydar leaders were key figures in mobilizing Biqa'i Shi'ites to join Faysal's Arab armies.[78] Ba'labak became a central stage for armed resistance and civil disobedience against the French.[79] The French succeeded, however, in crushing the resistance and incorporating Biqa'i Shi'ites into Grand Liban in 1926. In 1927, the French quelling of the Great Arab Revolt in Syria demoralized the peasants, and a decade later the Haydar leaders defected to the French camp.[80] Meanwhile, to placate the Biqa'is, the French founded an agricultural bank to give loans to peasants and a department to enhance the production of eggs. They also changed the drain system and water canals, but their irrigation projects had limited success.[81] In 1935 and 1936, they lifted certain taxes relating to the importing of agricultural machines and reduced the tax on animal herds.[82] A few roads were built linking the major towns to each other and ultimately to the central Beirut-Damascus highway. The French also took a special interest in the ancient Roman ruins of Ba'labak, renovating them in 1935.

In the South, Shi'ite social bandits started to gain momentum after World War I, launching attacks against French posts and pro-French Christians who assisted the French army or personnel. These bandits were groups of rural rebels from various social backgrounds and with some connections to elite figures. They were also relatively organized, forging ties to peasants and dignitaries interested in challenging French colonial authorities.[83] In the South, among the most effective were the bandits led by Sadiq Hamza (Hamzeh), Adham Khanjar, and Mahmud Bazzi. Hamza and his supporters targeted French soldiers, stealing their weapons and horses and attacking Christian villagers that allegedly collaborated with the French.[84] Their attacks at times paralyzed the French administration, especially with respect to the collection of taxes from both Christians and Muslims in the South.[85] They practiced self-governance in areas that fell under their control and collected a safety tax from the landed dignitaries—money paid in return for safety and preservation of property.

Banditry was a way of living when earlier systems of Ottoman economic production, social support, and authority had collapsed. Bandit leaders were local chiefs (carrying honorific titles such as *emir* and *bey*) with Shi'ite and Sunnite backgrounds.[86] Their activities and outlook had much in common with Ottoman feudatories, yet without fiefs, tax-farming rights, or state supervision.[87] In the South, bandits emerged from a mixed nomadic and sedentary base, expressing allegiance to Faysal and gaining some dignitaries' temporary support. Peasants, intellectuals, and dignitaries held mixed views about the bandits, ranging from admiration to repulsion.[88] On the one hand, the bandits' anti-French activities were claimed as part of southern colonial history and popular national culture. On the other, the bandits were condemned for acts of random violence against local southerners—in particular, Christian civilians.[89] According to Sabrina Mervin, the elites felt unsettled by what they branded as an "anarchistic" force that undermined their place in society.[90] Yet prior to the escalation of the bandits' attacks on Christians, the elites supported the bandits' resistance to the French. Exemplifying the change in the attitudes toward the bandits, Sayyid Hasan, the son of Muhsin al-Amin, embellished the bandit Khanjar's heroism in his short story "A Lute of Fire,"[91] but he became dismayed by the bandits' massacre of Christian civilians in the southern town of 'Ayn Ibil, discussed in the next section. Overall, the bandits were a true example of political uncertainty, fragmentation of authority, and colonial dislocation. To this picture, one must add Shi'ite peasants' confrontation with Zionist settlers. In March 1920, a group of armed Jewish settlers in the South led by Joseph Trumpeldor (1880–1920), a Zionist Socialist leader, assisted the French soldiers who were being pursued by the locals.[92] Several Shi'ites and Jews died, including Trumpeldor.

Vivid hopes for unity with Syria were evident among the peasants.[93] These hopes converged with the interests of several—but not all—southern notables.[94] In family gatherings and social and political meetings, two notables of the literati, Ahmad Rida (d. 1953) and Sulayman Zahir (d. 1960), showcased the unity cause.[95] A handful of provincial leaders such as Kamil al-As'ad supported the struggle against the French in the 1920s, but they achieved only short-term political goals. During this phase of the struggle, the leading maraji' (exemplars, sing. marja') seemed united against the French detachment of the South from Syria. Sayyid Mushin al-Amin, who resided in Damascus, advocated Shi'ite-Sunnite unity against the French, thus cultivating the respect of Sunnite national leaders in Damascus.[96] Sayyid Sharaf al-Din, who was situated in Tyre, promoted his religious leadership in a more provincial and Shi'ite-based milieu. He took advantage of peasant discontent and banditry to undermine the French and force them to offer religious dignitaries such as himself power and resources. Owing to his liaison with the bandits, however, the French sentenced him to exile in absentia. A few years would pass before Sharaf al-Din would attempt a rapprochement with the French. He remained thereafter on good terms with the French military governor of South Lebanon, Zinovi Pechkoff.[97]

Bandits' Assault on 'Ayn Ibil and French Reprisal

Bandit leaders, religious scholars, and dignitaries congregated in Wadi al-Hujayr in the South in 1920 to discuss future forms of resistance to the French and to address the bandit attacks on Maronite Christians. Most southern sources and French reports blamed the bandits' acts of violence against Maronites on the *marja'* Sharaf al-Din's encouragement and financing.[98] Anti-French bandit activities had initially served his interests.[99] He had wanted the French to know that the Shi'ites could be mobilized by religious leaders to obstruct their plans. On April 5, 1920, following the meeting in Wadi al-Hujayr, Mahmud Bazzi's group of bandits attacked the Christian town of 'Ayn Ibil, killing approximately 100 people and wounding 100 more.[100] A close look at the conflicting historical accounts reveals new dimensions in this incident.

Sharaf al-Din's opponents may have exaggerated his role in the bandits' attack on the Christians.[101] For one, the alliance between two socially antagonistic entities—the bandits and Sharaf al-Din—was only temporary. Sharaf al-Din, as noted earlier, benefited from the bandits' threat to the French, but there is no reason to believe that all of Bazzi's activities were directly commanded by Sharaf al-Din. Then, after reconciling with the French, Sharaf al-Din negotiated a better position for himself, aiming to become a central link between the colonial government and the Shi'ites. In exchange for Sharaf al-Din's conformity to their policies, the French appointed one of his children mufti in Tyre in 1931 and another one judge in Ba'labak in 1936.[102]

Following the bandits' attack on 'Ayn Ibil, French troops led by General Nieger launched a military campaign against Shi'ite rebels and civilians alike, using air force. They bombarded Bint Jubayl and several adjacent villages, setting them aflame. Southern Shi'ites were put on trial, and French punishment was collective.[103] The army looted and demolished many homes, arrested scores of Shi'ites, and executed approximately thirty rebels. Furthermore, the French imposed a heavy tax as a financial punishment of all southern villages in the amount of 100,000 golden pounds, thereby draining peasants' coffers for decades.[104] The French thus reasserted their control over the area and temporarily silenced the Shi'ites' call for unity with Syria. Their close surveillance and onerous taxation of the area made their colonial rule oppressive, especially in comparison to the French Mandate in Mount Lebanon and Beirut.

Contesting Grand Liban

The spokesmen for unity with Syria did not always express a clear or coherent vision of what such unity entailed. More important, the drive for unity went through different phases. In the late Ottoman period, pro-tonationalist Arab notions of statehood and sovereignty overlapped with Muslim and Ottomanist ones. On April 24, 1920, a group of southern leaders and notables demanded unity with Syria under Faysal's leadership.[105] They rejected the French Mandate categorically. Others were ambivalent about joining Grand Liban even though they doubted Faysal's ability to defeat the French and establish his rule in Syria.[106] Southern delegates who met with Faysal could not dispel these doubts. Some believed that Faysal advised the southerners to acquiesce to French rule because he was unable to launch a military campaign against a European power. Another group of southerners believed Faysal was ready to send military and medical supplies in support of a jihad (holy war) against the colonizers.[107] Even after the British made Faysal king in Iraq, some remained convinced that a unified socioeconomic network linking the South to Syrian cities was the only guarantee of security and growth.[108] When southern elites could not achieve such unity, they called for a noncentralized government in 1926,[109] petitioning the French authorities to treat the South as an autonomous administrative unit separate from Grand Liban yet part of the French Mandate government.

Pechkoff assured his superiors in France that the Shi'ites in Grand Liban elected their own deputies and judges and enjoyed an independent civil status.[110] If annexed to Syria, he noted, they would cease to exist as a free and separate community. In fact, however, the French themselves chose most of the parliamentary deputies, and the Shi'ite courts had emerged earlier in the late Ottoman period in connection to the Tanzimat modernizing reforms rather than French accomplishments. Despite the French administrators' attempts to bolster their image as the protectors of the Shi'ite "persecuted minority," many southerners rejected Grand Liban and demanded unity with Syria. Since the late Ottoman period, the Shi'ites of the South and the Biqa' had been resentful of the economic and political dominance of Mount Lebanon with its Druze and Maronite Christian leaders.[111] The Ottomans had given Mount Lebanon a semiautonomous administration in 1861, known later as Petit Liban. This administration articulated the Maronites' ascendancy and paved the way for growth in their entrepreneurial weight and investments in the silk industry. After the San Remo conference on April 25, 1920, which mandated French rule over Grand Liban and Syria, the South became part of Grand Liban. Maronite leaders supported the formation of Grand Liban after guarantees that the French would preserve their privileges.[112] In contrast, the Shi'ites in the South felt that their inclusion in Grand Liban would force them once again to compete on unequal grounds with Mount Lebanon as they had under Petit Liban. Southern notables and scholars complained that Petit Liban had benefited from the Shi'ites' "attachment" to it and that the Shi'ites continued to suffer from such an "attachment."[113] They added, "We pay taxes, but little if any is spent on us. We came to realize that our rights are wasted with it [Petit Liban]. We are not given the jobs that we deserve."[114] This position, however, did not prevent members of the Shi'ite elite from declaring their support of Grand Liban in order to promote their political and economic interests. They declared that in the spirit of "concord" they "[saw] no harm" in joining Grand Liban.[115]

Interest in unity with Syria persisted throughout the 1930s. Religious intellectuals played no small part in agitating against the French through cultural clubs and intellectual associations. A prominent association, the 'Amili Youth, joined literary critics and religious modernists who advocated Syrian-Arab nationalism and challenged the landed elites' authority. The 'Amili Youth espoused anticolonial resistance, arguing that integrating the South into Syria rested on "natural" historical factors, but Grand Liban was a French invention. The Syrian Unity Party (Hizb al-Wahda al-Suriyya), a political organization that emerged in 1935, attracted clerics and leading scholars such as Rida, Zahir, Ahmad

'Arif al-Zayn.[116] It emphasized the cultural and economic links between the South and Syria in opposition to the Lebanese Unity Party (Hizb al-Wahda al-Lubnaniyya), which promoted Libanism and defended the polity of Grand Liban.[117] The advocates of Libanism, in particular the Maronite elites made up of patriarchs and entrepreneurs, tried to persuade the French to keep the South outside the boundaries of Grand Liban.[118] They wanted instead to have the Biqa' Valley and Tripoli in the north annexed to Grand Liban and Beirut.[119] They did not see the South, with its large Muslim population and meager economic resources, as being vital to their interests in the new polity.

Libanism and Shi'ite Dissent

As the French colonizers thwarted national aspirations for a Syrian Arab state under Faysal, champions of Libanism were providing ideological justification for Grand Liban and drawing upon Eurocentric perceptions of the Oriental Muslims and Christians. In 1917, Shukri Ghanim, a Maronite Christian, championed the cause of Grand Liban as a non-Arab nation— referred to at times as "Phoenicia"—with roots in the pre-Islamic past. Like other Libanists, he had adopted French colonial and Jesuit missionary ideas about the "exceptional" cultural qualities of pre-Islamic Syria and its Christians. Another Libanist, Nadra Moutran, described Lebanon as both "Christian and French." The Muslims, he reflected, could not rival the Christian minority, which was one-third of the population, because this minority had control over trade and key resources and owned vast lands. Moutran argued that even though Muslims formed two-thirds of Syria's population, they were divided among themselves. Jacques Tabet, son of a wealthy Christian family from Beirut, studied at the Jesuit University of Saint Joseph in Beirut and maintained close ties with French economists there. The advancement of Christians, he reflected, depended on their autonomy, which can be fulfilled under Grand Liban. Tabet noted the Christian's mercantilist "disposition" and flexibility as opposed to the Muslim's "xenophobic" outlook.[120]

Michel Chiha, a Maronite entrepreneur, became a central figure in the committee that the French charged with drafting the Lebanese

Constitution.[121] Approved by the French high commissioner in 1926, the constitution tried to find a Lebanese nationalism acceptable to all, including the Shi'ites, a "community" that had taken shelter from Sunnite persecution in the mountainous regions of what is now Lebanon. Chiha and the committee he represented argued that Lebanon's diverse "communities" such as the Druze and the Maronites had also sought refuge from religious and ethnic discrimination at the hands of Sunnite Muslim rulers. The perception of Lebanon as a "shelter" resonated with French colonial arguments for why the Shi'ites as a "persecuted minority" should embrace their new "freedom" in Grand Liban. A major proponent of Libanism, Chiha declared that Lebanon's birth was a sublime attempt at coexistence among diverse religious traditions and races. He turned the separation among religious sects into a communalist virtue and distinguished among these communities on the basis of both sect and class. He organized the Lebanese provinces hierarchically according to their contribution to Grand Liban's "civilizational" role, singling out Mount Lebanon as the national heartland. Mount Lebanon, though previously impoverished, Chiha reflected, had emerged into "a solid and powerful social and cultural structure that offered the Lebanese diaspora the most brilliant [figures] and best representation."[122] Mount Lebanon represented the alliance between the propertied elites and the financial bourgeoisie, an alliance that Chiha imbued with moral values and national ideals. He envisioned Lebanon as a commercial and financial center that would remain the friend of France and a neutral member of the Arab region. He expected Lebanon to achieve mercantilist urbanity following Western civic codes and legal models, hoping the Lebanese would overcome "provincial" customs that threatened such urbanity.[123] Libanism was presented as a civilizing sentiment in an Arab-Islamic region. This sentiment, according to Chiha, allowed the Lebanese, in particular the "adventurous" Maronites, to achieve modernism and progress.

The relationship between Maronite leaders and the French was not without tensions and disagreements, however.[124] Yet the Maronite professionals and religious leaders identified with French culture and language to varying degrees.[125] The Lebanese nation, Patriarch Ilyas Huwayyik argued, was distinguished by its "adoption of the language, moral values and customs of French culture."[126] The French eventually fulfilled Maronite hopes for decision-making power and ascendancy in state posts.[127] Patriarch Antoine Arida argued that it was possible for all religious groups to belong to Grand Liban if they were to acknowledge the privileged association of Grand Liban with Christianity.[128]

Libanist emphasis on the Christians' "modernness" paralleled a colonial narrative about impediments to Muslim progress. A French report in 1930 noted that the Muslim Shi'ites of the South were culturally inferior owing to their rural livelihoods, which "naturally isolated them from the rest of Lebanon" and kept them unexposed to superior civilizing influences from "outside." Because of the difficult terrain and lack of roads and crossable tracks, the French report noted, the heart of the southern countryside remained sheltered from positive external cultural stimuli. The prospects for southern economic and intellectual development were "consequently retarded." The Shi'ites lived a "dull" life based on the habits of a "sedentary and underdeveloped population," which survived through only one work pattern, the exploitation of limited arable land. The southern people, the report continued, were subjugated to the tutelage of small feudal and religious lords and left their villages only to go to the closest market. They "know only" the villages adjacent to them and seemed ignorant of others farther away, even by name. The Shi'ites, the report reflected, had only a few schools, whereas the Christians in the South, "thanks to the Jesuits Schools of father Pelissier," had at least one school in each village.[129] These reflections were not made to justify French plans for economic or educational development in the South. No such plans existed, especially because the South was given low priority in furnishing the foundations of Grand Liban.

During the 1930s, Shi'ite peasants continued to dispute Libanism and membership in Grand Liban.[130] Yet a few Shi'ite political and religious leaders gradually adapted aspects of Libanism—namely, the claim that Lebanon possessed unique historical qualities and was a final home for southern and Biqa'i Shi'ites. At the same time, though, these leaders contested Maronite political supremacy and colonial discourse about Muslim and Shi'ite inferiority.[131]

A Shared History: The South and Northern Palestine

To complete our historical account of the Shi'ites under Grand Liban, it is important to highlight the shared experiences of the peoples of the Biqa' and Damascus, on the one hand, and those of the people of the South and Galilee (northern Palestine), on the other, who found themselves in separate national states after 1919–20. Prior to the French Mandate, the Shi'ites were part of a regional socioeconomic setting that crisscrossed Damascus and northern Palestine, respectively.[132] Several towns in Acre and the South (Jabal 'Amil) were part of one political administration.[133] A French security officer in Sidon reported that the "population of South Lebanon is even more sympathetic to the Arabs of Palestine since the two have commercial relations and family links together. Around 2,000 to 3,000 individuals, originally from Sidon resided permanently with their families in Palestine and earned their living there."[134]

For the southerners, it was Haifa not Beirut that was the center of commercial activities. Many had relatives in Haifa or traveled to it for business.[135] The Palestinian lira circulated among southern hands more frequently than the Lebanese lira.[136] Shoemakers of Bint Jubayl and leather producers of Mashghara in the Biqa' Valley found an eager Palestinian market for their commodities. A number of cities—such as al-Nabatiyya, Bint Jubayl, and 'Udaysa—served as linking posts or intermediary markets between the south and northern Palestine.[137] The Monday and Thursday markets at Al-Nabatiyya and Bint Jubayl cultivated vital trade links among the economies of the south, Damascus, and northern Palestine. The southerners found in these regional streams a sense of economic stability and social identity.[138]

A few years following the establishment of Grand Liban, however, the markets of Bint Jubayl, Marji'yun, and al-Nabatiyya started to disintegrate. As a consequence, thousands lost their jobs, including 30,000 craftsmen who left Bint Jubayl in 1928. Beirut's port replaced Haifa's for Syrian trade and transit.[139] Business investors in Beirut and Mount Lebanon protested in 1930 against British development projects in Haifa's port, fearing future competition and declining profits. In the meantime, capitalist enterprises in the South were limited and could not compensate the southerners for what they had lost with Haifa.

During the 1930s, the Palestinians' outrage at the British support of Jewish immigration into Palestine and the fear of Zionist national aspirations resonated in the South. The southerners were caught in the middle of the struggle between the British and the French over fixing a boundary between Grand Liban and Palestine. They lost seven villages and their agricultural lands.[140] A poem composed by the scholar Sulayman Zahir highlighted these conflicts,

> Let not the children of Zion
> Feel confident in [their] hopes
> For Balfour's promise is no guarantee
> One asks Britain what her hands have committed
> What does it pretend by giving settlements to Zion
> They [Zionists] trampled over prosperous Arab lands
> In the name of educating and civilizing.[141]

The southerners deeply felt the 1936–39 revolt in Palestine against British imperialism and Zionism.[142] Shi'ites, Sunnites, and Christians in the South took to the streets, facing injury and death, to protest against the colonizers. Meanwhile, a southern resistance to Zionist settlements grew in several villages.[143] Palestinians came to al-Nabatiyya to buy arms during the early months of the revolt.[144] Shi'ite supporters of the revolt intercepted trucks carrying food and ammunition to Zionist settlers.[145] The city of Bint Jubayl became a refuge for Palestinian fighters.[146] Young southerners answered the call for help from Shaykh Muhammad al-Ashmar, a Palestinian resistance leader.[147] Meanwhile, Haj Amin al-Husayni, the Palestinian mufti, was forced out of Jerusalem by the British and escaped to Bint Jubayl in 1936. He came to Tyre to meet Sayyid Sharaf al-Din. The French authorities tried to prevent the meeting but faced a huge crowd in support of the Palestinian resistance and al-Husayni.[148] Massive demonstrations denounced Zionist nationalism but also condemned colonial economic policies and the French imposition of the Régie.[149] When three Shi'ite fighters returned in 1938 from Palestine, the young and old rushed to hear about their encounters and to learn about the condition of the Palestinians.[150]

Fawzi al-Qawuqji, the leader of the later Arab Rescue Army (Jaysh al-Inqadh al-'Arabi), which aimed to defend Palestine against Zionist occupation in 1948, noted in his memoirs that the South was one of the central platforms for the Arab-Israeli War. Shi'ites took part in the battles between the Rescue Army and the Zionists.[151] Many fled their houses following a Zionist massacre against the people of Hula, close to the Palestinian border.[152] The southerners' break with northern Palestine occurred definitively in 1948 when the Zionists succeeded in establishing the State of Israel.

Summary

Before the onset of French colonial rule in Grand Liban, 'Amili society under the Ottomans witnessed a greater social stratification marked by the rise of the notables, who rivaled the landed chiefs, acquired modern education, and expressed nascent Arab nationalist leanings. Ottoman land and administrative reforms enhanced the notables' political sway and increased a few peasants' profit. The reforms, however, could not secure formal ownership of land by peasants or end the abuses of powerful chiefs who were intermediaries between the Ottoman state and the peasants.

Following the French annexation of the Biqa' and Jabal 'Amil to Grand Liban, several social bandits emerged. The Shi'ite bandits in the South rejected French colonization of Syria, expressing mixed Ottomanist and Syrian loyalties as well as commitment to Faysal's Arab government in Syria. Many southerners sympathized with anti-French banditry and underscored the national heroism of its leaders. The bandits' increased militancy, however, troubled Shi'ite elites and intellectuals, who condemned the bandits' anarchism and their zealotry against Christian civilians allegedly cooperating with the French. The bandits were dispersed following the French execution and exile of their leaders.

Between 1918 and 1920, the majority of Shi'ites preferred unity with Syria under Faysal over a French-mandated Grand Liban.[153] Once the regions with a Shi'ite majority became part of Grand Liban, the Shi'ites felt marginal to the urban bourgeoisie of Beirut and resented competition with a favored child of the French mandate—Mount Lebanon. A handful of notables were recruited into the French administration, but no major economic ventures parallel to those in Mount Lebanon existed in the Shi'ite regions to draw these regions' elites into the sphere of the European market and the heart of the Lebanese polity. The Shi'ite elites felt undermined by the Libanists, in particular the Maronites, who enjoyed distinct economic and political privileges. Maronite patriarchs and entrepreneurial elites stressed the Christians' unique disposition to modernity and their profound links to the French culture. At the same time, the emphasis on the Muslim Shi'ites' parochialism and lack of progress evident in colonial discourse reinforced Libanism, augmenting the Shi'ites' alienation from the nascent polity. Nonetheless, a segment of the Shi'ite political and religious elites came to adapt elements of Libanism, portraying Grand Liban as a haven for "minorities" and the homeland of Biqa'i and southern Shi'ites. These leaders, despite this adaptation or perhaps because they had gotten their foot in the door, as chapter 2 further illustrates, confronted Maronite supremacy and protested its exclusive claims to modernity.

Finally, the British colonization of Palestine and the militant Zionist operations in northern Palestine and the South disrupted further the shared social history and economic links between these regions. These developments helped constitute Lebanese Shi'ites as a religious minority—against the possibility of union on the basis of Arab or economic ties across borders. Indeed, the Palestinians' crisis and tragedy had a more profound manifestation in the South than in any other part of Grand Liban. It had major implications for the spread of nationalist and leftist resistance to Israel in future Lebanon.

2

Education, Modernism, and Anticolonial Struggle

The threat to religion in colonial and postcolonial Islamic society, as well as the challenges of modernism to Islamic institutions of learning and the shari'a experts, the clerics, had significant implications for Lebanese Shi'ites. These developments were inextricably tied to the form of polity established in Lebanon and the latter's integration into the capitalist world economy. This chapter focuses attention on the main socioeconomic forces and political and intellectual trends in Lebanese Shi'ite society from the 1920s to the late 1940s.

The first section focuses on economic and political developments. It examines the conditions and implications of the Bint Jubayl revolt in the South against the French in 1936. It assesses the shifts and ambiguities in the Shi'ite demands for unity with Syria, which continued through most of the 1930s. The peasants, supported by a group of notables and 'ulama, protested against the tax penalties, the imposition of the tobacco monopoly, and French coercion of political activists. This chapter revisits the Shi'ite communal leaders' endorsement of Grand Liban and their renunciation of unity with Syria in the conference of al-Tibi in 1936. It delineates the rise of a youth culture that identified with peasants and advanced a local "indigenous" modernism against most of the elites who eventually chose to join Grand Liban. And, finally, it highlights the Shi'ites' precarious place in the sectarian-secular system of independent Lebanon in 1943.

Socioeconomic discontent, modernism, and confrontation with French colonial policies provide the context for the cultural developments discussed in the chapter's second section. The latter deals with intellectual

27

developments, highlighting the challenges posed by modern secular education to Lebanese Shi'ite scholars and *talaba* (students of the Islamic sciences) at Najaf's seminary in Iraq. Najaf held great significance for Shi'ites as the site of Imam 'Ali's shrine and center for Shi'ite legal scholarship established by al-Shaykh al-Tusi (d. 460/1067). Its intellectual prominence varied over time but by the nineteenth century it became the foremost center for Shi'ite legal studies in the world, shaping through its graduates the clerical politics of the Shi'ite world. These *talaba*, drawn mostly from the South, became dissatisfied with the seminary during the 1920s and expressed increased disaffection with clerical vocations, instead turning to careers in literature, teaching, and journalism. In the middle of the struggles against British and French colonialism, some *talaba* investigated European secular thought and found justification for renewing Islamic traditions. A few aspiring *'ulama* gravitated toward Marxist thought, which set in motion rich, multifaceted, and poignant discussions about the place of Arab-Islamic traditions in a modern world.

Socioeconomic and Political Transformation

Punitive Taxes, the Tobacco Monopoly, and Political Repression

European colonialism and national liberation were not just the subjects of intellectual investigation in southern cultural and educational associations. They also had immediate bearing on the lives of Lebanese Shi'ites—in particular, southern peasants. By 1936, the peasants and rural workers of Bint Jubayl were in open revolt against French colonial rule and were joined by a number of notables and religious scholars.[1] Several historical conditions led to this revolt.

The southerners were under duress following the civil crisis in 'Ayn Ibil and French punitive measures since 1920. People complained about the arbitrariness of colonial taxation and demanded the implementation of a standard taxation scale free of class, religious, or provincial biases.[2] They paid in-kind taxes to the French army stationed in the South and taxes on certain endowments as well as on livestock and construction. Others suffered from paying high custom tariffs that hindered their trade with northern Palestine and Syria. Southerners complained also about the invasion of their markets by foreign commodities and wanted custom protection for their local products. The French further imposed certain fines indiscriminately for major and minor violations.[3]

The French authorities reinstated a monopolistic policy in 1935 on all aspects of tobacco production and sales in the new Lebanon and founded the Régie Co-Interessee Libanaise des Tabacs et Tombac (the Régie) to administer the monopoly.[4] The people of the South and Lebanon at large relied primarily on tobacco cultivation after tobacco replaced silk as the primary cash crop following the steep decline in silk production during the mid-1920s. French monopolistic plans suffocated 170 local factories that had sprung up earlier in Ottoman Mount Lebanon, preserving only thirty of them, labeled "principal manufactures."[5] The tobacco workers who were laid off in the late 1920s after the mechanization of the Syro-Lebanese cigarette industries received no compensation from the Régie.[6]

Thousands of peasants and seasonal workers sought jobs mainly in the growing tobacco production, and to a lesser extent, in the olive oil, marble, and stone industries.[7] Lebanese political leaders and deputies tried to protect the burgeoning tobacco industry by appealing to the French authorities to increase the custom tariffs on imported foreign tobacco. The French turned a deaf ear to these demands.[8] The low custom tariffs put Syro-Lebanese tobacco growers and workers in fierce competition with the regional and international market, which led to decline in local production, the smuggling of foreign tobacco, the lowering of tobacco prices in Lebanese markets, and eventually the decrease in state revenues.[9] The crisis paved the way for the French to reinstate the tobacco monopoly in 1935, which became integral to its hegemonic colonial system. This development set off a wave of protests in Syrian and Lebanese cities and towns. Outcries against the monopoly overtook several Lebanese towns and cities, where in this instance Maronite and Shi'ite farmers joined hands.[10] A large sector of the national elites—Christian and Muslim—supported the tobacco-grower peasants and workers in protest against the French. Bint Jubayl played a central role in the revolt, as did the village of 'Aynatha.[11] (See map 2.) In the congregation of workers that followed, southerners carried to the center of the Régie plant in Beirut a yoke and a pick axe in a coffin, which symbolized the death of the means of their production and source of live-lihood. They presented the Régie administration with a list of demands pertaining to the production and sale of tobacco. The French imprisoned several protesters and passed sentences on some without trial.[12]

In the southern city of al-Nabatiyya, the word *monopole*, as one union leader put it, was like a "ghoul that stripped workers at the cigarette companies and tobacco farmers from their bread."[13] Al-Nabatiyya's lands and those of adjacent towns were suitable for planting tobacco because they had no trees.[14] It was in these areas that the peasants fought fiercely against the Régie, facing imminent death at times.[15] Pechkoff tried to alert his French superiors to problems with the tobacco monopoly and seemed to have justified the "disappointment" felt by the peasants.[16]

Southern grievances also included fiscal inequalities, decrease in local production, and shortage of portable water.[17] Transportation networks in the South improved little under the French, either. Major roads were dug to link the South to coastal cities in other parts of Lebanon, but they were unpaved. The method for water distribution was inadequate, and the irrigation system and water wells needed renovation. Schooling and health facilities were poor. Only a small number of Shi'ites attained cleri-cal-administrative posts in the state bureaucracy. Under these conditions, it was difficult for common southerners to commit themselves to Grand Liban. Along with the reinstatement of the Régie, these conditions revived the call for unity with Syria.

Intraelite competition over parliamentary posts was also part of the background to the Bint Jubayl revolt. In 1934, the city of Bint Jubayl grew weary of French meddling with the elections to promote their favored notables to parliamentary posts.[18] The people of Bint Jubayl had nominated 'Abd al-Latif al-As'ad and Yusuf al-Zayn to run for parliament offices in 1934. They lost to Fadl al-Fadl and Najib 'Usayran, who were backed by the French. When al-Fadl died, al-As'ad was nominated a second time to run for the post but failed again.[19] The southerners were furious and accused the French of tampering with electoral votes to extinguish their hopes for a true political representation. Men and women organized popular demonstrations and held meetings to mobilize against Pechkoff.[20] Armed confrontations erupted between al-As'ad's supporters and the colonial authorities. By blocking democratic Shiʻite representation, the French had fueled the anger of wide southern sectors.[21]

The Revolt of Bint Jubayl, 1936

All of these streams of dissent joined in one major current at the end of March 1936. Tobacco farmers and intellectuals from the ʻAmili Youth association, supported by a few notables and religious scholars, petitioned the central government in Beirut to fulfill the farmers' demands to annul the Régie monopoly. Muhammad Saʻid Bazzi, a local pro-French dignitary, refused to endorse the petition. Reiterating a common French view, Bazzi paid homage to the French for having "liberated" the Shiʻites from Ottoman oppression and made them free to practice their religion.[22] His statements fell on deaf ears, for the protestors found them irrelevant to the crisis in sight. Our account of the succeeding incidents of the revolt was drawn from Lebanese historical accounts and the French sources, as well as the memoirs of a few ʻAmilis. While memoirs are not sources for "pure data," they draw attention to the attitudes and sensibilities of the rebels. They are also a window on the later production of mentalities.

As mourners gathered at Bint Jubayl's *husayniyya* (an edifice or hall where religious services and ceremonies are held) to commemorate ʻAshura on the tenth of Muharram 1936, news broke out about the French arrest of resistance leader Hajj ʻAli Baydun. Angry protestors, including women as well as men, marched to the *saray* (city hall) and forced his release from prison. The next day the French police arrested thirty-three young men from Bint Jubayl and took them to the city hall. Women started to shout nationalist slogans, and the men followed their lead, reciting inflammatory poems: "The young shed their blood when traitors entered our country." Hundreds of southerners from adjacent towns and villages—in particular, ʻAynatha—joined the protest. They brought their shovels and together opened a large hole in the prison walls. The police shot at the crowd, killing three young men and wounding two others.[23] Indignation and anger at French brutality were echoed in Damascus, where the *marjaʻ* Sayyid Muhsin partook in a general strike against the French, which Syrians in other cities joined as well.

Pechkoff described the rebels as "fanatic Muslims" who acted "only through blackmail, or funds from the People's Party of Syria."[24] His analysis of the revolt deserves close attention. He surmised that the 'ulama, the notables, and heads of the families in the South had been respected for a long time, but that now they appeared to have lost all control over the youth. He drew a link between the increase of political disturbances and the youths' breakaway from paternal control.[25] What is certain from the southerners' own sources and Pechkoff's notes is that the revolt reflected a marked politicization of family life and attested to the dynamism of a youth culture pushing against filial duty and class privilege. Pechkoff considered patriarchal and family authority beneficial for the organization of society. Here and elsewhere he implies that colonial subjects were beset by irrational drives, much like disorderly children who needed paternal supervision. Notwithstanding this view, his report also outlined the main political and economic motives for the revolt. The southern demand for unity with Syria, he noted, was fundamentally tied to ending economic exploitation and French occupation. The activists supporting unity with Syria persuaded the "ignorant masses [farmers] of Bint Jubayl that recovery of the country cannot be attained without achieving unity with Syria, and with other Arab countries."[26] Pechkoff embellished the xenophobia of the agitators, who "rekindled" the "ancient fanaticism of the Muslims" to create a "Muslim movement with their co-religionists of Syria."[27]

When accounting for women's active participation in the Bint Jubayl revolt, the French report stated that they were merely complying with the wishes of the patriarchal head of the family. The French, for instance, were convinced that the men purposely placed the women at the front lines of clashes with the police to heighten the men's courage and keep them from declaring defeat at the hands of the French. This colonial construction of the "Muslim woman" overlooked the importance of women to the rural economy and tobacco production, which pushed them to revolt along with the men.[28] Southern women were touched directly by the reinstatement of the Régie monopoly because they were involved in labor-intensive planting of tobacco and traditional manual fabrication of cigarettes.[29] Moreover, workingwomen gained the lowest wages at the Régie. Several women who suspected their husbands would not join the Bint Jubayl revolt ridiculed them or tried to persuade them to join the anti-French resistance.[30]

Pechkoff was reviled by thousands of southerners who suffered from oppressive taxes, imprisonment, and political repression, but he also apparently demonstrated his disdain for his subjects on many occasions. One account has it that many indigent southerners hoping to slacken French oppression attempted to show their respect for Pechkoff by visiting him on July 14, Bastille Day in France. During the visit, Pechkoff refrained from shaking their hands and sat at a distance, instead placing his sword on a chair that separated him from the visitors. They walked up in line and one by one bent down and kissed the sword. Southerners also went to Pechkoff's office requesting permission for construction, usage of land, buying or selling products and goods. One account has it that Pechkoff would call his trained dog to come into the office where visitors waited their turn to talk to him, then order the dog to leave the office, and once again command him to come back and sit in a corner without making the slightest move. Southerners understood Pechkoff's show with the dog as a warning to them. It was his own way of letting them know that he expected them—his colonized subjects—to obey his orders as a trained dog would. Louis Nur, Pechkoff's secretary, confirmed the show with the dog but denied that it was meant to denigrate the southerners. Nur, who seemed to have admired Pechkoff, did not provide an alternative interpretation, however.[31]

The weeks following the quelling of the revolt brought more police coercion and the incarceration of anti-French activists. A general strike and street processions erupted in which women chanted slogans and children whistled in defiance of the authorities. The people of Bint Jubayl tried to put pressure on Muhammad Bazzi to communicate their grievances to the French. Bazzi had already left Bint Jubayl and was residing in ʿAyn Ibil, the Christian village protected by the French following the 1920 massacre.[32] Meanwhile, the French reinstituted the Régie by force, causing a drastic loss of working hands in agriculture. Immigration came "like a current," dragging young people to West Africa.[33] What money they were able to send brought some relief to southern families, but the long-term benefit took decades to materialize when class mobility and increased investment in the southern economy became evident.

Conforming to Grand Liban?

After quelling the revolt, the French tried to get southerners to declare their loyalty to Grand Liban and abandon ideas of unity with Syria. On April 10, 1936, several southern notables met at the house of provincial leader Abd al-Latif al-As'ad in Tibi (al-Tayyiba) to decide on a collective course of action vis-à-vis the French.[34] Most attendees were lukewarm toward unity with Syria. Many of the notables, provincial leaders, and the *'ulama* argued that joining Grand Liban was the only option left for southerners to obtain personal security and economic relief. The peasants knew that without concrete support from the upper classes, they did not have the means to sustain a long-term rebellion against the French. Pro-French leaders, though few in number, gained decisive power over the rest, owing to the question of economic relief and prisoners' release.

The attendees of the meeting in al-Tibi asked the French authorities to fulfill sixteen central demands in return for the southerners' loyalty to Grand Liban. The top three urgent demands were that the French free Bint Jubayl's prisoners, investigate the unjust treatment of southerners in connection to the revolt, and reduce police coercion. The next three demands were requests to modify certain clauses in the Régie's bylaws regarding freedom of planting tobacco. The petitioners asked the French to fix the buying price of tobacco at thirty liras per kilogram (as opposed to the price that would be decided upon the discretion of the Régie agents), acquire certain quantities for export, prohibit the purchase of foreign tobacco, and offer general amnesty for contravention of the Régie regulations. The attendees at al-Tibi also asked for the implementation of a standardized (not arbitrary) fiscal regime, eliminating arrears taxes implemented in 1935, reducing taxes on buildings in cities and construction in villages, and lowering the *aghnam* (taxes on animal herds) by 50 percent.[35] The southerners then asked the French to found an agricultural bank, protect local production, and search for outlets for their produce. They suggested building an agricultural school at the center of the South and called for reform of the public functions of government and the provision of services to each Lebanese community in proportion to its size. They also asked the French to establish a plenipotentiary in al-Nabatiyya and Bint Jubayl and to move the Ja'fari courts to Tyre and Marji'yun.

Peasant voices emerging in the al-Tibi memorandum expressed their willingness to cease the struggle against the French if given respite from political and economic punishment. Southerners urged the French to construct asphalt roads; build official centers for summering the cattle at Marji'yun, Shib'a, al-Nabatiyya and Tibnin; open schools for boys in locales where none existed, as well as secondary schools at Sidon, Tyre, Bint Jubayl, and al-Nabatiyya; purify drinking water; build new water canals; and execute irrigation projects at al-Qasimiyya, Tyre, and Marji'yun. They expressed their need for regional health clinics and dispensaries, prevention of deforestation, maintenance of electric power, and development of the sewage system.[36]

The peasants seemed to have lost most of the elite figures in the South to the French, and they were unsure about the level of support from and efficacy of Syrian Unity Party leaders. At this juncture, they were more concerned about resolving their pressing socioeconomic problems than struggling for unity with Syria. It should not be concluded, however, that the al-Tibi demands sealed the southerners' full and clear commitment to the Lebanese "nation." Rather, it framed the contradictions and tensions wrought in this type of national affiliation. Accepting Lebanese citizenry was at the time a means to end colonial oppression.

The Secular-Sectarian System and Shi'ite Representation

With the end of the Ottoman Caliphate, Islamic law, or the shari'a, ceased to form the basis for legislative, judicial, or executive legal regulation at the state level. The Lebanese constitution integrated Swiss, French, and Italian legal codes, which defined the modern secular rubric of the state.[37] At the same time, the religious demands of the diverse Muslim and Christian communities and their clerical representatives were given expression through family law. The state also supported religious activities in public spaces and managed their plurality and competing manifestations. The state's secular rubric was also infused with a particular sectarian arrangement identifying each sect's political shares and posts within the organs of the state.

The Shi'ites' representation in the government did not correspond to their proportion in the Lebanese population as a whole.[38] In 1925, the census showed that there were 101,637 Shi'ites in Lebanon, a somewhat smaller sect than the Maronite Christians (178,257) and the Sunnite Muslims (122,678).[39] Despite these numbers, the Representative Council (which acted as a parliament) of Grand Liban gave the Maronites ten seats, the Sunnites six, the Shi'ites five, the Greek Orthodox four, the Catholics two, the Druze two, and the minorities one.[40] The council's sectarian divisions and competitions, its lack of any legislative authority, and its inability to address political problems hindered the Shi'ites' integration into the emerging nation-state. The class dimension of this political "equilibrium" was such that the Shi'ite notables and landed dignitaries dominated the few parliamentary seats available to the Shi'ites, and they were always drawn from the al-Zayn, al-As'ad, al-Fadl, Bazzi, 'Usayran, al-Khalil, Hamada, and Haydar families. Complaints about the inadequate political representation of Shi'ites had been made as early as 1928 when Yusuf al-Zayn and Sabri Hamada walked out of the Representative Council, demanding that government designate a minister seat for Shi'ites on a par with the main sects in Lebanon. In its 1932 census, the Lebanese state used a "restrictive citizenship policy" to ensure Christians' numerical dominance in order to thwart demands for greater representation from the Muslim sects.[41] The census factored in Christians who had immigrated and resided permanently in other countries as resident citizens of the Lebanese Republic.[42]

The first two presidents of Lebanon—Bichara el-Khouri (1946–52) and Camille Chamoun (1952–58)—promoted Lebanon as a liberal, pro-Western, service-based polity in which the Maronite elite and a few Sunnite, Druze, and Shi'ite allies enjoyed political and economic dominance. The power-sharing formula that emerged in independent Lebanon was such that the Maronites controlled the presidency and the military, the central bank, the Supreme Court, the Ministry of Information, the civil service, and the chairmanship of the Lebanese University.[43] On the basis of the 1943 Lebanese National Pact, the Sunnite bourgeoisie controlled the

prime ministry. Legislative power was given to the Shi'ite landed bourgeoisie and notables through the post of parliament president. Liberal economic policies forced agricultural production to respond to the needs of
the international rather than the local market, encouraging the rise of a
modern banking system and communication and transportation network
tying Lebanese and Arab markets to Western production. This economy
was justified and protected by what Gran describes as an "ethnic-tribal"
equilibrium—otherwise called "sectarianism."[44] The "equilibrium" or parceling of power and resources among the sects was capable of diluting
horizontal divisions and maintaining the hegemony of the bourgeoisie
over lower social groups. It also created incentives for competition among
families of the same sect.

Maintaining a sectarian balance in the legislative body of the state,
however, did not mean that all sects enjoyed an "equal management of
the state."[45] Executive power devolved largely to the Maronite bourgeoisie and came to dominate legislative power. This feature derived from the
constitution, which gave the Maronite president of the Lebanese Republic
advantages over other branches of the state. The Shi'ite leaders and businessmen were among the weaker elements in the national alliance that
formed the basis of the 1943 Lebanese Pact. Two years following Lebanese
independence in that same year, the post of parliament chair, which had
been designated for Shi'ites, was occupied by a Greek Orthodox leader,
prompting angry denunciations from Shi'ite leaders.[46] By 1947, the situation had changed, and the Shi'ites had ten deputies in Parliament out of
fifty-five for all of Lebanon.[47] Although parliamentary representation for
Shi'ites was drawn from the Biqa' and the South, Rashid Baydun (who had
moved to Beirut from the South) ran as deputy for Beirut and Ahmad al-
Husayni for Mount Lebanon. In the following decades, the Shi'ite middle
class began to grow, and émigré businessmen started to invest in the Lebanese economy. The question of political representation made these groups
throw in their lot with the lower classes at times against the leadership of
notables such as 'Usayran and al-As'ad.

The Shi'ites' relationship to the Lebanese government was characterized by skepticism and frustration. There were persistent complaints about
the lack of basic amenities in peripheral Shi'ite regions. Under Bichara

el-Khouri government (1943–52), the minister of water and electricity, Munassa, whose name derived from the Arabic verb root "to forget" (*nasiya*) was satirized in popular lore: "Munassa ate his soup and forgot to turn on the light."[48] The government had little credibility: "Oh government of deceit, where did you take [our] sustenance / We will not stop the strike until [President] Bishara comes to us on foot."[49]

To complicate things even further, approximately 100,000 Palestinian refugees ended up in the South from among the 700,000 that the new Israeli government had expelled from their homes in 1948–49.[50] As later chapters show, the Palestinian crisis became a significant factor in the Lebanese Shi'ites' political radicalization and restlessness.

Intellectual Developments

Education

Young boys were sent to the *kuttab* schools of Jabal 'Amil that specialized primarily in teaching the Qur'an and incorporated the study of calligraphy and arithmetic.[51] A range of elementary classes in Arabic grammar, reading and writing, mathematics, and logic supplemented the study of the Qur'an. After this stage, some students studied at one of the local 'Amili and Biqa'i madrasas (schools) founded by a Shi'ite scholar, and some attended Ottoman public schools. These madrasas rarely had *waqf* (religious endowments) for supporting teachers and students. They received financial aid from provincial leaders and benefactors. Founded for the most part by legal scholars, they taught the religious-legal sciences: Arabic philology, morphology, rhetoric, logic, and Islamic theology. The latter consisted of five doctrinal points—the belief in unity, divine justice, the necessity for prophets in human society, the continuation of divine guidance through the infallible Shi'ite Imams, and the belief in resurrection on the Day of Judgment.[52] The madrasas also taught theology (*kalam*), metaphysics, jurisprudence, law, Qur'anic exegesis, arithmetic, history, and literary arts.[53]

Shi'ite students also frequented the Ottoman public schools, particularly from the 1860s on. These schools with their "new pedagogy" were absent from the Jabal 'Amil before Midhat Pasha was appointed Syria's *vali* (governor) from 1878 to 1879.[54] Midhat Pasha founded the *amiriyya* (state or public) schools, which included the *rushdiyya* (primary schools) in the centers of the subdistricts and the *i'dadiyya* (preparatory school) in the centers of the districts and provinces.[55] Shi'ite scholars remembered Midhat Pasha favorably and praised him for preserving Muslim pietistic traditions, encouraging the social-educational autonomy of Syria's Arab population, and securing religious endowments for learning.[56] Several Shi'ite scholars taught at the new public schools, offering courses in Shi'ite doctrine, law, and jurisprudence.[57] More Shi'ites could have benefited from Midhat Pasha's initiatives if the schools had been built within Jabal 'Amil instead of the coastal centers. During this period, secular fields of knowledge became increasingly relevant to the madrasas.[58] History, linguistics, and, more particularly, literature started to gain independence from the madrasa and seminary curricula if they did not become domains for contesting the study of the shari'a and clerical service.

At the major seminary in Najaf, Shi'ite *talaba* pursued advanced clerical expertise. The seminary was traditionally a center of learning that hosted several madrasas founded by various religious scholars. Although Islamic madrasas varied considerably in their curriculum and subjects of study across time and geographical location, Najaf's seminary focused on the legal-religious sciences to prepare students for clerical vocations. Those who wished to become mujtahids spent no less than fifteen years of study if their means permitted.[59] A mujtahid derives his rulings on the basis of the Qur'an, the hadith (reports preserving the Prophet's and Imams' sayings and doings), the consensus of the Shi'ite *'ulama* (which includes indirectly the Imams' opinions), and reason.[60] Shi'ite believers voluntarily choose to follow the rulings of one or more mujtahids and abide by his legal opinions on questions pertaining to worship and social transactions.

The number of Syro-Lebanese Shi'ites who became mujtahids and muftis dropped dramatically in the first half of the twentieth century. Students complained about deteriorating life conditions at the seminary that had reached a critical level in the early 1930s. They noted a decline in the contribution of legal or discretionary monies (*al-huquq al-shar'iyya*) and gifts to Najaf's seminary, especially by merchants and landholders in and around Najaf.[61] Some provincial chiefs ended their patronage of students, withdrawing yearly student stipends. A handful of students lived off the rent of an apartment or house they owned or relied on a portion of the revenues of agricultural land. The rest were in despair.[62]

A southern seminarian, Ahmad Mughniyya, recounted some of these experiences. After his father died, he was raised by his brother, 'Abd al-Karim, a religious scholar and teacher at Najaf's *hawza*.[63] After being in the seminary for a while, Ahmad discontinued his studies and set out for Ma'raka in southern Grand Liban. His father's lands had formerly been planted with figs and olives but had fallen into disuse and could not provide him with a source of livelihood. Owing to the lands' low value, he could not sell them. Without scholarly credentials or a college degree, he could not acquire a white-collar job. His family's scholarly status seems to have prevented him from manual labor available to workers and peasants. So for the following four years Ahmad continued his religious studies under his brother in Najaf, remaining dependent on him and even falling into debt. When his brother died, he lost his main source of financial support and traveled to Senegal to work, but to no avail. He went back to Lebanon and then traveled to Baghdad, where he taught Arabic language and literature for two years at a Jewish school, the Shammas Secondary School. In 1949, the Iraqi government interrogated him along with Husayn Muroeh, a fellow southerner teaching at the school. Accused Communists, they were forced to leave Iraq permanently.[64] In the South, he finally obtained a stable job as a schoolteacher.

Reforming the Seminary

Discussions of modernism, secular education, and religious reform began to consume the southern *talaba* and scholars at the Najaf seminary during the 1920s and the 1930s. The seminary was thus not merely a center for traditional training in law and jurisprudence, but also a hub of ideas about the changing political and intellectual world. The semistructured program of study at the seminary, which allowed students to choose their instructors and subjects within each stage, also allowed them to navigate outside the seminary's scholastic boundaries. Some students traveled to

Baghdad, where they interacted with leading nationalist and Marxist Iraqi intellectuals, poets, and artists.

Southern *talaba* and ʿulama expressed their frustrations with a dysfunctional curriculum, weak teaching methods, and textbooks deemed archaic by the modern student. They derided the books aimed at teaching Arabic, "which in addition to their complicated meanings and long sentences, were badly printed on paper of poor quality."[65] Some *talaba* studied works of jurisprudence before learning the prerequisite subjects for it, such as Arabic grammar and lexicography.[66] The *talaba* also complained about the lack of a grading system or formal exams to evaluate student performance. Since the medieval period, scholars had given the *ijaza*, or license, to their students to teach and transmit their knowledge of the foundational texts they have successfully covered and commentaries on them. In the twentieth century, however, students felt that this system of evaluation was incompatible with empirical accountability and quantitative methods known to modern universities.[67] These contradictory observations about Najaf's seminary reflected the complex historical experiences of Iraqi society during the 1920s and the 1930s. Central to these experiences were Ottoman educational reforms, the British occupation of Iraq, and the rise of the modern nation-state.

To accommodate demands for reform and solve administrative problems at the seminary, the *marjaʿ* Muhammad Husayn Kashif al-Ghitaʾ set a fixed schedule for classes and established committees for administering exams at regular times.[68] He also assigned salaries according to instructors' rank and the quality of teaching.[69] The *talaba* who were comparing Najaf's seminary to European colleges did not find the mode or momentum of the *marjaʿ*'s reforms sufficient to deem the curriculum on the whole "modern," however. Students also asked that the seminary establish a reading club for books in diverse disciplines and issue a journal on scientific and religious ideas committed to ideal "human values" and to the "truth" away from religious "fanaticism" and "parochial" conduct. These demands clearly reflected the *talaba*'s increasing adaptation of liberal modernist ideas about the functions of education. Finally, the reformists urged the seminary to allow the education of women.[70] The insistence on having the seminary open its doors to women was supported by proofs and examples of Muslim women who had been tutored in the religious sciences and literature since the medieval period. Outside Najaf's seminary, however, southern thinkers debated this question extensively, with some advocating Western liberal views about Muslim women's lamentable lack of rights. The poet Musa al-Zayn Sharara maintained that women were enslaved by men and kept intentionally ignorant and without "freedom." They were laborers who were transformed into "containers" for reproduction and acted as unpaid maids for their extended families, husbands, and children. Sharara attacked the restriction in women's public roles and their seclusion, a practice that was prevalent among the elite. Even though he and Sayyid Muhsin al-Amin were allied together as "reformists," Sharara saw the majority of the 'ulama as an impediment to modernism. "Turbaned" men, he commented, cursed him severely for his views, as if he "was the slayer of the grandson of the Prophet and his family in Karbala'!"[71]

At Najaf, the 'ulama for their part confronted Europe's scientific ideas, their secular foundations, and European claims to cultural superiority. They elucidated how scientific modes of thought either violated or agreed with Islamic religious cosmology and beliefs. Meanwhile, scholars and seminarians addressed the thought of the Enlightenment and debunked materialist theories that had shaken Europe, including Darwin's theory of evolution.[72] Universalism represented the objective and permanent existence of scientific truths—truths that provided the most superior mode of knowledge.[73] The jurists and clerics in Najaf who questioned the values of the Enlightenment apparently rejected the newly found philosophy of progress and reason.[74] The reformist talaba and scholars, however, adapted some of these values, struggling with the seminary's program and cultural attitudes. The mujtahid Muhsin 'Abd al-Karim Sharara from Bint Jubayl illustrates this point.

Sharara, like many scholars in Najaf, followed closely the legal and educational reforms at the Sunnite seminary of al-Azhar in Egypt.[75] He was preoccupied with questions of relevance and utility of religious learning in a modernizing world and proposed a new administrative structure for Najaf's seminary inspired by the reforms at al-Azhar. Sharara rejected the seminary's pedagogical methods, accusing the "poor selves hiding under the turbans" of contributing to the decline of a luminous intellectual center such as Najaf. He argued that medieval and early modern scholars had been well versed in science and rational theology, which were now unknown to Najaf's seminarians. Contemporary jurists, he complained, were unable to instruct students in legal questions that required expertise in astronomy and mathematics, such as calculating the direction of prayer or inheritance portions.[76] In other words, Sharara wanted the study of the natural and applied sciences be "brought back" to the Islamic madrasa where it had belonged since the medieval period.[77] Whereas secular modernism was demanding separation of the fields of science from philosophy, law, and literature, Sharara envisaged the modernity of the seminary in terms of bringing these fields together in one rubric. He had great hopes for building a "university" in Najaf that integrated up-to-date educational methods and administrative principles. As a consequence, he aimed to strengthen the religious sciences and protect them from the encroachment of Western secular learning precisely through the adaptation of certain modernist values and educational methodologies.

In addition to religious modernism and the reformation of seminary education, several southern *talaba* and scholars espoused literary modernity. The latter had been evident since the late Ottoman period and in the twentieth century when it lent itself to nationalist discourse and notions of ethnic-linguistic purity.[78] Southern modernists saw Arabic language and literature as vital areas of control for producing artistic and aesthetic values of nationalism. At Najaf's seminary, an increasing self-consciousness about poetic composition and literary criticism was reflected in the discussions about what constituted "good" and innovative writing.[79] There was nothing new per se about religious students learning to appreciate or write poetry—they had done so steadily since medieval times. However, what was new was literature's independence from the Islamic sciences as well as its nationalist features. The three seminarians Husayn Muroeh, Muhammad Sharara, and Hashim al-Amin devoted much energy to questions of literary modernity and national struggle against European colonialism. They formed a literary association in 1925 that rejected "the existing conditions in [the] Najaf [seminary], socially and intellectually."[80] The southerners in Najaf discussed essays by literary modernists such as Taha Husayn and Muhammad Husayn Haykal published in the Egyptian journals *al-Hilal* and *al-Siyasa*. They analyzed the literary components of the speeches and poems elegizing the anticolonial Egyptian leader Sa'd Zaghlul.[81] A major public organ of literary modernity and nationalism for Shi'ites was *al-'Irfan*, a journal founded in 1909 by Ahmad 'Arif al-Zayn.[82] Described by a southern scholar as "the message of the homeland," *al-'Irfan* maintained vivid exchanges between Arab intellectuals and discussed current political developments. Young writers and readers of *al-'Irfan* felt they were part of a new cultural vision.[83] The journal was known popularly among women and men as *al-Kazeeta* (the Gazette). *Al-Kazeeta* succeeded in crossing class boundaries as it was read in social gatherings to the learned and illiterate alike. The southerners "used to think that the whole world was *al-'Irfan* because it was the only window on [Arab–Islamic] tradition (*turath*) and modern knowledge. If our generation had the opportunity to know what existed outside Jabal 'Amil, then this owes to *Al-'Irfan* magazine, for it took the hands of the first intellectuals of Jabal 'Amil and encouraged them to write and endeared education to them."[84]

Overall, however, Najaf was not the stagnant center that some modern reformists made it out to be. The seminary continued to hold an aura of legitimacy, and the *'ulama* remained in the eyes of some modernists the principal sources of moral guidance and national leadership.[85] 'Ali al-Zayn, a southern scholar, noted that "to be serious, any revolution has to start with a critique of the leaders and the *'ulama* because their role is the most important in society."[86] Yet colonialism and the modern state stripped the shari'a of its comprehensive power in Islamic society and confined the *'ulama*'s role to the area of family law. Aside from the decreased justification for seminary education under these conditions, Najaf's jurists strove to renew young people's interest in Islamic learning and to resolve the seminary's administrative problems. Several southern seminarians, however, eventually turned away from a clerical vocation and took off their turbans.[87]

Religion, Modern "Progress," and Marxism

Political philosophies and ideas of historical change found their way into Najaf's seminary in Iraq, but none put out lasting roots like Marxism. The efforts spent by the Marxist *talaba* in adapting facets of Western secularism to Islamic traditions enriched the intellectual landscape of Najaf but also complicated the relationship to senior clerics. The latter's authority derived from the protection and renewed application of the shari'a or functions of it that were not overtaken by the modern nation-state. Up until 1950, however, there was no definitive rift between the Marxist seminarian and the cleric. Sayyid Hasan al-Amin's reflections on the place of Marxism in southern intellectual life confirm our views. He stated that the relationship between Marxist thought and the ideas at the religious seminary at Shaqra', his hometown, was confrontational on the social level, but constructive and dynamic on the literary-intellectual level. Marxism at the time, Sayyid Hasan explained, "did not entail a severance with Arab–Islamic tradition [*turath*] but rather a severance and an engagement simultaneously." He gave the example of Husayn Muroeh, a Marxist inspired by the ideas of the *marja'* Sayyid Muhsin on religious modernism. Muroeh "established an open discussion with Marxism, not a relationship of [blind] following."[88] Mutual exploration and fluid social and scholarly exchanges abounded between the "Marxists" and the "clerics." In this section, as well as the following chapter, the ideas promoted by Communists from clerical families demonstrate clearly that the Marxists and the clerics were both interrelated and internally diverse.

Several religious modernists and Marxist thinkers emerged not only from the South's French-styled public schools, but also from the Syro-Lebanese madrasas and Najaf's seminary. The Marxists were preoccupied with defining modern progress and "negotiating" its manifestation in Islamic society. Karl Marx, like several European thinkers of the nineteenth century, promoted the idea of "progress" yet expressed divergent positions on whether human progress is inevitable and necessary. In *Capital*, he emphasizes the necessity of circulating new findings among societies with varying degrees of material and social development.[89] For him, progress in the "economic formation of society" has critical implications for culture and its transformation. Robert Nisbet points out that Marx condemned imperial British rule in India at the same time that he considered it a necessary historical mechanism (part of the contradictions of capitalism) to compel future human development under communism.[90]

Despite the secular foundations of Marxist thought, the seminarians who adopted Marxism found it unsettling to authorize a progressivist trajectory—the ideas that societies in the future will achieve more than contemporary societies can achieve and that preserving and maintaining the "old" were tantamount to failure. Islamic traditions of religious-legal knowledge did not lend themselves to this trajectory. To authenticate an account of what the Prophet said or did, the Shi'ite 'ulama need to trace it back to the Prophet and the Imams through a reliable chain of transmitters. Moreover, the earlier the evidence for a legal concept or social practice in medieval Islamic society, the more authoritative it is. The understanding of "progress" in its Enlightenment context as a positive evolutionary advancement in human society was untenable for the Marxist religious intellectuals, so they reinterpreted "progress" to yield contextual rather than fixed criteria for modernity. They claimed, for instance, medieval Islamic achievements in science and philosophy to be part of modern progress. Muhammad Sharara, a southern seminarian who adopted communism, tried to impress on Najaf's clerics the importance of establishing a rich and competitive academic world, much on a par with its medieval Islamic counterpart. He said: "We want to return to an Islamic age where students moved from the jurist's pulpit to the historian's podium and from the astronomical lab to the geographer's map."[91] Supporters for intellectual renewal and modernization, he noted, must recognize "that the old has a splendor in the face of which much of the splendor of the new . . . fades."[92] Like Muroeh, Sharara emphasized the centrality of rationalist traditions and secular scientific production to Islam in order to legitimize elements of Western modernity.[93] He hoped the seminary would reflect the concerns of the modern world around it, a world defined by socioeconomic divisions, colonial realities, and nation-states.

Muroeh drew other connections between modernity and Islamic culture. For him, the form and content of Islamic tradition (turath) undergo constant transformation but preserve a discursive unity from past to present. As such, originality (asala) and modernity (mu'asara) fall into a dialectical relationship with each other marked by interdependence rather than absolute contradiction. He also argued that modern European achievements had to be seen in the wider context of an incremental development of world civilizations—including the Islamic one.[94] Muroeh made an important adjustment to the modern Eurocentric correlation between a secular world and advancement in the natural sciences. He argued that rationalist methods of inquiry and scientific production had flourished in Islamic society at a time when the state and religion were one and when religion was not separate from society. European society, which had received and adapted this production in the medieval period, was unprepared, historically speaking, to benefit from it, possibly owing to the separation between the Vatican's religious leadership (which encouraged the reception of Greek thought) and the European states. This separation, as well as feudalism, may have led European thinkers to focus on metaphysics (God's nature, the Trinity) as a field of investigation unrelated to science. Even though this feature does not comprise "an absolute distinction" between western European and Islamic society, Muroeh noted, it may offer one explanation for the advancement of the medieval Islamic traditions.[95]

Peter Gran suggests that Muroeh "interrupts the Enlightenment evolutionism" by drawing up "parallels between medieval and modern periods or superior phases of human production."[96] Of course, science itself was not the product of Western modernity; it had developed much earlier. Muroeh's statements reflect the view that if science existed and developed before the modern period, and if Islam had a pioneering role in it, then legitimizing premodern forms of knowledge is part of creating new ones. This view reflects unease with the Eurocentric logic of progress. Immanuel Wallerstein argues that non-Westerners' attempt "to appropriate progress for part or all of the non-Western world" ended with the attempt to preserve the idea of progress but to extract Europe out of it.[97] But the important question for us is not whether the concept of progress is Eurocentric in origin. Rather, we are concerned with what became of the concept in other societies and historical contexts. Whenever "progress" was evoked, it could not be a mirror reflection of this origin. We are interested in the tensions that "progress" carried for Muslim thinkers, why it was advanced, and how it was reinterpreted on the basis of discursive Islamic traditions. Reinterpreting progress and temporality would allow religious modernists and Communists to achieve something quite concrete—namely, industrial modernization and agrarian reform. They hoped to reorganize economic relations on a modern basis without accepting all the cultural implications of the Enlightenment narrative. Communism also became for many a rubric for decolonization and secularization of the Lebanese state. Secularism, as Gran argues, was not merely a "tactic" for the Communists. It was instead the stepping-stone for a modern culture, which "meant fighting Europe but adopting the principles found in Europe, on which science and social science could proceed."[98] The need to modernize, Muroeh suggested, could be resolved by drawing upon the very resources of Islamic tradition and selective elements of Western modernity.

Summary

From the French perspective, the Shi'ites were less essential to the national project of Grand Liban than the Maronites, the Sunnites, and even, to a lesser extent, the Druze. Even though the open struggle of the South against the French ended, its conflict with Libanism and its efforts to fit within Grand Liban had just started. Al-Tibi conference, far from sealing peasant loyalty to Grand Liban, exposed their precarious citizenry. Meanwhile, a youth culture that identified closely with the peasants challenged the authority of the landed elites at the same time as it agitated against the French Mandate. As we show in other parts of the book, the nationalist elites attempted in the following decades to boost their interests and draw new political alliances across Christian and Muslim sects. In fact, the Shi'ite entrepreneurial-business elites who aspired to decision-making power at the state level were quite amenable to Lebanese nationalism, albeit a modified one.

European cultural domination and colonial rule sanctioned universalizing ideas about modern progress that could be achieved through scientific knowledge and reason. A generation of Shi'ite *talaba* drew upon these ideas, questioning the relevance of a clerical career to a modernizing world. Those who called for the "reform" of Najaf's seminary and their valorization of the secular sciences as nothing more than the resumption of Islamic theological and scientific traditions that unqualified jurists and rigid bureaucrats had discontinued. The crisis brought by universalizing ideas notwithstanding, these *talaba* were advancing localized demands and solutions. They were articulating a justifiable view that interrelated sacred and secular activities and forms of knowledge were integral to being Muslim and to Islamic experiences historically.

Out of this local modernism emerged also a religiously grounded Marxism. The religious modernists and the Marxists emerging from the *'ulama* families fitted particular features of Western modernism to Islamic tradition using distinct cultural resources. At the same time, they expressed unease with the narrative of linear evolutionary progress, insisting instead on the simultaneity of renewal and conservation. They also doubted that scientific knowledge and reason alone could have revelatory powers. Thus, although the religious modernists and the Marxists were not "autonomous" agents of modernism,[99] they did not reproduce European experiences of modernity or congruent European arguments for its justification. Rather, the Shi'ite thinkers looked for ways to negotiate modernity from within their local tradition and to reinterpret "progress" on the basis of the personal, intellectual, and historical materials available to them at a particular time.

The senior seminary jurists had good reason to challenge the reformists' arguments about the practical benefits of secular knowledge. They doubted that a "safe" cooperation could exist between the secular sciences and the shari'a sciences. The integral ties between modernity, secularism, and the nation-state meant to these jurists further marginalization of clerical activity and erosion of one of the last cultural institutions for regulating public religion. Dissatisfied *talaba* departed slowly but surely from Najaf's seminary and the madrasas of the South, leaving their turbans and religious cloaks behind.

It is useful to note here that this same preoccupation with modernism and reform is evident even today in Hizbullah's and Fadlallah's Islamist arenas, albeit in new forms. The rise of these Islamists went hand in hand with a revalidation of Najaf's seminary and its educational and cultural role. They present the shari'a and not modern secularism as the true engine of social renewal guaranteed by *ijtihad* to arrive at modern legal rulings.

As chapters 3 and 4 show, the Islamists are indebted to rich and complex discussions by the pre–World War II religious modernists, Marxist seminarians, and Communists about Islamic culture. These groups suggested varied forms of modernism to empower Islamic-Arab society against European imperialism and Western hegemony. The Marxists' approaches to the Enlightenment and Western modernity form a critical part of the intellectual material discussed and disputed by the Islamists in Lebanon since the late 1970s.

3

Communists in the *'Ulama*'s Homes

Economic Shifts, Religious Culture, and the State

The Left is rarely accounted for in the study of Shi'ite political history or Islamism in Lebanon even though Marxism shaped the lives of several seminarians and religious intellectuals there.[1] The early Lebanese Islamists have adapted during the 1970s and the 1980s distinct Communist critiques of imperialism, the economy, the Lebanese state, and the Palestinian question. This chapter thus brings Marxism and communism to the center of the discussion of the political and intellectual currents that shaped Shi'ite society in Lebanon. It starts by highlighting the historical factors that led seminarians and members of the *'ulama* families in South Lebanon to adopt Marxist thought and to join Communist organizations.[2] Political analysts generally treat communism as a purely secular experience antithetical to religion and rarely examine its local form and manifestation. Southern communism, as this chapter suggests, expressed an affinity with Shi'ite eschatological and doctrinal traditions. This chapter notes how several leftists and their sympathizers saw communism not only as a program for secular political change and economic improvement, but also as a moral system resonating with Shi'ite emancipatory and spiritual symbolisms.

This chapter also delineates the socioeconomic conditions of the Shi'ite countryside that led to opposition to the state and subsequently to the espousal of leftist demands in the decades following the independence of Lebanon in 1943. The state's economic policies contributed to the deterioration of rural life in the South and the Biqa' (Ba'labak and al-Hirmil) and the rapid growth of Beirut at the expense of the countryside.

51

The radicalization of thought and action took place in response to these specific conditions of political-economic crisis in Lebanon. Meanwhile, the Communists' role in mobilizing the unions against capital, their confrontations with the state, and their reevaluation of Arab nationalism had important implications for southern Shi'ites.

Finally, to give a vivid account of these developments, the chapter offers the reader a portrait of two Shi'ite Communists from the 'ulama families: Sayyid Ja'far Muhsin al-Amin (d. 1981) and Husayn Muroeh (d. 1987).

The Appeal of Communism, 1920–1943

The attraction that Marxist thought held for a generation of seminarians and members of Shi'ite clerical families during the 1930s and the 1940s was tied to historical conditions first in the South and second in Iraq (in particular Najaf and Baghdad), where many southern seminarians lived a good part of their lives. We start with the change in the socioeconomic activities and power of the religious elites in the South. The destruction brought by World War I, the dominance of the European markets, and the colonial partition of geographical Syria into separate polities had debilitating effects on the economy.[3] The relative prosperity that the Shi'ite 'ulama had witnessed in the late nineteenth century came to an end with the French annexation of the South to Grand Liban in 1920, as well as with land fragmentation. Moreover, financial contributions to Najaf's seminary by Iraqi merchants and large landholders diminished, which restricted further the educational opportunities of Shi'ite students traveling to Najaf.

At the same time, other factors brought decisive support for communism. The French imposition of the tobacco monopoly, the Régie, in 1936 radicalized many Shi'ite peasants and workers against French capitalist enterprises and the Lebanese authorities.[4] A sector of the notables and members of the 'ulama impacted by the monopoly joined the protests of Shi'ite tobacco farmers and workers. Communism also promised to resolve problems in labor, land reform, and agricultural development in the countryside attributed largely to the landed elites' exploitative practices.[5] Moreover, Lebanese peasants and workers quickly felt the economic realities of European colonialism. Yusuf Yazbik, one of the founders of the

Lebanese Communist Party, discussed in 1923 the necessity for communalizing the land through revolutionary struggle.[6] The Communists called in 1931 for abolishing the privileges of foreign companies and cancelling the debts that the French imposed on the Lebanese and Syrian peoples.[7]

The Shi'ites' economic problems in the South became entangled with colonial rule and political marginality in Grand Liban. We discussed in chapter 2 the precarious representation accorded to the Shi'ites in Parliament and the state. Here we look at colonial disruptions. Southern peasants considered the European occupation of Greater Syria and the militant activities of the Zionists in Palestine as the central causes of unemployment, the dissolution of local markets, and decrease in the value of the land.[8] The Communists affiliated with the Syrian-Lebanese Communist Party (Al-Hizb al-Shuyu'i al-Suri al-Lubnani), founded in 1924, publicized their views about the interconnections between colonialism, Zionism, and impoverishment of working families—interconnections that resonated with southern experiences.[9] Communist leaders such as Farajalla al-Helou saw Zionism in 1944 as "a colonialist movement whose economic goals are exporting capital to Palestine and neighboring countries and transforming them to a market for investment and selling of goods."[10] To the role of colonialism one should add the disillusionment of the Arab nationalists with Faysal's leadership in Iraq. Other developments in Iraq were also significant in encouraging Communist leanings; we discuss them in the following section. Meanwhile, the Lebanese Communists, Muslim and Christian, challenged the state, accusing the Chamber of Deputies (Majlis al-nuwwab) in 1931 of being a "tool in the colonizer's hands" and demanding its annulment.[11] Southern Communists such as Sayyid Ja'far Muhsin al-Amin and Ahmad Gharbiyya agitated against the state's economic regulations, demanding new labor laws and improved work conditions, particularly for teachers.[12] Early Communist Shi'ites advocated scientific socialism against capitalism and expected technoeconomic advancement to improve peasants and workers' lives. They also hoped a socialist democracy would secularize fully a political system based originally on sectarian divisions.[13] In theory, Marxism was attractive in providing "rational" proofs for freeing the lower classes and destroying privilege.[14] Soviet communism soon prevailed among the members of the Lebanese Communist

Party as a program for social and economic development.[15] It offered an alternative model of modern development to that of capitalist Europe, which the southerners associated with colonialism.

Another important factor in the growth of southern Communist leanings was the political and intellectual milieus of Najaf and Baghdad. Iraqi cities were roiling with questions about national identity, economic reform, political rule, and anticolonial struggle against the British in the 1920s and the 1930s.[16] The question of unity with Syria was already on the minds of the southerners, who were fighting their own battles against the French, and thousands of Iraqi Shi'ites lent their numbers to a jihad, an armed defense, against British occupation in 1920.[17] Meanwhile, national support for King Faysal vanished gradually in the face of his ineptness against British policies, giving way to a socialist critique of Arab nationalism among many Shi'ite intellectuals.

Baghdad was a primary site of Marxist ideas and Communist activism.[18] The Shi'ites formed the widest and highest elements of the Iraqi Communist Party (ICP, Al-Hizb al-shuyu'i al-'iraqi). The central factors accounting for this development were a greater proletarianization in urban cities, expansion of state education in rural regions, and the limited size and role of the Shi'ite bourgeoisie in Iraq who otherwise embraced Arab nationalism.[19] During the mid-1940s, jurists in Najaf warned against the popularity of communism among the Shi'ites and praised the efforts of the Iranian government in preventing its growth.[20] The Communists, however, continued to rally support for their ideas. They partook in the revolution that brought 'Abd al-Karim Qasim to power in Iraq on July 14, 1958, and played a critical role in shaping public opinion about the revolution through the Iraqi press.

Communism and Shi'ite Religious Culture

The reasons highlighted in the previous section for the appeal of communism among the southerners remain incomplete without an illumination of the local texture of Communist ideals and their interface with Shi'ite religious culture. During French rule in Lebanon, an affinity grew between communism and elements of Shi'ite doctrine and eschatology, particularly on questions of power and social justice.[21] Shi'ite societies have expressed skepticism about the legitimacy of any state or temporal authority but the Mahdi's (the Imam in occultation).[22] Even though communism is not millennial per se, the idea of the dissolution of the state as a Communist utopia possibly linked up with messianic Shi'ite expectations.[23] The notion of a Communist egalitarian haven, a society of justice and freedom, resonated with the belief in a Shi'ite utopia of a new righteous order established by the Mahdi. Disengagement with the state, resistance to it, and the struggle to transform it are present in Twelver Shi'ite history, yet the reasons for any of these actions depend on the historical context.

Revolutionary change also tied in with features of the Karbala' tragedy. Karbala', as explained in chapter 1, was the battlefield where Imam Husayn was martyred while aiming to assert the rights of the *ahl al-bayt* (the Prophet's progeny through 'Ali and Fatima), which in time came to mean more broadly the altering of an unwanted political system through activism. It was not unusual, therefore, for Shi'ites in Grand Liban to read Imam Husayn's martyrdom as a Communist struggle against capitalist exploitation and European domination.[24] These threads had a clear affinity. Among the *ulama* of the 'Amili countryside who upheld values of reciprocity, collective responsibility, and pietism, attraction to communism may have also reflected an aversion to the individualism and materialist values they associated with capitalist ideals.

Shi'ite Communists expressed varied engagements with religious belief and practice. They were a mix of observant and nonobservant Muslims, and only a few were avowed atheists who insisted that "religion" impeded modern "progress" and class solidarity.[25] To be sure, most of them aimed to privatize religion, separating decisions about the economy, judicial system, education, national defense and the like from the domain of the shari'a and the activity of its experts, the jurists. For the most part, the Communists were active in the religious life of southern towns and at their *husayniyyas*, particularly during 'Ashura.[26] In popular culture, early pious and austere Muslim personalities were imbued with protosocialist qualities to confirm Islam's stand against the avarice of the ruling elites, their indulgence, and their indifference to the welfare of believers.

Some leftists and sympathizers drew proofs for a socialist "morality" from Imam 'Ali's sayings, in particular his letter to Malik al-Ashtar al-Nakha'i (d. 658) when he appointed him governor of Egypt.[27] The "*ahd Malik*," or oath, that Malik made to Imam 'Ali, represented for some Shi'ites a valid objection to the exploitation of the poor and the creation of class differences.[28] In this letter, Imam 'Ali advises Malik, "If the authority of your position engenders vanity and arrogance, then look at the grandeur of God's dominion above you." He urges Malik to be "just with God" and "with the people [giving them what is their due]" and asks him to make the "most beloved of affairs" that which is "the most comprehensive in justice, and the most inclusive of popular contentment, for the discontent of the common folk (*al-'amma*) undermines the contentment of the elite (*al-khassa*)." In a statement that sympathetic audiences of the left evoked and linked to peasants' welfare, he tells Malik, "Let your cultivation of the land outweigh your concern with the collection of the tax" and urges him to tend to the needs of the "lowest class . . . the destitute, the needy"[29] Abu Dharr al-Ghifari (d. 652), a companion of the Prophet, was known to have condemned the misuse of the treasury funds, suggesting that surplus has to be distributed among the needy.[30] In popular tradition, southerners have it that Abu Dharr, who supported Imam 'Ali's claims to the caliphate, was responsible for the growth of Shi'ite sentiments in the South. The emphasis on Abu Dharr's austerity and righteousness in the early historical sources made some leftists refer to him as "the first socialist in Islam."[31]

It would be a mistake to conclude from this picture that Shi'ite religious culture encourages unconditional affiliation with the Left. Rather, this culture is engaged with under particular historical conditions. Certain features and symbols of this culture connect to the way social class is lived and how relations of power are experienced at a particular time and place. The Shi'ite lower classes considered the Lebanese state and the nationalist elites supporting it directly responsible for their economic hardships and political marginality. Business and entrepreneurial sectors of Shi'ite society also took up the theme of Shi'ite subordination, however. They talked about the need to reverse marginality but were thinking more specifically about their class-based aspirations for national ascendancy and decision-making authority in the government.

Sayyid Ja'far Muhsin al-Amin: From the Madrasa to a Life in Red

A biographical account of Sayyid Ja'far al-Amin, a Shi'ite Communist from a major clerical family in the South, illustrates the themes of anticolonial resistance and modern reform discussed so far and elucidates how Communist ideals were fitted into the local religious culture during this period.

Signs of Marxist leanings appeared all of the sons of the *marja'* Sayyid Muhsin al-Amin: Hashim, 'Abd al-Muttalib, and Ja'far. The southerners would say that Hashim went to Najaf in pursuit of knowledge and came back "a first rate ideologue" in Marxism.[32] 'Abd al-Muttalib also expressed Communist views but did not join a political party out of respect for his father's position as a religious authority.[33] Sayyid Ja'far was by far the most politically active of Sayyid Muhsin's sons.[34] His childhood was marked by a painful separation from his manumitted Ethiopian mother, his stepmother's antagonism toward him, and his father's passive guilt.[35] Sayyid Ja'far's feelings of isolation in a society that scorned his mother's status and color seemed to have encouraged his radical critique of social norms that he expressed at times through satirical humor.[36]

In 1918–19, as 'Amili bandits were active against the French army, Sayyid Ja'far's family moved from Shaqra' to Damascus. There Sayyid Ja'far joined the 'Alawi School, founded by his father in 1902, and strove to keep up with his religious-legal studies. He seemed to have welcomed new reforms at his school that ended the wearing of the *qunbaz* (a long-sleeved garment open in front and fastened with a belt) and the *qabqab* (wooden clog).[37] With the outbreak of the Great Syrian Revolt in 1925, the family moved back to Shaqra', staying there for four to five years. Sayyid Ja'far joined the fifth grade of al-Nabatiyya's elementary school in 1927, but he could hardly cope with the requirements of its French curriculum. Nonetheless, he proceeded with his studies, expressing for the first time open rejection of traditional clerical learning. He apparently convinced some students to join him in discarding their turbans, which were tied around their Turkish fezs.[38] In 1930, Sayyid Ja'far became a teacher at al-Nabatiyya's first public school.[39]

Sayyid Ja'far's intellectual inquiries were shaped by Iraqi thinkers and poets such as Muhammad al-Habbubi, 'Ali al-Sharqi, and Mahdi al-Jawahiri, whose works were published in *al-'Irfan*, the journal that left its imprint on a generation of southerners.[40] He also followed closely the debates on women's domesticity and public roles in the magazines *Minerva* and *al-Mar'a al-Jadida*.[41] He participated in several poetry competitions and started his comic newspaper, *Abu al-Kashakish* (Mr. Gaudy).[42] His editorials and essays reveal a keen interest in workers and peasants' lives, social traditions, and practices. They also tackle a range of local economic problems facing the southerners. Sayyid Ja'far's poems "A New Reign and a Rich Life" and "To an Intellectual" attest to the enthusiasm that communism evoked in him.[43]

Al-Nabatiyya's milieu and location joined him with thinkers and workers who shared socialist goals. They awaited the issues of the Lebanese Communist newspaper *Sawt al-Sha'b* (People's Voice) and read the essays of Russian writer Elie Ehrenburg, who, according to Sayyid Ja'far, expected "the spirit of optimism and the hope in the triumph of humanity to shine."[44] In the spring of 1944, Sayyid Ja'far was instrumental in founding a branch of the Syrian-Lebanese Communist Party in al-Nabatiyya.[45] He reminisced that he and his friends were not afraid to publicize their affiliation with the party.

> even though communism during those days barely offered what could prevent starvation. In addition, it involved neck breaking. He who embraced it exposed his feet to the whips of the government, his livelihood to interruption, and his reputation to denigration. In addition, Communists were considered infidels because they were fighting Hitler, whom the majority of this country considered as they would the awaited Mahdi for this people. . . . Until now, we have not forgotten the sword awarded to Mussolini in those days carrying the words "Sword of Islam" in appreciation for his heroism in subjugating Ethiopia and destroying its independence![46]

The Communists, Sayyid Ja'far noted, confronted a prevalent "irrational" support for Nazi Germany in defiance of the French and British colonizers.[47]

Sayyid Ja'far's memoir describes the southern Communists' aims in broad terms: "to eliminate stagnation and rigidity and to look for a better and more beautiful future for all."[48] Communism received a welcome in and around al-Nabatiyya.[49] The reason for its popularity, Sayyid Ja'far commented jokingly, was that not many men in al-Nabatiyya "wore a fez or a turban," the headgear of landed dignitaries and clerics, respectively. He felt assured that Communist modernism could reverse the deplorable economic, educational, and medical conditions of the southern country-side. He also saw in Communist modernism an antidote to rural deterio-ration, economic exploitation, and European colonialism.[50]

A decisive setback for the Communists in Lebanon came in 1947 when the Soviet Union supported the United Nations' decision to partition Pal-estine between Jews and Arabs,[51] despite Arab governments' insistence on the integrity of Palestine and view of the Jewish demands as baseless. Because of the Soviet position on the partition, the Lebanese police sought the Communists in their homes, harassing and physically coercing them to end their activism.[52] This treatment, however, did not prevent the Com-munists from cultivating support for their cause at social gatherings and religious congregations. And the continuing popular appeal of Commu-nist ideals was evident in antigovernment protests led by women, men, and children. It was common for the Communists to overturn the gov-ernment's ban on the celebration of Labor Day whenever it coincided with or was close to the tenth of Muharram, the day when Imam Husayn was martyred. The occasion also helped them force the government to release political prisoners. At the beginning of Muharram, the residents around the government offices at the city hall would declare a state of emergency. There was "no authority above theirs [the mourners] in the first ten days [of Muharram]," stated Ahmad Gharbiyyeh. "They held funereal councils [*majalis 'aza*'] for al-Husayn, and most of them were from us, the Com-munists. . . . [W]e would walk toward the city hall at night where those detained were kept . . . and lamentation would start by the ritual cursing of those who committed injustice against the house of the Prophet. . . . [W]e did not leave the city hall's prison until all those detained were released."[53] Such references to 'Ashura and Imam Husayn were common for Com-munists of Sayyid Ja'far's generation. The affinity between certain Com-munist goals and Shi'ite emancipatory symbolism was simply one shade of southern communism at the time.

Civil activism that addressed small-scale health and socioeconomic needs absorbed much of the Communists' energy in the South. Sayyid Ja'far and his comrades pressured municipal and national officials to address these needs.[54] He maintained that democracy and progress are achieved by collective civil responsibility as much as by a transformation of the state. In the late 1940s, the Communists in al-Nabatiyya established a bookstore and turned a hotel into a school for teaching the illiterate to read. To pay for the hotel rent, they worked in the tobacco fields.[55] Sayyid Ja'far reflected excitedly, "It was a memorable day in al-Nabatiyya when teachers, university students, craft workers, and traders were seen farming and carrying water on donkeys without complaint."[56] The Communists also raised money for the beleaguered Syrian citizens after the French attack on the Syrian Parliament in 1945.[57]

Sayyid Ja'far experienced his share of political harassment and imprisonment. In 1946–47, a provincial Communist leader in al-Nabatiyya urged the Lebanese Ministry of Education to force Sayyid Ja'far out of his school post and to take action against him at the disciplinary court.[58] In what Sayyid Ja'far felt was a "betrayal" by his own party, the ministry succeeded in removing him from his post and transferring him to Shumustar in central Biqa', where he worked as a public-school director.[59] Shattered by party officials' complacency, Sayyid Ja'far emerged from his "red" life, "a broken cavalier."[60] Thereafter he satirized party bureaucrats and accused them of using Marxism "as a cover for [their] insecurities."[61] He withdrew from the party but immersed himself in projects for peasant educational and social development.

Rural Disintegration and State Policies, 1943–1964

Following the independence of Lebanon in 1943, the state's economic policies and sectarian features contributed to rural disintegration, which in turn encouraged antistate struggles and leftist leanings among the Shi'ite population. Under the first two Lebanese presidents, Bichara el-Khouri (1946–52) and Camille Chamoun (1952–58), liberal economic policies forced agricultural production to respond to the international market's needs instead of the local market's. Lebanon's rural regions suffered from major socioeconomic problems that the reforms of President Fouad Chehab (1958–64) did not effectively resolve. These regions—the Biqaʿ, the North (in particular, ʿAkkar), and the South—exhibited common features of underdevelopment, population growth, unemployment, and high rates of illiteracy in the mid-1950s.[62] They possessed particular sectarian features as well. The Biqaʿ had a large Shiʿite constituency, followed in size by the Christian communities—both Catholic (Maronite) and to a lesser extent Greek Orthodox—and then by the Sunnite and Druze communities. The South, as noted earlier, is predominantly Shiʿite but has a significant Maronite (Catholic) population and a smaller Sunnite one. The North has a mixed Muslim and Christian population of various religious denominations, with a majority of the latter.

In the South, the agrarian economy revolved more specifically around the planting of tobacco and absorbed a significant part of the Lebanese labor force, around 30,000 farmers living under semi-feudal relations.[63] Labor activism and militancy were tied mostly to the grievances of tobacco workingwomen and men involved in planting and manufacturing.[64] Agricultural labor was also necessary to cultivate wheat, barley, millet, sesame, lentils, beans, peas, watermelons, vines, fig trees, olive, and citrus.[65] The sugar-beet industry and cultivation absorbed large numbers of workers and farmers in the central Biqaʿ Valley, predominantly a Muslim area.[66] Government discrimination against Muslim regions and failed development plans pushed émigrés and entrepreneurs to take over the agribusiness in the South, tying it to the demands of the international market.[67] In the Biqaʿ and ʿAkkar, wealthy émigré Shiʿites, along with Palestinian and Beiruti entrepreneurs, established capitalist farms that grew citrus, potatoes, and sugar beets.[68]

Land shortage and el-Khouri and Chamoun economic policies contributed to the disintegration of the Biqaʿ and the southern countryside.[69] In the mid-1950s, the government extended its support to industrial regions close to the capital city, but only to strengthen banking, transportation, finance, and tourism.[70] Despite the increase in industrial output between 1955 and 1961, industrial undertakings were insignificant to the economy because the government reinvested its profits in the services rather than the productive sectors.[71] The same historical forces that accounted for the enlargement of some sectors owing to "economic liberalism" caused sharper class inequalities and boosted urban centers at the expense of the rural regions.[72] The government's aversion to progressive taxation, economic reform, social welfare, and trade unionism threw the lower classes into critical periods of inflation and poverty.[73]

Those engaged in agriculture, although estimated at 40–50 percent of the population, earned no more than 19 percent of the total provisional national income in 1950, whereas the industrial population, although estimated at the time at only 8 percent of the total population, earned 13 percent of total income.[74] Integrating Lebanon into the world market forced a decrease in peasant workers from 48.9 percent in 1959 to 18.9 percent in 1970.[75] Although the government took a few measures to improve irrigation and enlarge the size of agricultural land,[76] the small peasant landholder and farmer were controlled by market interests through a hierarchy of landowners, traders, bankers, and ultimately foreign business.[77] The heavy reliance on foreign clientele in organizing the economy blocked agricultural developments that would sustain rural life.[78] Meanwhile, foreign capitalists who pushed for an expansion in Lebanese banking activities in the 1950s also controlled investment initiatives, preventing some of the credits and resources to be reinvested in the economy.[79] The educational infrastructure also suffered in the 1950s. For instance, only thirty-one teachers served a body of 14,000 students from ages six to eleven at the public schools of Tyre, a major city in the South.[80] Between 1960 and 1966, this picture started to change somewhat when one public school was built in each village, and many more teachers were recruited.[81] This expansion in public education, as well as urbanization, contributed in part to upward social mobility but also to civil activism against the state. Many Shi'ite teachers, journalists, and intellectuals pushed for economic and political reform through Syrian nationalist, Arab nationalist, and Marxist organizations.

Without agrarian reform in the Biqa', population growth caused land shortage. Around 2 percent of the Biqa's agricultural workforce was made of small proprietors who hired laborers and rented small lots (1955–56). Tenancy and farm labor were the dominant patterns, and "the individual farmer" was "in the minority."[82] The sugar beets' industry did not achieve adequate expansion and thus failed to absorb more peasant workers in the Biqaʿ. Its production depended on the whims of the world market rather than on local need. The health and educational facilities in the Biqaʿ were pitiful.[83] In forty-five towns, mules were the major source of transportation. Running water was available to only 5 percent of the inhabitants.[84] As opportunities for economic growth evaporated, unskilled workers and peasants became more restless.

The breakup of land ownership owing to inheritance and sale created many tiny lots that were insufficient for the subsistence of a rural household (a family of five). In 1961, around 92 percent of peasants owned five or less hectares, whereas less than half of one percent owned from fifty to a hundred hectares.[85] Capitalist development favored the rise of fewer landlords, who increased their fortunes rapidly.[86] These conditions contributed to the alienation of peasants, compelling them to sell their lands to become agricultural laborers or move to the city.[87] The steady movement of peoples from village to city was not a sign of rural overpopulation, as one economic analyst posited.[88] The demographic pressures could have been adequately absorbed through an aggressive development plan to preserve rural society.[89] Meanwhile, by the mid-1950s Shiʿites became arguably the largest Lebanese sect, thus adding pressure on the infrastructures of the Biqaʿ and the South.[90]

In response to the Muslim lower classes' increasing opposition to the state, President Chehab tried to solve the problem of economic growth in rural Muslim regions.[91] For example, he initiated the building of new branches for the Régie in al-Nabatiyya and al-Ghaziyya in the South.[92] But these branches did not specialize in manufacturing, as the central branch in Beirut did. The latter exhibited the full line of production—sorting tobacco leaves, manufacturing, packing, and marketing cigarettes—so Beirut continued to offer most opportunities for employment. Meanwhile, Parliament kept receiving numerous petitions voicing the southern tobacco peasants and waged workers' grievances.[93] Under these conditions, labor unionism and Communist activism spread, and a few capitalist ventures collapsed, having devastating effects on the lower classes. A marked breakdown in relations between workers and employers at several industrial sites made 1963 for instance "the year for the spread of strikes" as the Lebanese daily *al-Nahar* declared.[94] Indeed, the 1960s witnessed increasing instances of state violence against workers.[95]

Chehab tried to achieve a Muslim-Christian balance in the productive economic sectors, including industry. His reforms absorbed elements of the Shi'ite bourgeoisie but failed to halt Shi'ite migration to Beirut or deflect institutionalized imbalance in sectarian allotments. After him, President Charles Helou (1964–70) continued some of these reforms, but unlike Chehab he permitted the provincial leaders to increase their power base.[96] The boom that the private economic sector previously witnessed was interrupted by the Intra Bank crisis of 1966 and by intense labor protests.[97] Meanwhile, renewed civil conflicts and Muslim-Christian schisms emerged in connection with the 1967 Arab-Israeli War. Among the Shi'ites, the bourgeoisie grew even as poverty and displacement (especially in the South) caught up with the lower social sectors.[98] The number of Shi'ites seemed preponderant in low-income occupations and reached the highest percentage (32 percent) of all the Lebanese who received less than the minimum wage (3,000 lira per year).[99]

All these developments encouraged antistate attitudes and leftist activism. Whatever steps the government took to regain legitimacy, a southern writer reflected, "the people will call for its downfall" if the crisis of inflation were not solved.[100] The Shi'ite clerics felt a mounting pressure to address antistate sentiments and the appeal of secularism and secular-based reforms to the lower and middle classes. Young Shi'ites were turning increasingly to the Communists, the Syrian nationalists, and Arab socialists, who offered a host of secular solutions to the Shi'ites' socioeconomic problems. Muhammad Jawad Mughniyya (d. 1979), a prominent southern *mujtahid*, supported the demands made by southern leftists and unionists against the government and the large landholders.[101] True, he had challenged Marxist theory on the question of religion, but he also accepted its critique of capitalism. He also shared the leftists' doubts about the uprightness of certain clerics, whom he described as "reactionary" and self-serving.[102] The landed elite, Mughniyya maintained, were the main cause of the crisis of unemployment and exploitation of the poor in the South.[103] He encouraged the 'ulama to rise against the injustices perpetrated by the notables and the deputies and put their weight behind labor activists and peasant protests in the South. He blamed the spread of secular ideologies among the Shi'ites on the immoral conduct and ignorance of a few clerics.[104]

Communist Activism against the State

The Communists demanded, among other things, state reform through the elimination of sectarianism, the rationalization of state bureaucracy, and the amelioration of electoral laws. To counteract sectarianism and weaken clerical control of family law, they advocated civil marriage across sects and called for the replacement of religious courts with civil courts.[105] They formed civil and political organizations that agitated against the bourgeoisie and their allies in powerful landed elites and offered alternatives to sect-based organizations. And they aimed to replace the multiple electoral districts with one and to elect Parliament candidates who obtained a proportional representation (in proportional representation, candidates who obtain the highest number of votes are elected, irrespective of their sectarian affiliation or the province they come from). [106]

The Communists' approach to the Lebanese nation-state informed their political program and activism. Mahdi 'Amil (d. 1987), a Shi'ite ideologue of the Lebanese Communist Party, articulated the basis of the Communists' resistance to the state's economic and political foundations. The Lebanese state had contradictory facets in that it was both secular and sectarian, 'Amil argued. In contrast to the enthusiasm that Chehab's reforms stirred among liberal nationalists, 'Amil proclaimed their tendency to strengthen the sectarian structure and protect the bourgeoisie. The reforms, he argued, appeared at a time in Lebanon's development when the bourgeoisie needed to reshape itself in the face of class unrest and popular dissent. Chehab's reforms did not aim to prevent sectarian divisions or to improve the relationship between the state and labor. Rather, they attempted to create a few outlets for lower-class frustration without undermining the major capitalist enterprises supported by the state. Yet capitalist processes themselves faced major challenges. In order to achieve capitalist growth, the state under Chehab would theoretically benefit from breaking its alliance with the landed provincial leaders who are enforcing sectarianism, but the state, 'Amil noted, was unable to break this alliance because the provincial leaders and the bourgeoisie were interdependent. In a postcolonial sectarian state such as Lebanon, a purely bourgeois-based reform was unachievable, 'Amil reflected. The Chehabist project simply brought a new balance of power among aspiring classes (such as the émigré Shi'ite bourgeoisie) within their locales and in the state. For the Communists, this project simply failed to absorb the mounting pressure from the lower classes.[107]

During the 1950s and 1960s, the trade unions loyal to the Communists were active among the workforce of the textile, tobacco, steel, and oil refineries, as well as some food industries.[108] Communists were present chiefly in the unions of Lebanese teachers, press and printing-press workers, steelworkers, writers, students, taxi drivers, fishery workers, and farmers, and in art and popular-culture associations. The unions demanded from state officials improvement in workers' salaries and working conditions and the protection of Lebanese farmers and consumers. They asked the government to provide funding for small industries, to support cooperatives, and to fight inflation and monopolies by pharmaceutical, oil, and flour companies.[109] They demanded that tenants be shielded from erratic and quick increases in rent and struggled to reform public education at the primary, secondary, and university levels. They urged the government to extend financial aid and stipends for students and unify the curricula at public and private schools. Communists struggled persistently to force the government to subsidize bread, gas, school textbooks, and medical benefits.[110] During the 1960s and the 1970s, Communists—students and professionals such as teachers and lawyers, as well as industrial workers—in various social arenas and in women's associations devoted a great deal of energy in support of civil marriage, which put them in a direct clash with clerical leaderships and state officials.[111] Communist programs, however, were not just focused on urban workers but also remotely targeted rural workers such as those in the North and the Biqa', who formed the largest productive pool in Lebanon.

Shi'ite activists appeared in a host of leftist organizations, most importantly the Lebanese Communist Party, the Party of Socialist Lebanon, and the Organization of Communist Action.[112] Numerous Shi'ite unionists and leftists partook in civil and militant struggles against the state to reform the political system and to improve labor conditions. For instance, they played a prominent role in the 1963 and 1965 strikes by the tobacco workingwomen and men at the Régie in Beirut. [113] More than 300,000 Lebanese relied on the Régie for their livelihood, including 45,000 tobacco farmers. [114] The most obvious reason for the strikes was that from 1955 to 1965 the annual sale of tobacco increased almost twofold, but workers' wages and benefits remained the same. [115]

When the Régie workers started a major strike in 1965, the company's union, the Union of the Régie Workers and Employees (URWE, Ittihad 'ummal wa muwadhdhafi al-riji), tried to diffuse it. [116] Communist involvement in this strike was repeatedly stressed in police and government reports. [117] The police had found Communist documents and flyers among Régie workers such as 'Ali Subayti (a Shi'ite), Ilyas al-Dibs (Greek Orthodox), 'Ali 'Awada (Shi'ite), Nimr Saliba (Greek Orthodox), and Musa Husayn (Shi'ite). [118] The strikers also coordinated their acts with the leftist association of the labor movement, the Federation of Workers' Liberation Front (Jabhat al-taharrur al-'ummali), which attacked the government fiercely. The Communists encouraged the strikers to ask for a 15 percent increase in their salaries instead of the 8 percent allotted by the government. [119] The Ministry of Information and state officials thus argued that Communist workers posed a "threat to their colleagues" and had enticed them to continue with the strike. "Leftist extremists," they noted, were also behind the workingwomen's "invasion" of the administrative building of the Régie in Beirut. [120] The newspapers controlled by the government ran editorials with headlines such as "Workingmen and Women Are Sacrificed for Leftist Extremists" and "The Communists Exploit the Strike of the Régie Workingmen and Women," and they claimed that Communist agitators placed "women at the forefront of the [strike] lines." [121] The size of the army force deployed at the Régie's plant in Beirut and the roads leading to it in response to the 1965 strike indicated the serious challenge that such strikes posed to the state. The strike included among its top demands that temporary workingwomen be paid minimum wage according to the labor law and that workingwomen be given wages equal to those of men at the same rank. [122] Kamal Junblat, the leader of the leftist Progressive Socialist Party (Al-Hizb al-taqaddumi al-ishtiraki) with its Druze Muslim majority, gave unconditional support to the Régie workers and with that support strengthened the Communists' position. Junblat stated that what the workers demanded from the Régie amounted to a small fraction of the illicit profit that "the rich and the covetous elite accumulated."[123] *Al-Anba'*, the party's newspaper, presented the Régie crisis as a symptom of the fundamental struggle between the Right and the Left in Lebanese society.[124] Overall, the 1965 Régie strike underscores the growth of labor unionism and Communist activism against the state, which drew a significant part of Shi'ite industrial workers, students, teachers, and intellectuals.

The Communists and Arab Nationalism

The ideological shift that the Lebanese Communist Party made in 1968 on the question of Arab nationalism was a landmark in the party's history. The party reviewed its rejection of Arab nationalist movements and decided to support those tied to the anticolonial struggle and armed resistance to Israel. This ideological shift further popularized Communist political programs among the Lebanese youth, including the southerners. A brief historical background for this transformation is useful.

Following the Soviet Union, the Lebanese Communist Party acquiesced with the UN resolution in 1947 that stipulated the division of Palestine into two states, an Arab one and a Jewish one. The Soviet Union looked favorably at Israel as a potential democracy that could prompt socialist change in Arab Middle Eastern societies.[125] The leader of the Syrian-Lebanese Communist Party, Khalid Bakdash, argued that British and American capitalist interests had drawn a wedge between Jewish and Arab laborers and tried to divide the Communists. Jewish laborers, he added, were led astray by the Zionist capitalists and made to serve their interests, which in turn were tied to the West.[126] The party also disengaged with the Palestinian national question and Arabism as forms of bourgeois thought with antimodern dispositions.[127] It held, for instance, an ambiguous position on the pan-Arab unity between Syria and Egypt and hailed the collapse of this unity in 1961.[128]

However, Third Worldist critiques of Soviet communism were also emerging after the Stalinist era in the mid-1950s and finding some resonance in the Arab world.[129] Several Communist leaders in Asia, Latin America, and Africa were revisiting Marxism in the light of their local experiences and historical conditions. Challenging "Eurocentric" Communist proposals, these leaders emphasized instead the revolutionary features of national struggle against colonialism in the Third World. A new generation of leftists criticized the Lebanese Communist Party for failing to harness the progressive elements of Arab national resistance to European hegemony. Anticolonial nationalism, the revisionist leftists argued, could form a counterweight to antidemocratic bourgeois impulses in Lebanon and Syria. 'Amil wrote about this period: "[H]aving isolated itself by withdrawing from the right national path, and from the nationalist popular masses, the [Communist] [P]arty was unable to play its role in leading the national struggle of these masses."[130] The party's social programs, 'Amil added, were disconnected from national-based movements that called for the secularization of the state.[131] This relationship changed a year after the second Arab-Israeli War in 1967, however, when the Communists validated Arab national struggles for liberation and lent their unconditional support to the Palestinian cause.[132] A number of leftist organizations promoted armed resistance against Israel through guerilla warfare modeled after the Vietnamese revolution. Pan-Arabists, however, continued to find the Communists' position unsatisfactory because they "never called for the obliteration of Israel."[133] Arab chauvinist arguments had limited effect on communism's appeal to Lebanese Shi'ites, though. Rather, the crisis of the state, on the one hand, and rural displacement leading to proletarianization, on the other, secured a firm place for Communist programs in several social and political arenas in Lebanon. Leftist journalists, thinkers, unionists, and artists brought to the public sphere a powerful discourse against the state and capital and achieved through their parties and civil spheres ways of organizing peoples around class issues and political demands.

Husayn Muroeh: The Mujtahid Who Never Was

A description of the social background and ideas of a major Shi'ite Communist of this period, Husayn Muroeh (1908–87) brings the historical trajectories described to life. Muroeh's writings reflect a Marxist attempt to modernize Arab-Islamic tradition (*turath*) by stressing its relation to political economy and both the national and international structure of power.

Muroeh, a cleric's son from Haddatha in the South, became one of the ideologues of the Lebanese Communist Party in the 1960s (see map 2). Despite his excellent academic performance and desire to become a *mujtahid*, Muroeh realized a year after he arrived in Najaf in 1924 that he may never fulfill his father's dream that he would become a cleric. [134] He returned to Lebanon for some time, looking there and in Damascus for a stable career in journalism or teaching, but to no avail. He then returned to the seminary, where he spent fourteen years pursuing his studies in the Islamic legal-religious sciences.[135] Senior southern ʿulama had high expectations of him and offered to support him financially as he continued his seminary education. Muroeh was still part of a shifting world where social status and self-esteem were tied to success in the classical system of Islamic learning, but where there were no guarantees for a stable career otherwise promised by a modern secular education.

In the 1930s, Muroeh, by this time married and with three children, continued to move between two worlds—the seminary and urban Baghdad. In Baghdad, he would change his appearance by taking off his religious garb and turban.[136] On his way back to Najaf, he would don them again. This regular shift between two styles and two appearances exposed his attachment to both worlds and the need to be validated by both—a need borne out of the hope that the two worlds would be reconciled in a new vision, a "reformist" vision not dissimilar to that of Sayyid Muhsin, the leading southern *marjaʿ*. But Muroeh, without realizing it, had already moved on a trajectory beyond that attempted by Sayyid Muhsin. The seminary was not the place for such a vision. Muroeh searched for the means and opportunity to leave the "circle of religious study to the wider environment, to continue—together [with Muhammad Sharara]—the movement of opposition and confrontation on the level of society as a whole, guided by scientific analysis of the social and ideological reality inside that society itself."[137] In this statement, made several decades after leaving Najaf, Muroeh was referring to his increased confidence in Marxist theory. In

1938, because of his more obvious secularist views, he was expelled from the seminary on accusations of heresy, after which he contemplated committing suicide.[138] Despite his Marxist leanings, he evidently still had deep ties to the seminary or at least high hopes of becoming a jurist. But he had to start new life in Baghdad.

During the 1930s, Muroeh's essays and public speeches showed a few traces of Marxist analysis. They also conveyed, however, a deep sense of Islamic piety and Arab-Syrian patriotism, as well as an appreciation of literary modernity.[139] He praised King Faysal in a public speech, urging him to fulfill his national obligations toward Iraq and the Arab peoples.[140] He placed Iraq's struggle against Anglo-American imperialism within the framework of an international anticolonial movement spreading through Asia and Africa.[141] He also addressed the Palestinian question. British colonial oppression and Zionism in Palestine, he proclaimed, were the sources of the calamity that beset the Arab national "dream" of unity. He wished the Palestinian crisis would induce a national "awakening" among the Arabs.[142] Muroeh argued that political and economic conditions must compel Arabs, irrespective of language or religion, to unite.[143] Muroeh did not offer a coherent picture of the form of political rule or Arab unity he envisaged. His writings also carried at the time paradoxical elements— secular modernism, chauvinist nationalism, and religious faith. For instance, he expressed admiration for the esprit de corps and European military training in building up the youth.[144] He also argued that the dismissal of Arab spiritual values and religious faith impaired the character of the Iraqi nation.[145] Yet at the same time he investigated the approach that Arab writers should take toward Western literary modernity. Writing about the Iraqi literary movement, he argued that modeling itself after its European counterparts could help the movement flourish without erasing its local or distinctive "personality."[146]

Muroeh's perturbed steps oscillated between Marxist and religious thought in "a struggle that was painful and enjoyable at once."[147] Baghdad's intellectual life sparked intense discussions about Arab nationalism and communism. Among the Communists there, the most noteworthy in connection with Muroeh was Husayn Muhammad al-Shabibi (1917–49), a Shi'ite from Najaf and one of the founders of the ICP. Muroeh was sufficiently intrigued by Marx's *Communist Manifesto* and Lenin's *State and Revolution* that he decided to maintain his relationship with al-Shabibi, yet in secret because at the same time, he was participating in the activities of the nationalist party al-Istiqlal (The Independence), a staunch enemy of the Iraqi Communists.[148] During a nationwide uprising against the Portsmouth Treaty, signed on January 15, 1948, Muroeh decided to support the Iraqi Communists publicly, expressing his confidence in their political vision and plans. The Portsmouth Treaty promised the evacuation of British troops from Iraq but caused an outrage among the Iraqis for permitting the British to take over Iraq's air bases during any future war, as well as to inspect Iraqi military activities. In 1949, in response to the Communists' protests, the government instigated a campaign against them and their sympathizers, which forced Muroeh out of Iraq and into Lebanon.

In Lebanon, Muroeh read the works of Ismai'l Mazhar and Shibli al-Shumayyil on Darwinian evolution and the role of natural laws in human development and historical change.[149] He found "the religious interpretation" of change in nature and society unsatisfactory. Embracing a secular outlook, he denied society's need for the *'ulama* and disapproved of the clerics' role in shaping human conduct.[150] Meanwhile, his Marxist literary analysis sparked the interest of a few Communists who invited him to contribute to *al-Tariq* (The Path), the Lebanese Communist Party's periodical. This invitation opened wide the party's doors to him in the early 1950s.[151] Muroeh remained active in the party until 1987, when he was assassinated in his house in Beirut. Communists accused the Shi'ite-based party AMAL of his assassination.[152]

Husayn Muroeh's intellectual transformation went through several complex phases. His contribution to Islamic Marxism, postcolonial theory, and the study of tradition appears primarily in his book *Al-Naza'at al-maddiyya fi al-falsafa al-'Arabiyya al-Islamiyya* (Material Tendencies in Arab–Islamic Philosophy), which he started to write in the late 1960s.[153] Revolutionary change in Arab society, Muroeh suggested, required a transformation not only of the economy, but also of culture, as a vital domain for colonial hegemony.[154] Colonial systems spread idealist attitudes that exaggerate the importance of the individual and the educated elite. These systems impede the "progress" of nascent nations (like those in the Arab world) and impair the connection between the individual's freedom and society's freedom within the world order.[155] Through Islamic Marxism, Muroeh tried to authorize secular modernism and direct it away from its Western colonial manifestation. At the same time, he stressed the importance of fitting modernism to Islamic discursive traditions, challenging at times "the mechanistic materialism that marred" the Soviet Orientalists' view of history.[156] Therefore, he did not consider the domain of culture a pure reflection of material forces. Ideas could become partially independent of the material forces that had originally shaped them. Muroeh rejected also the liberal-national frameworks of inquiry that treated modern features of Arab-Islamic tradition as extensions of the past. In contrast, he saw tradition as developing constantly in relationship to the historical location and social activity of humans involved in thinking about it. The past is revisited and understood in relationship to the present. The "materialist" historical method allowed Muroeh, as he noted, to understand tradition in its constant dynamic movement and to acknowledge its relative rather than absolute value. It further uncovered the ties between the "democratic tenets" of the traditions of each nation-state and the international democratic tenets of contemporary human thought as a whole.[157]

To sum up, Muroeh joined the ranks of the religious modernists in Najaf when he was still a young student. He advocated at the time selective adaptations of liberal European ideas by Muslim societies. His experiences in Iraq made him doubt that clerical leadership could secure a stable source of livelihood, become meaningfully connected to the struggles of the day, or generate a viable argument for secular modernism drawn from within the Islamic tradition. Meanwhile, he recast some of the features of the Enlightenment, in particular the notion of "progress," to fit the experiences and needs of a decolonizing society and its Islamic traditions. His commitment to communism was deepened by the Lebanese Communists' embrace of anticolonial struggle in the 1960s, as well as by their programs that aimed to reform the economy, combat the alliance between the landed elites and the bourgeoisie, and secularize the state.

Summary

The appeal of communism to the *'ulama*'s sons was shaped by a shift in the class conditions and rural economy of the South. It was also influenced by anticolonial struggle, disappointment with Faysal's leadership, and political marginality in Grand Liban's sectarian polity. Communists in the South hoped to create a modern material and social culture that did not follow the patterns of European capitalism. Soviet communism offered one solution for problems of agricultural deterioration, economic exploitation, and sectarianism. Sayyid Ja'far al-Amin and Husayn Muroeh offered localized readings of Marxism that moved away from party confines to local experiences of communism. As noted earlier, popular sectors on the left and their sympathizers saw communism not only as a secular political program, but also as a moral "belief" reinforcing Shi'ite notions of social justice and expectations of a utopian order.

Southern rural life continued to deteriorate when the government made only minor efforts in agrarian reform, instead promoting commerce and tourism at the expense of agriculture and industry.[158] The political system sustaining these policies organized Lebanese citizens hierarchically as endogamous sectarian entities.[159] The Communists demanded the removal of sectarianism as a condition for economic equity and democratic political representation for all Lebanese constituencies. Mahdi 'Amil suggested that capitalist ventures were hampered by the state's commitment to sectarianism. The state, he maintained, was caught in a formidable contradiction: it could only reinvent itself as a "bourgeois state" through its existence as "a sectarian state."[160] This contradiction explained, noted 'Amil, why Chehab's reforms failed to halt sectarian inequalities.

The Shi'ite countryside faced critical economic challenges and political transitions during the 1960s. The lower classes, transformed decisively by rural dislocation, urbanization, and expansion in public education, expressed new forms of resistance to the state. The Communists and unionists demanded effective labor laws, free medical benefits, student financial aid, and prevention of monopolies by medical and food companies. They led demonstrations against broader sociopolitical problems, demanding the elimination of sectarianism, secularization of state bureaucracy, and educational reform.

The dynamism of leftist culture in the South and the continued appeal of secular Communist ideals to the youth during the 1960s and the 1970s soon faced a formidable challenge, however. As chapters 4 and 5 show, an organized clerical opposition to the Communists was making inroads into Shi'ite political life. The opposition found its strongest advocate in Iraq through the *marja'* Sayyid Muhsin al-Hakim and in Lebanon through the charismatic cleric Sayyid Musa al-Sadr.

4

The "Shi'ite Communist," the Clerical Movement, and the Islamists in Iraq

In chapters 2 and 3, we saw how a number of Lebanese *talaba* and aspiring *'ulama* at Najaf's seminary adapted elements of secular modernism and, more specifically, communism. In this chapter, we delineate two interconnected sociopolitical currents that appeared during the late 1950s at the Shi'ite seminaries in Najaf and Karbala': antisecularism and modern Islamism. These currents were shaped by the conflict between clerical authority and the Communists—a conflict that left its mark on the ideas and experiences of the Lebanese Islamists in Najaf such as Muhammad Husayn Fadlallah; Shaykh Subhi al-Tufayli, one of the founders of Hizbullah; and Sayyid Hasan Nasrallah, the present leader of Hizbullah.

The preponderance of Shi'ites in the labor movement and the Iraqi Communist Party (ICP) had significant consequences for Najaf's seminary and its leading jurists. This chapter revisits the broad idea expressed by clerics and Islamist thinkers that Communist atheism and disdain for religion was the primary motive for the jurists' radicalization as well as the rise of Islamism. This idea is probed through a distinction between, first, atheism and secularism and, second, the shari'a (nomocentric or legally based traditions) and popular religion as well as Sufi and philosophical traditions.[1] Many Shi'ite Communists and sympathizers evidently drew versatile associations between a secular organization of society and local religious culture. These associations rather than atheism per se undermined clerical authority and disrupted the implementation of the shari'a perceived by the jurists as the kernel of Islamic belief. Overall, this chapter shows that three interrelated factors drove activist and militant clerics to attack the Shi'i Communists—namely, the affinity between Communist ideals and local religious culture; Communist socioeconomic programs; and secularization of family law, education, and political representation.

The early Islamists defined Islam and Muslim identity as the public enactment of the shari'a, which is antithetical to secular society. The latter, originating in the West, could lead to cultural displacement and disintegration of Islamic society. By and large, the early Islamists rejected forms of belief that are not bound by the shari'a's legal, doctrinal, and ritualistic demands. They also questioned an open engagement with Islamic discursive traditions—in particular, the mystical and the philosophical. The Islamists argued as such that one has to live by the shari'a in its full sociolegal dimension in order to realize the true life of a Muslim.

Communist social and economic programs posed a major threat to the power and financial interests of the Shi'ite jurists and seminary leaders. These programs stressed agrarian reforms that would limit abuses by the large landholders, decrease taxes, offer governmental loans, and, more importantly, give small lots of land for landless peasants. They also supported secularization and state-directed initiatives to privatize religion and prevent the clerics from shaping questions of political representation, public education, and family law. Shi'ite support for these programs inside and outside the seminaries led to the growth of an Iraqi clerical movement that defended the jurists' interests and distinct aspects of public Islam. This chapter highlights the leading role played by the *marja'* Sayyid Muhsin al-Hakim in the clerical movement and his efforts in combating communism. To illustrate the character of the clerical movement and the nature of the Islamists' dispute with communism, the chapter ends with a portrait of a prominent jurist Muhammad Baqir al-Sadr, who directed the first comprehensive attack on communism in Najaf and promoted Islam as an alternative spiritual, political, and socioeconomic system. He challenged the universalistic ideas projected by the Enlightenment at the same time as he refitted elements of Western modernism to Shi'ite jurists legal activity. His advocacy of a modernist Islam paradoxically triggered clerical denunciation of Western and leftist "influences" on Shi'ite jurists like him.

The Shi'ite Jurists and the Communists

From the mid-1940s and through the 1950s, thousands of Shi'ites considered communism a medium for national liberation, economic reform, and modernism—a modernism that argued against a capitalist and colonizing Europe.[2] Communist struggles against British colonialism were intertwined with demands for economic reform and political secularism. During the mid-1940s, leading *'ulama* in Najaf such as Muhammad Husayn Kashif al-Ghita' and 'Abd al-Karim Zanjani were agitating against the spread of communism among the Shi'ite youth. They urged the government to follow the lead of Reza Shah Pahlavi in Iran and curtail communism.[3] Meanwhile, a few jurists in Najaf cooperated with the British to prevent the spread of communism at the seminary. The British allowed the mujtahid Muhammad al-Khalisi to return from exile in Iran to Kazimayn in Iraq with the stipulation that he pursue his anti-Communist activities.[4] The Communists, however, continued to rally support for their ideas among the Shi'ites, where stark inequalities existed; a few ranked among the most affluent in Iraq, and many among the poorest.[5]

The Communists devoted their attention in the 1940s to national liberation and succeeded in eliminating several stipulations in the Anglo-Iraqi Treaty of 1930 and in implementing an election law to achieve democratic representation.[6] They stressed the role of British interests in prohibiting the formation of political parties, unions, and cultural clubs reflecting the concerns of common Iraqis. They also focused on strengthening the youth movement and organizing the peasants.[7] The dominance of foreign capital and colonial enterprises, in their view, impeded Iraq's agrarian development. They warned against the effects of the international market on rural production and deplored the prevalent feudal relations and the loss of peasant lands. The peasants were disgruntled by British-led initiatives to transform tribal chiefs into influential sedentary landlords.[8] They had been forced to pay rent for the land on which they worked as well as government taxes and certain dues for the tribal chiefs and *sarakil* (landlord's foremen), payments that totaled half or more of the total yield.[9] The Communists denounced the egregious interest rates on loans taken by peasants to produce the crops. The latter were then sold at a quarter of their value.[10] The Communists demanded the distribution of small lots of land to landless peasants, the extension of government loans, and the lifting of customs and taxes as well as illegal rents by the chiefs.[11]

Around 2 percent of propertied Iraqis owned two-thirds of agricultural land in the late 1950s.[12] The Communists' attempt to introduce tenancy reform, tenure stability, land redistribution, peasant cooperatives, and so on won them sufficient support among the Shi'ite peasants in the 1950s as to worry the large landholders among the chiefs and the clerical leaders. The peasants of the Shi'ite tribe al-Azayrij, some of whom had Communist affiliations, revolted in the South in 1952 following the government's decision to allot the lands customarily owned by the tribe to the powerful chiefs.[13] Husayn al-Shabibi, the Communist leader from Najaf, insisted that the "national question is in its essence a peasant cause," and others raised the slogan "Land is owned by the person who cultivates it."[14] Liberation from colonial rule had to be tied to the elimination of feudalism and peasant poverty as well as to the upgrading of relations of production. Despite their efforts, the Communists could not organize the peasants as effectively as they had hoped owing to government surveillance, police harassment, and intransigent beliefs.[15]

On his part, Sayyid Muhsin al-Hakim rejected Communist demands for land reform and defended the interests of the large landholders, some of whom were sponsors of Najaf's seminary. To compensate for the scarcity of the financial sources coming from Iran, the seminary leaders had turned to funds from Iraqi landholders.[16] Al-Hakim insisted that land reform violated the Islamic foundations of private property.[17] He considered the lands redistributed under government economic reform as "lands taken by force." He issued a legal injunction (fatwa), declaring that praying on such lands is prohibited.[18] When news about the fatwa reached some peasants, they demanded a written proof of it, for they doubted that their *marja'*, al-Hakim, would prevent them from improving their conditions or would justify their exploitation by the large landholders. Other peasants, Faleh Jabbar notes, "denied such a *fatwa* [against agrarian reform] was issued at all, saying that al-Hakim was too wise to take such a position."[19]

These accounts illustrate the moral expectations placed on al-Hakim's actions, but also the contentious nature of agrarian reform. Other influential jurists obliquely succored the landholders, causing common Shi'ites to mistrust them and to turn to the Communists.[20]

By 1955, the Shi'ite Arabs formed the largest group (44.9 percent) in the ICP.[21] Shi'ite teachers, medical doctors, and intellectuals occupied important party posts. The Communists dominated student unions and "Cultural Committees" at several schools and colleges and shaped various social, literary, artistic, and political arenas.[22] They devoted much attention to the dissemination of Marxist principles and concepts through newspapers, journals, and periodicals, which caught the attention of the British and the Iraqi monarchy under Nuri al-Sa'id.[23] The British were actively combating communism, and along with their European allies tried to draw Syria into the Baghdad Pact, ratified in 1955.[24] In 1956, Communist uprisings spread in reaction to the tripartite attack on Egypt by Britain, France, and Israel following Gamal Abdel Nasser's nationalization of the Suez Canal. Hanna Batatu notes that the most dynamic of these uprisings occurred in Najaf and Hayy, a town southeast of Baghdad.[25] From Najaf, they spread to Kufa and eventually reached Baghdad, Mosul, Kirkuk, Sulaymaniyya, and Arbil.[26] In Najaf, the intensity and duration of the uprisings can be attributed to the sharp class differences between the powerful landowners and the peasants as well as to Najaf's relative resistance to centralized state authority.[27] The Najafis, Batatu writes, "never reconciled themselves completely to the fact of government" and defended their own people against encroachment or attack. Kinship and clerical ties notably sheltered the Communist demonstrators at times and carried sway with the local police and provincial administration. For instance, a judge whose son was a Communist gave mild sentences to the Communists who appeared before his court. Sayyid 'Ali Salman, a Communist of the Najaf Party Committee, who came from a *sayyid* family that formed a major municipal faction in Najaf up until World War I, seemed to have cast a mantle of protection over Communists in Huwaysh, one of four quarters in Najaf's old town, where it was "impossible to track or arrest a Communist." The Najafis seemed also to have sheltered Communist physicians in appreciation of their free services for the poor.[28]

Shi'i Shuyu'i (Shi'ite Communist)
and Secularization under Qasim's Regime

The Communists partook in the revolution that brought 'Abd al-Karim Qasim to power on July 14, 1958, and played a critical role in shaping public opinion through the Iraqi press. From the beginning, Qasim's regime was pulled in various directions by the Communists and various groups of Arab nationalists, such as the Ba'thists, the Nasserites, and the Iraqi nationalists.[29] The curious expression "Shi'i Shuyu'i," meaning that "the Shi'ite is typically Communist," became popular during the 1950s and the 1960s. It revealed how religion and even ethnicity were framed in the nationalist discourse of the Nasserites and Ba'thists against communism.[30] The former were enraged by Communist denunciations of bourgeois national culture and of the glorification of Arab "civilization" by both Nasserties and Ba'thists. The latter presented communism as a Shi'ite phenomenon, implying that a Shi'ite, unlike a Sunnite, was hostile to Arab culture.[31] The "Shi'ite" was represented also as having close ties to Persian culture and Iranian intellectuals and was thus an "unauthentic" Arab. Perhaps the label "Shi'ite Communist" also pertained to the ICP's early approach to the Palestinian question. The Arab nationalists proclaimed that the ICP had gone against national sentiments by supporting the United Nations' decision to partition Palestine into an Arab and an Israeli state.[32] Even though the Communists revoked this decision later and partook in major anticolonial struggles, they continued to be presented as anti-Arab. The Communists were in favor of *qutri* (regional) nationalism and opposed pan-Arabism and Arab unity, noting the differences among Arab countries in terms of economic development, social composition, and shape of government. They also questioned the imposition of Arab unity from above by government leaders rather than the achievement of it from below by the lower classes.[33] Instead of Arab unity, the Communists advocated social cooperation among the Arab working classes and the building of regional Arab markets. The depiction of Shi'ite Communists as anti-Arab ran parallel to Najaf jurists' denunciation of them as atheists beyond the pale of Islam.

Communist ideas had traveled from the urban Shi'ite neighborhoods of Baghdad to Najaf's seminary.[34] Destitute and politically marginalized, many Shi'ite migrants to Baghdad lent their numbers to the ICP.[35] Under Qasim, the Communists continued to attract Shi'ite workers, students, teachers, physicians, and intellectuals.[36] They also felt confident enough to confront clerical campaigns against them. Public disputes between the Communists and their opponents escalated at times into physical tussles in Najaf's quarters.[37] Meanwhile, a group of clerics and *talaba* led by al-Hakim were forming an organized movement to combat Communist programs for secularization and agrarian reform.

This movement was evidently deeply shaken by Qasim's issuance of the secular statutes by means of the 1959 Code of Personal Status. The Communists considered the code a "great legal achievement" in the process of building a national government devoid of sectarian and ethnic-based arrangements.[38] It signaled a new phase in secularization pertaining to family law—in particular, questions of marriage, divorce, and inheritance.[39] Najaf's senior jurists, however, found women's enhanced power under the new code—especially in matters of divorce and inheritance—irreconcilable with the shari'a.[40] For these jurists, the most alarming aspect of the code was the amalgamation of personal-status law drawn from the Ja'fari and Sunnite schools of law. Muhammad Bahr al-'Ulum, a prominent scholar in Najaf, prepared a thorough critique of the code, arguing that its fixed legal stipulations might lead to the closing of "the gate of *ijtihad*," which is the basis for legal renewal in the Ja'fari school of law.[41] The jurists criticized the clauses relating to witnesses in marriage, conditions for polygamy, and, more important, intestate succession, which removed a male heir's right to receive a double share of the legacy.[42] High- and low-ranking clerics rose in a political offensive against the Communists, fearing that the latter's secular vision would erode their functions, their authority, and the foundations of Islamic society.[43]

The Question of Atheism

Atheism was not a principal theoretical commitment in the ICP, nor did the Communists seriously implement it.[44] It was not stated in the party's official documents, nor did it appear as a main objective in its programs.[45] Leninist atheism had an active and pervasive character in building the

Communist Soviet state and society.[46] It was decisively antireligious and stressed the view that humans are enabled by their will, organization, and reason, which can be impeded by religion.[47] Even though the ICP drew upon the framework and international politics of Soviet communism, hardly any influential Iraqi Communist adopted its wide-ranging atheism.[48] The Iraqi Communists, for instance, did not attempt to utilize scientific data on the origins and evolution of the human species to establish proofs against religion. The Communist-dominated cultural committees at schools and colleges during the 1950s and the 1960s did not promote scientific atheism per se. A few Communists associated atheism with the ability to control material conditions and hence to achieve power over human thought and values.[49] It is also true that a handful of essays printed in the Communist periodical *al-Qa'ida* between the mid-1940s and the late 1950s denounced religion as the "sigh of the oppressed creature" and denied the existence of God.[50] These views, however, had little sway at the popular level. Yusuf Salman Yusuf, known as "Fahd," the first secretary general of the ICP in 1940–41, strove to show that the ICP's communism was not atheistic and that it had drawn even "clerics and their sons" to it.[51] The ICP's second official organ, the journal *Kifah al-Sha'b* (The People's Struggle), which first appeared in 1940, stressed transitional rather than final ends. For its catchphrases, it turned not to the "Communist Manifesto but to the Qur'an and to 'Ali ibn Abi Talib, the fourth caliph of Islam."[52] It is difficult to ascertain whether the journal's religious language was a calculated effort to attract followers. A more plausible view is that Communist programs adapted to local culture. The atheists who rejected belief in God and the metaphysical dimensions of human reality were indeed present in the ICP, but they were elite thinkers who did not supply the public image of communism in Iraq in the 1950s and the 1960s.

On their part, Shi'ite Communists expressed varied engagements with religion, drawing links between Marxism and Shi'ite doctrinal and eschatological traditions. A number of 'Ashura' reciters (*rawadid*, pl. of *radud*) who led chest-beating sessions, poets elegizing Imam Husayn, and individuals who worked at the shrine of al-Rawda al-Haydariyya were Communist.[53] Husayn Muhammad al-Shabibi, whose father had spent his life as an orator at the Husaynid pulpit in Najaf, was a leading Communist and anticolonial activist.[54] He became a member of the Political Bureau of the ICP's Central Committee and was executed by the mandatory regime (under the British) along with Fahd in 1949. Communists and their sympathizers in Najaf and Karbala' participated regularly in the commemorative rituals of 'Ashura', which generated a debate about it within the ranks of the ICP during the mid-1950s. One view warned that objecting to these rituals or discouraging their performance would isolate the Communists from society. Another view pointed to the utilitarian aspects of these rituals, noting that they could "be turned . . . to good account."[55] A prevalent approach to the 'Ashura' ceremonies, however, was one of accommodation based on a particular reading of Marxist-Leninist views about the collective beliefs of peasants and working classes. Supporters of the ceremonies interpreted Lenin's statement "Act where the masses are" as pointing to the importance of adjusting Communist activism to the sentiments of a critical mass that can lend its support to communism. Another argument rested on the moral significance and political meaning of the historical 'Ashura' and Husayn's martyrdom. One Communist reflected: "Didn't Husain revolt against injustice?" He noted that this revolt would encourage the peasants to think about injustice and tie it to the Communists' ideas. These ideas were more readily accessible to the public during 'Ashura' than at any other occasion.[56] A further reason for participating in the ceremonies was practical. During the ceremonies, the Communists were able to communicate their ideas and programs to mourners and pilgrims with little difficulty because the government and the British had prohibited congregations and public gatherings except during religious ceremonies.[57] In Karbala', the Communists participated fully in 'Ashura', holding their procession known as "al-'Abbasiyya" and reciting folk poems with leftist overtones.[58] The few uncompromising secularists in the ICP, however, suggested that accepting participation in 'Ashura' and other religious ceremonies should be only temporary because the ultimate aim was to eliminate "the social roots of religion."[59] Beyond such talk among a handful of Communists, uprooting "religion" was nowhere evident. At the base, the Shi'ite Communists were a mix of pious believers and secularists who drew upon Islamic traditions and local religious culture.[60] What is clear, however, is that the terms *religion* and *religiosity* expressed by these Communists did not carry the same meaning or implications as they had for the influential jurists. To illustrate this distinction, we turn to questions of religious culture and anticlericalism among the Shi'ite Communists of Iraq.

Communism, Anticlericalism, and Religious Culture

As explained earlier, central socioeconomic and political factors drew rural and urban Shi'ites to communism. At the same time, particular doctrinal and eschatological features of Shi'ism nurtured an affinity with Communist ideals during the colonial and postcolonial periods. For many Shi'ites, Marxism became a secularized form of Shi'ite messianism—that is, the fulfillment of justice on earth, marked by material ease and spiritual realization. Many Communist Shi'ites were seen expressing broad sympathies for *ahl al-bayt* and honoring *wilayat* 'Ali, his rights in political rule, and religious leadership.[61] Other Communists saw Shi'ism as a vehicle for political protest against illegitimate systems of authority. Such protest was tied to the historical Shi'ite rejection of the Islamic governments established after the death of Imam 'Ali. In the modern colonial period, this protest bestowed "sacredness" on antistate opposition and brought a sense of triumph in the defeat of British rule and the Iraqi monarchy in 1958.

Several local Shi'ite orators and poets in Najaf and Karbala' who composed and recited devotional poetry for *ahl al-bayt* were Communists or sympathized with the ICP.[62] Sacred Shi'ite figures and symbols made a commanding and versatile appearance in Communist Shi'ites' poetry and essays.[63] Imam 'Ali was depicted as a just ruler defending the poor, and Imam Husayn was characterized as a warrior who dies fighting against an immoral order. These sacred figures also assumed modern secular features. Muzaffar al-Nawwab (b. 1934), a famous Communist born to a Shi'ite family in al-Karkh in Baghdad, illustrates these views. In a poem that circulated widely among Iraqis, he recites the following.

> I belong to the hungry and those who will fight
> . . . and [I belong] to Muhammad on condition that he enters Mecca
> with arms
> . . . and I belong to 'Ali unconditionally.[64]

Here, al-Nawwab intervenes in the original historical narrative where Prophet Muhammad enters Mecca in peace. He makes his commitment to the Prophet conditional upon an armed entry into Mecca that dislodges its elite and the social basis sustaining it. But he declares his unconditional loyalty to "'Ali," for he approves of 'Ali's actions. In the poem "From the Special Secret Notebook of the Imam of Singers," al-Nawwab evokes the Imam's "secret" knowledge, a theme that runs deep in Shi'ite traditions, but he also reconfigures this knowledge. Al-Husayn is introduced as "the Imam of Singers," and the poet appears as the keeper of his secret text. A number of clerics, in contrast, would consider such a depiction of al-Husayn as an infringement on the Imam's sacred status. Al-Nawwab also redraws in poetry the spiritual and historical ties that form a bond between him and al-Husayn, revealing, "and there are matters and matters that join the South, the head of al-Husayn and me."[65] The poet here sees himself being formed by Shi'ite martyrdom (the head) in the face of injustice and marginality (the South).[66] His reinscription of sacred components of the Karbala' narrative into the poetry is undoubtedly a secular depiction of the religious tradition.[67] These components are relocated from the tradition to a modern culture, which can then be shared by Sunnite, Christian, or Jewish Communists.[68] Nonetheless, among the Shi'ite readers and reciters, this poetry unleashes new religious experiences. The sacred symbolism of Karbala' is not abandoned even though it is connected to Communist ideals. In al-Nawwab's poem "Standing Between the Heavens and Imam al-Husayn," the event of al-Husayn's martyrdom becomes the actual seal of the Qur'anic revelation:[69]

> You [al-Husayn] are a revelation continued after the Prophet
> ... You are more alive than us
> Aren't you al-Husayn the son of Fatima and 'Ali?
> ... [Y]our tears were the seal of what was revealed.[70]

Many Communists engaged with Shi'ite doctrine and ritual, but they resisted the shari'a or disregarded it, thus provoking the clerics. Al-Nawwab's poems reflect the struggle that emerged between the clerics and the Communists over culture:

And they say that I have been extreme in my belief
About the sovereignty of the poor,
In excess, indeed I am
They reproach [me] that I blow fire in the [Islamic] tradition
I only refuse the metal scraps from the jurists
For there is a difference between the tradition and a hiss sound of it.[71]

Al-Nawwab likens the jurists' admonitions to the hissing sound of a snake and contests the claims they lay to the "tradition." Although Communist adaptations of religious culture left Najaf's jurists perplexed, the Communists' anticlericalism fueled their anger.[72] Communism seemed to offer Shi'ites a moral-spiritual order and not merely a secular program for political and economic change.

Shi'ite Communists expressed at times moral outrage at the impiety of certain jurists. They publicized the view that Islamic piety is not attainable through the clerical profession. The popular poem "Where Is My Right?" by Muhammad Salih Bahr al-'Ulum (1908–92), a Communist from a prominent family of *'ulama* in Najaf, expresses this outrage. The poem denounces those clerics who claim that class divisions (*nizam al-tabaqat*) are God given[73] and accuses affluent jurists of exploiting the peasants and workers, using "religion" to ensnare them. Al-'Ulum asks

How can the majority continue to watch this mockery?
The people toil without wage to serve a few persons
And millions of victims among peasants and workers
Continue to be struck by injustice calling out: Where is my right?

A few Communists also drew upon Islamic philosophical and Sufi traditions as alternative sources of spiritual authority to nomocentric traditions—that is, legal traditions tied to the regulation and implementation of the shari'a.[74] This was the case of Hadi al-'Alawi (d. 1998), a Maoist from Karradat Maryam in Baghdad whose grandfather was a Shi'ite *faqih* (jurist). He seems to have memorized the Qur'an and the *Nahj al-Balagha*, which combines the sermons, letters, and sayings of Imam 'Ali, then pursued broad readings in Islamic history, law, and exegesis, and obtained a degree in economics. Al-'Alawi explored distinct facets of religious faith but rejected clerical approaches to the shari'a. He curiously considered communism a philosophy of conscience rather than a reasoned conviction, for it emphasizes an emotion of love for people and an abhorrence for "the state, the rich and the clerics."[75] Al-'Alawi, like other Maoists, turned to the Islamic traditions and questioned the assimilation of Western liberal humanism by Iraqi intellectuals, including Soviet-modeled Communists.[76] Whereas Maoist reforms in China involved a rejection of folk religious beliefs and mythology, Arab Maoists expressed a keen interest in peasant culture and religious traditions.[77]

The jurists confronted in public and in their writings the view that Communist ideals were embedded in the Qur'an and the hadith.[78] Muhammad Jawad Mughniyya, a Lebanese *mujtahid* who studied in Najaf, gave precedence to Islam over communism in embedding values of "equality" and "social justice." He discussed the "Islamic" incumbency upon the wealthy to provide for the needy. He supported his arguments by revisiting the biography of Abu Dharr al-Ghifari (d. 652), one of the Prophet's companions and a supporter of Imam 'Ali known for his asceticism and denunciation of corrupt rulers. Mughniyya curiously did not challenge the modern meanings of "justice" and "equality" or the socialist connotations given to them by the Communists. Yet he insisted that Abu Dharr's outlook is uniquely Islamic and stands apart from communism, socialism, and capitalism. It is "Qur'anic-Muhammadan, neither Eastern nor Western. It is work for God's house."[79] Jurists such as Mughniyya seemed well aware that Marxism competed with Islam not only on the basis of its organization of social and economic life, but also as a system of morality. Against the arguments of Nietzsche and Marx, Mughniyya insisted that the natural basis for morality was religion. He also tried to revalidate clerical guidance, proclaiming that society cannot dispense with the 'ulama, who must in turn carry Islamic values of modesty and austerity.[80] As the following sections make clear, some clerics were nonetheless touched by Marxism, drawing upon its methods and principles in interpreting Islam.[81]

The Communists retrospectively embellished complex connections between secular projects and Shi'ite hadiths, eschatology, and popular historical narratives. Many young Shiʿites felt enchanted by this locally shaped Marxism, which inevitably disrupted Najaf's clerical authority and were responded to with intensified clerical attacks on the Communists under the leadership of Sayyid Muhsin al-Hakim.

Najaf's Jurists against Communist "Heresy"

The clerical discourse of *takfir* (proclamation of blasphemy) against the Communists was developed in response to the atheistic tenets of Marxism–Leninism and the Soviet Communists' formal declarations on religion. A group of *ʿulama* and tribal chiefs allied to the seminary leaders decried "the lack" of religious faith among the Communists and branded them as transporters of European culture.[82] The mujtahid Mirza Mahdi al-Shirazi (d. 1960), for instance, wrote several fatwas proclaiming the Communists blasphemous and thus arguing that even the meat sold by a Communist butcher was prohibited to Muslims.[83] The actual basis for the denunciation of the Communists was not atheism, but rather economic reform, privatization of religion, and the confinement of the shariʿa to civil life and state legislation. Given the clerics' role in implementing the shariʿa, the Communist attempt to restrict its application, as the clerics saw it, was tantamount to blasphemy and pure materialism. Moreover, the emergence of the Communists at a place such as Najaf, an international center of Shiʿite religious authority, implied defection from Islam and with it the failure of the seminary itself. It should be noted here that the discourse of *takfir* involved at one level diffuse and erratic reproof to communism and at another level the issuance of specific fatwas furnishing the legal grounds for the Iraqi Communists' "heresy" and "blasphemy" as well as the punishment that awaited them.[84] The view that the Communists "profaned" Islam through secular, Western, and Marxist inquiries was broadly shared among the clerics, as can be illustrated in their treatment of Husayn Muroeh and Hadi al-ʿAlawi.[85] Muroeh, whom we discussed in chapter 3, did not question the doctrinal or metaphysical bases of Islam beginning with the existence of God and Muhammad's apostleship. He also held a few *ʿulama* in high esteem and maintained good ties with them. Yet several clerics and early Islamists considered his attempt to reconceptualize Islamic tradition on the basis of Marxism antithetical to a pietistic understanding of this tradition.[86] Al-'Alawi was described by his disciples and friends as a "devout Muslim" who was shaped by Sufism and rational theology (*kalam*).[87] Unlike Muroeh, however, al-'Alawi attacked the clerics openly. In his writings on early Islamic history, he denounced Muslim leaders for having committed moral transgressions and even criticized the Prophet for approving these transgressions.[88] These views clearly ran against pietistic attitudes toward the Prophet and the emphasis on his infallibility, and for the jurists they were pure blasphemy. In effect, secular frameworks of inquiry, anticlericalism, and aversion to the nomocentric dimension of Islam could potentially trigger clerical accusations of heresy against the Communists.[89]

The question of Communist "heresy" took a distinct form under the leadership of al-Hakim and his clerical movement, which became institutionalized in 1958 through the founding of the 'Ulama's Assembly in Najaf (Jama'at al-'Ulama' fi al-Najaf al-Ashraf).[90] Al-Hakim relied on certain funds to launch systematic attacks on the Shi'ite Communists, their families, and friends. Beyond furnishing the legal Islamic grounds for their atheism (*ilhad*), al-Hakim and his followers used violence as well as civil organs to try and remove the Communists from Shi'ite society.[91] The opportunity would soon present itself for President Qasim to dispute the national and international politics of the Communist leaders in Iraq. After Qasim's first public denunciation of the Communists on July 19, 1959, the clerical movement developed its plan of attack against the Communists. Seven months later, on February 15, 1960, al-Hakim issued a fatwa proclaiming communism "irreligious and blasphemous."[92] He also solicited supplementary fatwas with similar content from clerics 'Abd al-Karim al-Jaza'iri, Abu'l-Qasim al-Khu'i, and 'Abd al-Hadi al-Shirazi shortly after. There is no evidence, however, that any of these fatwas diminished the Communists' popularity in Shi'ite locales.[93] Nonetheless, unlike the erratic reproofs to communism, the fatwas were a source of alarm for many Shi'ites because they could potentially legitimize the persecution of the Communists.

Al-Hakim's struggle with the Communists over culture, as we explained earlier, was tied to political and socioeconomic conflicts.[94]

The mounting demand among the lower Shiʻite classes for economic and legal reforms as well as the mobilization of workers and peasants after 1959 received the support of many Najafis, including ʻAshura' organizers and attendants at the Haydariyya shrine.[95] Several orators who sympathized with the Communists dominated the Husayni pulpit, which seminary groups affiliated with Sayyid Muhsin al-Hakim branded as the "atheistic pulpit."[96] Al-Hakim's assault on the Communists antagonized these sympathizers as well as some of the local jurists who were part of the Movement of Peace Supporters (Harakat Ansar al-Silm al-ʻAlami), an anti-imperialist movement linked to the World Movement for Peace and supported by the Soviet Union.[97] These jurists did not share al-Hakim's zealous dislike of the Communists and feared that the Iraqi government would use the clerics' fatwas to persecute the Shiʻites.[98] In response, al-Hakim directed media attacks against local jurists such as Muhammad Husayn al-Hammami and Muhammad Husayn Kashif al-Ghita' and tried to pressure the former in 1959 to write an anti-Communist fatwa.[99] Al-Hammami refused, explaining that some political parties might use his fatwa as a pretext to "purge" the Shiʻites, given the great number of Shiʻites in the ICP.[100] In 1959, however, al-Hammami, al-Shaykh ʻAbd al-Karim al-Mashita, and Muhammad al-Shabibi died, which facilitated the politicization of the *marjaʻiyya*, the seat of highest religious and legal authority, in Najaf, at the hands of al-Hakim. He was now able to pursue his financial interests and drive for power undeterred, drawing alliances with Reza Shah and the Baʻthists.[101]

In 1963, al-Hakim issued another fatwa describing the Communists as *murtaddun*, defectors from Islam, whose punishment must be death.[102] He argued that any person who "understands" communism and upholds it should be killed, but the one who considers communism a form of assistance for the needy should be detained and informed about its heretical reality then forced to repent, which might save him or her from death.[103] Al-Hakim's fatwa seemed to have been solicited by a Baʻthist official who told al-Hakim that he wished to follow Islamic rulings on the punishment for 11,600 Communists, including 9,000 in Nuqrat al-Salman prison, 70 percent of whom were Shiʻite. It is curious that a "secularist"[104] government such as the one in Iraq under Abdul Salam Arif, with strong Baʻthist features, would seek an Islamic justification for executing Communists and the endorsement of the *marja'* himself. The state evidently hoped this step would both create internal schisms among the Shi'ites and shake the support for Najaf's jurists. In the long run, extending religious sanctity to state violence undermined the Shi'ite jurists and the seminary itself.[105]

The Clerical Movement and the Early Islamists

The rise of the clerical movement and the formation of Islamism in Najaf and Karbala' occurred for several reasons: the appeal of communism, the pressure exerted by common believers to modernize the clerical profession and to politicize the jurist's functions, and clerical conflicts with the nation-state and secularism at large. Against secularization processes, advocates of public or political Islam at the seminaries insisted on the comprehensive nature of Islam and on its ability to traverse all domains of the believer's life, be they the social, political, or economic.

The Shi'ite clerics participated in the anticolonial struggle against the British but shifted their focus later to questions of political representation and employment.[106] The leading *maraji'* supported the political "neutralization" of the seminaries in order to safeguard the jurists' integrity.[107] The senior jurists, for instance, disapproved of membership in political parties or state-based organizations.[108] This "neutralization" was also believed to facilitate the balance of power among multiple *maraji'*, who somehow shared collectively in sociolegal authority. From the late 1950s, however, a group of Iraqi, Iranian, and Lebanese *talaba* and clerics challenged the seminary's "neutrality" and questioned the shifting alliances of the *marja'iyya*. Meanwhile, the only marginal participation of Najaf's clerics in the national struggle for liberation in 1957–58 affected their following negatively.[109] Some argued that Najaf was losing its young audiences to Arab nationalist and Communist ideologies because of the *'ulama's* political detachment. During this period, no less than twenty-three Iraqis were reading the Communist Party's periodical in comparison to other party periodicals, whose circulation reached only 10 percent of this figure.[110] Meanwhile, around 500,000 demonstrators had called for a greater Communist representation in government in May 1959.[111] Thus, aside from combatting communism, the clerical movement hoped to renew interest in legal studies and to attract finances for the seminary.[112]

The clerical movement took definite form with al-Hakim's founding of the 'Ulama' Assembly in Najaf in 1958, which included around twelve jurists in addition to al-Hakim, its leader.[113] Muhammad Baqir al-Sadr, a young and dynamic jurist, was instrumental in shaping the assembly's weekly public statements.[114] He made clear "use" of leftist populist slogans such as "the toiling masses" and "the shameless class-based order."[115] The assembly's political goals were to protect the interests of the mujtahids in Najaf and Karbala' and to cultivate ties between them and Iraqi groups opposed both to communism and to president Qasim. Soon after the rise of the 'Ulama's Assembly in Najaf, another association, the Free Group of 'Ulama' (Jama'at al-'Ulama' al-Ahrar), was formed in Najaf by Shaykh 'Abd al-Karim al-Mashita as a counterforce to al-Hakim's movement and its objectives.[116]

A small group of scholars in the clerical movement considered the combatting of communism a precondition to attracting the youth to a modernist and revolutionary faith promised under Islamism. Curiously, this group pushed against al-Hakim's intellectual conservatism and the indifference of the *marja'iyya* (as an institution) to the Shi'ite struggles nationally and internationally. Baqir al-Sadr and his student Muhammad Husayn Fadlallah, who represented this group, went past al-Hakim's goals to promote political Islam as a substitute for communism.[117] They considered the Islamic Da'wa Party, which appeared in Najaf around 1958, a suitable platform to achieve this aim.[118] Shaykh Subhi al-Tufayli, a member of the Da'wa Party at the time and first secretary-general of Lebanon's Hizbullah, explained later that the glue that held the early members of the Da'wa Party together was fighting Communist "atheism that shook Iraq's society at its roots" during Qasim's rule.[119] Sayyid Mahdi al-Hakim, the son of Muhsin al-Hakim, and Talib al-Rifa'i, his close confidant, took part in the early planning and general direction of the Da'wa Party.[120] Meanwhile, al-Rifa'i drew Baqir al-Sadr into the party, after which Baqir al-Sadr became its main ideologue.[121] The latter's ideas about public Islam developed in part through his exploration of Marxism and confrontation with the Communists. He stressed, for instance, the need to rationalize

Shi'ite beliefs as well as to find a material historical basis for them.[122] He suggested to Muhsin al-Hakim that the party hold public forums where the jurists and the Communists would argue their positions.[123] Al-Hakim disagreed, for he did not appreciate Baqir al-Sadr's intellectual concerns or, for that matter, his Islamist activism. This activism, he feared, would undermine Baqir al-Sadr's role as a *marja'* at the seminary and in Shi'ite society at large.[124] Possibly under pressure from al-Hakim, Baqir al-Sadr distanced himself from the Da'wa Party at least officially in 1961.[125] Al-Hakim's view of Baqir al-Sadr did not imply that al-Hakim was apolitical, but rather that his politics were confined to specific goals—namely, preventing secularization and rural economic reform, boosting his own power, and securing new financial resources for the seminary.[126]

The growth of the 'Ulama's Assembly ironically resulted from the Qasim government's relaxed attitude toward Najaf's clerical leadership.[127] Up until 1968, the Shi'ite seminaries experienced one of their most dynamic periods intellectually and financially.[128] The *'ulama* expanded their educational activities and participated in new sociopolitical forums.[129] The clerical movement did not initially express its antagonism toward Qasim, who acknowledged the integrity of the clerical community, offering money to al-Hakim to build new schools and homes for the poor.[130] It was owing to Qasim that the 'Ulama's Assembly attained access to a radio station to publicize its Islamic teachings and vision.[131] Qasim, whose mother was a Shi'ite, expressed public deference to al-Hakim, at least before the latter started to mobilize the *'ulama* against his reforms. Despite Qasim's dispute with the Communists and his support of the clerics, al-Hakim started to campaign against him, this time forming ties to the Ba'thist *'ulama* in Najaf, particularly through his son, Muhammad Rida al-Hakim.[132] With the support of the British government and American intelligence officers, the Ba'th Party toppled Qasim's government on February 8, 1963, and executed him. The Communists were decisively weakened by their own political oversights and the assaults on them by the clerical movement and the Ba'th Party. During its fifth year in power, the Ba'th regime (1965–2003), after having imprisoned, tortured, and killed thousands of Shi'ite Communists, turned against the Shi'ite *'ulama* and the Islamists, despite its ties to these groups before coming to power.[133] Under Saddam Husayn's leadership, the regime closed down a number of madrasas, confiscated religious endowments, and prohibited religious processions.[134]

Despite these developments, Islamists praise al-Hakim's "combative" (anti-Communist) *marja'iyya* and consider it a turning point in the seminary's history.[135] These admirers also avoid reference to al-Hakim's antagonism toward Ayatollah Ruhollah Khomeini during the latter's stay in Najaf from 1965 to 1978. Khomeini was disappointed to see the cautiousness and condescension of Najaf's jurists toward him.[136] One source has it that al-Hakim publicly ridiculed Khomeini's call to rise against the shah, suggesting to other jurists the need to distance themselves from Khomeini. Al-Hakim had by this time established strong ties to the shah and described him in one interview as "the symbol of the Shi'ites" in Iran.[137] Khomeini's speeches on *wilayat al-faqih*—that is, the legitimate role that a qualified jurist can play in Shi'i society as the deputy of the Hidden Imam, resonated with a few clerics in Najaf, but it was not until years later that the Iraqi clerical movement paid homage to him.[138]

Under the Ba'th regime, Islamist activity went underground, and Najaf's intellectual dynamism and scholarly growth were severely impaired. In the 1970s, the seminaries' revenues plunged, and the *'ulama* agitated for solutions to their financial and administrative problems.[139] Meanwhile, pressure from Iranian and Iraqi seminarians on the leading jurists to rise against oppressive regimes mounted. Finally, Sunnite-Shi'ite sectarianism encouraged by the Ba'th regime also helped the seminary leaders mobilize Shi'ites in the countryside and urban centers against the demise of major Shi'ite educational and economic institutions.[140]

Muhammad Baqir al-Sadr:
Morality, Economics, and the *Marja'iyya*

This chapter has so far elucidated the Iraqi Communists' engagement with Shi'ite religious culture and the clerics' and Islamists' struggle against them. This section draws attention to the intellectual dimensions of this struggle through the political formation and writings of a major Islamist jurist, Muhammad Baqir al-Sadr. The attempt to create a modernist clerical leadership through the *marja'* underpins Baqir al-Sadr's rejection of the seminary's traditional aloofness from political embroilments in Iraq and the Muslim world. As will become clear, he used the methods and tools of the Shi'ite juridical tradition itself to justify a modernist public Islam. The tradition's moral grounding in turn was emphasized in the fight against capitalist and Communist economic systems and social theories. Baqir al-Sadr's methodology and proposals further reveal the dialectical relationship that existed between Marxism and political Islam.

Baqir al-Sadr was born in 1935 to an Arab Shi'ite family that enjoyed historical links to Lebanon, Iran, and Iraq.[141] He was raised in al-Kazimiyya in Baghdad and moved at the age of eleven to Najaf with his family, where he pursued his legal-religious learning, exhibiting special scholarly abilities and an original mind. He authored specialized and simplified works of jurisprudence that conveyed the breadth of his knowledge as well as his intent on making legal theory and logic accessible to modern-day talaba.[142] Baqir al-Sadr also produced works in law, logic, history, Qur'anic exegesis, philosophy, and "Islamic" economics.

Early on Baqir al-Sadr criticized the political detachment of the marja'iyya and believed that the cleric should play an active sociopolitical role in Shi'ite society. There is reason to believe that Khomeini's attempt to mobilize the jurists in Najaf against the Iranian government reinforced some of Baqir al-Sadr's leanings. Yet it was not until al-Hakim passed away in 1970 that Baqir al-Sadr openly contacted Khomeini and lent support to his Islamist proposals.[143] Baqir al-Sadr agitated against the regime of Saddam Husayn in the late 1970s, issuing a legal injunction that declared affiliation with the regime's political party, the Ba'th, abominable. He believed it was incumbent upon Iraqi Muslims "to liberate themselves from this gang [Saddam's regime] and establish a righteous, unique, and honorable rule based on Islam."[144] Baqir al-Sadr's sister, Amina, known as "Bint al-Huda," joined her brother in public agitation against the Iraqi government, particularly during the Shi'ites' 1977 Safar uprising in southern Iraq.[145] She established religious schools for girls in al-Kazimiyya and Najaf and spread the call for public Islam against cultural Westernization and secularism.[146] She was put to death with her brother, Baqir al-Sadr, in 1980, sparking public outrage in several Shi'ite regions.

Baqir al-Sadr went to great lengths to debunk the foundations of capitalist and socialist thought, maintaining that the Islamic system is the only viable alternative for material development, happiness, and human salvation. European imperialism, Baqir al-Sadr argued, prevented Islam from functioning as a comprehensive system of ideals and practices as it had during its inception. Marxist socialism and capitalist forms of democratic representation had taken precedence over Islamic principles.[147] Islam had consequently lost its power as a moral and sociopolitical force.[148] The disruption to Islamic society caused by these ideologies and European colonialism demanded confrontation and combat, hence revolutionary change.[149] Baqir al-Sadr articulated such change through the militant activities of the Da'wa Party, and his polemical discourse against capitalism and communism in *Falsafatuna* (Our Philosophy), published in 1959, and *Iqtisaduna* (Our Economics), published in 1961. In the former work, Baqir al-Sadr refuted the "dialectical logic" of Marxist theory, which considers human knowledge about nature and society to be based on physical and material causes. Human knowledge, he maintained, is not the product of observation and empirical proof because the latter function simply as tools for applying the rational precepts originally existing in the human mind.[150] In contrast to Marxist "dialectical logic," the rational method (*al-miqyas al-'aqli*) espoused by Baqir al-Sadr, assigns value and meaning to human knowledge, which is in turn derived from a divine source. The rational method is capable of pointing to nonmaterial realities and confirming the message of Islam. Humans attain "happiness" through their drive to gain divine benediction, which Islam offers to each person. Baqir al-Sadr ultimately combined particular idealist and materialist positions, noting that if humans "possess necessary knowledge about several objective rules and truths," they can construct metaphysics on a philosophical basis.[151] In other words, philosophy confirms revelation, and what is known through reason is enjoined through scripture. In this way, Baqir al-Sadr insisted that God's existence could be proven through modern science.[152]

Baqir al-Sadr realized that for any Islamist movement to compete with communism, it would have to address economic relations, state legislation, and social justice.[153] His propositions lay claim to an Islamic moral economy that resists neoliberal practices and wards off the values shaped by global capitalism that had overtaken Muslim societies. Whereas many leftists argued that Islam supports socialist ideals, others questioned the mere existence of "Islamic economics," let alone its noncapitalist qualities. Hadi al-'Alawi, for instance, claims in a later work that early Muslim exegetes downplayed limitations set by scriptural sources on accumulation of wealth and private property. After these modifications, Islam permitted the right in private ownership, as well as modern capitalist economic transactions. More important, al-'Alawi notes that when the jurists came to cooperate with the dynastic rulers, the shari'a tended to serve the powerful and sustain inequalities.[154] Baqir al-Sadr in contrast confirmed Islam's inherent commitment to social justice at the same time as he justified private ownership, discussing its modern "psychological" basis. The shari'a, he added, is equipped to defend the believer against state exploitation and the abuses of private interest.

Baqir al-Sadr's economic project, laid out in *Our Economics*, hoped to replace Western economic models with an Islamic one. Islamic economics, Baqir al-Sadr explained, is defined by three central features: first, manifold private–public forms of ownership; second, monitored economic freedom; and third, social justice. The last two perhaps reveal his compromise with communism, stressing the need to limit private interest for the benefit of public interest. Islam, he explained, accommodated various forms of private and public ownership as well as state ownership, combining capitalist and Communist economic modes. Rarely has an Islamist thinker delved so seriously into communism as Baqir al-Sadr has, yet his assertions about private property and surplus value are on the whole weak. For one thing, he rejected the Marxist view that the labor exerted in producing commodities forms the core of capitalist profit—that is, the surplus value. He considered the value of human labor to be of a "subjective psychological" nature and claimed that raw material has an objective value and an exchange value independent of the labor added to it before it is turned into a commodity. He applied the same logic to agrarian labor, arguing that the amount of labor that the peasant spends to make the land cultivable does not always yield profit. As such, human labor in and of itself cannot be the basis for the value of agricultural products.[155] Aside from the shortcomings of such arguments, they seem to justify the objections to agrarian reform raised by the large landholders and their clerical allies. With respect to capitalism, Baqir al-Sadr tried to set limits for the commercial and financial practices of businessmen and bankers in contemporary Islamic states. For instance, he dismissed the view that the element of risk (*mukhatara*) justifies the investor's demand for a good percentage of profit in a commercial venture. He also denied an investor's right to collect interest (*riba*) on a commodity or its equivalent indirectly from the agent in order to account for the change in their exchange value between the time of the transaction and a future period. Accounting for this value, however, has been the normal practice in several Islamic banks, including Saudi Arabia's. Indeed, Baqir al-Sadr's vision of Islamic banking did not agree with the overriding forces of globalized capitalism in the 1970s, which witnessed the expansion of the oil-producing sectors' finances in Iraq and the Persian Gulf states.[156]

Like several Islamist thinkers, Baqir al-Sadr expressed a fundamental objection to the postcolonial nation-state. The modern nation-state, with its secular roots, is incapable of fulfilling the Muslims' aspirations, he noted, and must therefore be replaced by an Islamic state. When Khomeini launched the Islamic Revolution in Iran, Baqir al-Sadr called on the Arabs to support it.[157] Unlike Khomeini, however, Baqir al-Sadr defined an "Islamic state" broadly and focused his energy on developing new political functions for the highest clerical post, the *marja'iyya*. The state can be led by jurists or lay politicians alike, according to Baqir al-Sadr, but all must be bound by the policies of the *marja'iyya*.[158] In six essays collectively titled *Al-Islam yaqud al-hayat* (Islam Directs Life), Baqir al-Sadr discussed the principles of Islamic governance and the relationship of the *marja'* to the state.[159] The *marja'* emerges as a main witness of the revelation and an essential guide (*shahid*) for the believers after the Prophet and the Imam. Political succession (*khilafa*) is entrusted to those who are its legitimate inheritors among the oppressed of the *umma* (Islamic community) and who want to reverse the conditions of their oppression. Baqir al-Sadr speaks of the Imam as the protector of "the revolution" that culminates in the formation of the "monotheistic society" overcoming

European imperial intrusions and secularization. The *marja'*, however, is the *umma*'s political guide as long as it is dominated by "idolatry" and oppression.[160] Baqir al-Sadr suggested that this "righteous *marja'iyya*" must be turned into an institutional office with an international political scope.[161] The *marja'* must modernize the seminary and the clerical community, relying on a supervisory organization with expertise in all juridical fields. The *marja'* is expected to establish communication links among all Shi'ite areas and agencies in order to spread public religion through learning, cultural projects, and political activism.[162]

Baqir al-Sadr's ideas, in particular those popularized in *Islam Directs Life*, featured prominently in the instruction of young Lebanese Islamists during the 1980.[163] Yet it was through one of Baqir al-Sadr's students, Muhammad Husayn Fadlallah, discussed in chapter 8, that the discourse on modernist Islam and its revolutionary potential found an enduring place among Lebanese Shiites.

Summary

The threat of communism to Najaf's leading jurists and clerics, as this chapter has shown, did not derive from any discernable spread of scientific atheism or irreligious ideas and practices. Far from copying Soviet communism on the question of religious faith and metaphysics, the Iraqi Communists tried to refit their secular programs to the socioreligious arrangements of Iraqi society.[164] Flippant or contemptuous attitudes toward religion were somewhat present among intellectuals but, many rank-and-file Communists were observant Muslims who venerated the Prophet and the Imams and participated in public religious rituals. The legal ground upon which several jurists attributed "atheism" to the Iraqi Communists was Marxist theorization on religion and not Iraqi Communist activities per se. How do we account, then, for the clerics' political mobilization in Najaf and Karbala' against Communist "blasphemy"? The chapter highlighted three interconnected factors impelling this mobilization. The first was the appeal of communism to residents of Najaf and the *talaba* at the heart of its luminous seminary. The association between local religious culture and communism disrupted the *'ulama*'s power and ability to generate conformity to the shari'a and the legal culture. Resistance to the nomocentric traditions of Islam was augmented by anticlerical voices denouncing powerful jurists' greed and moral collapse. The local Communists evoked Shi'ite emancipatory statements against economic exploitation and colonial subordination. Even though the Communists reshaped the doctrinal and eschatological materials in secular frameworks, they awakened new religious sensibilities. But Islamic accounts of the Imams and pious Muslims were read as proto-Communist texts embodying principles of equity, social justice, and compassion for the poor.[165] All these experiences undermined the spiritual resources of the 'ulama who had shaped a meaningful social and scholastic world for centuries.

The second factor was Communist socioeconomic programs—in particular, land reform and the redistribution of large landholdings to reverse the situation of landless peasants. Sayyid Muhsin al-Hakim defended the landholders' interests through legal injunctions, declaring that land reform violated Islamic foundations of private property. Despite placing much confidence in the *maraji'*, the peasants increasingly supported Communist programs for redistribution and development of cultivable lands after 1958. The Communists considered al-Hakim to have prevented an improvement in peasant conditions and to have suppressed the rights of marginal groups, including lower-class women.[166]

The third factor was secularization in the fields of family law, education, and political representation. The Communists aimed to prevent clerical authority from regulating social and political life. Talal Asad deconstructs the view that secularism merely seeks to separate state from religion and thus is impartial to the manifestations of religion in the public sphere.[167] Here suffice it to note that the Iraqi Communists were convinced of the "neutrality" of secularized public spheres and the necessity of safeguarding them from the clerics. In fact, they feared that the clerics' ability to renew the shari'a would produce laws that traverse social, political, and economic domains. Far from being neutral, the Communists promoted a distinct vision for reorganizing these domains.

Sayyid Muhsin al-Hakim prepared the ground politically and financially for launching the clerical movement against communism in Najaf and Karbala'. Even though he sought to achieve greater power as a *marja'*, he did not advocate state leadership for the jurist or an Islamic state. The secular legal reforms introduced by Qasim's government and their pervasive effects on *ijtihad* and family law were blamed largely on the Communists. As al-Hakim became the sole surviving *marja'* in 1960, he elevated communism to a heretical theology whose advocates had to be eliminated physically to protect a "godly" society. In a famous fatwa, he made licit capital punishment for communism and helped the Ba'thist state accomplish the mass execution of Communists in 1963. A few Shi'ite jurists, however, despite pressure from al-Hakim, refused to issue similar fatwas. It was only a matter of time, though, before the Ba'thist state started persecuting the Shi'ite jurists and Islamists alike, leading to Najaf's decline as an international center for clerical training.

Despite their adversarial relationship with Iraqi communism, Islamist ideologues such as Muhammad Baqir al-Sadr adapted leftist discourse about revolutionary change and Third Worldist approaches to European imperialism. At the same time, there was a conscious attempt to modernize clerical thought and rationalize religious belief. This synthesis preceded the onslaught on secularism, which the Islamists perceived as a neocolonial entity eroding the fabric of Islamic society. For the Iraqi and Lebanese Islamists, the shari'a was to remain the main system of moral reference and political legislation simultaneously. Baqir al-Sadr saw the jurist ultimately as a catalyst for Islamic cultural modernity. As chapter 5 shows, there were diverse models of Islamic modernity proposed by religious thinkers and clerics during the second half of the twentieth century. One such model was proposed by the cleric Sayyid Musa al-Sadr, who rose to prominence among the Lebanese Shi'ites in the late 1960s. Against secularism, he endorsed the sectarian framework of the Lebanese state and urged the Shi'ites to embrace modern citizenry and express loyalty to the state. To succeed in his political project, Sayyid Musa, too, had to confront the Shi'ite Left.

5

Shiʻite Discontent

Sayyid Musa al-Sadr and the Left

The discourses of Shiʻite empowerment and modernism articulated by the cleric Sayyid Musa al-Sadr (1928–78) had major consequences for the Lebanese Shiʻite left and its secular initiatives. The Movement of the Dispossessed (Harakat al-Mahrumin) launched in 1974 by Sayyid Musa marks the first public forum for the co-optation of the Left and the entry of the cleric to the center of political life. It inspired new connections between religion and power and must be considered a precursor to the Islamist movements of Hizbullah and Fadlallah and a rallying point for skeptics of secularism.

This chapter outlines the social processes engulfing Lebanon in the 1970s. In the South, Israeli assaults resulted in a fragile security and livelihood for thousands of Shiʻites. Israel's occupation of the South from 1978 to 2000 radicalized young Shiʻites, who had joined the Palestinian resistance movement, as well as leftist and nationalist (Arab) parties. One form of dispossession—namely, Palestinian statelessness—resonated with the Shiʻite lower classes' economic grievances and political marginality. New waves of Shiʻite migration from the countryside to Beirut followed the outbreak of the Lebanese Civil War (1975–91) and expansion of Israeli military operations in the South. Experiences of displacement and impoverishment among the migrants in the Beirut suburbs encouraged Communist opposition to the state, unionism, and labor militancy. Sect-based and even family- and village-based social arenas provided vital services for the lower classes in the absence of state-sponsored programs. Scholars of modern Lebanon have, for the most part, stressed the prevalence of sectarian activity among the Lebanese but rarely the ways in which sectarianism was resisted or adhered to in unison with other affiliations, in particular social class.[1] The activities of the Shi'ite tobacco workers at the Régie illustrate the way class interest and religious affiliation worked together and against each other in various contexts.[2]

A large portion of this chapter is devoted to Sayyid Musa's clerical leadership and efforts to weaken the Communists, suppress leftist opposition to the state, and enhance the cleric's political functions. His advocacy of national modernism was coupled with a practical accommodation of the Lebanese state, a state that implements sectarianism but possesses secular legal procedures and rules of function and administration. By accepting the foundations of this state, Sayyid Musa hoped to institutionalize clerical guidance and to empower the Shi'ites as a sect. His efforts at privatizing Islam were at variance with Islamist advocacy of public and political Islam found among several Iraqi and Iranian clerics. The initiatives Sayyid Musa took in 1969 to create the Supreme Islamic Shi'ite Council acknowledged state restrictions on the shari'a, which was confined to personal-status laws. At the same time, the council allowed the cleric to play a vital role in mediating between the Shi'ites and the state.

The last section in this chapter sheds light on the Shi'ite-based AMAL party, originally founded by Sayyid Musa in 1975 to forestall Palestinian Liberation Organization (PLO, Munazzamat al-Tahrir al-Filastiniyya) activities in the South, as well as to protect Shi'ite land from Israeli occupation. The emergence of AMAL should also be understood within the context of the looming civil war. The Communists' ambiguity about resuming armed resistance in the South and AMAL's assaults on them backed by Syria, as this chapter shows, had destructive consequences for the Shi'ite Left.

War, Displacement, and Political Conflicts in the South

The 1967 June war between Israel and Arab countries brought the number of Palestinian refugees in Lebanon to 1.3 million.[3] Of this number, around 100,000 Palestinians settled in Lebanese camps in the South, the North, Beirut, and the Biqa'. In the South, an armed resistance against

Israel formed roots in 1969 organized by the PLO. Meanwhile, two events ignited the rage of depressed social sectors against the Lebanese state between 1966 and 1969 and encouraged support for the Palestinians: the bankruptcy of Entra Bank, which had launched major investments in Lebanese commerce, and Israel's defeat of the Arab armies in 1967.[4] In a short time, the Entra Bank had garnered the trust of Lebanese and Arab capital, attracting no less than 18,000 clients whose total deposits came to 9 million lira. Its unexpected bankruptcy was a serious setback for the private economic sector, as well as for the workers in the twenty-five companies and financial institutions that Entra Bank helped sustain. Lebanese capitalists were thrown into a fierce confrontation with radicalized workers who lost their jobs or faced an uncertain future. Meanwhile, tens of thousands of students protested against tuition increases, the outcome of the Arab-Israeli wars, and American intervention in Arab regional politics.[5] The economic and political challenges facing this generation of southerners popularized not only communism, but also Pan-Arabism of the Ba'thist and Nasserite types. Many expected the rise of Jamal 'Abd al-Nasser against Israel and Western imperial policies to yield better conditions for the Arabs. Several Shi'ite thinkers at the time identified with Nasser and his anti-imperial stance.[6]

Following the formation of the PLO, Mosha Dayan, defense minister of Israel, threatened to set the Lebanese South aflame if Palestinian commando operations did not cease. The Israeli army boosted its military operations, launching air raids and gradually moving into southern civilian locales and border villages. On May 9 and 10, 1970, Israel raided the area and shelled it with napalm.[7] Pondering over the government's indifference to Israeli attacks on the South, Zahra al-Hurr, a woman poet, wrote the following.

Lebanon, I am a human being in a nation
That has not accepted that we are humans
. . .
Disease has spread and devoured the land of 'Amila [the South]
Have you not, oh Lebanon, anyone to console us?[8]

Without the army's backing, many southern Shi'ites turned to Palestinian organizations for defense against Israel. Many Maronite leaders and some Muslim ones, however, blamed the crisis in the South on the PLO and its supporter, the Lebanese National Movement (LNM), a coalition formed at the brink of the civil war and made up of secular national and leftist parties.[9] Indeed, a few leaders accused the PLO and the LNM of giving Israel a reason to transform the South into a war zone. These two groups feared, however, that Israel would seize more Arab land and uproot its people if the resistance in the South ended. Around 250,000 southern Shi'ites had already left for Beirut's suburbs by 1974, when agricultural work was paralyzed in the South, businesses slowed, and schools closed following incessant Israeli attacks.[10] A poem by an anonymous "Son of the South" (Ibn al-Janub), titled "Sad Honey and the Tragedy of Exodus," weaves themes of collapse and desertion.

Do not ask me, brother, how I left
. . .
I saw others running so I started to run
. . .
I wish to have died at the front door before departing . . .
Is not the taste of death in our gasping South
Richer than the taste of children's bread and shame?[11]

Israel took advantage of the Lebanese Civil War to launch a large-scale military operation in the South three years later. This new assault proved taxing to workers in industrial occupations such as carpentry, machine repair, printing, construction, and shoemaking. A number of firms and tourist businesses started to lay off workers, at least 3,000, within a few days after the attack. Factory owners did the same to maintain their high profits. They asked the government's permission to dispense with half of their workforce or to decrease workers' salaries by half.[12]

Despite the popular support for the Palestinian cause, the Shi'ite southerners' relationship to the PLO at the time was not one of pure cooperation or harmony. Owing to state neglect and the PLO's resources and organizational capacities, the latter's leaders dominated the political scene in southern Lebanon. The PLO commanders were acting more independently of local Shi'ite activists and leaders, who accused them in turn of greed and abuse of power.[13] Deputy Sayyid Ja'far Sharaf al-Din, son of the mujtahid Sayyid 'Abd al-Husayn Sharaf al-Din, for instance, expressed his disillusionment with the PLO in the late 1970s and criticized "its violations and sabotage of the Palestinian cause."[14] As conflicts erupted between the PLO and Shi'ite activists, the latter started looking for alternative mediums of political expression.

Emigrants and Suburban Poverty in Beirut

As rural settings disintegrated in the South and the Biqa', Shi'ites fled to the capital city for survival, shelter, and jobs. Earlier, in the 1950s, people from the Biqa' had settled in the eastern suburb, and those who came from the South settled in the southern suburb. During the 1970s, the neighborhoods Burj Hammud and al-Nab'a, received families from Ba'labak and al-Hirmil, as well as from al-'Arqub, al-Khiyam, al-Tibi, Bint Jubayl, al-Zahrani, and al-Nabatiyya in the South.[15] Population increase and dramatic urbanization, compounded by government incompetence, brought further disappointment to the working classes. The change in the sectarian character of East and West Beirut illustrates the profound transformations caused by rural deterioration and forced migration to the city. Al-Nab'a, the quarter in East Beirut to which tens of thousands of Biqa'i Shi'ites migrated, grew into a heterogeneous milieu, hosting Armenian Christian and Palestinian craftspeople, as well as Syrian, Egyptian, Pakistani, and Bengali workers.[16] Leftist parties such as the Lebanese Communist Party and United Democratic Youth (Ittihad al-shabab al-dimuqrati) had a vivid presence there, as did the Syrian Nationalist Party.[17] Most of Bint Jubayl's residents in al-Nab'a were cobblers organized into a syndicate and affiliated with the Lebanese Communist Party and the Socialist Arab Ba'th Party (Hizb al-Ba'th al-'arabi al-ishtiraki), which split up the Ba'th Party in 1970.

When assessing the social divisions in Lebanese society in the late 1960s and early 1970s, only a handful of scholars have discussed the role of class antagonisms in shaping political action.[18] Fuad Khuri, writing in

1969, insisted that the basis of political conflicts in Lebanon was not class interests, but "sect interests."[19] He treated "sect" and "class" as two mutually exclusive entities, ignoring the complex ways in which they interacted outside the rubric of the state. The Shiʻites lent their numbers in large part to secular ideological parties emphasizing class and political interests, but they in equal numbers were members of sect-based and communal-based associations.[20] Majed Halawi accurately notes that the urban Shiʻite poor "became conscious of belonging to a wider social class seeking to restructure an unjust order that systematically marginalized them."[21] They articulated the alignment of imperialism and sectarianism in Lebanon as a way for the upper classes to strengthen their dominance. Other workers perceived socialism to be a solution to their problems.[22] Emile F. Sahliyeh speaks persuasively of the sizable "Shiʻi membership in the revisionist, radical and revolutionary parties (and their militias)," noting that far more Shiʻis were to fall "during the civil war of 1975–1976 than members of any other group in Lebanon."[23] The Shiʻites were equally present in civil arenas that sustained a critique of the state, led protests against economic discrimination, and launched social programs to protect marginalized groups.[24]

By 1971, almost half of the Lebanese Shiʻites became concentrated in Beirut's suburbs.[25] Three years later the number of Shiʻite migrants in West Beirut and its suburbs reached 260,000 (76 percent) out of a population 304,000 in that area.[26] With the deepening of the Lebanese Civil War and the domination of right-wing Christian militias over East Beirut, all Muslims of the eastern suburb were forced to take refuge in the southern suburb, where they eventually settled.[27] The expansion of the domestic industry and development of urban centers formed the new social and economic landscape for the migrants. Proletarianization was one aspect of the transformation that took place for "the more fortunate" ones, Halawi notes, because many more joined the ranks of the "unclassified urban poor" who became the inhabitants of "the belt of misery," a heavily populated slum area encircling Beirut.[28] Civil strife and uprootedness after 1975 made the adaptation of displaced migrants to urban life extremely complicated. Some illegally built small rooms on public properties belonging to the local municipalities. Others rented small apartments or bought a few square meters where they built modest lodgings. The average family consisted of seven members, living at times in a one-room or two-room shanty apartment, with a small kitchen and a bathroom.[29] Sayyid Ja'far Sharaf al-Din transferred the licenses of the fourteen public schools in Tyre to the southern suburb.[30] The transition from rural to suburban life was marked by contradictory pulls: the emergence of new labor patterns, as well as the reinforcement of village-based residential patterns. Industrialization was gradually shaping the outlook of Shi'ite workingwomen and men.[31] Wage labor became increasingly feminized; Shi'ite women composed 42 percent of the Régie female workforce in 1969. They became the largest group of workingwomen, followed by their Maronite counterparts.[32] Challenge to and reinforcement of preindustrial values (filial piety and patriarchal restraint) occurred simultaneously.

The absence of national welfare institutions forced the Shi'ites to turn to family ties, provincial associations, and political parties to improve their life conditions.[33] At the same time, the forces of urbanization and public education shaped new sensibilities among migrant Shi'ites, who disputed state sectarianism and its economic configurations. The aspiration for change among the lower and middle classes, however, was hardly fulfilled through provincial and parliamentary representation. The electoral system prevented rural migrants from becoming fully integrated in the political life of Beirut because these migrants were required to cast their vote in their town or city of origin, no matter how long they had lived in Beirut. They therefore could not elect their own political representatives in Beirut who could defend the migrants' interests and promote their views. Many agitated against the government, turning to Arab nationalist and leftist parties for solutions to their political and socioeconomic grievances. Among the Communists, the masculinized culture of Lebanese labor activism proved an impediment to the recruitment of industrial workingwomen.[34] It is worth noting that the workingwomen (mostly Shi'ite) at the Ghaziyya branch of the Régie in the South went on a wildcat strike in 1970 independently of Communist leadership and the union's decision.[35]

In an atmosphere rife with conflict and restlessness, Arab nationalists and leftists in the southern suburb faced a new contender in the political and social struggles: the religious leader Sayyid Musa al-Sadr. A mix of religiously observant and secular Shi'ites from the lower and middle classes rallied around him. Sayyid Musa also gained the support of a few *talaba* and clerics who identified with Sayyid Muhsin al-Hakim's anti-Communist movement in Najaf. They hoped that "the man of religion" would counteract secularism, partake in the sociopolitical affairs of modern society, and mediate between the Shi'ites and the state.

A Modernist Cleric from Iran: Sayyid Musa al-Sadr

Sayyid Musa came from a clerical Lebanese family in the South, but he was born and raised in Iran. Despite his degree in law from Tehran University, he entered clerical service, stating succinctly that modern society needs the guidance of the *'alim*, religious scholar. He spoke of the moral void or "gaping hole" that had opened up in modern society and that had to be filled up by the religious scholar. Without the intervention of the cleric, the "hole" would be filled up by secular politicians.[36] In 1959, Sayyid Musa received an invitation from Sayyid 'Abd al-Husayn Sharaf al-Din to come to Lebanon and manage the Shi'ites' religious affairs.[37] It was the *marja'* Sayyid Muhsin al-Hakim, however, who chose Sayyid Musa formally to be his representative in Lebanon.[38] Some *'ulama* were perplexed by the news, including perhaps Shaykh Muhammad Jawad Mughniyya, a distinguished mujtahid with superior credentials. Sayyid Musa's political maneuvers and ambitions may have also become a source of controversy in Lebanon. Prior to his collaboration with an anti-shah opposition group in Iran, he seemed to have defended the shah's international image and distinguished it from his domestic one, where "he was seen as a tyrant."[39]

During his tenure as cleric, Sayyid Musa oversaw the integrity of the legal procedures at the Ja'fari courts, launched charitable projects, and spent much energy resolving communal conflicts. Many parliamentary deputies in the South and the Biqa' resented his increasing popularity among the middle and lower classes.[40] Facing significant adversity from the Shi'ite elites and leading scholars, he sought alliances with Sunnite leaders in order to build his power base. Shi'ite deputies were traditionally allied to their Sunnite counterparts in the South, exhibiting intramarital ties, as was the case between the al-As'ad (Shi'ite) and al-Sulh (Sunnite) families, as well as between the al-Zayn (Shi'ite) and Salam (Sunnite) families.[41] Sayyid Musa appreciated the sociopolitical import of such ties. He also participated in forums dedicated to "reducing inter-Muslim differences" and communicating Shi'ites' and Sunnites' shared intellectual experiences. Juristic unity between the Shi'ite and Sunnite schools of law, he suggested, is essential for achieving national and social unity. Juridical differences seemed less contentious than doctrinal ones, but Sayyid Musa joined a number of scholars in Iran and the Arab world in maintaining that doctrinal differences do not justify acts of hostility. Ali Shari'ati, a leading Iranian intellectual, praises the *maraji'* such as Sayyid Muhsin al-Hakim, Sayyid Ja'far Sharaf al-Din, and Jawad Mughniyya for drawing vital links with reformist Sunnite scholars. In his view, the strength of their public exposition of Imami Shi'ism did not undermine their "enlightened" demeanor toward Sunnism.[42]

Modernizing the Shi'ites, Claiming the Nation-State

Sayyid Musa's discourse on Shi'ite modernism and national identity formed an integral part of his outlook and clerical leadership in Lebanon. The ideas and line of reasoning that inform his discourse can be best illustrated through his mediatory role in a major communal conflict. Several families in Ba'labak and al-Hirmil came to loggerheads in 1970, and the fight escalated into civil strife. Sayyid Musa decried the "primitiveness" of their revengeful acts and their "tribalism" at a time when the Shi'ites were plagued by the enemy and economic hardship. He inquired irately: "What is the meaning of escalating the wave of revenge and turning to primitive animosities in the face of grave problems such as the [Israeli] occupation and poverty?"[43] Without despairing, however, he appealed to their communal virtues, their "valiant" and "noble" spirit, which would guide them to seek reconciliation.[44] Chivalry and courage must be spent in protecting Lebanon's borders, he urged. At the same time, however, he held the Lebanese state responsible for the Biqa'is' undisciplined conduct, their "tribalism": "We are here in Beirut, in the North, in the threatened South, in the destroyed villages, among the dispersed. . . . Even if the state had left you, due to fear, or collapsed due to ethical hypocrisy and bankruptcy in vision, how could you desert yourselves, your happiness, your honor, your humanity, and your citizenry?"[45]

All Shi'ites must make personal sacrifices in times of great emergency and national misfortune, he said. The feuding parties must make God their arbiter, seeking reconciliation and embracing the "path of Jerusalem" and the cause of the needy.[46] It is unlikely that Sayyid Musa considered the liberation of Jerusalem or Palestinian land a vital concern for the Lebanese Shi'ites. Rather, Jerusalem formed the rallying symbol, evoking historical injustices committed by Israel against Islam. Sayyid Musa was no stranger to the connections that the Shi'ites made between their political marginality and Palestinian statelessness. He was concerned, however, with the national duty of protecting the southerners from Israeli aggression and occupation of their land.

The points Sayyid Musa raises in the speech quoted from here resonated with his broad view that the Shi'ites would become "modern" when molded into national subjects. The Biqa'i Shi'ites' "unruliness" appeared to him as an impediment to modernism, self-governance, and civic responsibility. Becoming modern leads to happiness (sa'ada), the happiness promised in a national society. One's humanity is fulfilled through citizenry rather than through what Sayyid Musa saw as the pull of "primordial" affiliations. Happiness is a function of proper citizenry, of becoming amenable to state laws. In a remarkable way, Sayyid Musa was caught in a contradiction as he urged the Shi'ites to be loyal citizens of a disloyal state, one he blamed for failing to fulfill its duties toward them. He encouraged the Shi'ites to embrace a "reformed" Libanism, one that rejected Maronite domination but accepted sectarianism as a means to bargain for a fair Shi'ite share in state posts, civil service, and employment. This political vision was justified by the growth of the Shi'ite émigré bourgeoisie who had a vested interest in reconfiguring their relationship to the Lebanese state and hoped to shape state policies and enhance its access to economic resources.[47]

The pursuit of national happiness—that is, turning Shi'ites into citizens of the Lebanese nation-state—was wrought with difficulties. Thus, Sayyid Musa's 1970 speech suggests that in the state's "absence" the Shi'ites must rely on civil regulation mechanisms to govern themselves. Shi'ite self-discipline and self-governance were necessary in the face of precarious security rights, economic rights, and political rights owing to state discrimination. From another angle, Sayyid Musa's national happiness involved the assimilation of certain Libanist elements that underpinned the state. The Shi'ites were not part of the foundational myth of Grand Liban, but Sayyid Musa had to argue that they could be part of it.[48] Solving the Shi'ites' economic crisis seemed to Sayyid Musa a necessary condition for nurturing "Libanist" loyalties and hence for entering a "modern" world. He probably felt that the Shi'ites' identification with the Palestinians stymied efforts at developing their national loyalties. The Shi'ites were not stateless like the Palestinians, he possibly reasoned, and as such they had to position themselves inside, not outside, the state, replacing rejection with compromise.[49] A few years later this approach did not seem tenable. Sayyid Musa realized soon enough that not everyone would receive the "benefits" of Lebanese citizenry. He then openly challenged the state and considered the liberation of southern land from Israel key to political normalcy. This normalcy would in turn shape a distinct national identity.

The Mahrumin Movement and the Left

The famed *mahrumin* movement led by Sayyid Musa against the government on May 25, 1970, unfurled banners that denounced political marginality, economic deterioration, and the plight of South.[50] Sayyid Musa's fiery oratory whipped up popular fervor, and the movement spread nationwide, becoming a defining moment in Lebanese history. The momentum for the *mahrumin* movement was naturally linked to larger developments taking place in Lebanon at the time. Despite Sayyid Musa's magnetism, he was hardly the cause for the Shi'ites' "awakening." As earlier chapters clearly show, the Shi'ites were already in the middle of a maelstrom, confronting the state and exhibiting tremendous dynamism in labor protests as well as leftist and nationalist movements.[51] Yet the *mahrumin* movement was more directly shaped by an episode of intensive Israeli attacks on the South that led to the displacement of an almost 50,000 southerners. The movement also overlapped with labor radicalism and political unrest in other parts of Lebanon. Noteworthy among these events were

the pro-Palestinian street demonstration in April 1969, the popular uprising in May 1969 against the national entrepreneurial elites, and the 1970
'Akkar insurrection.[52] Then a few years later thousands of tobacco growers
marched in protest from al-Nabatiyya in the South to the Arab University
in Beirut.[53] The mounting crisis brought the convening of the Congress
for Tobacco Growers (Mu'tamar muzari'i al-tabgh) in April 1974, which
demanded, among other things, job security, health insurance, formation
of a syndicate for tobacco growers, and governmental protection of the
Lebanese cigarette industry.[54]

What Sayyid Musa brought to the scene with the *mahrumin* movement was a sectarian delineation of Shi'ite rural and suburban traditions
of protest and restlessness. He harnessed the lower classes' discontent and
power and tied them to sectarian deprivation. Many Shi'ites were expressing mixed notions of "class" as an organizing principle of human society
and partook in major confrontations with capital and the state against
inflation, lack of health security, wretched work conditions, and political
marginality.[55] No movement or clerical leader could muster a wide-based
following without co-opting features of this leftist Shi'ite culture. Sayyid
Musa was no exception, even if he intended to attenuate the transmis-
sion of the Left's political messages. Having argued that the Biqa'i Shi'ites
needed to be saved from civil lethargy, he felt the southerners needed to
be dissociated from radical Communist and Arab nationalist activism. He
brought Islam and Lebanese nationalism together as a counterforce to the
Left. Unlike Marxism, religion, he stressed, was an "authentic" cultural
feature of Islamic society.[56] Shaykh Hani Fahs, a contemporary cleric and
admirer of Sayyid Musa, noted that the latter aimed to "remove the Left's
exclusive custody of Shi'ite activism, prevent it from investing in a project
that destroys the state, and preserve the Left only in the framework of a
labor–social opposition that leaves the [Shi'ites'] national roots intact and
remedies the branches through a realistic and rational method that makes
violence unlikely."[57]

The pressure on Sayyid Musa to find tangible solutions to the lower
classes' grievances was mounting. The example of the Shi'ite tobacco workers at the Ghaziyya factory in the South helps illuminate this picture and
shows the limitations that the state placed on Sayyid Musa's bargaining

power. The temporary workers of the Ghaziyya factory, mostly Shi'ite women, started their strike on June 23, 1970, demanding that the Régie improve their work conditions and, most importantly, grant them permanent status so that they could obtain health benefits.[58] The workingwomen sought the assistance of Sayyid Musa, asking him to petition the government on their behalf to fulfill their long-standing demands.[59] By turning to a popular religious leader, especially one who espoused the cause of "the dispossessed," the workingwomen hoped to find a sympathetic ear. They waited for hours in front of the building where the Supreme Islamic Shi'ite Council met because Sayyid Musa declined to speak with them at first, supposedly because they were not wearing head covers. When the women persisted, the council's staff handed them head covers, after which Sayyid Musa met with them, promising to mediate their concerns to government officials. He was nonetheless suspicious of attempts to alter the political system or challenge it through labor unionism or militancy. He hoped to alleviate the pains of the Shi'ite lower classes without altering these classes' fundamental conditions or severing his relation with the state. Sayyid Musa's lukewarm support of the workingwomen was compounded by his lack of leverage in bargaining with the state. He came back empty-handed from a meeting with government officials. The council's staff afterward asked the women strikers to move their protest to the headquarters of the General Federation of Workers (GFW, Al-Ittihad al-'am li-al-'ummal).[60] After several months of campaigning, the Lebanese government and the Régie proposed a modest solution to the crisis, which the strikers accepted.[61]

In spite of Sayyid Musa's discourse on "the dispossessed," he was also amenable to the interests of the Shi'ite bourgeoisie, who in his view needed to adopt "Libanist" loyalties in order to increase their bargaining power with respect to the state.[62] The Shi'ite bourgeoisie had limited access to power in comparison with their Maronite and Sunnite counterparts, and, as such, they did not benefit fully from the state's liberal economy. As Shaykh Fahs explained, the émigré Shi'ites returning from African and Latin American countries who invested their capital in Lebanese business ventures needed the state to be "their guarantor."[63] He candidly remarked that Sayyid Musa wanted to ensure that the state become such a "guarantor" and hence permit the Shi'ite bourgeoisie to achieve higher status in the administrative bureaus and ministries.[64] Sayyid Musa ultimately did not challenge the national status quo but rather the "misapplication" of the sectarian principle in the hope of offering the Shi'ite elites a greater role in the country's politics. The *mahrumin* movement voiced the lower classes' grievances, co-opting some demands that the local Communists had made for decades. Focusing on the plight of Shi'ite agricultural and industrial laborers (including construction workers), the movement called for the curtailment of feudal and capitalist entrepreneurial exploitation. Economic stability and security for the southerners were not realized, the movement's leader declared. He also stressed the Shi'ites' rights in adequate political and administrative representation. In a short time, the movement attracted diverse groups such as leftists from the Popular Front for the Liberation of Palestine (Al-Jabha al-sha'biyya li-tahrir Filastin), Leninist and Maoist activists, and, later, Khomeinists, as Waddah Sharara notes.[65] Sayyid Musa made sketchy remarks in praise of the Left as "a force of change" and tried to acknowledge the leftists' involvement in struggles for socioeconomic reform. His movement, however, was the earliest serious encroachment on the Shi'ite leftists. He presented the leftists (in particular, Shi'ite Marxists) as lacking faith in God: "I am not harsh against the Left as some might think. Rather, if we define the Left as a force for change, then I consider myself one of its pillars. However, I do not trust him who does not believe in God, for faith in my opinion is not an abstraction."[66] Sayyid Musa implied that he, a man of faith, should be trusted more than the Communists. The latter, however, describe a different scene, in which the discourse on atheism aimed to discredit the Communists and facilitate the cleric's political functions.[67] Sayyid Musa assumed that by weakening the Left he could negotiate new sectarian rights for the Shi'ites with the Lebanese state. The Communists, for their part, denounced sectarian politics, Sayyid Musa's ambiguity on anti-Israeli resistance, and his instrumental use of leftist slogans to co-opt the Shi'ite Left. They also accused him of mystifying the conflict between Shi'ite labor and the state.[68] Within a decade, however, the alleged followers of Sayyid Musa were found writing on Tyre's walls, "He who kills a Communist enters Paradise," and making physical threats and forays against the Communists.[69]

Without any impetus from Sayyid Musa, the *mahrumin* movement took on a life of its own, becoming a vehicle for political Islam and state delegitimation even if it aimed in principle to bargain with the state. Despite his silence on the subject of Islamic governance, Sayyid Musa was concerned with bolstering religious authority and muffling secular sensibilities in the public sphere. He also disseminated Muhammad Baqir al-Sadr's anti-Communist ideas and arguments in the *husayniyyas* and scholarly circles.[70] Curiously, the early Islamists had criticized Sayyid Musa for his initial rapprochement with the Christian Right and feared it would sabotage the resistance to Israel in the South.[71] It was only after the unfolding of the *mahrumin* movement that many Islamists lent their support to Sayyid Musa.[72] They seemed to welcome his attacks on secularism.

In his enthusiasm, Shaykh Hani Fahs applauded the *mahrumin* movement for achieving its aim "in entering forcefully in the state structure."[73] Yet Fahs's assertions run against clear evidence that no change in the political or economic configurations relevant to the Shi'ites occurred at the time.

The Supreme Islamic Shi'ite Council and Secularism

A new chapter in the relationship of the Shi'ite clerics to secular leftists unfolded with the entrance of Sayyid Musa, who sought to renew Islamic faith in modern society. His interface with secularism was multifaceted, as evidenced by the politics of the Supreme Islamic Shi'ite Council and his view of sectarianism. By and large, clerics such as Sayyid Musa feared that secularism would render religious guidance ephemeral and marginalize the clerics as transmitters of God's law. His recapitulation of the Libanist notion of sectarian "coexistence" encouraged "public performance of piety, and therefore, simultaneously the performance of religious difference," as Roschanack Shaery-Eisenlohr suggests.[74] In other words, Sayyid Musa found sectarianism useful for protecting Shi'ite observances and hence the cleric's authority. He concurrently recognized the limits on public religion placed by a modern nation-state like that of Lebanon, whose constitutional laws were inspired by the French Civil Code rather than by sacred laws. Under this state, sectarianism was organized around secular laws and inscribed into the Lebanese constitution. Therein rested the secular-sectarian nature of the Lebanese state and one of its contradictions that proved useful to Sayyid Musa for augmenting religious difference.

Under modern states, jurists were requested to fit areas of the shari'a with the states' legal apparatuses instead of placing it in competition with them.[75] The state used secular procedures to organize the economy, education (to some extent because religious schools remained intact in Lebanon), health, dispensation of justice, bureaucracy, and the army. It wrested away many of the sociolegal functions of clerics—in particular, Muslim ones, who saw the shari'a trimmed down to the Code of Personal Status. The latter formed a small body of laws pertaining to marriage, divorce, child custody, and inheritance.[76] In 1969, Sayyid Musa succeeded in pressuring the Lebanese government to found the Supreme Islamic Shi'ite Council, extending further legitimacy to his clerical leadership. It is misleading to view the council as a vehicle for the application of the shari'a as it was known before the rise of modern nation-states. Rather, the council had to restrict the application of the shari'a to the personal-status laws (*qanun al-ahwal al-shakhsiyya*), which was in turn necessary for the secular organization of the state.[77] The family (*al-'a'ila*) and the sect (*al-ta'ifa*) received vivid legal articulation in this rubric. This articulation allowed a cleric such as Sayyid Musa to speak for both family and sect. The state also expected the Shi'ites to be more properly supervised through the council. The birth of the Supreme Islamic Shi'ite Council, as such, was not a small event. For many, it embodied the necessary bridge to the state and hopes of social betterment through sectarian bargaining and sustained institutional pressure. In this respect, the council's emergence suppressed other forms in which the Shi'ites had already represented themselves. Its presence made it seem as if they were making their first legitimate entry into official Lebanese history.

Although Sayyid Musa conformed to the secular framework of the Lebanese state, he recoiled from leftist secular proposals, especially the elimination of state sectarianism, the founding of civil courts, and the promotion of civil marriages across religious lines. To a Shi'ite audience with varied secular sensibilities, his declaration that there is "no difference between those who call for secularization [such as the LNM] and Israel" seemed overpitched. Secularism, Sayyid Musa cleverly argued, would threaten the integrity of the resistance against Israel: "When we cease to fight Israel [because of such secularization], we will be defeated and destitute."[78] State sectarianism appeared to guarantee the continuation of religious-legal guidance and the clerics' political power. The destruction that could be unleashed in Lebanon by secularization, particularly among the Muslims, was comparable, Sayyid Musa cautioned, to the destruction caused by Israel's creation and its occupation of Arab lands. Notwithstanding this view, the program of secular political reform proposed by the LNM in 1975 received many Shi'ites' support.[79] The LNM demanded that resources and power sharing be based not on one's religious identity, but rather on principles of equity and merit. AMAL, the party formed by Sayyid Musa, rejected the LNM's reform program and upheld instead the constitutional document proposed by right-wing president Sulayman Franjiyya in 1976 and approved by the Syrian regime of Hafiz Asad.[80] The constitutional document paid lip service to state reform and reiterated the need for equal representation between Christians and Muslims in government. It reinforced and defended political sectarianism in Lebanon.

After Sayyid Musa's disappearance in 1978, the Supreme Islamic Shi'ite Council conformed itself to being a state organ despite occasional disagreements between it and the state. Sayyid Musa's discourse on national identity and modernism found resonance in the writings of Shaykh Hani Fahs.[81] Fahs opposed Communist, unionist protests, as well as armed and civil movements that tampered with the state's legitimacy. The original Shi'ite rejection of temporal authority in the absence of the Mahdi, according to Shaykh Fahs, can be reformulated to produce a sustained critique of the state to achieve reform.[82] Critique, he insisted, is effective if directed internally not externally—that is, not from outside the state, but from within it. His assertions ran against both Communist and early Islamist views that "reforming" the state from within is pointless and would reproduce the same practices.[83] According to these views, these practices were responsible for protracted civil crises and wars in the first place. One might argue that Shaykh Fahs overlooked Sayyid Musa's actual practices. Having stressed Shi'ite national integration and loyalty to the state, Sayyid Musa found himself in the paradoxical situation of creating an armed militia at the brink of the civil war in 1975.[84]

AMAL's Leadership and the Communists

AMAL built on the legacy of Sayyid Musa's movement and invested in an image of itself as the protector of the Shi'ite sect and the defender against Israeli assaults as well as Palestinian control. AMAL originally did not entertain a particular ideology and lacked coherence, which supports Richard Augustus Norton's view that AMAL's activities varied in nature from one southern town to another.[85] It did, however, distinguish itself as a sect-driven party, posing a fierce challenge to the LNM's proposed reforms and to the Left at large. It refused to see the South overtaken by leftist organizations that buttressed the joint Lebanese-Palestinian resistance movement. It decided to align itself with Syria, which controlled much of Lebanon's internal politics from the mid-1970s to the early 1980s. With the full backing of Syria, AMAL fought both the PLO and the LNM and helped impair leftist activism in the South.[86] Meanwhile, Syria gained enough power to crush the Palestinian organizations in Lebanon, thus weakening their leftist supporters in the South and Beirut.[87] AMAL went so far as to participate in the National Salvation Front (Jabhat al-inqadh), which Lebanese president Ilyas Sarkis established during the 1982 Israeli invasion and which sought to fulfill American and Israeli demands to end the war with Israel.[88]

AMAL and the Supreme Islamic Shi'ite Council drifted apart, developing distinct courses of action, despite cordial relations. Yet the two stood united when they feared a growth in the Islamists' power and a possible subversion of the council by Ayatollah Ruhollah Khomeini's supporters.[89] Islamist leanings appeared within AMAL itself when around 1982 Husayn al-Musawi, inspired by the Islamic Iranian Revolution, formed an Islamic wing of AMAL, which maintained close ties to Iran.[90] Following

Israel's invasion of Lebanon in 1982 and the departure of the PLO, the Communists launched a national movement to liberate Lebanon from Israeli occupation.[91] They soon found in AMAL's leaders their most dangerous foes. They or Islamic AMAL and other clandestine Islamist groups became involved in the campaign, which led to the death of several Communist teachers, journalists, and workers. Two prominent Shi'ite Communist thinkers—Husayn Muroeh and Hasan Hamdan (known as "Mahdi 'Amil")—were assassinated in 1986 and 1987, respectively. Meanwhile, the crisis of the Communist Party in the Soviet Union in late 1980s tied to the restructuring of its economy (perestroika) forced Lebanese Communists to reassess their programs, political commitments, and options.

Until the late 1980s, AMAL remained the dominant political party among the Shi'ites.[92] To AMAL, then, devolved the leadership of the resistance in the South against Israel after pushing the leftists out.[93] In AMAL's dictum, resistance to Israel conveyed its resolve to rebuild and reconstruct the Shi'ites' lives.[94] It did not, however, mean perpetual struggle against Israel to achieve victory. AMAL's success in the South is contrasted, as Norton notes, to its failures in Beirut, where it strengthened the power of the mercantile bourgeoisie, leaving the problems of the rural and urban poor unattended.[95] AMAL's alliance with Syria helped it provide the Shi'ite bourgeoisie with a number of political gains. Without challenging the national status quo, it secured new positions in public administration and a greater representation in the government. It also provided new funds through the Council of the South (Majlis al-janub), and bank loans for rebuilding the infrastructure of the South. Despite these changes, the poor in the South and Beirut received only sporadic assistance, and those in the Biqa' were in dire conditions.

Summary

The Shi'ites of the Biqa' and the South experienced steady economic deterioration and sociopolitical dislocation that released waves of migration to the city. The impoverished eastern, southern, and western suburbs of Beirut extended like a ring around half of the metropolis, inspiring the appellation "the belt of misery" (*hizam al-bu's*). The Shi'ites who joined

Beirut's poor suburbs in the late 1960s came face to face with new ethnic, classed, and gendered hierarchies. The suburbs were home for Syrian, Egyptian, and South Asian immigrants and Lebanese unskilled and skilled workers of various religious backgrounds. Feminization of labor accounted for the appearance of numerous Shi'ite workingwomen in Beirut's major industrial enterprises. Despite the significance of these experiences, the electoral system continued to be reinforced by sectarian undertones. The system forced migrant Shi'ites to vote in their rural provinces rather than in Beirut, their new home, in order to preserve the sectarian "balance" of each electoral district. Unable to elect their own candidates in Beirut, radicalized Shi'ites could not translate their social reality into political power. Notwithstanding this system, sectarian cohesion was forcefully challenged through class-based and ideologically shaped arenas in the public sphere during the 1960s and the early 1970s. Sectarian networks, religious authority, and family ties were frequently used to negotiate better living conditions and access to educational facilities, economic aid, and cultural development. When the Ghaziyya workingwomen failed to resolve their labor grievances through Sayyid Musa's efforts, they demonstrated their power as workers and as women through a wildcat strike.

The Shi'ites remained outside the imagined constitution of a modern bourgeois metropolis such as Beirut. The fair number of bourgeois Shi'ite families that moved to prosperous areas of the city barely altered the prevalent Lebanese discourse of Shi'ite "provinciality." The Shi'ite middle class had expanded through immigration to Africa and South America, public education, and urbanization, creating civil arenas that contested the political dominance of the traditional landed elites and denounced the state's apathy toward the crisis in the South. Meanwhile, the growth of a Palestinian-Lebanese civil and armed resistance against Israel had particular implications for southerners. Palestinian statelessness spoke intimately to common Shi'ites, who experienced their own political marginality as a form of statelessness. These conditions and the events surrounding them shaped the Shi'ites' formation as national subjects. Common Shi'ites decried government indifference toward their safety and welfare, frequently challenging the Libanist principles upon which the state had been founded. Lebanon's "exceptional" sectarian equilibrium and economic "liberalism" came under attack, as did its disentanglement from regional Arab conflicts. As the Shi'ites emerged into a major Lebanese constituency, they remained underrepresented in the cabinet, Parliament, and public administration. New strata of Shi'ite émigré businessmen and the petite bourgeoisie pushed to reverse this situation. These social groups saw in the AMAL Party a suitable medium for attaining a greater role in the government.

Leftist activists, thinkers, and sympathizers had become a significant if unsteady force in Shi'ite society during the 1960s and the 1970s, thus taking power away from the provincial elites. Communist Shi'ites were vocal against the state's organization of the economy, privatization of medical health and education, and the sectarian basis for political representation. They fought long battles to ameliorate labor laws and give permanent status and health benefits to industrial workers. There were successes and failures along the way, but Communist intersectarian arenas and joint Muslim-Christian activism were increasingly difficult to sustain after the outbreak of the civil war. The civil war at the same time put a great deal of strain on the relations between the Palestinians and southern Shi'ite leaders. These relations turned sour when the PLO leadership expanded its activities independently of the local activists and their priorities.

A serious encroachment on the Shi'ite Left appeared through the clerical leadership of Sayyid Musa al-Sadr and his *mahrumin* movement. Sayyid Musa embellished the discourse of Communist "atheism" and denounced leftist demands for political and legal secularism. At the same time, he validated the principle of sectarian "balance," hoping to negotiate greater rights for the Shi'ites on its basis as well as to turn them into "modern" national citizens. By accepting a different version of Libanism, Sayyid Musa surmised, the Shi'ites could become loyal citizens. He himself had conformed to the secular requirements of the state's legal apparatus, which organized the economy, labor, education, public justice, public administration, and the army.[96] This apparatus confined the shari'a to a body of personal-status laws that curbed religion and privatized it in the public realm. It was within this sectarian-secular arrangement that Sayyid Musa negotiated an active political role for the cleric. His rejection of secularist doctrines and practices beyond this point arguably disclosed the ambiguity of his modernist initiatives, however. This ambiguity had plagued the Muslim clerics as administrators of the shariʻa from the time when modern legal codes appeared with the nation-state. The following chapter highlights other aspects of the interface of religion and the state and examines the relation of secularism to modernity.

The *mahrumin* movement signaled a temporary breakdown in relations with the state and a co-optation of local Communist demands. Through the movement, Sayyid Musa presented all Shiʻites as one subaltern group, the "deprived" or "dispossessed," thus channeling class conflicts by guiding them into institutional forms offered originally by the state. As a consequence, more Shiʻites started to view their political marginalization rather than economic inequities as the chief basis of their "deprivation." To some extent, the *mahrumin* movement overshadowed the way Shiʻites had presented themselves earlier as unionists, feminists, civil rights groups, and anti-Libanist reformists. But inasmuch as the *mahrumin* movement co-opted some Communist demands, disputed leftist secularism, and revitalized the cleric's place in modern society, it can be considered a precursor to the Islamist movements of Hizbullah and Fadlallah.

Following the disappearance of Sayyid Musa, the AMAL Party exploited anti-Palestinian sentiments and Syrian support to prevent the PLO from continuing its armed resistance in the South. In 1982 and following Israel's invasion of Lebanon, the PLO departed to Tunisia, an event that along with Syria's calculated self-serving policy in Lebanon undermined the Shiʻite Communists.[97] To be sure, the public support for the leftists in the South depended in no small measure on armed resistance against Israel. As chapter 6 shows, the Communists' indecision over continuing the resistance and the assaults leveled at them by AMAL and Syria contributed to the Islamists' popularity. Indeed, the rise of Hizbullah spelled peril to the Shiʻite Left.[98] Despite AMAL's anti-leftist agitation, it did not have the ideological resources to shake their legacy in the South. In contrast, the Islamists attracted the lower classes through a formidable network of social services and economic and medical aid. Their grassroots leaders and charismatic clerics presented the Communists as materialists carrying Western disruptions deep into Islamic culture. They embellished political Islam as a modernist and revolutionary force leading to liberation from Israeli occupation and Western cultural hegemony. Wrestling dialectically with Marxism and local communism, the Islamists introduced new ideas and sensibilities to the public sphere.

6

Political Islam and the Formation of Hizbullah

It is helpful to remember that "the Islamists" in this study are the advocates of political and public religion in the Hizbullah and Fadlallah movements along with their interconnected arenas. The arrival of the Islamists on the Lebanese scene and the growing popularity of their ideas and practices were shaped by the socioeconomic deterioration and political marginality described thus far. Beyond that, the Israeli occupation turned out to be the most significant factor in the radicalization of the Shiʻite lower classes, who turned to Islamic solutions following the Communists' decline and AMAL's contentious politics. The occupation left the Shiʻites with a lingering sense of resentment against American sponsorship of Israel and hastened the rejection of the hegemonic values of Western modernism. We have seen how young seminarians denounced their *marajiʻs'* detachment from the political struggles of the day. They also excoriated them for failing to reconcile Islamic legal principles with modern society and offered to promote "modernist Islam" as a source of spiritual and political authority.

Transnational clerical communities played no small part in embellishing the features of this "modernist Islam." In Iraqi and Iranian circles, Lebanese *talaba* drew upon concepts of Islamic governance and advocated jihad (sacred struggle) against oppression. They also set up forums for the refutation of Marxism and secularism and erected new madrasas for the revival of religious education. The founders of Hizbullah were particularly concerned with the Iranian revolutionary model, adapting Khomeini's theory of *wilayat al-faqih* (deputyship of the jurist) to fit the local aims of their liberation movement against Israel. They considered the struggle for liberation inseparable from the recovery of public religion in Islamic society. Meanwhile, Iranian funding allowed the Lebanese Shi'ites as a whole (and not only the Islamists) to change the picture of poverty[1] that existed during the 1930s and the 1940s.

To avoid repeating information covered in previous studies on Hizbullah, this chapter offers a concise account of its political ideology, program, and social composition.[2] It discusses the appeal of Islamist ideas to young Shi'ites and illuminates the associations they made between the tragedy of Karbala' and the plight of the Palestinians. It also explores new dimensions of martyrdom evoked by the Islamists during the last decade of the twentieth century, which ended with the liberation of most of the South from Israeli occupation.[3] The main occurrences of the post-liberation period are also closely assessed: first, the assassination of Prime Minister Rafiq al-Hariri on February 14, 2005; second, the 2006 Israeli war on Lebanon; and third, Hizbullah's unprecedented use of armed intervention to thwart an internal threat to the Islamic *muqawama* (resistance) in 2008. This section investigates the implications of Hizbullah's effective partnership with AMAL, its increasing sectarian performance, and its move away from civil protest to armed action not only against its political opponents, but also sometimes against its own civilian supporters' towns and neighborhoods. Information about this period was obtained from Lebanese and Arab newspapers, interviews with key informants, and observations on regular visits of research sites in Beirut, the South, and the Biqa' during 2005, 2006, and 2007.[4]

Finally, this chapter offers a biographical sketch of the Islamist leader Sayyid Hasan Nasrallah, Hizbullah's secretary-general. A perusal of his speeches and the writings on him conveys the local sources of his radicalism and religious sensibility and highlights the role that Iraqi and Iranian Islamist thought played in shaping his political vision. Among devotees, Nasrallah acquired the image of an honest and fearless public servant, imbued with the Imami ethos of martyrdom.

The Rise of Hizbullah

The U.S. Marines arrived in Lebanon along with the Multinational Peacekeeping Force in August 1982, less than two months after Israel's invasion of Lebanon. A U.S. memorandum was issued during the same year to secure public support for Israeli military activities and long-term political plans in Lebanon.[5] Israel's invasion paralyzed the agrarian economy in the South, laid siege to Beirut, and killed thousands of Lebanese and Palestinian civilians.[6]

In 1982 and 1983, the Lebanese started to hear references to "Hizbullah," the Party of God, which evoked confusion and apprehension. On October 20, 1983, a suicide bomber trained and supported by the Iranian government drove through the headquarters of the U.S. Marines base in Beirut, killing around 246 persons.[7] The organization Islamic Struggle (al-Jihad al-Islami), whose connection to the nascent Hizbullah is unclear, claimed responsibility for the act. As Augustus Norton suggests, between 1982 and 1986, Hizbullah was "less an organization than a cabal."[8] Until the late 1980s, the party drew upon AMAL's Islamist elements and members of clandestine militant Islamist groups. It was also tied to members of the Da'wa Party, including those close to Sayyid Muhammad Husayn Fadlallah.[9] In this nascent phase, al-Jihad al-Islami, along with militant Lebanese–Iranian groups, kidnapped several Europeans.[10] The kidnappings, condemned by Shi'ite liberals and the Lebanese media, debilitated commercial and financial sectors owing to a decline in investments and business profits.[11] Hizbullah's members also threatened store owners to end their sale of alcoholic drinks and demanded that seaside resort owners close down their beaches during the first ten days of the month of Muharram when 'Ashura' is observed.[12] The businesses of those who did not comply were subsequently vandalized or destroyed. The condemnation of such acts of arbitrary violence by diverse civil arenas may have forced the nascent Hizbullah to revise its methods. The party reemerged after 1986 with a new structure, political program, and local leadership, building alliances with a few secular organizations in the public sphere.

Hizbullah introduced itself to the Lebanese public as an Islamic resistance movement in a Third World country that had suffered from the oppressive policies of the United States and the Soviet Union.[13] The name *Hizbullah* was inspired by a verse in the Qur'an (5:56): "And whoever takes God and His messenger and those who believe for a guardian, then surely they are the party of God [*hizbullah*] that shall be triumphant."[14] The organization challenged Western perceptions about humans' relationship to nature and society and presented Islam as a counterforce to these perceptions and a revolutionary means for "progress" and creativity. At the same time, it advocated militancy against Israel to achieve liberation. The United States, Hizbullah's leaders declared, is the principal cause of Israeli oppression and much injustice committed against Muslims.[15] American complicity in Israel's violations of international law, they staunchly stated, taught the Muslims that there is no relief through diplomacy or negotiation. Rather, jihad and sacrifice alone would lead to liberation in the South and freedom from American hegemony. Hizbullah also espoused the ideals of the Iranian Revolution and Khomeini's theory of *wilayat al-faqih* (deputyship of the jurist).

A brief explanation of this theory helps clarify Hizbullah's views. In its classical form, Shi'ite theory considers political authority void and illegitimate in the absence of the Mahdi, who derives his legitimacy from Prophet Muhammad himself.[16] In time, this theory led to a transfer of power and social leadership to the Shi'ite jurists, who interpreted the Imams' statements and transmitted their rulings to believers. These believers at times held messianic expectations of the return of the Mahdi and his establishment of a just government. Khomeini, however, suggested an adjustment to classical Shi'ite theory that would allow Shi'ites to legitimize and participate in government.[17] He maintained that a jurist with special qualifications can become the full legitimate deputy of the hidden Imam. This deputy can then establish a legitimate government on the Imam's behalf until his reappearance.[18] This revisionist theory, known as *wilayat al-faqih*, bestowed on the jurist charismatic and institutional authority. From the viewpoint of Hizbullah's thinkers in the 1980s and thereafter, *wilayat al-faqih* legitimized an array of economic and political activities needed for their movement. Their commitment to *wilayat al-faqih* continues today, recognizing the Iranian leader Ayatollah 'Ali Khamenei as the Imam's designated deputy after Khomeini.[19]

In terms of its structure, Hizbullah is composed of the Central Council (al-Majlis al-Markazi), consisting of almost 200 cadres and founders who elect the Consultative Council (Majlis al-Shura), which consists of seven members.[20] The party's decisions are issued and implemented through the legislative, executive, and judicial units; the Jihad Council (Majlis al-Jihad) and the politbureau, which combines council members and the party's parliamentary deputies.[21] The Consultative Council is the highest decision-making unit in the party and is elected every three years.[22] Its current members are Sayyid Hasan Nasrallah, secretary-general; Shaykh Na'im Qasim, deputy-secretary; Shaykh Muhammad Yazbik; Sayyid Hashim Safi al-Din; Sayyid Ibrahim Amin al-Sayyid; Hajj Muhammad Ra'd; and Hajj Husayn Khalil.[23] It is unclear whether decisions in the Consultative Council are made on the basis of a majority vote, but Nizar Hamzeh notes that if no agreement can be reached on a particular question, the question is turned over to Khamenei as the deputy of the jurist and one of the main maraji' for Hizbullah.[24] In addition, a group of jurists who follow Khamenei's legal opinions give direct advice to Hizbullah.[25] Nasrallah has also turned to Sayyid Fadlallah at times for informal advice.

Hizbullah established a central base in Beirut's southern suburb (al-Dahiya al-Janubiyya), two bases in Ba'labak and al-Hirmil in 1985–86, and the South in 1989–90, particularly in Iqlim al-Tuffah, which is adjacent to the city of Sidon and the Palestinian camps.[26] From the time it emerged, it posed a major challenge to AMAL, and the two soon clashed, first in the South and later in the southern suburb. By 1987, the neighborhoods of al-Khandaq al-Ghamiq, Wadi Abu Jamil, Mintaqat al-Fanadiq, and Hayy al-Lija in Beirut held many of Hizbullah's followers.[27] Meanwhile, from the husayniyyas and mosques in the South and Ba'labak, the Islamists preached to a curious audience about God's omnipresence, religious morality, and sacred struggle against the Israeli occupiers.[28] Nowhere was the new reality of Islamism more evident than within the Shi'ite family. Family life became politicized as parents fought with their children over their political affiliations and siblings became divided over their support for Communist, Syrian nationalist, Arabist, or Islamist ideas.[29]

Also by this time, Hizbullah had ended an episode of clashes with AMAL, solidified its base in the southern suburb, and turned its efforts to social and economic planning. The Syrian government feared the growth of Iran's power in Lebanon and tried in 1987 to strengthen its own ally, AMAL, against Hizbullah. During this time, Hizbullah's secretary-general, Shaykh Subhi al-Tufayli, negotiated thorny issues with Syrian president Hafez Asad, after which the relations between Hizbullah and AMAL were pacified.[30] Despite the broad religious similarities between Syria's leaders and Hizbullah, differences abound. For one, the Syrian government is anti-Islamist, having dismantled a number of Islamic political organizations.[31] Hizbullah's rising popularity and Iranian pressure on Syria eventually convinced the latter to form a strategic bond with Hizbullah that in the long run would strengthen its regional power.[32] Syria's alliance with Iran protected the space within which Hizbullah grew and nurtured its local interests, and Hizbullah has maintained strong ideological and political bonds with Iran but has been somewhat autonomous in conducting its national politics.[33]

Between 1988 and 1989, Hizbullah launched its major civil projects in economic, social, educational, and medical relief for the Shi'ite poor. The building of co-ops, clinics, and pharmacies, hospitals, and sports facilities won it many followers.[34] The Islamists devoted much attention to raising cultural awareness about "revolutionary Islam" through educational programs at the seminaries and at the schools known as "Madaris al-Mahdi."[35] The Islamist media publicized selective aspects of Israeli and American societies, underpinning the Knesset's politics, Israeli brutality against the Palestinians, the dilemmas of American liberalism, and distortions of Palestinian history by Zionist writers. It also disputed features of Jewish political philosophy and expressed diffuse anti-Semitic views.[36] Meanwhile, Islamic art, photography, and religious iconography linked Hizbullah to the Islamic Revolution in Iran, communicating themes of sacrifice, triumph, and redemption.[37] Hizbullah's defense of Palestinian civilians against AMAL's assaults, its devotion to the liberation of the South, and its contribution to medical and economic relief spoke intimately to poor peasants and displaced urban migrants. Hizbullah possessed "moral values," people would say, which roused curiosity as well as support for the party in diverse civil arenas.[38] AMAL's image fared poorly in comparison.[39] Despite the political gains that AMAL achieved and the governmental funds extended to it to rebuild the South, the social abuses and extortion activities committed by several of its leaders and its overall reconciliatory approach toward Israel undercut its popularity. As AMAL became part of the status quo in Lebanon, many of its followers started to look for an alternative political organ. These conditions may have convinced most of Hizbullah's leaders in 1991–92 to partake in parliamentary elections despite their reservation about the Ta'if Accord (1989). Overseen by Saudi Arabia and shaped by Syria and the United States, the accord had ended the Civil War, aiming to restore the Lebanese state and to reconstruct the country after the war.[40] It stipulated an equal distribution of parliamentary seats and government positions between Muslims (treated as one group) and Christians (treated as one group).[41] The Council of Ministers, presided over by a Sunnite Muslim, was now given more executive powers than previously. It also increased the term of office for the Speaker of the House (parliament president), a position reserved to Shi'ites, to four years. In theory, the accord promised the gradual elimination of sectarianism and a balanced developmental policy in all parts of Lebanon. This objective, however, was not fulfilled. In fact, the accord reinforced the state's sectarian character precisely as it aimed to "balance" Christian and Muslim representation in Parliament.[42] It preserved the presidency for Maronite Christians and ensured Maronite presence in the cabinet and Parliament.[43] It strengthened, however, the ministers' executive power at the expense of the Maronite president. Large segments of Maronite Christians expressed apathy toward the elections that followed the accord.[44]

Maronite leaders were not the only ones displeased with the Ta'if Accord. Islamist leaders such as Fadlallah criticized its constitutional framework, which in his view bolstered sectarianism.[45] He would tolerate it, however, for the sake of national unity. Hizbullah had initially challenged the accord, but in 1991 most of its leaders moved decisively to accommodate it.[46] Shaykh Subhi al-Tufayli, however, continued to reject it, arguing that Hizbullah was losing sight of its original commitments to change the state system.[47] He feared the consequences of participating in a political system predicated on secular governance, profound inequities, and sectarian competition. If Hizbullah were to partake in elections, it would be forced to accept the system's rules of engagement and enter into alliances that undermine Islamist ideals. The rift deepened between al-Tufayli and the rest of the party, leading to al-Tufayli's dismissal from the party's Consultative Council and the realignment of new figures—namely, Sayyid Hasan Nasrallah; Shaykh Na'im Qasim; Muhammad Fneish, a prospective deputy at the time; Deputy Muhammad Ra'd; and two clerics, Hassan 'Abdullah and 'Afif al-Nabulsi.[48] In the 1992 elections, Hizbullah won eight deputy seats: four for Ba'labak, one for Mount Lebanon, one for Beirut, and two for the South.[49] This development was a turning point in the party's history, recasting its role as a national political actor. Aside from its decision to participate in the elections, Hizbullah strove to strengthen its alliance with Syria. Al-Tufayli, again in opposition to the main Hizbullah view, considered an alliance with the Syrian government harmful and hypocritical because Syria was attempting to gain American approval.[50]

The lower classes constituted Hizbullah's mainstay during the first decade of its existence. Yet the party's social composition changed, reflecting middle-class elements after the 1992 elections. Hizbullah's ability to wrest several parliamentary seats in 1992 and launch a few economic projects attracted the business and entrepreneurial Shi'ite classes, who now saw a new opportunity for sectarian power and political representation.[51] Lebanese émigrés in Sierra Leon and the Ivory Coast, many of whom were nonpracticing Muslims, started to donate money and invest in Hizbullah's institutions.[52] Engineers formed the party's largest professional sector in the late 1990s, and most of the merchants in the southern suburb of Beirut became affiliated with the party.[53] Southern towns' economic activity and production patterns seemed to shape their approaches to the Islamists. Rural workers in the interior villages such as Marji'yun and in Sidon's inland area turned in large numbers to Hizbullah.[54] Cities such as Tyre, Sarafand, and al-Zahrani, as well as coastal regions connected directly to the tourist economy and the service sector, tended to follow AMAL, however, possibly owing to AMAL's impartiality to public piety.[55] Members of an older Shi'ite bourgeoisie in western Beirut from the al-Zayn, Baydun, and Makki families seemed to maintain a distance from both AMAL and Hizbullah.

In 1997, Hizbullah faced a serious dilemma when thousands of peasants and community leaders in the Biqa' started the Revolt of the Hungry (Thawrat al-Jiya'), led by al-Tufayli, against Prime Minister Rafiq al-Hariri's economic policies. The crops planted in the Biqa' as an alternative to marijuana yielded poor returns for the peasants, who asked the government in vain for funds and new investment plans.[56] Despite Syrian threats, around 30,000 people joined the demonstrations, engaging in civil disobedience and urging their fellow Lebanese to refuse the payment of taxes.[57] The revolt, which spread to Beirut, worried Hizbullah's leaders, who saw a major section of the Shi'ite population mobilized by their opponent, al-Tufayli.[58] And despite Hizbullah's attempt to diffuse tensions between the two major Shi'ite regions, the Biqa' and the South—with the Biqa'is complaining about the significant attention southerners received from the government and the deputies—the tensions persisted.[59] Sheikh Khudr Tulays, a Shi'ite deputy who supported the revolt, tried to reconcile the protestors and Hizbullah, declaring, "We all are Hizbullah and . . . there is no fear of rifts [within Hizbullah from the revolt]."[60] In reality, some protestors accused Hizbullah of acquiescing to al-Hariri's government and dismissing the Biqa'is' grievances.[61] Others blamed the Iranian government for advising al-Hariri to quell the revolt.[62] On their part, Hizbullah's leaders reservedly acknowledged the demonstrators' demands but "not the means they used" to achieve them—revolt and demonstrations.[63] They aimed in the long run to avert the threat of another uprising in Ba'labak and al-Hirmil that could dispute their power. Beyond relief efforts, they worked to implement development plans for that region, extending agricultural loans to farmers.[64] The plans were insufficient to revitalize the Biqa' economy, but they helped absorb some of the complaints directed against Hizbullah.

The Israeli Occupation and Memory of Injustice

Struggle against injustice occupies a central place in Shi'ite historical memory. The source of struggle has risen and receded depending on social divisions and relations of power and the cultural meanings given to them at different periods. The Karbala event evoked disempowerment, but also revolt as a means to change an illegitimate form of rule and hence social reality.[65] It thus accommodated new ideologies and religious discourses even if it appeared originally as a struggle to recompense Imam Husayn for his sacrifice and restore his family's rights in succession to the Prophet. For instance, Shi'ites drew analogies between the cause of Imam Husayn and the plight of the Palestinians. Waddah Sharara, a Lebanese scholar illuminated this feature in the late 1960s: "Hussein c'est la Palestine, Yazid n'est qu'une préfiguration du sionisme dans cette perspective, divers aspects de l'itinéraire de Hussein sont repris et développes en correspondance avec des éléments du drame Palestinien."[66]

The association between Karbala' and Palestine has run deep in southern culture and over time has been articulated by secular nationalists, leftists, and, more recently, Islamists. The mujtahid Shaykh Mughniyya reflected that the calamity of Karbala' "was painful and grand, [and] reflected in it was the calamity of all humanity. The epic of the Palestinian people is also painful and grand because the Zionists wanted to dispense with them."[67] The southern literary climate has also been shaped by Palestinian literature and its revolutionary elements. To be sure, when Ghassan Kanafani (d. 1972), the Palestinian writer and activist was assassinated, several southern intellectuals elegized him. 'Abd al-Muttalib al-Amin, for one, looked to Kanafani as a poet-prophet whose words become an act of creation:

> You were the word
> All things, all things the word
> Like the bud and solidity
> Like rocks and roses
> There is no beginning without the word
> Nothing without the word
> No glory without the word.[68]

In the 1960s and early 1970s, government officials and business entrepreneurs viewed with suspicion such identification with the Palestinian cause and feared it would unify disgruntled Palestinian and Lebanese groups and fuel antistate protests.[69]

The Israeli invasion of 1982 and its protracted occupation of the South stimulated new forms of Shi'ite and Palestinian collective memory. Israeli soldiers planned regular provocations of the townspeople during their social gatherings and religious ceremonies. They interrogated, tortured, and imprisoned anyone suspected to be in the resistance and used different forms of punishment against their family members. Determined to subdue the resistance, the occupiers also attacked Shi'ite spiritual figures and religious symbols. A notable example was the desecration of the *husayniyya* and the destruction of the Qur'ans in Ma'raka.[70] But apart from causing rage among the southerners, the Israeli soldiers' public display of hostility for the Islamic scriptures and traditions only helped focus attention on religion. It encouraged a consecration of radical models of Shi'ite piety.

A few months following the invasion, the PLO left Lebanon for Tunis, and the Palestinian camps became disarmed. The Lebanese Forces, a right-wing Christian militia, in coordination with the Israeli army, carried out a massacre of 4,000 Palestinian civilians—women, men, and children—in the Sabra and Shatila camps in Beirut.[71] The massacre left a deep impression on many Shi'ites and seemed to strengthen their conviction that UN declarations and conventions about human rights would not prevent Israel from perpetrating such crimes. They considered the United States the main culprit in the continuation of Israel's offensive assaults on the southerners and the Palestinians. In the years that followed, Hizbullah organized memorials for the remembrance of the Sabra and Shatila massacre.[72] Shaykh Raghib Harb (d. 1984), a prayer leader from Jibsheet and one of the early Islamist activists in the South, strove to raise awareness about the occupation and Zionist ideology.[73] Harb was troubled by some Shi'ites' complacency toward the occupation and the amicable exchanges between a few merchants and the Israeli soldiers. At the *husayniyya* of occupied Jibsheet, he would speak about Israeli "dream theft: We are forbidden from wishing for justice to spread among people even for a moment. . . . We have been robbed of our dreams even."[74] Beyond robbing them of their blood, children, and livelihood, he added, "Israel [has] robbed us of the desire to be what we hope to be." For Islamists such as Harb, the Palestinians and southerners' plight seemed part of one and the same predicament— namely, Zionist colonialism and American hegemony. Around 200,000 Shi'ites left their homes in April 1996 in reaction to Israeli Defense Forces (IDF) military operations against the resistance led by Hizbullah's guerilla fighters.[75] Israel moved to solidify its occupation through a large-scale air raid named the Grapes of Wrath and attacks from land and sea for more than two weeks, leading to the death of 165 civilians.[76] After incessant shelling of a UN refugee base in the southern town of Qana, 100 children, women, and men were killed. Norton captures the religious sentiments aroused by this incident: "Qana is the Karbala of the twentieth century; it is a land made holy by the Lord Jesus and contaminated by the Zionist Satan (enemy of God)."[77]

During the occupation, young Shi'ite fighters volunteered for suicide missions against Israeli targets in the South. Fadlallah insisted that such missions should not be described as acts of suicide but rather as examples of martyrdom. Suicide, he argued, is an individualistic act aimed at relieving the self from the responsibilities that come with social existence.[78] In contrast, the martyr decides on self-sacrifice to alter an oppressive reality for the benefit of all members of society. In this act, the martyr chooses the greater rewards of a saintly afterlife over passivity and moral death in this life. Through martyrdom, a person shares in the grace of Imam Husayn as a redeemer of justice for believers. Nasrallah evoked other dimensions of martyrdom following the death of his eighteen-year-old son Hadi in combat at the hands of the Israeli army in September 1997. Martyrs, he pointed out quite serenely, "have a special place in God's affection. At the Last [Day of] Judgment when the good and the bad will stand before God, the martyrs are allowed to plead for their family members."[79] The power of *shafa'a* (intercession)—that is, pleading with God on behalf of believers—devolved originally to Prophet Muhammad and the Imams. Here, however, the martyr is allowed to bring God's forgiveness and mercy to the living and the dead. Graced by his sacrifices, the martyr lays claim to a divine power that enables him to elevate the status of his family members on the Day of Judgment.[80] The Qur'an conveys in sura 3, verse 169, that martyrs are "alive": "Think not of those who are slain in Allah's way as dead. Nay, they live, finding their sustenance in the presence of their Lord."[81] Based on Shi'ite purification and burial rituals, when the martyr is found dead, his body does not receive *ghusl*, washing.[82] He is to be shrouded and buried with his blood on his body as a testimony to the sacrifice he made in the path of God.

The Islamists advocated militant self-liberation, casting doubt on American plans for "peace" that seem tailored to suit Israel. They accused the United States of aiming to co-opt and pacify the Palestinians in the Occupied Territories through precarious peace agreements with Israel. Shaykh Na'im Qasim, Hizbullah's deputy-secretary, considered these agreements part of a method to legitimize the Israeli occupation. The Oslo Accords, the Palestinian-Israeli agreement promulgated in September 1993, Qasim commented, provided Israel with peace and security guarantees but offered the Palestinians vague assurances on the question of sovereignty and national rights.[83] Under U.S. auspices, he added, Israel was granted control over the negotiations, thus allowing it to manipulate the accords in order to prevent Palestinian self-rule. From Hizbullah's perspective, the conflict is not over borders between two neighboring countries, but over Israel's "uprooting" of the Palestinian people and establishment of its state at their expense.[84] Hizbullah's *Second Political Document* or manifesto, delivered by Nasrallah in November 2009, renewed the Islamists' commitment to the Palestinian cause and the *jihadi* impetus against Israel. It devoted a separate section to Jerusalem and al-Aqsa Mosque that stressed the unique religious and spiritual import of al-Aqsa Mosque for Muslims around the world. Al-Aqsa is a principal niche for prayer, the third holy place after Mecca and Medina, and the site of the Prophet's spiritual night journey (*isra'*). Aside from disrupting Muslim traditions, the founding of a Zionist state on Palestinian land is "a crime against humanity committed by the West." Zionism, the manifesto states, is "a racist movement, both in thought and practice," nurtured originally by colonial powers, "using religion and employing religious sentiment to achieve its aims and goals." The manifesto denounces the initiatives taken by George W. Bush as well as by Barak Obama to make the Palestinians acknowledge the Israeli state and thus legitimize it. If the whole world acknowledges Israel, Nasrallah declares, Hizbullah would never do so. The manifesto discusses the shortcomings of the "hegemonic order" shaped by American policies and the dilemmas of the Israeli state: "A natural and inevitable conclusion is that this artificial usurping entity [Israel] will live an existential dilemma. It [Israel] will agonize its leaders and supporters for being an artificial entity, incapable of staying alive or persevering, and as such [it will be] prone to demise."[85]

The manifesto defends the armed resistance against the occupation in the Palestinian territories, arguing that it can "bridge the gap of strategic superiority" possessed by the West. "Fierce capitalism," American hegemony, and globalization have suppressed Muslim aspirations for freedom and nurtured unjust political systems in the Middle East. The manifesto also stresses the goals already achieved by the Palestinian and Lebanese resistance against Israel, mocking "the negotiation option" and its meager results in comparison to *jihadi* struggle.[86] It summons a collective Islamic-Arab support for the Palestinians to help them liberate themselves from the occupation.

Stressing the tragic consequences of the refugee problem for the Palestinians and the Lebanese alike, it urges the Lebanese authorities to alleviate the sufferings of the Palestinians in the camps who are deprived of the basic conditions for a tenable livelihood, as well as civil rights.[87] In August 2009, Hizbullah's deputies voted in Parliament to remove discriminatory state laws against the Palestinians, stressing their right to work and to receive both social security benefits in certain jobs and health-care coverage.[88] But Hizbullah's ability to push for further changes or intervene on behalf of the Palestinians in the camps has been limited by pragmatic considerations, not the least of which is appeasement of its ally, Michel Aoun, the Maronite leader of the Free Patriotic Movement (al-Tayyar al-Watani al-Hurr).[89] Overall, through their thought and practices, the Islamists have stressed common experiences of injustice and a shared memory of occupation with the Palestinians.

After the Liberation: National Disputes and Armed Conflict

During its formative period, Hizbullah relied predominantly on proselytizing about public religion and revolutionary Islam, using public debate in social, political, and educational forums.[90] It also exercised a level of coercion when establishing its headquarters in the southern suburb and used armed intervention against AMAL not only to spread its influence but also to confront acts of extortion and corruption.[91] The complex relation of public religion to civil society (or the public sphere) is closely examined in chapter 7. Here, we note that the Islamists' initial entry into the public sphere was marked not only by civil debate, but also by conflict. In 1985–87, a strong wave of civil and political condemnation surfaced in connection to AMAL, assisted by units of the Lebanese army and backed by Syria, laid siege to the Palestinian camps.[92] Hizbullah extended its support to the Palestinians, with Fadlallah condemning the siege, which led to the death of many civilians and the destruction of whole neighborhoods in the camps in Beirut. Curiously, Hizbullah's violent clashes with AMAL helped the Islamists gain recognition in several civil arenas. Yet when coercion and acts of violence by Hizbullah became readily employed in place of civil debate after 2005, they threatened the uncensored spaces of the public sphere. Hizbullah's actions, given the reality of sectarianism and the deep national divisions arising in the postliberation period, gradually undermined the democratic forces of civil society. After 2005, Hizbullah strengthened its alliance with a past opponent, Nabih Berri, the leader of AMAL, only to face three major challenges to its *jihadi* stance against Israel. The first was the assassination of Prime Minister Rafiq al-Hariri on February 14, 2005. The second was Israel's invasion of Lebanon in July 2006 following Hizbullah's kidnapping of two Israeli soldiers from northern Israel. The third was the attempt by the Lebanese government, assisted by the United States, to dismantle Hizbullah's communication network in 2008.

Following the assassination of al-Hariri in 2005, his supporters accused Syria, Hizbullah's ally, of the crime, calling for a UN-led investigation of the assassination and the formation of an international tribunal to put the murderer(s) on trial.[93] This initiative was spearheaded by the newly appointed prime minister, Fuad al-Sanyura, Sunnite leader Sa'd al-Hariri, Druze leader Walid Junblat, and Maronite leaders Samir Ja'ja' and Amin al-Jumayyil.[94] They represented the pro-Lebanon coalition (supposedly versus a Syrian-Iranian Hizbullah coalition) known as the "March 14 Bloc" (Arba'at 'Ashar [min] Adhar). Hizbullah feared the United States might use the international tribunal to incriminate the Islamists and so, along with AMAL and Michel Aoun, formed an opposing coalition known as the "March 8 Bloc" (Thamani [min] Adhar). Hizbullah preferred a national or Arab investigation instead of an international one, but the March 14 Bloc rejected its proposal. Al-Hariri's supporters considered Hizbullah's objection to an international investigation a sign of the Islamists' lack of national loyalty and their conspiring with Syria and Iran against their assassinated leader, al-Hariri. These supporters had defended al-Hariri as the champion of neoliberal economic prosperity, political stability, and the reconstruction of Beirut.[95] In support of the March 14 Bloc, the mainstream media in the Arab gulf countries cautioned against the threat of "political Shi'ism" and the "Iranization" of Hizbullah.[96] To this end, a few Sunni-based Lebanese organizations in the South, the North, and Beirut stood firmly behind Hizbullah. Meanwhile, Fadlallah devoted much effort to cement a Sunnite-Shi'ite unity in Lebanon and the region.[97] The March 14 Bloc leaders argued that the continuation of the *muqawama* (resistance) in the South was driven by Iranian regional interests and attempts to turn Lebanon into an arena for proxy wars. Hizbullah's national demands were in this context seen as a means to achieve Shi'ite hegemony. Islamist leaders rejected accusations of "Iranization" despite ideological ties to Khomeini's Islamic Revolution and to Khamenei.[98]

Several Sunnites were not convinced by Hizbullah's statements and proceeded to articulate the March 14 Bloc's "fears." Radwan al-Sayyid, a prominent Sunnite scholar, argued that Iran's support for armed groups such as Hizbullah disrupts their allegiance to their national states. He was convinced of the "Iranian threat" posed by the "spread of Shi'ism" in Sunnite Arab communities.[99] The exaggeration of "Sunnite fears," however, aimed to reduce the populist support for the *muqawama* and for Nasrallah among Sunnite Arabs and to deflect the political nature of the conflict. The March 14 Bloc feared also that Iran's power in the region would be enhanced through Hizbullah and hence challenge Saudi interests. These considerations were augmented by the sectarian bids for domination inscribed by the state. These sectarian bids made it difficult for the Sunnites, who formed a major part of the March 14 Bloc, to see Hizbullah as anything other than a means for Shi'ite hegemony.

In July 2006, Nasrallah was planning to release more prisoners held by Israel and forestall a U.S.-Israeli attack on Hizbullah.[100] The latter had been expecting such an attack in connection to the issuance of UN Security Council Resolution 1559, which called for the withdrawal of all foreign armies from Lebanon and the disarmament of all Lebanese and non-Lebanese militia groups.[101] Syria withdrew from Lebanon while Hizbullah tried to resolve the issue of disarmament by participating in a "national dialogue" over Lebanon's national defense strategy. Hizbullah's leaders argued that they would not give up their arms because they formed a *muqawama* and not a militia group as defined in the Ta'if Accord. It is possible that the UN's failure to remove Hizbullah's weapons through national pressure led the United States and Israel to contemplate a war against it to achieve this goal. American officials tried to secure internal support for an Israeli military strike against Hizbullah.[102] Hizbullah, however, decided to strike first, launching in July 2006 an operation known as "Fulfilled Promise" (al-Wa'd al-Sadiq), which resulted in the kidnapping of two Israeli soldiers from northern Israel. The George W. Bush administration supported Israel's massive air raids in Lebanon, hoping to dismantle Hizbullah's military infrastructure. Those air strikes involved the use of artillery-fired cluster bombs as well as the "smart bombs" produced by the United States and banned by international laws and despite warnings from Human Rights Watch.[103] The Bush administration refused calls for immediate and total cease-fire between the two sides that were coming from the international community and regional Arab countries in the first weeks of the conflict.[104] Aside from using phosphorous weapons that cause chemical burns, Israel dropped more than a million cluster bombs in the last days leading to the cease-fire.[105] Large areas in the South and Beirut's suburbs became unlivable. The raids deliberately targeted highways, major bridges, and the airport. The southern town of Qana lived through a second tragedy on July 30 when Israeli air raids, having failed to inflict damage to Hizbullah's bases, turned to civilian targets. An Israeli aircraft fired upon a building used as shelter by several families in Qana, killing at least sixty-five people, twenty-eight of whom were children.

The Israeli war against Lebanon in July 2006 brought the Lebanese together for the duration of the war. The resolve of the Islamic resistance in the face of "the most dominant military force in the region—the Israel Defense Forces" united the Lebanese against Israel, commented U.S. Deputy Secretary of State Richard Armitage.[106] After the war, however, the Lebanese once again stood divided. Hizbullah (aided by Iran) faced enormous political and financial pressures to compensate civilians for loss of residence and work. Although many agreed that Israel had failed to achieve its goals and praised the Islamists' perseverance, the *muqawama*'s future operations after this war were in question.[107] Earlier sympathizers with Hizbullah felt that the party's *jihadi* activity exceeded the requirements of the *muqawama* and that it was self-destructive and came with a high price for the Lebanese. As thousands of Shi'ites tried to put their lives back together, the rift grew deeper between the supporters and opponents of the *muqawama*. In this atmosphere, Hizbullah Islamists' willingness to tolerate criticism from other organizations and actors in the public sphere diminished.[108] Shi'ites who expressed reservations about Hizbullah's practices were readily labeled "traitors" by Islamist acquaintances and neighbors.[109] Members of Hizbullah engaged in a *takhwin* discourse (accusations of treachery) against their Shi'ite critics and denied them certain social and economic services. Moreover, Shi'ites living in areas dominated by party members felt a greater pressure to conform to the expectations of Islamist clerics about religious observance, dress code, and social conduct.

When it became clear that the Sanyura's government (July 2005–July 2008) sought to implement the UN Security Council Resolutions to disarm Hizbullah and hold an international tribunal, the Islamists and their allies decided to launch an *i'tisam*, sit-in, in Beirut in early December 2006, which attracted more than 800,000 Lebanese. Hizbullah called for the formation of a "national unity" government representing all groups to address the country's social and economic problems. Nasrallah did not offer a particular vision for such a government but hoped the Lebanese from different regions, "religions, and ideologies" would confront local and international challenges together for the time being.[110] Numerous protestors set up tents in the business district of downtown Beirut, promising to continue their sit-in until Sanyura resigned. The *i'tisam*, however, did not succeed in bringing the two blocs together to negotiate their differences, and the country seemed to be heading toward another national crisis. The national crisis was augmented in no small way by popular sectarian frenzy, which had found new forms of legitimacy among the Lebanese youth.[111] The sight of Shi'ite activists claiming the business center of urban bourgeois Beirut unleashed raw class and sectarian hostility, not the least through the caricatured presentations of the Shi'ites as "unclean," "pastoral," and "rowdy."[112]

In 2008, the March 14 Bloc, supported by the government and the United States, decided to use its executive powers to dismantle Hizbullah's military communication network by declaring it illegal. Nasrallah gave the government forty-eight hours to reverse its decision, but to no avail. On May 7, 2008, the Islamists, AMAL, and pro-Syrian groups embarked on an armed retaliation against the March 14 Bloc. Using machine guns and artillery, they assaulted their opponent's party offices in Beirut and Mount Lebanon and the homes of central party figures and burned down some stores. The more problematic actions, however, were the armed attacks against civilian neighborhoods of mixed political affiliations, such as Ras Beirut and Choiefat. Indeed, the use of violence against civilian targets jeopardized the democratic forces of civil society, which ironically lent the Islamists support in the first place. Meanwhile, ideological conflicts pushed the sectarian divisions to a breaking point causing recurrent violence and the failure of peaceful democratic practices. Around thirteen days later, representatives of the two blocs met in Qatar and signed the Doha Agreement on May 21, 2008, which ended this episode of civil strife, as well as the sit-in. During this period, Shi'ite journalists and intellectuals critical of the March 8 Bloc faced new pressures. AMAL's forced removal of Sayyid 'Ali al-Amin from his post as *mufti* of Tyre and Jabal 'Amil pointed in this direction.[113]

The March 14 Bloc condemned Hizbullah's "state inside the state" and considered its espousal of *wilayat al-faqih* a stark infringement of the Lebanese state's legitimacy and sovereignty.[114] The bloc's enthusiasts argued that Hizbullah lacked the features of a bona fide social movement because it functioned outside the official state rubric and set up its own alternative institutions and structures. Another group of critics rejected both the anti-secular and *jihadi* features of the *muqawama*, suggesting that the Lebanese state is the only guarantor of stability for its citizens against Islamist projects such as Hizbullah's.[115] The Islamists, in return, held the government responsible for neglecting the Shi'ites' economic grievances and for its ineptness in extending safety and security to southerners against the Israeli occupation.[116] This situation, they argued, had forced the Shi'ites to build an infrastructure of social and economic organizations and the *muqawama*. Critics of this "infrastructure" unpersuasively responded that the problems of the Shi'ite poor could be resolved through the legal and administrative institutions of the state.[117] Other critics of Hizbullah risked making the circular argument that the responsibility for the state's weakness lay in Hizbullah's ability to undermine it. The arguments in support of and against the *wilayat al-faqih* in particular deserve a thorough examination in connection to public religion and civil society, as discussed in chapter 7. Here, it is useful to mention that the Islamists have more or less suspended serious discussion about the implications of *wilayat al-faqih*, affirming rather ambiguously their nationalist stance and lack of interest in establishing an Islamic state.[118] In recent years, Nasrallah and Hizbullah's deputies have asserted that the attack on *wilayat al-faqih* is a religious offense and a violation of the freedom of belief.[119]

Hizbullah continues to face critical challenges in Lebanon relating to the scope of its militancy, its commitment to public religion, and religion's implications for modern citizenry. A serious critique of Hizbullah's thought and practices has come from 'Abbas Baydun, a Shi'ite intellectual and former Communist. Hizbullah's "revolution" is "more genuine than the state," Baydun maintains, but its ability to grow and alter political reality is doubtful. He explores Hizbullah's model of resistance, noting the inspiration it drew from the Vietnamese revolution and the "heroism" achieved by its own young fighters during the 2006 war. Baydun, however, hesitates to confirm the Islamists' overtly optimistic expectations about the resistance. The Islamists, he argues, like a host of radical leftists and nationalists before them, have often been morally driven to side "with unsuccessful causes and battles."[120] Their "idealism" and "morality" commits them "to impossible revolutions that often turn to a free praise of the revolution as an end in itself, without seeking a political or practical gain."[121]

Hizbullah has not outlined a vision of economic reform or expressed a coherent view of the government's economic policies. Contradictory class pulls appear clearly among the Islamists. The lower and lower middle classes are opposed to economic liberalism and the state's role in it, whereas upper-class Islamists support liberalism and privatization projects.[122] Aside from transforming Lebanese state enterprises into privately owned companies, privatization has involved short-term investments in the public sector and the private administration of public companies, as is the case with two Lebanese cell-phone companies, Liban Cell and Cellis.[123] In 2004, the two companies received government approval for their outrageous subscription fees. At the time, monthly subscriptions to cell phones cost around $11.70 per month in Syria and around $5.50 in the United Arab Emirates, but in Lebanon they reached a staggering $37.50 per month.[124] Hizbullah made no official statements promoting economic privatization. It did not object to it, either, though, as when Lebanon received 7.5 billion dollars in 2007 through the Paris III Donor Conference, conditioned on privatizing major public institutions and bringing fiscal "reform."[125] Hizbullah's member, Minister of Energy and Water Muhammad Fneish, even seemed to have recommended the full privatization of electricity production as a solution to the deteriorating performance of the Électricité du Liban owing to poor management, corruption, and electricity theft.[126] He claimed that such problems would be avoided in private companies responsible for the operation and maintenance of power plants and the importation of fuel oil. He looked favorably at the model of Zahle Electricity Company, one of a handful of companies operating under concession contracts. Privatization initiatives may also appear in the form of a partnership between the private and public sectors. The government of the prime minister at the time, Najib Miqati, is seeking approval for a law on partnership between the public and private sectors supported by Hizbullah's representatives.[127] The partnership aims to generate money for the state, but it has opened the way for bargaining among deputies over profits from commission and bribery.[128]

Sayyid Hasan Nasrallah: Piety and Revolutionary Islam

Migration and displacement shaped the childhood of Sayyid Hasan Nasrallah (b. 1960) whose family moved from the southern town of al-Bazuriyya to al-Karantina then to al-Nab'a, two impoverished neighborhoods sitting at the cusp of Beirut's "belt of misery."[129] While still in elementary school, Nasrallah worked during his spare time at his father's grocery store, where a picture of Sayyid Musa al-Sadr hung on the wall.[130] Through the *mahrumin* movement, which left an indelible mark on him, the young Hasan saw the cleric turn into a charismatic political leader and protector of the Shi'ite sect.[131] Nasrallah, the eldest of nine children, showed little interest in common teenage pastime avoiding sports such as soccer and swimming. He did not grow up in a clerical family, but he followed the teachings of the Qur'an and the Shi'ite hadith, expressing piety and artless simplicity. He spent much of his free time at the mosques in the suburbs of East Beirut and read used books on Islam that he bought from peddlers at the Martyr's Plaza in Beirut.[132]

He was to experience the earliest calamities of the Civil War in 1975–76 when the Shi'ite quarters of al-Nab'a were destroyed by the militia of the right-wing Christian-based Lebanese Phalange Party (Hizb al-Kata'ib al-Lubnaniyya). Nasrallah's family fled to al-Bazuriyya, where southerners appeared as a mix of radicalized nationalists and leftists joined together with the Palestinians in the National Front that protested Maronite hegemony of the state, sectarianism, and economic inequities. Nasrallah's family struggled to find new sources of livelihood as he completed his secondary education at a public school in the nearby city of Tyre. At the age of fifteen, he became an AMAL officer in al-Bazuriyya, where popular political sentiments lay with the Communists. For Nasrallah and his brothers, AMAL appeared to hold the promise of reversing the conditions of the "deprived" and of empowering the Shi'ites as a sect. On the lower floor of a *husayniyya* building in al-Bazuriyya, he formed an Islamic group that fought against the Communists.[133] A year later, in 1976, Nasrallah had set his mind on pursuing a seminary education in Najaf.

As part of an eclectic network of clerics, Muhammad al-Gharawi, the local prayer leader of Tyre's mosque, helped Nasrallah pursue his religious-legal studies in Najaf by recommending him to Muhammad Baqir al-Sadr. The latter turned over the task of educating Nasrallah to his own student, Sayyid 'Abbas al-Musawi, a Lebanese Islamist from the Biqa'. Penniless, Nasrallah received a stipend to buy food, clothes, and books through al-Musawi's aid and so completed an intensive two-year program of seminary education and legal-political training. Al-Musawi, the mentor, nurtured a fatherly bond with Nasrallah and a camaraderie that culminated in the future formation of Hizbullah in Lebanon.[134] The principles promoted by the Da'wa Party were undoubtedly evident in al-Musawi and Nasrallah's outlook. Al-Musawi did not seem to have given serious consideration to Khomeini's proposals during the latter's sojourn in Najaf between 1965 and 1978. Instead, the clerical movement's views and Baqir al-Sadr's lectures, which made their way into the collection *Islam Guides Life*, offered "proselytes" such as al-Musawi and Nasrallah "proofs" of the legitimacy of political Islam.[135] Some of these lectures outlined Islam's revolutionary capacity, the necessity of achieving the Islamic state, and a pious social order superior to communism and capitalism.[136] Baqir al-Sadr discussed the Islamic state's ideological makeup and its general ethos based on the administration of justice at the hands of Imam 'Ali, "the exemplary revolutionary in Islam."[137] What started for Nasrallah as an impulsive anti-Communist sentiment in Lebanon became in Najaf an integral feature of his political vision. He was convinced that the Islamists must replace the Communists in Shi'ite society and prevent them from "destroying" the fabric of Islamic society with its "accommodations" to neocolonial Western thought, in particular secularism.

When in 1978 Saddam Husayn's regime clamped down on Islamist Lebanese *talaba* in Najaf, Nasrallah fled to Lebanon.[138] He continued his legal-religious studies at the al-Imam al-Muntazar Seminary in Ba'labak founded by al-Musawi. Nasrallah's duties consisted of schooling the cadres in the meaning and aims of jihad.[139] The "Islamic revolution" started to take local tones not merely as a recovery of the Islamic *umma* against conditions of "indirect colonialism," but also as a removal of Maronite hegemony in Lebanon. Islamists described "sectarianism" as "a despicable weapon" used by Western colonialists to weaken the Islamic movement.[140] Up until this point, Nasrallah had not severed his ties with AMAL, becoming its delegate for the Biqa' in 1982, the same year Israel invaded Lebanon. This situation changed soon thereafter, though. Nasrallah deplored AMAL's participation in the National Salvation Front, which had led to the election of Bashir Jumayyil to the presidency and the promulgation of a peace agreement with Israel.[141] As he stressed *jihadi* Islam against Israel, so did he reject AMAL's precarious approach toward the Palestinian cause and its rapprochement with right-wing Christian leaders. Nasrallah's brothers remained part of AMAL but at the age of twenty-two he set out to form an alternative political party—namely, Hizbullah.[142] In 1987, he joined its Consultative Council and became its chief executive officer. When al-Tufayli became the party's secretary-general in 1989, Nasrallah pursued further legal-religious education in Qom, Iran. He probably received certain political training while in Iran and established contact with Khamenei.[143] The armed clashes that erupted between AMAL and Hizbullah during the same year, however, forced him to return to Lebanon, where he resumed his political and military assignments, particularly in Beirut. In 1992, a year after al-Musawi was elected secretary-general of Hizbullah, he, his wife, and one-year-old child were assassinated by Israeli forces. When this happened, Nasrallah, owing to his strong relations with the party's base and unique bond with al-Musawi, was, at the age of thirty-two, elected secretary-general of Hizbullah in al-Musawi's place.[144]

Nasrallah's militancy owes no small part to the government's weakness and the failed Arab League declarations and UN resolutions in defending the South from Israeli attacks. With the assistance of Iran, Nasrallah organized a guerilla movement against the occupation, which bore fruits in the late 1990s. As the last decade of the twentieth century came to an end, Nasrallah's reputation as a visionary and military strategist was widespread among the Shi'ites. In April 1996, the Israeli Air Force launched Operation Grapes of Wrath, which conducted, over sixteen days, around 1,100 air raids and massive shelling of civilian and military targets in south Lebanon. With this operation, Israel hoped to halt the sporadic shelling of northern Israel by the Islamists.[145] The martyrdom of Hadi, Nasrallah's eldest son, in September 1997 endowed the father's leadership with elements of redemptive suffering and sacrifice. Nasrallah declared that he could now "look into the eyes" of the mothers and fathers who had lost their loved ones. Hizbullah, he added, is a *jihadi* movement that is honored by the martyrdom of its clerics and children.[146] He drew a personal link between militant struggle and the pietistic traditions of *ahl al-bayt,* explaining, "We are used to death, and our dignity is derived from the martyrdom God grants us."[147]

In the years that followed, Nasrallah implemented an ambitious plan against the Israeli army that led to its withdrawal from all southern lands (except the Shib'a farms, Kafarshuba hills, and parts of al-Ghajar town) in May 2000.[148] Faith and divine guidance, he announced, have emboldened Hizbullah's fighters in front of a formidable enemy. The liberation of the South became the linchpin of the *muqawama*'s national popularity. The 2006 Israeli war on Lebanon, however, had the opposite effect nationally. Some Lebanese groups had by this time already condemned the "glorification of death" and martyrdom in Hizbullah's movement.[149] They saw Nasrallah's role in the 2006 war equally as an unjustified *jihadi* venture. Nasrallah argued, however, that militancy and piety were essential for self-liberation; thus, armed popular resistance based on faith, will, and popular support is the surest and best method for fighting Israel. On July 16, 2008, Israel received the bodies of two soldiers in return for the release of four Lebanese prisoners.[150] Nasrallah's ability to negotiate the release of a large number of Arab prisoners from Israel was a significant achievement in Arab and Muslim eyes, adding to his popularity in the Arab and Muslim worlds. His Lebanese critics, however, saw these acts as transient gains coming at a great cost to Lebanon.

In recent times, sectarian boldness and Shi'ite assertiveness have characterized Nasrallah's youngest followers, who have no memory of the Civil War or the Israeli occupation. Their new social world has diluted the ideals of the early Islamist movement. Nasrallah has also been awakened to the problem of drug addiction among the youth and to the effect of money and power on Hizbullah's veterans.[151] He reminds the latter of the austerity and piety of the Islamists' grassroots movement, deploring the lavish display of Land Rovers among some of the party cadres. In the meantime, Nasrallah's calm demeanor has changed with the provocation of Shi'i–Sunni schisms and the shoring up of "Sunnite fears" against an alleged plan to boost "Shi'ite" power and Iranian interests in the region.[152] He has tried to appease both opponents and allies simultaneously with his party's conformity to the state's constitutional rubric, renouncing efforts to remove or ameliorate its sectarian structure or electoral system. Meanwhile, the deep national divisions over al-Hariri's assassination in 2005 and the repercussions of the international tribunal continue to absorb much of Nasrallah's energy.[153]

Summary

Displaced and radicalized lower-class Shi'ites were the earliest affiliates of Hizbullah and the mainstay of the *muqawama*, resistance, against Israel in the South. They were inspired by Ayatollah Ruhollah Khomeini's Islamic Revolution and Muhammad Baqir al-Sadr's vision of modern Islamist society. The formation of Lebanese Islamist men and women as actively pious and self-reliant civilians was not simply a "revival" of inherent values or dispositions in Islam. Rather, Islamism was shaped by historical developments particular to the Lebanese Shi'ites: socioeconomic displacement, political marginality, and subordination under the Israeli occupation. As such, the South should be seen as the primary milieu for political Islam. The *muqawama*, initially nurtured by leftist and nationalist traditions, became a highly organized well-funded operation under Hizbullah. The struggle against Israel was imbued with a high moral purpose as a form of defensive jihad and sacrifice in the path of liberation. Martyrdom was expected to transform the Islamist fighter into an intercessor who pleads with God for his family members on the Day of Judgment in order to remove their sins. Meanwhile, southerners continued to link together Karbala', the South, and Palestine as places of memory, stressing shared experiences of injustice, oppression, and occupation.

As it consolidated its power in central Shi'ite locales, launched ambitious economic projects, and partook in national elections, Hizbullah started attracting the Shi'ite émigré bourgeoisie of entrepreneurs and businessmen as well as professionals such as engineers, doctors, and teachers. To further its aims and compete effectively with its political rivals, Hizbullah began to conduct particular transactions with the Lebanese state, evident through its adjustment to the Ta'if Accord and participation in national elections. These transactions did not undermine Hizbullah's militancy or commitment to the *muqawama* but rather reinforced them. Whereas Shaykh Subhi al-Tufayli rejected such transactions categorically, Sayyid Muhammad Husayn Fadlallah argued that they must remain "temporal and transitional" because the state's sectarian structure and procedures are contradictory to Islam. In the postliberation period, however, Hizbullah showed less interest in economic and political reform, at least with respect to the following questions: the amelioration of electoral laws, the securing of government protection for Lebanese farmers and industrial workers, and the elimination of sectarianism as the basis for parceling posts in the administration and civil service. It became more invested in sectarian politics, seeking political allies who could protect the *muqawama* against mounting national opposition, as well as regional and American threats. Hizbullah's sectarian domination over the Shi'ites was sealed in 2005 by an endorsement of a past rival, Nabih Berri, the president of Parliament. This development signaled the beginning of a new phase in Hizbullah's domestic activities and in the development of its political program.

After 2005, Hizbullah's ability to increase the appeal of political Islam in the public sphere and rally support for the *muqawama* declined. The change was triggered by its effective domination of Shi'ite politics and the deep political and sectarian schisms caused by the assassination of President Rafiq al-Hariri and suspicion of the Islamists' and Syria's involvement in it. To these elements, one must add the conflicting feelings of triumph and tragedy that the 2006 Israeli invasion and Hizbullah's role in repulsing it evoked in the Lebanese people. On the one hand, Hizbullah was able to harness the Vietnamese model of combat and guerilla warfare more effectively than the Lebanese-Palestinian groups and the Communists in the South. The moral capital that the Islamists derived from defying the powerful Israeli army was greater than even the concrete gains made by the *muqawama*. The reputation of the Israeli army was shaken. On the other hand, Hizbullah came face to face with the limits of its *jihadi* thrust and guerilla warfare given the deployment of the UN forces along most of the Lebanese-Israeli borders. As a consequence, it is unclear what the future holds for the *muqawama*, which has changed from a liberation movement to national defense by military means.[154]

From 2006 until 2008, Hizbullah faced increasing governmental, regional, and international pressure to disarm the *muqawama*. The *muqawama*'s supporters argued, however, that the Lebanese government is incapable of protecting the southerners from Israeli aggression or preserving the sacrifices of the martyrs who liberated the South. The wish to disarm the *muqawama* also became entangled with fears of Shi'ite sectarian power, thus unleashing civil strife and deep national divisions. When the March 14 Bloc, represented by the prime minister, decided to dismantle Hizbullah's communication network, the latter launched an armed campaign in areas loyal to the bloc. Unlike Hizbullah's earlier civil protest in downtown Beirut, its use of armed force against civilian targets at this time jeopardized its place in the public sphere and undermined the Islamists' ability to enrich civil arenas that lie outside the state and that articulate the concerns of marginalized and minority groups.

Beyond highlighting a personal history, the biographical sketch of Sayyid Hasan Nasrallah given here stresses his formation as a major Islamist leader in the Middle East. Rural deterioration, displacement, and the Israeli occupation helped popularize public religion and draw the young Nasrallah closer to militant Islam. The key motive for his radicalism, it seems, was the futility of UN resolutions, peace negotiations, and diplomacy in the face of the Israeli occupation and violations of international humanitarian law. Nasrallah hailed Sayyid Musa al-Sadr's antisecular and anti-leftist practices before turning to Islamist doctrines proposed by Muhammad Baqir al-Sadr and the Da'wa Party, as well as to the Iranian revolutionary model offered by Khomeini. He also embraced the *hawza* education after it had declined among prominent clerical families in the South and the Biqa'. Yet, unlike the conventional *talaba* who spent years seeking advanced training in law and jurisprudence, Islamists such as Nasrallah sought a shorter program of study that meshed with political Islam. They also explored the possibilities for liberation offered by *jihadi* Shi'ite Islam. Nasrallah's teenage hostility toward the Communists took a more definitive form through his association with the clerical movement in Najaf and members of the Da'wa Party. Islamists of his generation considered Marxist secularism a neocolonial Western trend capable of destroying Islamic society.

As a political strategist, Nasrallah was instrumental in rallying diverse constituencies across the nation around the *muqawama* and taking pragmatic decisions to protect it. Meanwhile, the conflicts that emerged around the international tribunal to investigate al-Hariri's assassination and its final report have been taxing for Nasrallah. Having expressed confidence in his ability to thwart a future Israeli attack, he seems unsure how a Shi'i–Sunni schism can be prevented, a schism that may escalate into a Civil War, involving Sunnite groups preoccupied with eliminating the "Shi'ite threat."[155]

7

The Islamists and Civil Society

The Islamists' entry into the Lebanese public sphere introduced new religious sensibilities and ways of rethinking modernism that ultimately challenged the sphere's prevalent liberal and leftist secular discourses. This and the following chapter delineate the transformation of the public sphere in Lebanon after a fight with, and defeat of the Left aided by the civil war and Israeli intervention.

By the mid-1990s, Hizbullah had turned into a social movement expanding in a relatively uncoerced public space. This chapter delineates central features of the Hizbullah and Fadlallah movements, which contributed to civil society for more than fifteen years, stretching roughly from the early 1990s until 2005. The Islamists made use of public discourse to emphasize the inseparability of active faith from the liberation of the South and the modernization of Islamic culture. They shaped new civil arenas where faith-based organizations assumed functions formerly belonging to the state. The chapter gives an overview of these organizations' activities and draws attention to efforts in controlling the disruptions caused by globalization. It delineates the Islamists' approach to globalized technologies such as television and Internet and explores the nature of their engagement with globalized environmentalism.

In the period focused on here, Hizbullah's movement underwent a significant change as the Islamists' ability to resort to civic debate, peaceful resistance, and protest against their opponents diminished. This change can be attributed to the continued production of sectarian violence in Lebanon and Hizbullah's reliance on armed force to protect itself and the *muqawama*, as well as its recourse to sectarian mobilization, to achieve its goals. As Hizbullah dominated Shi'ite politics, it integrated a heterogeneous group of followers made of founding members and newer ones for whom the main attraction of Islamism had less to do with its ideals than with the political ascendancy of "the Shi'ites." To these followers one must add the mix of Shi'ite allies from AMAL and Christian allies belonging to the Free Patriotic Movement.

This chapter looks closely at two principles of sociopolitical and moral conduct that shaped the Islamist arenas of Hizbullah and Fadlallah during their formative period: piety and sacrifice. These principles drew the ethical boundaries of the "society of the resistance" (*mujtama' al-muqawama*) and were justified by the thrust for the liberation of the South. They allowed the Islamists to negotiate new relations with diverse constituents of the public sphere who shared their commitment to civic responsibility and social justice.

The ethical boundaries of the resisting society and its moral purpose were reflected in women's acts as much as in men's. This chapter sheds light on women's active piety and participation in sacrificial acts for the preservation of the resisting society. It explores experiences of death and self-sacrifice (suicide missions), specifically during the Israeli occupation of the South, which heightened women's observance of ritual purity and public prayer. Women tried to ensure that norms of sexual purity were not transgressed, and they expected much benefit from their piety. Women who lost their sons in combat expressed public approval of their death, drawing upon Shi'ite traditions of redemptive suffering and made new connections to Shi'ite models of female piety.

Civil Society and Political Islam

There are several definitions of civil society and diverse theoretical formulations of the origins, components, and historical function of a public sphere.[1] More important, there is disagreement about locating and speaking of a civil society in an Islamic context, past and present.[2] The arguments about the absence of an Islamic civil society are in part based on a mechanical application of features of Western civil society to Islamic society. They reflect equally a lack of appreciation for the multiple experiences of Western modernity itself.[3] In the past decade, a number of scholars have

tried to overcome these limitations by redefining civil society compara-
tively within and outside the Western context and to raise new points that
seem useful for writing this chapter.[4] New critical readings of "civil society" and the "public sphere" have a wide spectrum of examples of public
spheres in both Western societies and Islamic societies.[5] More specifically,
these studies challenge Weberian conceptions of a civil society formed
through secularized voluntary associations seeking individual autonomy
against the state in the phase of late modernity.[6] They also investigate
Jürgen Habermas's liberal bourgeois sphere, its homogeneity, its special
claims to equality and rationality, and its neglect of conflict. More important, they challenge Habermas's attempt to invest the bourgeois sphere as
a "normative category" tied to the tradition of the Enlightenment.[7] Critics of the Habermasian model question the neglect of religion and of its
role in shaping the modern public sphere.[8] Talal Asad is concerned with
how discursive religion, which inhabits a public sphere, seeks empowerment and aims to change the relationship with secularism and the nation-
state.[9] Meanwhile, a host of studies on contemporary Muslim countries
has explored aspects of civil society, politics, and the media, questioning
the centrality of Western individualism to the emergence and function of
the public sphere.[10] These studies prove to be useful for exploring similar
features in Hizbullah's civil arena.

It is important to emphasize that the observations and conclusions
we advance in this chapter about the nature of Hizbullah's civil society
do not necessarily apply to other Islamist movements in the Middle East
or outside it. The Islamists discussed here are the Shi'ites in Fadlallah's
circles and in Hizbullah's movement. It is necessary to start with the local
historical reality of Hizbullah's movement (referred to hereafter as "the
movement") and occasionally refer to the literature on Islam and civil
society by way of illuminating, comparing, or differentiating aspects of
this activist faith-based movement from others. We feel justified in speaking of an Islamist civil society in Lebanon as an autonomous public arena
unmonitored by the state, distinct from sectarian, provincial, and familial
networks, but which intersects with them. It is an arena that produces
forms of civic responsibility as part of religious morality. The term *public sphere* is used here interchangeably with *civil society*, which includes

student associations, labor unions, women's social organizations and political committees, religious organizations, political parties, as well as groups coming together on questions such as cultural identity, class, gender, or social development. The Lebanese public sphere is composed of multiple arenas or spheres that to varying degrees have discursive connections to the state.[11] A number of institutions and voluntary associations are the mainstay of Hizbullah's and Fadlallah's arenas. Their civil actors are located outside the state's rubric and its regulatory economic and political organs, expressing a range of needs and human aspirations.[12]

Social conflict and power are significant in the formulation of civil arenas, including Hizbullah's. Discord and coercive acts were as much part of the early Islamists' civil engagements as communicative reasoning and negotiation of difference.[13] During this formative period, the Islamists brought a degree of pluralism to the public sphere through a greater inclusion of actively religious Shi'ites from lower- and middle-class rural backgrounds. The movement's civil institutions, seminaries, and schools communicated a world of religious ideas and sentiments born out, not aside from, an engagement with power. Civil society as such has implications for the attainment of power and may intersect with practices involving the state.[14] As such, some scholars note the complex relations that exist between civil society and violence.[15] Acts of violence have at times facilitated the entry of marginalized groups into the public sphere and given them a voice against the normative delineations and preferences of this sphere. The early Islamists undeniably engaged in violent clashes with their opponent, the leftists and AMAL, and used coercive means to build a base in Beirut, such as intimidating landowners to sell their property in the southern suburb.[16] At the same time, they spread their ideas through voluntary associations and institutions, using proselytizing, public discourse, and political socialization. After 2005, the movement, following a series of historical events, replaced civil protest with increasing coercion and armed intervention, which impaired the democratic elements of the public sphere, whose general constitution aims to minimize coercion and to control arbitrary violence.

Jose Casanova argues that religious movements, which stand in a problematic relationship to modernity, can nonetheless contribute to the public sphere if they remain committed to its rules of engagement. These movements, which adapt to or recognize "some of modernity's values as their own," evoking moral norms against the state or the economic system, remain within the rubric of a democratic tradition of modernity.[17] Casanova's separation of secularization and modernity, however, poses a set of problems, as Talal Asad has shown.[18] The Islamists' approach to secularization is discussed in chapter 8, together with their relation to the modern nation-state. Here, suffice it to note, that Hizbullah's Islamism carries dissonant elements of modernism that need to be constantly reworked in connection to new historical conditions. To arrive at safe conclusions, one also needs to analyze the movement over a longer period of time. After all, the Islamists have been part of Lebanese society for less than three decades. In recent years, the movement's support for the rules of civic engagement has been uneven.

Islamists and Leftists in the Public Sphere

The public sphere that the early Islamists entered in the 1980s was constituted by liberal, secular nationalist, and leftist arenas, among others. Shi'ite schoolteachers, unionists, academics, writers, religious intellectuals, and artists were prevalent in these arenas. The early Islamists shared important sensibilities with the inhabitants of several of these arenas, including an aversion to governmental economic policies, state sectarianism, and Western policies in the Middle East. At the same time, they contested the public sphere's adaptations of "Western" ideas of secular modernism and liberal democracy. The crucial point of contention with the secularists was the latter's advocacy of the privatization of religion and the restriction of the role of clerics and the shari'a in state legislation and public life. Of these secularists, the Communists became a primary target of Islamist attack, which made them responsible for "the spread of atheism and materialism" in Shi'ite society.[19] The Communists, for their part, insisted that democratization and economic development in a multisectarian society such as Lebanon required the tapering off of religion and the narrowing of the extent to which clerics could shape questions of polity, legal rights, and the economy.[20] Shi'ite "enchantment" with Communist revolutionary ideals and its ethical reasoning were a formidable challenge to the Islamists.[21] Indeed, there was a time when municipal councils, charitable associations, and school boards commented on the Communists' sense of civic responsibility and moral rectitude.[22] The romanticized image of the Communist was buttressed by the latter's role in the armed struggle against Israel in the South. Slowly but surely, the Islamists reduced this image by condemning the Communists' indifference to piety and God's law and, hence, to Islamic legal obligations and prohibitions.

Public faith and political resistance went hand in hand in the formation of the Islamist subjects who in time assumed a distinct place in the Lebanese public sphere.

Family life in the South became politicized, and the conflicts between the Communists, AMAL members, and the Islamists were out in the open.[23] At family gatherings, schools, social clubs, and universities, the Islamists insisted on the Communists' blasphemy and the falsity of their "Western-derived" ideas.[24] Hizbullah's women and men argued about the type of books to be read, the clothes worn, the foods to be eaten, the rituals to be observed, and the music permitted. These civil exchanges between Islamist thinkers and adversarial groups undoubtedly involved confrontation and at times coercion.[25] The Islamists did more than argue their vision for a faith-based society. They started to dominate important social arenas through two major lines of action—a militant approach to Israeli occupation and the building of civil organizations for medical and economic relief.[26] The Islamists' success in liberating most of the South by 2000, coupled with the achievements of their welfare programs, appealed to a group of Communists who saw them as part of a larger revolutionary tradition encompassing the Palestinian resistance and leftist–nationalist struggles in the South.[27] These Communists discussed Hizbullah's success in harnessing the "Vietnamese model" and lent support to its anti-imperial *jihadi* dimensions.[28] They came together with the Islamists on the necessity of armed struggle against Israel and the need to "democratize" international space, resist American domination, and transform regional policies pertaining to marginalized groups. But these Communists' support for Hizbullah seemed conditional upon the latter's long-term plans for reform—in particular, the elimination of sectarianism as a basis for political representation, civil service, and electoral choices.[29] Hizbullah evidently had not pushed for such reforms.

Several constituents of the Lebanese public sphere stood to preserve secular ideas, which they argued were threatened by the Islamists' "anti-modernism."[30] The latter have seriously engaged with modernity, but they are not alone in harboring unresolved tensions with it, as becomes clear in chapter 8. But if greater civil society leads to democratization, then the empowerment of the Islamists has for better or worse forced the Lebanese to hear the voices originally coming from the "periphery." The upcoming sections focus on the way the Islamists enriched civil society, the ideas they projected, the moral sensibilities they cultivated, and the dialogues as well as the dissension they raised in the Lebanese public sphere.

Bequest and Investment: Islamist Civil Organizations

Family, village, and party associations are the site of autonomous civil activities and self-directed services outside the state. In the South, where rural traditions of civil organization interwove with nationalist and Communist activism, Shi'ites volunteered their time and efforts to improve social facilities, health conditions, and education. Those organized into secular parties continued to utilize village, family, and sectarian channels to resolve a host of economic and social problems. These channels were, at times, the only means to reach civilians.[31] Fadlallah's and Hizbullah's organizations reflected some of the same patterns and activities, but at a much wider scale, guaranteeing continuity in delivering social and economic services. Indeed, the Islamists took self-reliance to a whole new level through substantive funding from Iran, long-term planning, and effective organization.[32] Thousands of Shi'ites, young and old, were contributing money to the Islamic resistance not only through almsgiving and *khum*s (the one-fifth taxation), but also through a "Piggy Bank" found in houses, schools, and commercial centers.[33]

Self-reliance is probably the most diffuse and complex feature of Hizbullah's and Fadlallah's civil organizations.[34] It is seen as a defense against state neglect as well as a means to nurture collective responsibilities undermined by "modern" individualism. Mirvat Talib, a kindergarten teacher at one of the al-Mahdi schools, was concerned for the youth "in modern times" because they seemed to avoid their responsibilities toward their families and rarely volunteered their time in collaborative social work.[35] Parents were advised to prevent child idleness and attenuate their commitment to the child's individual needs.[36] Self-reliance also tied into the Islamists' emphasis on activating civil responsibilities when the state and international political organizations are ineffective. The "culture of the resistance" (thaqafat al-muqawama), al-Shaykh Mustafa Qasir, director of Hizbullah's educational board, maintained, is formed when civilians find solutions to their problems through their own initiatives instead of waiting for governmental or international agencies to act. One is forced to rely on oneself to achieve justice and autonomy because the "international order" is "without justice."[37] He pointed to the Palestinians who developed their own resistance to the Israeli occupation instead of waiting for Arab or international initiatives.

Islamic traditions of charitable contribution and philanthropic work are manifest through several Lebanese organizations and combine at times with political or cultural claims. For example, the Islamic Orphanage Center (Dar al-Aytam al-Islamiyya) in Beirut emerged in 1929 as a Sunnite welfare organization for social relief and aid and relied heavily on women's voluntary labor and civilian, as well as institutional contributions. In post-independent Lebanon, the Orphanage Center has expressed its rejection of sectarian conflict and its interest in disseminating "moral values" and enhancing "the humanitarian principles of Islam such as justice and tolerance."[38] It has also promoted itself as a vehicle for "progress and modernity" but does not specify what those terms entailed. In comparison, Hizbullah and Fadlallah's charitable organizations advocated Islamist sociopolitical principles rooted in the shari'a and its modern renewal. These organizations embodied the piety of resistance as both a civil practice and a political-cultural project.

In 1978, Fadlallah founded the al-Mabarrat Charitable Organization, an organization for charity and benefaction. It launched several social, economic, and cultural programs through schools, institutes, and welfare organizations, as well as through the Persons with Special Needs Organization and health centers that include two hospitals.[39] Al-Mabarrat's

Health-Cultural Center in al-'Abbas in Yatir (the South), for instance, includes clinics for obstetrics and gynecology, emergency services, and dentistry, as well as a pharmacy and rooms for audiovisual presentations and training students in information technology.[40] The Institute al-Hadi cares for the deaf and the blind. The Persons with Special Needs Organization uses advanced psychological methods and speech therapy to help children who have difficulties reading, writing, or learning mathematics. It also helps children with hyperactivity and attention deficit disorder.[41]

In 1984, two important Hizbullah organizations, the Islamic Health Committee and Struggle for Construction (Jihad al-Bina'), were founded in the southern suburb of Beirut through Iranian funds and investments by affluent Shi'ite émigrés in West Africa. In 1987, Imam Khomeini's Relief Committee managed the crisis caused by fleeing refugees from the South to the southern suburb.[42] Hizbullah provided medical aid for Shi'ites through mobile clinics and subsidized pharmacies.[43] In 1988, the Islamic Health Committee founded the clinic Dar al-Hawra' for Obstetrics and the al-Rasul al-A'zam Hospital in Beirut and the Imam Khomeini Hospital in Ba'labak. Families of martyred Hizbullah fighters and their children received social and economic relief from the Institution of al-Shahid.[44] The Struggle for Construction brought the southern suburb its independent water resource between 1990 and 1994.[45] It also provided constituents with the means to buy an apartment or rebuild their homes, which had been destroyed by Israel, and launched ambitious construction projects for urban development.[46] The Good Loan Organization (Mu'assassat al-Qard al-Hasan) offered interest-free loans for those committed to the movement and the principle of *wilayat al-faqih* (discussed in chapter 6).[47] These pious institutions fostered "the resisting society" as self-reliant and resolute in the face of hardship and death. It is a society capable ideally of withstanding the demolition of its homes, the loss of stable employment, and the disabling of educational and social development caused by Israeli attacks.[48] It is also a society that embraces Islamic religious-legal obligations and resists secularization as part of a broad resistance to Western cultural domination. Hizbullah's civil institutions compensated for the deficit in state aid and services as well as for government discrimination against rural Shi'ites.[49] Water and medicine cannot wait for government

planning and execution, Islamist leaders argued.[50] The Islamists were trying to secure water and medicine for civilians and were seen constructing
roads in the South despite Israeli shelling. In the southern suburb, Hizbullah's organization, Struggle for Construction, carried out garbage collection in the 1990s then turned it over to al-Hariri's government and the
Sukleen Company. Islamist thinkers insisted that the practical functions
of civil institutions as well as their cultural role must remain independent
of the state.[51]

Hizbullah's Emdad Committee devoted its efforts to creating jobs for
the mass of unskilled workers. It trained many in handicraft and technical professions useful for a rural economy as well as in small industries.
The al-Husayn b. 'Ali and al-Rasul al-A'zam technical academies provided stipends and fellowships for students to pursue specialized training
in Arab and Western countries.[52] Around 6,261 destitute families were
able to achieve economic independence by 1992.[53] The Iranian government paid millions ($60–120 million per year) for the Emdad Committee
to provide uprooted Shi'ites with food supplies and home furniture. By
the mid-1990s, voluntary contributions from Islamists and sympathizers internationally were made to the Emdad Committee.[54] Investments in
housing projects and business enterprises such as fisheries and bakeries,
as well as clothing industries, also helped replenish Emdad's resources.[55]

In the Biqa', Islamist civil projects were incapable of absorbing the staggering economic crisis that precipitated the Revolt of the Hungry in 1997.
Sometime after the revolt, Hizbullah organized a series of workshops on
the Biqa's economy and made new investment plans in that region on the
basis of advice from financial and economic experts. Hizbullah's statistical surveys concluded that around 53 percent of Ba'labak and al-Hirmil's
people in the northern Biqa' lived below poverty level.[56] Agricultural production and its related tasks formed a major source of livelihood for the
people of Ba'labak and al-Hirmil.[57] Poor irrigation plans, the high price of
fertilizers and insecticides, and the lack of loans were compounded by a
marketing crisis in the globalized economy. In an attempt to extend aid
and relief to the Biqa', the organization Iranian Struggle for Agriculture
(Jihad al-Zira'a al-Iraniyya), gave $17,000 in 2001 to establish local medical clinics in Shmustar and al-Nabi Sheit.[58] The Center for Agricultural

Counsel (Markaz al-Irshad al-Zira'i) established and supervised licensed agricultural co-ops. By 2002–2003, Hizbullah restored several water passages and systems in Ba'labak, including a recycling water station, and brought drinking water to two major Biqa'i towns, al-Yammuna and 'Uyun Arghash.

Critics of Hizbullah argued that its deputies did not seriously pursue economic reform lest it jeopardizes its alliances with parliamentarians who supported state privatization plans and upheld the sectarian power-sharing "formula."[59] Reformists accused the Islamists of overlooking the Biqa'i's economic demands during two consecutive parliamentary rounds and of expressing lukewarm support for the workers' and farmers' demonstrations.[60] Hizbullah's leaders, however, blamed the government's economic policies. Two years after the Revolt of the Hungry, the government put at risk the livelihood of Biqa'i families when it agreed to give several Arab countries tariff exemptions on agricultural products exported to Lebanon.[61] Farmers in the Biqa' asked the government to change the time of year during which it imported products such as garlic, onion, and potatoes from Egypt so it would not overlap with the farmers' season in the Biqa'. The farmers also welcomed the importation of rice and cotton from Egypt, which are not produced in the Biqa'. Hizbullah's leaders discussed the limits of their development programs in the absence of adequate governmental protection for Lebanese farmers.[62] But the Islamists' overall support for privatization and the absence of a comprehensive economic plan for reform may have added to the Biqa'i farmers' predicament.

The Islamists and Globalization

The increasing dependence on civil organizations to generate labor and resources attests to the crisis of the modern state in Lebanon. For citizens of a weak state, innovative educational prospects and globalized health and communication technologies are hardly affordable.[63] The Lebanese government cannot partake in the global economy, let alone manage its immediate or long-term manifestations.[64] Hizbullah's institutions and al-Mabarrat have tried to control the disruptions of globalized economic processes and ideas.[65] The Islamists' reliance on Iranian aid, volunteer labor, and welfare practices, including *zakat* (almsgiving), seemed crucial for insisting on cultural and religious difference. To protect and nurture this difference, pious activists in al-Dahiya, the South, and the Biqaʿ seemed propelled to acquiesce to the effects of globalization. They evidently were not concerned with neoliberal capitalist globalization and have utilized global financial institutions to generate profit. They warned, however, against the type of cultural homogenization that they equate with Americanization. The idea of cultural mobility was not particularly acceptable to Hizbullah because it meant sameness produced by the domination of Western culture over Muslims. By attending to the immediate economic and health needs of displaced and poor Shiʿites, the Islamists were able to popularize their own interpretations of globalized cultural texts. Jonathan Inda and Renato Rosaldo suggested that the disjuncture caused by globalization involved the refitting of some of its features into a new body.[66] Facets of globalization are not automatically or passively internalized but rather are "reinscribed" and activated through local and national forces. This process was evident among the Islamists as they refitted globalized commercial, communicative, and health features to the needs of their civil arena.

The Islamists' civil arena had provided meaningful ties between believers and their local urban and rural environments, which went against the tendency of globalization to make local choices and events adapt to realities in remote places on the globe.[67] Consumerist American items did not enter the Islamists' public spaces easily. Globalized food and fashion sensibilities among the youth were in particular redirected. Icons of globalized American food culture, such as McDonald's and Kentucky Fried Chicken, were accommodated and sometimes replaced by eateries selling *halal* hamburgers, chicken burgers, cold cuts, and hot dogs. The soft drink ZamZam, made in Iran, was popular among Fadlallah's and Hizbullah's followers who boycotted a number of American goods, including Coca-Cola.[68] As the Islamists tried to be rooted in the local material and social culture, they, unlike other Lebanese constituencies, were careful about what they accommodate and justify.[69]

The public media shaped by the Islamists was the site of complex forms of globalization. Hizbullah's TV station al-Manar, with its Internet site, negotiated Islamist sensibilities with diverse audiences and facilitated their spread among the youth. Hizbullah's cultural programs and reality shows decentered Western military superiority and elevated the Shi'ite martyrs to superhuman levels. Al-Manar's popularity in Persian Gulf countries and overseas pushed the station to provide additional support for the increasing number of Internet users since 2001.[70] Hizbullah's own Internet site has evolved significantly, thus creating an extended virtual space where believers feel united in their commitment to public religion.[71] For sympathizers and curious onlookers, these Internet sites offered a quick and condensed image of the Islamist civilian through presentation and interactive features. American and Israeli assertions about Hizbullah's terrorist character, for instance, are quoted on Hizbullah's official site in order to counter them with images of Israeli assaults on Palestinian civilians and Lebanese children.[72] Israeli electronic attacks on Hizbullah's Internet site have led to a greater realization of the "power" transmitted by this virtual space. With this realization, after 2000 Hizbullah's media specialists started to direct cyber attacks on Israeli sites such as the Tel Aviv Stock Exchange and the Israeli Knesset.[73]

Al-Mabarrat and Hizbullah's organizations have shown a selective interest in globalized research and discourses on the ecology and the conservation of the environment.[74] "Preserving the environment" is in part motivated by globalized information about the connections among deadly diseases, environmental damage, and state policies. On the ground, the Islamists at the Struggle for Construction have attended to urgent environmental problems and tried to resolve them with the aid of the hydraulics and electricity, environment, and water authorities.[75] During parliamentary elections in 1996, the party's campaign promised the implementation of forestry measures to prevent aridity of land.[76] The Islamists, however, did not fulfill these promises, nor were they able to establish recycling factories or prevent water pollution by industrial wastes or soil pollution caused by unsupervised use of pesticides, insecticides, and fertilizers.[77] As they face increasing national and regional challenges, their ability to focus or invest in environmental preservation seems to be limited. For many, the environment comes into focus usually in connection with economic destruction and damage to southern Lebanese land, air, and water. As a consequence, the Islamists collaborate with environmentalists in projects that have a clear political dimension, such as the Pan-Arab Antiglobalization Gathering (PAAG, Al-Tajammu' al-'Arabi al-Munahid li-al-'Awlama), as well as the Lebanese Nongovernmental Organization Antiglobalization Gathering (Al-Munazzama al-Lubnaniyya Ghayr al-Hukumiyya al-Munahida li-al-'Awlama).[78] In a conference organized by the Euro-Mediterranean Partnership, twenty-seven states of the European Union and twelve of the southern Mediterranean agreed to nurture financial prosperity, cultural progress, and peace in the Middle East based on a two-state solution for the Palestinians and the Israelis.[79] The PAAG rejected American and international pressure to neutralize Lebanon as an actor in the Arab-Israeli conflict.[80] In connection with these primary political concerns, the Islamists have shared the PAAG's focus on the damage to the environment caused by globalization policies, including the privatization of the coast, the desertion of local markets for agricultural products, and the continuation of illegal construction.[81] They alerted the world to the detrimental effects of Israel's use of depleted uranium and cluster bombs. Meanwhile, they have also tried to "convince part of the international left" that they can be partners in confronting American policies that pose a threat to the welfare of "developing countries and to the environment."[82]

The "environment" is a diffuse entity for many civilians in the movement. It does not encompass attitudes and practices we formally associate with environmentalism. Priority is given to environmental demands that are tied to local needs and religious sensibilities. For the Islamists, environmental conservation has become a way to restore the Muslim's relationship to a natural world damaged by materialism. Nature is considered a necessary place to admire God's beauty, bounty, and power. To waste it or take it for granted is impious.[83] Rescuing the environment has thus validated the Islamists' warnings regarding the destructive features of Western modernism, individualism, and American consumerism. These meanings were evoked in the type of heritage tourism organized at al-Mabarrat, as well as in the reproduction of historic Arab-Islamic places in present settings. A subsidiary association of al-Mabarrat called the Traditional Courtyard Village (Qaryat al-Saha al-Turathiyya) worked to re-create "authentic" environments for believers in the middle of suburban

Beirut. A group of engineers and architects directed by Jamal Makki built a restaurant known as the Courtyard Village close to Beirut's airport.[84] The restaurant carried the architectural motifs of the village center, and its profit went to al-Mabarrat orphanages and institute employees.[85] Islamic entertainment parks, restaurants, private beaches, and community centers tried to bestow on everyday activities dimensions of godliness.[86] On bus tours and sightseeing trips, Islamist women visit Shi'ite shrines, mosques, and historical landmarks and experience leisure as part of a duty toward God and a diversion that comes with a religious reward.[87]

Public Religion and Rituals

Hizbullah's movement shaped a new public arena—first, through the power to provide provisions and medical relief and, second, through the ability to liberate the South from Israeli occupation. Owing to its principles of piety and sacrifice, the movement received a warm reception even from doubtful audiences. These principles eased the Islamists' negotiation of their ideas among skeptics of public religion.

During the 1980s, observant and nonobservant Muslims alike questioned the Islamists' "heightened" performance of public worship, purity, body and head covering, and the avoidance of physical contact between the sexes. For the Islamists, piety is not furnished through individualized or spontaneous spiritual ventures toward God. Rather, God is worshipped through a body of moral-legal edicts that ensure the exercise of what is "right," such as prayer and fasting, and the avoidance of what is "wrong," such as alcohol consumption and adultery.[88] Doing what is right is a public act involving a measure of private practice. This is elucidated in several statements made by the Imams especially 'Ali b. Abi Talib, al-Husayn b. 'Ali and Ja'far al-Sadiq revealing different features of *taqwa* (piety), which can be expressed by "abstaining from that which is forbidden" but can also go beyond it through individual efforts to acquire humility, patience, trustworthiness, and kindness.[89]

There are practical steps to be taken to achieve piety, and they are found in the rhythm of daily worship and purity rituals. With the advent of the Islamists, a semiautonomous culture of commanding right and forbidding wrongdoing, *al-'amr bi-al-ma'ruf wa-al-nahi 'an al-munkar*, began to flourish in several Shi'ite locales in Beirut, the South, and the Biqa'.[90] Fulfilling one's duties toward God then involves responsibility not only toward reforming oneself, but also toward reforming family members and the "community or society at large."[91] By the late 1980s, however, the Islamists were expressing the need to implement aspects of the shari'a in daily life.[92] Sayyid Muhammad Husayn Fadlallah's legal opinions on worship and social contracts became particularly popular. His concise legal work, *Ahkam al-Shari'a*, is "easy to carry around," its publisher explained, stressing its value to common believers as a reference work.[93] This new interest in public religion, however, evoked tensions and conflicts in the public sphere and within the Shi'ite family. In the light of such conflicts, Fadlallah argued that a believer whose family or spouse opposed public religion is exempted from fulfilling her or his religious obligations.

The movement's Islamists enjoined moral rectitude and ascetic norms.[94] Piety was gauged through the maintenance of public welfare and resistance to material temptations. The Islamists' "religious morality" was contrasted with the "corruption" of political parties such as AMAL and the Druze Party led by Walid Junblat.[95] At the time when Muhammad Fneish from Hizbullah became the minister of energy in 2005, the management unit employees for the oil refineries of Tripoli and Zahrani were receiving inflated salaries that exceeded their counterparts in the public sector. Employees were using state funds to "cover personal expenditure ranging from maids to car insurance and telephone lines." Fneish acted swiftly, lowering salaries and counteracting corruption. He also secured oil supplies from Algeria and Kuwait in 2005, which reduced the country's energy bill by $70 million.[96] These acts were considered a major accomplishment in the face of failing attempts to secure reliable and affordable fuel imports. Supporters of the movement also pointed to the Islamists' trustworthiness. During the Israeli invasion of 2006, Hizbullah's fighters preserved all valuables, including jewelry and money, that they found around destroyed or burned houses in the South and al-Dahiya. They returned them to their proper owners after the invasion. Critics of Hizbullah, however, consider these virtuous acts incidental and hardly manifest among the younger generation of the party's affiliates.[97]

Despite the Islamists' pious concern for the poor, they have supported worker and unionist demands only sporadically during episodes of conflict between Shiʿite labor and the state.[98] They have attributed class inequalities to ideological differences between "the oppressed," or God-fearing Muslims, and their opponents—namely, Israel and the hegemonic imperial order.[99] Thus, belonging to the resisting society has changed how class is lived and understood. Baqir al-Sadr's "Islamic economics," which inspired many Islamists in Lebanon, relied on Islamic legal proscriptions and moral obligations to protect citizens from the ills of the capitalist market discussed in chapter four. To redistribute wealth and prevent injustice against the poor, believers were advised to pay almsgiving, *khum*s, and channel *riba* (usury, interest) into public projects. The Islamists created an outlet for lower-class needs through their welfare and educational programs at the same time as they preserved the integrity of bourgeois capitalist ventures.

Despite Hizbullah's broad concern for the common person's well-being, its criticisms of al-Hariri's neoliberal economic policies were sporadic. Fadlallah, in comparison, remained consistent in his criticisms of al-Hariri's economic projects and political practices. Solidère, al-Hariri's multibillion-dollar construction company, had planned to rebuild downtown Beirut following the civil war.[100] But his neoliberal economic policies undermined the public economic sector and increased Lebanon's national debt dramatically. The latter rose from $2.5 billion to $18.3 billion in a few years (by 2011, it exceeded $50 billion) as al-Hariri made available state funds and private capital for investment.[101] In response, Fadlallah issued a fatwa in 1995 making the buying of shares in Solidère illegal under the company's current conditions: "I voiced my concern from a legal and humanistic viewpoint because the previous owners [of the properties] who had shops and legal rights in that area [downtown Beirut] were not satisfied with the [Solidère] plan, which bought their properties and confiscated their rights. The amounts they received [from Solidère] do not correspond to the [properties'] value, as they [the owners of these properties] say. As such, the Solidère company turned into a usurper [*ghasiba*] that violated the rights of these people in the legal sense of the term."[102]

Fadlallah also held the Parliament responsible for jeopardizing Lebanese citizens' private property when it legalized the Solidère.

Women's Piety and Purity

Women who joined the movement during the 1980s and the 1990s experienced changes in dress and demeanor, as well as in ablution and prayer patterns. There was a period of experimentation with hair scarves, Iranian-style black chadors (a body-length head cover tied or held under the chin and split open down the front), and gloves. There was also a transition from habitual performance of rituals to an active referencing of religious texts and jurists.

In the movement, women expressed a greater awareness of rules of avoidance (of certain foods), purity, worship, and the covering of the body and head. This awareness came at a time when many Shi'ites were experiencing Israeli occupation as a physical and psychological displacement ranging from denigration of Islamic symbols (the burning of Qur'ans) to imprisonment, torture, and death.[103] The resistance was made sacrosanct through the sacrifices of martyred men and the purity and sacrifices of women. In a revealing sentence, al-Tufayli would say about the weapons of the resistance, "It is a pure [religious] weapon that deserves ritual ablution before touching, for it has the breeze of freedom and pride. The men of the resistance are verses in the Qur'an."[104]

As young men were sacrificing their bodies to defeat the occupier, Islamist women were adding layers of separation between their bodies and the male public. They re-read Qur'anic verses and Shi'ite hadiths, promoting a new venture toward faith.[105] They drew upon doctrinal and eschatological literature to situate their political and human crisis. The self and the body politic mirrored each other in public performance of piety. The Islamist public conscience had to be constantly redrawn and with it norms of purity and veiling precisely because the transgression of these norms was inevitable and with it the threat to the integrity of the resisting society.[106] As Mary Douglas has noted, "The moral code by its nature can never be reduced to something simple, hard and fast."[107] It is clarified and elaborated upon in connection to actual situations and changing contexts.

Women's public observance of purity rites and veiling was an important elaboration of this moral code during the occupation of the South.

The resistance traversed gendered spaces. Women of active faith expressed the necessity of living morally, veiling, praying, and avoiding physical contact with men. The Islamists' militant march against Israeli occupiers came with a fear of transgressing God's laws. Women were preoccupied with preventing pollution of various parts of the body almost as a way to fortify the resistance. Even though women are not considered substantively impure (*najis*), getting sexually polluted may render them at least temporarily impure and can spread impurity to others.[108] To get rid of *janaba* (a state of sexual pollution), women (as well as men) must perform different types of ablutions depending on the pollutant and conditions of the pollution. Veiling and prevention of contact between the sexes are tied to a social concern with sexual pollution, which can annul one's *wudu'*, preparatory ablutions for prayer. It should be emphasized that women and men's intentions with respect to physical contact are not relevant to such a concern.

Public expressions of purity, avoidance rules, and body covering were indeed more extensive for women than for men because the former were in relations of subordination to men not only economically and sexually, but also ideologically and symbolically. As such, the responsibility of earning God's favors through these observances and rituals devolved primarily to women.

Sacrifice and Martyrdom

Sacrifice was central to the culture of the resisting society. It was expressed by a willingness to give up one's life for the well-being of society, to endure pain to lift injustice, and to take up volunteer work and public responsibilities without expecting direct material return. Islamist women and men's sacrificial acts shaped major civil arenas in the public sphere. Medical doctors, Judith Harik notes, were "ready to abandon far more lucrative practices in the capital [Beirut] for exceedingly low-paying work at the grass roots."[109] The Islamists expected their collective and long-term sacrifices to make crucial improvements in their life conditions. Much human effort at Hizbullah's organizations was provided through volunteer work, which comes with the expectation of social reciprocity and spiritual reward.[110] Lara Deeb delineates the importance of women's volunteerism in Islamist associations focused on providing food supplies for the poor and preventing child labor.[111] Even though donations were the major resource for Hizbullah's facilities, women, men, and even children contributed to fund-raising initiatives.

Self-sacrifice embodied the militant idealism of the resisting society and its highest spiritual values. Fadlallah explained that martyrdom (*istishhad*) is a sacrifice made by a person for the preservation and freedom of the collectivity.[112] Self-sacrifice was inevitable when no parity with Israel in terms of technological and military capabilities was possible. Martyrdom soon became the center of controversy in the Lebanese public sphere, and the Islamists were accused of nurturing "a culture of death" among the Shi'ite youth.[113] Fadlallah rejected the use of the term *suicide* (*intihar*) to describe the missions that young Shi'ites carried out against Israeli targets leading to their self-sacrifice.[114] He explained that "suicide" aims at bringing relief for the individual and an escape from one's problems, which is at odds with the motives and aims of martyred Islamists.

Probably the most distinctive feature of active piety in the late twentieth century was the way women appeared to have a central place in the offering and reception of sacrifice. Women revisited past narratives and eschatological illustrations of Karbala' to make sense of the present. Validating sacrifice ranged from women's selfless service to others in and outside the domicile to accepting the death of loved ones in combat.[115] Activist women at Hizbullah's welfare organizations struggled to meet high expectations, do extra work, and make the sacrifice personal.[116] Needless to say, unwaged social work and volunteerism were not new to Lebanese or Shi'ite women.[117] For decades, urban upper-class women had engaged in fund-raising and philanthropic services, and lower-class women had organized communal events involving food preparation and distribution.[118] There had been also no lack of piety or norms of communal responsibility before the movement spread.[119] What was new in the Islamists' civil society were the scope and implications of sacrifice for the resisting society during the Israeli occupation.

Young Islamists saw the offering of oneself for the protection of the collectivity as atonement for sins committed against Imam Husayn and his family. Of particular relevance in this context is the pledge taken in 684 by the Penitents (*tawwabun*) who were Kufan Shi'ites to sacrifice their lives to atone for their guilt of abandoning Imam Husayn.[120] The implications of sacrifice and sacrificial symbols among the Islamists are best illustrated through Douglas's view that "when someone embraces freely the symbols of death, or death itself . . . a great release of power for good should be expected to follow."[121] There is a sense of imminent reward and the expectation that favors will be showered on those who give up what they value the most. Khadija, a woman activist in the movement, expressed her disappointment that none of her sons had yet honored her by their martyrdom.[122] Women Islamists were inclined to see themselves as mediators and agents of sacrifice. They embraced rather than opposed death in order to avert a greater calamity.[123] The "mother of Wasim Sharaf" gave thanks to God for choosing her son to be a martyr and felt that the sacrifice she made was immense.[124] She reflected that "one day is not enough to honor the mother" and referred to two Islamic hadiths embellishing the sacrifices of mothers. One hadith has it that the Prophet asked one of his companions to fulfill his sick mother's wish to perform pilgrimage by carrying her on his back to circumambulate the Ka'ba. The Prophet pointed out to him that his act would fulfill only a small part of what he owes his mother.[125] Wasim Sharaf's mother evoked another hadith from Imam Ja'far al-Sadiq: "A man asked the Prophet, 'To whom shall I be dutiful?' He replied: 'Towards your mother.' Then I asked: 'And to whom after her?' He said: 'Your Mother.' I asked: 'And then to whom?' He said: 'Your mother then your father then the closer in order of kin.'"[126]

By evoking these hadiths, Sharaf stressed her self-worth through motherhood and society's debt to her. Zeina Zaatari discusses the meanings given to motherhood by Islamist women in the Hizbullah Women's Association in the South. A mother's responsibilities, Um Mazen reflected, do not entail only caring for a child's body by making it healthy through food and clothing but also tending the child's soul.[127] In the magazine *Ajyal al-Mustafa* and on the website of al-Mahdi schools, the overwhelming majority of poems and essays dedicated to young martyred men were written by women relatives, teachers, and friends. Women have turned to the examples of Fatima al-Zahra' and her daughter, al-Sayyida Zaynab, to draw inspiration and meaning. They recount how Fatima and Zaynab experienced misfortune, injustice, and loss of loved ones at the hands of their enemies, thus emerging into primary female models of sacrifice and courage.[128]

Fatima al-Zahra' occupies a central role in Shi'ite tradition.[129] We are concerned here with the way Fatima, a woman considered pure and infallible, epitomizes the whole Imami line and its collective tragedy. In a popular hadith discussed by Fadlallah, the Prophet was so greatly moved by Fatima's devotion to him that "he anointed the motherhood in his daughter with the words: 'Fatima is the mother of her father.'"[130] Fatima becomes the symbolic mother of Prophet Muhammad and his nurturer who also shares in his authoritative spiritual role. Her sacrifices allow her to reverse history on the Day of Judgment, when God fulfills her wishes, which revolve around her son al-Husayn. In one hadith, Fatima is placed by God on a "high station" and given power to avenge the martyrdom of Imam Husayn. God will make the following announcement on the Day of Judgment: "Cast down your glances and lower your heads, so that Fatima (peace be upon her), daughter of Muhammad, peace be upon him and his progeny, crosses the Bridge (al-Sirat)." The hadith adds that "People will cast down their glances and then Fatima, peace be upon her, will arrive seated on one of the highbred animals of Paradise, followed by seventy thousand angels. Then she will occupy a noble post at one of the stations of the Day of Judgment, dismount, and take the blood-soiled shirt of al-Husayn b. 'Ali, peace be upon him, in her hands, saying: 'O Allah! This is the shirt of my son, and You know what was done to him.' An announcement from God Almighty, will reach her: 'Oh Fatima, you have my benediction.' She will say: 'Oh God, Help me take revenge from those who killed him.'" Eventually, God fulfills Fatima's wishes, then she enters Paradise, along with her descendants and the partisans of the Shi'ites accompanied by angels.[131] Many of the movement's women who lost their loved ones have asked whether they have "paid their debt" to Fatima, using the word waffaytu (pay a debt, fulfill an oath). The women evoke a silent oath "to compensate" for Fatima's losses as if these losses were their own. Past and present collapse in women's renewed sacrifices as they seek atonement for al-Husayn's martyrdom. When Fatima Yasin, the wife of Nasrallah, first knew that her son Hadi had been killed in combat, she looked up and said: "Have I fulfilled my debt to you, Oh Zahra'?" She and her husband explained that their martyred son will intercede on their behalf to the house of the Prophet, and they will receive God's benediction. When Batul Khatun, Hadi's fiancée, saw the image of his dead body on television, she cried: "Our path is martyrdom for [our] land and its liberation from the occupier." The women who came to Hadi's funeral congratulated his mother for attaining such honor.[132] A close look at these statements reveals that in times of crisis these women seek healing through the suppression of individual pain and personal loss. Embracing death and its emblems are also expected to bring benefits in the natural and social worlds.

Al-Sayyida Zaynab is respected for her sacrifices and for raising the children orphaned in Karbala'. She is also admired for her courage in bearing the loss of family members. Sana' Abu Zayd, a treasurer at al-Mahdi school in Tyre, considered Zaynab's persona immortal and hoped to be able to atone and "pay back" (*uwaffi*) what is rightly hers.[133] Zaynab, like Fatima, bore witness to the sacrifices made by Lebanese Shi'ite women whose children endured prison and torture and died fighting against Israel. Zaynab's chastisement of the Kufans for reneging on their promises to her brother, al-Husayn, also kindles in believers the fear of disgrace. The *hadith* narrates, "I saw Zaynab, the daughter of 'Ali, peace be upon them both, and I had never seen a more eloquent woman with her modesty, as if she uttered the speech of Imam 'Ali (her father) . . . She signaled to the people to be silent, so the breathing faded away and the voices hushed. Then she said: 'Praise be to God and His blessing on my grandfather, the messenger of God. Listen, Oh people of al-Kufa, people of betrayal and disgrace, may your tears never dry and your moans never cease."[134] Zaynab's admonitions were evoked to stress the shame and pain, which false promises and cowardice brought to the Kufans and must therefore be averted through perseverance in the face of death.

The culture of redemptive suffering and sacrifice troubled some women in the Islamist resistance. They questioned the tendency to normalize martyrdom and suppress a mother's experience of individual loss. Samar, an urban middle-class woman cautioned against encouraging the martyrdom of sons and objected to women's investment in it.[135] She argued that glorifying self-sacrifice sent the wrong message about the reality of Hizbullah. She insisted that the movement valued individual life and that self-sacrifice must occur when it is the only remaining option during war with Israel. Samar referred to a few other women in the movement who shared her thoughts and who tried to negotiate the norms of the resisting society. Like her, these women did not seem to facilitate acts of self-sacrifice, socially or symbolically. These sentiments were expressed by Islamist men also following the liberation of the South in 2000. Planned acts of martyrdom (or suicide missions) declined dramatically.

Summary

The public sphere the Islamists inhabited was not equidistant for all civil actors, for it privileged particular groups and discourses over others. This sphere, in particular the arenas populated by the Shi'ites, favored secular Communist and nationalist (Arab and Syrian) ideologies. The Shi'ite leftists in general and the Communists in particular shaped a range of artistic, cultural, and intellectual associations, posing a particular challenge to the early Islamists. The Islamists condemned the Communists' secularization efforts and their confidence in humans' limitless capacity to change nature and society. They confirmed instead the teleology that behind the human will to change reality is God's will and behind the strength of the "resisting society" lurks God's benediction. In the meantime, the Islamists' civic responsibility and trustworthiness placed them far above AMAL's members, and it was only a matter of time before thousands of Shi'ites turned to Hizbullah.

Discord and conflict between the Islamists and diverse civil actors enhanced the democratic propensities of the public sphere as much as negotiation and reasoning did.[136] Playing out conflict and dissension to the extent of using violence is seen in certain situations as a way to gain a firm place in civil society.[137] A case in point is the Islamists' armed clashes with AMAL, which encouraged collaboration between the former and an array of political and civil activists who denounced AMAL's shady dealings and aggression against the Palestinians in the camps. This picture, however, changed in connection to the sectarian framework of Lebanese politics, Hizbullah's alliance with AMAL in 2005, and the national and international threats to the *muqawama*. The Islamists relied increasingly on coercion and violence to protect the *muqawama*, which impaired the public sphere's democratic forces.

The Islamists in the movement and in Fadlallah's circles emerged in the early 1990s as organizers of civil space, negotiating new relations with diverse constituents in the public sphere. The thrust for self-sufficiency at Hizbullah's institutions and at Fadlallah's al-Mabarrat helped control the disruptions of globalized economic processes and ideas even if it did not avert them. Moral principles of piety and sacrifice were transmitted through an array of social and economic organizations, traversing the domains of education, labor, art, technology, and leisure. The public perception of the Islamists as God-fearing, upright, and self-sacrificing civilians fostered in turn the movement's ideological domination of the Shi'ites. In times of crisis, the Islamists were able to shore up the local civil resources for the movement. Time will tell, however, whether these moral principles will have the same command on the movement's recent members as they did on its early ones.

Islamist women transformed acts of worship from habitual rituals to a conscious exercise of piety through the body and the self. The public expression of purity rites and avoidance rules and the covering of the body and head became elaborate among Islamist women. The responsibility of earning God's favors devolved primarily to women in a social structure where men were economically, politically, and sexually dominant. Accepting and offering sacrifice, in particular self-sacrifice, became constitutive of piety for Islamist women who saw themselves part and parcel of the resistance movement. The sons the women sacrificed would recompense Fatima, the mother of Imam Husayn, "the Prince of Martyrs" and the *ahl al-bayt* for their losses and the usurpation of their rights. The relevance of sacrifice cannot be understood aside from the predicament of death, imprisonment, and displacement experienced by Shi'ites for more than two decades in connection to Israel's occupation of the South. These experiences recharged Shi'ite redemptive suffering and atonement for Imam

Husayn's martyrdom embellished in eschatological hadiths. The suppression of individual pain and personal loss for loved ones became a way to have some power over pain. By welcoming death and its symbols, Islamist women felt more assured of the benefits that God could release in their social and natural worlds. At the same time, some women openly questioned the enthusiasm for men's self-sacrifice and the responsibility that devolved to women in facilitating the fulfillment of that sacrifice.

The "culture" of sacrifice, however, was the center of controversy in the Lebanese public sphere and became the subject of negotiation among Islamist women. In the following chapter, this and other features of Islamist thought and practices in Lebanon will be assessed in connection to modernity and the nation-state.

8

The Islamists

Modernity and Predicament of the Nation-State

The national character of Hizbullah, its claims to modernity, and its relation to the nation-state have been the subject of much debate. Assessing these issues adequately requires a reconsideration of the theoretical frameworks and conceptual tools that guide our understanding of public religion and secularism in Islamic society. To this end, this chapter explores the role of the shari'a in shaping public religion in Hizullah's movement and its implications for modern citizenry and relations to the Lebanese state. Owing to the chapter's thematic concerns, our discussion does not follow a chronological organization but rather offers a general assessment of these themes over time.

This chapter presents Hizbullah's evolving association with the Lebanese state since 1992 as a series of "transactions" aimed at protecting the *muqawama* primarily and buttressing Shi'ite demands secondarily. It examines the development in Hizbullah's approach toward the Lebanese constitution and political sectarianism in its second manifesto (2009), juxtaposing Islamist theory on sectarianism with practical politics. It also revisits the relation of public religion to Islamic governance, articulated differently by Fadlallah and Hizbullah's leaders and thinkers. A prevailing tendency is to view *wilayat al-faqih* (the deputyship of a jurist) as the chief factor in determining Hizbullah's aspiration for an Islamic state, as well as its lack of national "loyalty." Our discussions shift the focus from *wilayat al-faqih* to the renewal of the shari'a and engagement with power, assessing how these features shaped the Islamists' relation to the nation-state.

Fadlallah and Hizbullah's advocacy of Islamic modernism deserves close attention. Islamists have treated jihad and *ijtihad* (rational legal inference) as resources of cultural renewal and modernism.[1] Jihad is a militant force used to achieve liberation from occupation and aspires to defend the Muslim holy places in Palestine. It is also considered a "civilizing" force, asserting the rights of Muslims to resist Western cultural domination. For the Islamists, jihad aims to subvert the structure of power in an international space dominated by American imperial interests. In addition, *ijtihad*, or legal inference using rational procedures, allows Shi'ite jurists to modernize society from within, relying on the Qur'an, the hadith, and the consensus of the *'ulama* (which reflects the Imams' views). This chapter investigates the discursive connections between Hizbullah's local modernity and Western universalistic elements of modernity. Despite its resistance to Western hegemonic norms, Hizbullah has refitted some of these norms to address its local needs. This local modernity nonetheless carries contradictory elements evident chiefly through the Islamists' relationship to the nation-state.

Finally, this chapter offers a biographical portrait of Sayyid Muhammad Husayn Fadlallah (d. 2010), a leading jurist and advocate of modernist Islam. It highlights his intellectual and political makeup and the historical forces that shaped his ideas on public Islam and its relation to modern society and the state. Facets of his discourse on political and his ethical reasoning are explored as well as his commitment to interreligious and intra-Islamic cooperation in Lebanon and the Arab world.

Public Religion and the Islamic State in Hizbullah's Discourse

Since the early 1990s, Hizbullah's leaders have publicly declared that the historical conditions for establishing an Islamic state in Lebanon are lacking and that they will not impose such a state by force.[2] Nizar Hamzeh suggested that this declaration was based on the multireligious character of Lebanese society, which makes it difficult for the Islamists to establish such a state. Hamzeh was careful to note that Hizbullah's participation in Parliament did not entail an end to the goal of establishing an Islamic state.[3] Indeed, Hizbullah did not alter its central view that Islam is a perpetual revolution against injustice and that the Islamic Iranian Republic established by Khomeini is the truest embodiment of that revolution. An Islamic state remains the ideal and legitimate form of governance as well as the ultimate basis for justice.[4] Hizbullah's second manifesto reiterated that the doctrinal dimensions of *wilayat al-faqih* do not prevent the Islamists from becoming integrated into Lebanon's national life and its political system. It pointed to the Islamists' participation in the parliamentary elections as evidence of such integration.[5] A close look at Hizbullah's declarations and manifestos in the past two decades, however, reveal the precarious link between its movement and the nation-state and hence fail to lend legitimacy to the state. Fadlallah was more explicit than Hizbullah in denying legitimacy to the Lebanese state, dissociating himself from the "un-Islamic" qualities that manifest themselves in this state's structure.[6]

Hizbullah's approach to Islamic governance and *wilayat al-faqih* during its formative period and beyond has been the subject of extensive debate. One group of scholars argued that the project of an Islamic state is ephemeral to the Lebanese Islamists today.[7] According to Joseph al-Agha, since 1992, "Hizbullah has put to rest, once and for all, the issue of the establishment or implementation of an Islamic state in Lebanon."[8] Lara Deeb noted that "many of Hizbullah's constituents" have said they do "not want to live in an Islamic state."[9] Be that as it may, no such assertion was given among the party's cadres or official members because it would entail a self-negation, a renunciation of a central component of Islamist thought and practice—namely, the shari'a's inextricable relation to power and governance. Another group of scholars considered the theory of *wilayat al-faqih* and Hizbullah's ties to Iran a breach of national loyalty to Lebanon and its state.[10] This view overlooks the local roots of Hizbullah, but more so the dilemma of Lebanese nationalism and the crisis of the state that existed prior to the rise of Hizbullah. Perhaps we do well to remind ourselves that the Islamists are not the first or last political activists to consider the Lebanese state an artificial or illegitimate entity. Various Syrian nationalist, Arab socialist, and Communist thinkers have articulated this position, but without justifying these positions on the basis of sacred textual sources, as Hizbullah has done.[11]

For the most part, studies on Hizbullah have rarely accounted for the implications of implementing the shari'a (or what has been conceived to be the shari'a) in modern society and how it shapes one's engagement with the state. The precariousness of the state, citizenry, and national identity are themes that run deep in Lebanon's modern history. The Islamists were not alone in attempting to find solutions to the dilemma of the postcolonial modern state in its sectarian-secular form. Indeed, a host of Arab socialist, Syrian nationalist, and Communist thinkers advocated a replacement of this state or a fundamental amelioration of its political system during different periods.[12] There are, however, major differences between these political groups and Hizbullah. The latter rejects secularism as the basis for modern governance and considers shari'a the basis for the regulation of a citizen's life. The restoration of the shari'a is a critical feature of public religion, according to Hizbullah, and is best reflected in the educational socialization of young Shi'ites at al-Mahdi schools and Islamist seminaries.[13] The Islamists, however, face a social world where secular processes have eliminated or suspended many domains of the shari'a. Moreover, the authority of the state and its secular legal framework, which incorporates Western civil codes, are antithetical to Shi'ite *ijtihad* and the authority of the jurists, especially the *maraji'*. As such, public religion and the ideal of Islamic governance undermine Hizbullah's commitment to the Lebanese state irrespective of whether Hizbullah continues to uphold the belief in the deputy-jurist or not.[14]

Scholars differ in their analysis of Hizbullah's "approval" of the Ta'if Accord and the party's participation in parliamentary elections in 1992. Some see Hizbullah's acknowledgement of the accord and its entry into the Parliament as signs of its Lebanization.[15] If "Lebanization" means that Hizbullah is not a tool of Iranian politics and that it has emerged from local realities and historical processes relevant to Lebanon, then, indeed, our study has substantiated this argument. But we are specifically concerned with one connotation of Hizbullah's Lebanization—its conformity to modern nationalist formations and compatibility with the nation-state. Roschanack Shaery-Eisenlohr argues that Hizbullah is profoundly concerned with shaping the nation and that its transnational performance promotes a particular experience of being Lebanese. She is correct to note that Hizbullah embellishes a particular vision of the Lebanese *watan*, homeland, which carries discursive ties with an Islamic *umma* (nation) and with Arab patriotism.[16] In its second manifesto, Hizbullah notably discussed the ancestral roots it maintains in Lebanon, its patriotic spirit in the defense of Lebanon's sovereignty, and the martyrdom of its children in liberating Lebanese land from occupation. Lebanon is the *watan* for Shi'ite Islamists, the ties to which are confirmed by the *muqawama* itself.[17] Notwithstanding this assertion, Hizbullah's "nation" is set apart from the nation-state itself and its secular delineations.[18] The fundamental challenge that public religion and the shari'a in particular poses to the nation-state makes it difficult to consider Hizbullah's members simply as one group of nationalists among many.

To understand Hizbullah's approach to the state, one needs to examine its interest in power and its shari'a-bound moral society. We can start with the significant statement made by Dr. 'Ali Fayyad, a prominent Hizbullah spokesman, that "faith," as the foundation of the Islamist movement, "needs illustration."[19] It is an active and introspective faith, but it must be outwardly professed and publicly enacted in the form of legal obligations.[20] The illustration is made through the application of the shari'a in the areas permitted so far by the state. For instance, shari'a cannot be applied in areas of commercial or criminal law, which are controlled by the state. Yet legal opinions on activities ranging from the performance of prayer to the treatment of infertility shape new patterns of sociability and public expectations among Islamist women and men. In addition, Hizbullah's public religion is tied to the *jihadi* culture of the *muqawama*, confirming the interconnection between society and political authority. An Islamic state is the ideal rubric for living morally and practicing justice, according to the Islamist vision of Hizbullah adapted from the writings of Khomeini and other Islamist ideologues.[21] Preoccupation with power is integral to Hizbullah, whether the head of the Islamic order is a jurist, a *marja'*, or someone who consults and coordinates with them.[22] As a consequence, the present commitment to *wilayat al-faqih* may not be a crucial factor in assessing Hizbullah's approach to modern governance. Shaykh Subhi al-Tufayli and Sayyid Muhammad Husayn Fadlallah are good examples of clerics who rejected *wilayat al-faqih* but continued to reject the Lebanese nation-state and find its secular-sectarian features illegitimate.[23]

The "Islamic state," as Norton suggests, might not carry today the same characteristics outlined originally in Hizbullah's first manifesto, the Open Letter of 1985.[24] It is unclear, though, what type of Islamic state Hizbullah's leaders would build if the opportunity arose. The refitting of shari'a into the rubric of the nation-state, some fear, would destroy the latter's modern foundations. One, however, can make the opposite argument as well—that the refitting of shari'a into the nation-state's rubric alters fundamentally the former because this rubric disentangles shari'a from a range of informal socioeconomic and moral considerations and aims to homogenize the law through codification. These processes are alien to shari'a's original "organic structure," to use Wael Hallaq's words.[25] Today, Sunnite and Shi'ite Islamist thinkers have advanced several ideas for wedding modern citizenry to Islamic government, which will inevitably change what we call "shari'a."[26] The state model that may be relevant to Hizbullah is that of the Islamic Republic of Iran where not all areas of politico-legal regulation have been Islamized.[27] Rigorous legal Islamization prevails in the area of criminal law in contrast to "the failure of effective Islamization of the Judiciary."[28] In other words, it is difficult to know what aspects of shari'a will be modified and adapted to the nation-state if Hizbullah were ever to push for an Islamic state and succeed. In the meantime, Hizbullah has made particular transactions with the Lebanese state that allow it to be an effective participant in national politics and to shape decisions relating to the Shi'ites and the *muqawama*. Central to these transactions are Hizbullah's consent to the Ta'if Accord, participation in elections, and, more recently, accommodation of the Lebanese constitution.

The historical and geopolitical events of the past decade made it clear that the Islamists' parliamentary politics and *jihadi* militancy against Israel reinforced each other. Hizbullah's deputies confronted government decisions that threatened the *muqawama* and Palestinian struggles in the Occupied Territories. The Islamists were quick to mobilize their members and allies to subvert the cabinet's decision to dismantle its communication network in 2008. Hizbullah insisted on the independence of the *muqawama*, preventing the subordination of its military forces to state institutions, especially the Lebanese army. Shaykh Muhammad Yazbik, a member of the party's Consultative Council, argued that Hizbullah's refusal to forfeit its autonomous military status and become integrated into the Lebanese state is justified by the state's "unjust" foundations and "ineptness"—that is, its inability to defend itself against Israel. Sayyid Nawwaf al-Musawi, the director of Hizbullah's foreign relations bureau explained that the party's political forces will also be integrated into the military resistance in order to thwart any Israeli assaults on the *muqawama*.[29]

The 2009 manifesto delivered by Sayyid Hasan Nasrallah denounced the Lebanese state's "undemocratic" features, its lack of sovereignty, and its weakness in the face of Israeli aggression. It maintained the need to modernize the Lebanese political system through practices of impartiality, equality, and professionalism.[30] This position resonated with the aspirations of leftists and reformist nationalists, but it did not appear to be significant to Hizbullah's short-range plans. For one, Hizbullah did not suggest ways to achieve this goal and opted for the preservation of the present electoral and constitutional system in order to protect the *muqawama*, which reigned supreme on its list of priorities. The *muqawama* is committed to "national Lebanese interests," the manifesto stated, but it is derived primarily from "faith in God, reliance on Him, and belonging to the umma," the Muslim "nation." The *muqawama*, the manifesto declared, rises against global monopolies and American military domination and becomes the agency through which a "strong, competent state" can be achieved in Lebanon.[31] Hizbullah asserted that the shortcomings of a weak state could be compensated for by the *muqawama*, which succeeded in coordinating its activities with the national army in recent years. In other words, Hizbullah's *jihadi* impetus, which faced a major dilemma after 2006, may end up checking the state if national and regional conditions threaten the *muqawama*. As a consequence, Hizbullah's manifesto sent two somewhat contradictory messages to the Lebanese people: first, that the *muqawama* could destabilize the state to protect itself, and, second, that participating in the state without challenging its modus operandi has the chance of protecting the *muqawama*.[32] Overall, Hizbullah's second manifesto created new transactions with the Lebanese state aimed at safeguarding the *muqawama*, which it described as a necessity "as long as the enemy threatens our lands [and] waters in the continued absence of a strong, competent state."[33]

Hizbullah and Sectarianism

In the 1990s, Hizbullah's thinkers argued that sectarianism is symptomatic of European colonial practices and must eventually be replaced by a just Islamic political system.[34] At the time, a number of Islamists were outspoken against sectarianism, supporting reform in Lebanese electoral laws, public administration, and civil service.[35] The opposition to political sectarianism, however, was closely tied to the rejection of Maronite sectarian privileges, as Amal Saad-Ghorayeb notes.[36] Prior to the Islamists, the Communists, the Nasserites, and the Syrian nationalists were at the forefront of political organizations demanding the elimination of sectarianism. The Islamists came to accept these groups' broad view that resources and political-administrative positions should not be divided on the basis of sect.[37] Yet the Islamists' insistence on shari'a as a source of state legislation and their opposition to secularism sets them apart from these other groups. Several Shi'ite Communists advocated secular change not only in electoral laws and political representation, but also in the area of family law.[38] For the Communists, secular reform relegated religious activities to a private domain where they cannot "encroach" on government legislation. The Communists also favored the creation of civil courts parallel to the personal-status courts, which rely on a small body of codified religious laws to regulate marriage, divorce, child custody, inheritance, gifts, and *waqf* (religious endowment). The Islamists, in contrast, rejected the displacement of personal-status laws from the broader framework of shari'a and have lamented the way these laws were reduced and codified to fit the nation-state's rubric.[39] During the French Mandate (1920–46), the personal-status courts replaced the Ottoman shari'a courts. Being "of no use to the colonial powers as a tool for domination," the Islamic law of personal status, Hallaq argued, along with Islamic rituals such as worship and ablution, were saved from elimination.[40] Yet the removal of the personal-status courts without establishing alternative shari'a-based courts would, in the Islamists' view, deal a death blow to the last legal institution where "God's law" can be applied. As a consequence, Hizbullah did not perceive these courts as sectarian or, for that matter, divisive, and so rejected attempts by the state or the secularists to diminish even further the role of shari'a in regulating society.[41] Much like the leading jurists in Najaf who denounced the secularization impetus of Qasim's government, Lebanese Islamists saw the courts as necessary to protect the Islamic basis of family law and the function of the clerics in modern society. The Communists, in contrast, considered a secular legal system the adequate basis for a democratic society that can remedy civil strife and violence. Many Communists accepted the preservation of the personal-status courts but demanded that civil courts be formed and accorded an equal status.[42]

With respect to the sectarian parceling of political power, Hizbullah's statements against it have not been followed by a persuasive plan for administrative and electoral reform. Moreover, there has grown around Hizbullah a group of supporters and allies since the early 2000s who insist on obtaining a percentage of administrative appointments and financial resources in the name of sectarian rights. Having been appeased by Hizbullah for providing it with partial Maronite support for the *muqawama*, Free Patriotic Movement leader Michel Aoun has pursued unhindered his sectarian bid for such appointments and resources. AMAL in turn openly reached for profit in the name of the "sect's share" when Hizbullah was occupied with the *muqawama*. After the Ta'if, Nabih Berri sought to increase the share of Shi'ites in posts and resources in accordance with their demographic size and to capitalize on their role in the liberation of the South. Most leftist intellectuals and civil activists whose public activity was impaired by sectarian practices condemned Hizbullah's alliance with AMAL. 'Abbas Baydun noted in 2005 that Hizbullah must take responsibility for watching the spread of "sectarian greed" without preventing it or implementing a program for economic and political reform. He highlighted the risk that the alliance with AMAL poses to civil society: "What will Hizbullah do with the Shi'ites now that it has become their leader par excellence? Will it continue an alliance with AMAL, which monopolizes and marginalizes public life and the intellectual elites? Will it give a free hand to the ally-enemy [AMAL] in various interests, services, and in the state?"[43] 'Abd al-Halim Fadlallah, vice president of Hizbullah's Consultative Center for Studies and Documentation, offered the party's approach to political and economic reform. He argued that the Islamists may support certain labor demands or amelioration of electoral laws in the direction of democratic change but they would avoid outlining a comprehensive and distinct reform plan.[44]

Hizbullah's second manifesto described sectarianism as an impediment to "democracy" and suggested forming a committee to assess it. Nasrallah did not shy away from adding, however, that the committee's decisions would not be binding to Hizbullah. As Nasrallah asked the Lebanese to be "realistic," he declared that "cancelling sectarianism in Lebanon is among the most difficult tasks." This made it clear that Hizbullah had officially renounced political reform. The manifesto then sketched a "wish list" of seventeen economic, political, and social features that Hizbullah hoped the Lebanese state would strive to attain. Among these features were a modern electoral system, an impartial and effective judicial system, and an economy that relies on public productive sectors, especially industry and agriculture, offering citizens educational and medical services and encouraging women's contribution to society.[45] Meanwhile, Hizbullah found "consensual democracy" with its "balance" of sectarian representation the best political format for the current period. With probably unconscious irony, Hizbullah evoked liberal Libanist positions, expressing its respect for diversity and "pluralism." Sectarian "balance," the manifesto noted, is legitimized by the "spirit of the Constitution," more specifically the Ta'if Accord. In retrospect, the new transactions formed by Hizbullah with the Lebanese state in 2009 were an attempt to please its own allies and appease the March 14 Bloc by maintaining the status quo with respect to sectarianism and the constitution. These transactions ultimately confirmed the priority of defending the *muqawama* over other political goals that Hizbullah outlined originally in the first manifesto. Indeed, since this manifesto, antisectarianism has not been a serious force in shaping the Islamist subject or in producing Islamist organizations devoted to finding resolutions to electoral, constitutional, and economic dilemmas.[46]

Modernism and Islamic Legal Renewal: Jihad and *Ijtihad*

Having accepted the Western universalistic norm of "progress," the Islamists rely on a rationalist (*usuli*) tradition of jurisprudence to translate "progress" and thus furnish their own local experiences of modernism.[47] *Ijtihad* is the cornerstone of this rationalist tradition that gives syllogistic reasoning and logic an important role in deriving the law.[48] Both Fadlallah's and Hizbullah's Islamists have made *ijtihad* integral to their modernist projects, allowing them to derive new legal rulings on diverse areas of human activity. This process, they argued, guaranteed the modern renewal of the shari'a and with it Islamic society but without recourse to Western models.[49] *Ijtihad* rests on categories of reason derived from Islamic legal and theological traditions.[50] Human reason, however, cannot arrive at final truths independently. It assists the jurist in finding God's law within the boundaries of the Qur'anic text, the Imams' traditions, and the consensus of the 'ulama' (which have to reflect the Imams' views). To prevent the repetition of time-honored practices or the blind emulation of past opinions, most of the Shi'ite jurists, including Fadlallah and Hizbullah's clerics, consider the legal opinions of a deceased *marja'* void.[51] This approach is antithetical to literalist and puritanical legal approaches known to the *salafis*. The believer must emulate the opinions of a living *marja'*. If the latter dies while the believer is emulating him, the believer may continue to follow his opinions. A believer is in principle free to decide whose opinion to follow and which legal injunction to uphold. According to Fadlallah, the believer can also choose partial sections of several injunctions belonging to more than one jurist. Some religious scholars, however, such as the late Sayyid Hasan al-Amin, were skeptical about the qualifications of Hizbullah's clerics to use *ijtihad* or issue legal injunctions on questions of worship, jihad, or family law. Sayyid Hasan rejected the "politicized" application of *ijtihad* and its wide and indiscriminate use in society. He suggested that it only served to foster the Islamists' hegemonic aims. With Hizbullah, he protested, legal rulings multiplied and found an expanding "market."[52]

Subjective elements relating to a jurist's sociopolitical leanings or his personal preferences are undoubtedly of consequence to the exercise of *ijtihad.* Fadlallah explained that the mujtahids do not study a particular legal case collectively or lay out shared findings to arrive at the most prob-able opinion.[53] Rather, *ijtihad* is a personal endeavor, and the mujtahid's opinions are not based on objective factors, but rather subjective ones. The way a mujtahid understands the text, be it a Qur'anic verse or a hadith, is shaped by the circumstances he lives through and his own convictions.[54] As a consequence, the mujtahids may produce legal opinions that favor or suppress women's control over marriage and divorce and others that may restrict or encourage integration of Christians and Jews in Islamic society at a given time.

It may seem odd to present defensive jihad as another feature of Islamist modernism. Yet Lebanese Islamist thinkers see liberation embodied by jihad as a necessary condition for becoming "modern."[55] The impetus for political freedom and self-determination through jihad was necessary in the past to confront Israel's military superiority and to challenge American imperial domination geopolitically and culturally.[56] Early on, the Islamists stressed jihad's sacred dimensions as a religious duty incumbent upon all Muslims not only to liberate the South from Israeli occupation, but also to defend al-Aqsa Mosque and Jerusalem. They rejected attempts to "Judaize" Jerusalem, force out its native Palestinians, both Muslim and Christian, and build Israeli settlements.[57]

The Islamists have also legitimized jihad as a revolutionary means to eliminate a "greedy" and "unjust" "imperial order," thus adapting features of Third Worldism and Arab leftist militancy.[58] Fadlallah objected to American policymakers' indiscriminate depiction of all *jihadi* movements as "terrorist." These policymakers, he argued, reveal their true intentions to "pull out all roots of resistance that live in the conscience of the Muslim peoples against the force of international hegemony that aims to confiscate the wealth of nations and their strategic positions."[59] Islamic jihad, he added, is a "civilized" method used by a group or nation to defend its vital interests, freedom, and independence.[60] In making this argument, Fadlallah aimed to link jihad to a modern discourse about civility—in particular, the individual's right to freedom and dignity. Most Islamists took up these arguments in order to defend militant struggle and even acts of martyrdom to end the Israeli occupation of the South.

Shi'ite jurists historically advanced diverse opinions on defensive jihad and its conditions during the absence of the Imam.[61] Hizbullah's leaders follow Sayyid 'Ali Khamenei's rulings on jihad in his capacity as the deputy of the Hidden Imam. A concise work by Khamenei, *The Elements of Jihad in the Lives of the Imams*, emphasizes perseverance against adversity, steadfastness in faith, and revolt against one's enemies.[62] In principle, if Khamenei issues a fatwa calling for a jihad, it is incumbent upon Hizbullah's members to partake in it, and it can extend to both men and women. Young Shi'ites who are younger than the legal age and whose parents do not consent to their participation in jihad can undertake it without their permission. Khamenei seems to legitimize jihad for defensive purposes and the liberation of Muslim land from occupiers. He also stresses economic forms of jihad such as boycotting American products and companies that support Israel or undermine the welfare of Muslims. Khamenei explains that such boycotts are incumbent upon Muslims as long as they do not jeopardize one's life, health, or livelihood. Moreover, if one is in doubt as to whether particular American and international companies support the Israeli economy, then one is not under obligation to boycott them.

Hizbullah's Local Modernity: Unsettled Questions

Unresolved tensions in Hizbullah's local modernity are manifested through the renewal of shari'a in Lebanese society and the theoretical commitment to Islamic governance. We already discussed the conflict that exists between modern codified secular laws and shari'a. This conflict sets the nation-state, one of the hallmarks of modernity, apart from ideal forms of Islamic governance suggested by Khomeini and Muhammad Baqir al-Sadr, among others. As we illustrate in this section, this conflict expresses not only a protest against Western modernism, but also a subtle "longing" for a premodern world in which what we call "religion" was inseparable from the political, social, and economic organization of society.

Lara Deeb convincingly shows that Shi'ite Islamist women in Lebanon are seriously engaged with modernity. She argues, however, that this "modern-ness" must be understood separately from Western experiences of modernism. Scholars must focus on what "modern-ness" connotes to the Islamists instead of on whether "pious Shi'is" select or reject "aspects of a universalizing Western modernity" or if they do either.[63] The problem with this suggestion, however, is that Western modernity is a main point of reference for Islamist modernism. The universalistic norms of Western modernity are of consequence to the Islamists' own discourse and "semantics" about modernity and its manifestations.[64] A case in point is the discourse and even the lexicon that Fadlallah utilized in calling for "an enlightened Islamic thought open to the reality of modernism and even to the reality of modernity."[65] The popularity of Fadlallah's "liberal" legal fatwas among Hizbullah's women shows that it is difficult to sanitize the Islamist sphere by getting rid of globalized discourses of Western modernism including liberal feminism. The "West" is present in the Islamists' reasoning about modernism, particularly because the Islamists have from the moment of their inception been part of a *muqawama* against American hegemony and the Israeli occupation.[66] This struggle is considered part of the constitution of the modern Muslim. To what extent do these practices and views succeed in producing a coherent Islamic modernism? The discussion here tries to provide answers to this question.

Jose Casanova argues that public (nonprivatized) religion is not a threat to modernity but can enhance it depending on the type of public arrangement, ideas, and practices issued by the religion in question. He questions the assumption that secularization (as it is generally defined) is essential for the constitution of modern democratic societies.[67] Talal Asad points out however, that Casanova's analysis ignores the way modern "national societies" have been predicated on secular formations. He correctly notes that secularism is an essential feature of the modern nation-state. The removal of the secularization thesis, considered integral to modernity, can in fact impede the realization of modernity. For the Islamists in Lebanon, shari'a's relevance extends to various domains of social and economic activity, legal regulation, and educational philosophy. The modern state, in comparison, aims to privatize religion and prevent clerical authority from shaping decisions about the economy, justice, defense, domestic policies, and political administration. Asad accurately argues that for advocates of public religion, "the principle of structural differentiation—according to which religion, economy, education and science are located in autonomous social spaces—no longer holds."[68] The "restoration" of shari'a resolves part of the alienation felt toward the Lebanese nation-state, but in the long term it removes the Islamists further from the operation of the modern state, legally and administratively. This removal is more significant given that the Islamists have agreed to a particular interface with the state but do not consider it just or legitimate. In this respect, Hizbullah's unease with the nation-state and its secularized apparatus is an "antimodern" feature—and by "antimodern" we simply mean nostalgia for a past disrupted by processes of modernity. Hizbullah's "citizens" have as such an ambiguous relationship to the modern state.[69] To make things even more complicated, Hizbullah's movement has also expressed dispersed postmodern sensibilities.

Hizbullah's thinkers have contributed indirectly to postmodern critiques of modernity. Postmodernist theorists have stressed the interconnections rather than the "radical break" between modernism and postmodernism and ways in which some of modernist attitudes and sensibilities have been integrated into postmodernist thought.[70] When looking at Hizbullah, it is useful to keep these interconnections in mind. Postmodernists challenged the West's proclaimed progression toward democracy and freedom and attacked its geocultural exclusivism. Like postmodern critics, Islamist thinkers express their disappointment with Western modernity and argue that Western democracy promised an equality and happiness it could not deliver.[71] The Islamists in general stress the moral failure of the Enlightenment and the inability of scientific knowledge, divorced from God, to improve the human condition.[72] David Harvey, a social theorist, considered contradictions within capitalism responsible for producing postmodernist attitudes and sensibilities. He underscored the dilemma of "the Enlightenment affirmation of 'self without God'," which, "in the end negated itself because reason, a means, was left, in the absence of God's truth, without any spiritual or moral goal."[73]

Like postmodernists, the Islamists challenged Western humanism's repudiation of religion and questioned the emancipatory role it accorded to reason.[74] Hizbullah's thinkers stressed the inseparability of reason from God as the source of truth and meaning.[75] They considered the limitations placed on "reason" necessary to maintain a pious life and social harmony. Yet, the Islamists, unlike the postmodernists, affirm a set of ultimate truths and defend them. Therefore, they consider it necessary to intervene and regulate religious belief in society. Shaykh Mustafa Qasir, the director of Hizbullah's schools, argued that Muslim believers should resort to "the method of intellectual dialogue" to convert atheists to believers. "Reason," he argues, is common to all human beings, and Islam aims to help them "reach the Truth and become bonded with the Truth, nothing more." Qasir, like other Islamists, includes a range of attitudes under the label *atheist*, such as a lack of belief in God or the Qur'an or both and rejection of Islamic religious observances. He notes that an atheist should be assisted in realizing the veracity of Islamic beliefs through reasoning and the establishment of proofs "in an atmosphere of intellectual freedom." Reasoning, however, should be replaced by force if the atheist in question becomes "oppressive" or tries to advocate her or his views publicly.[76] It is unclear, though, how or when an atheist's acts are deemed oppressive. The use of force against the *atheists* is considered a legitimate part of the self-regulatory features of an Islamist society. The use of reason is thus ultimately tied to the justification and implementation of final religious truths.

The Islamists have not challenged capitalism per se, but they have resisted *"al-istikbar al-'alami," "*international hegemony" or "global arrogance," denoting the broad cultural and political domination shaped by late capitalism.[77] Hizbullah confronted American imperial policies and defied Israeli plans in the South joining other international movements of antisystemic dimensions.[78] Hizbullah can also be seen making a localized attack on systems of domination. All these features carry a postmodern element, but they are not sufficient to make Hizbullah a postmodern movement.[79] Postmodernism avoids metanarratives and metatheories of both a secular and a religious nature. The Islamists, however, accept a moral and political metanarrative that underscores Islam's "essential" and "superior" qualities. Islamism is held together by universal and transcendent truths that promise salvation to Muslims and freedom from Western domination.[80] In retrospect, Hizbullah's movement has engaged with modernity rather than approaching it superficially. At the same time, though, it carries subtle "antimodern" and postmodern features that disclose its unresolved tensions with modernity.

Muhammad Husayn Fadlallah:
Resistance and the Power of Juristic Reasoning

Sayyid Muhammad Husayn Fadlallah (d. 2010) occupied an important place in the Lebanese Islamist movement. His scholarly training and political leadership provide insights into the experiences and intellectual resources of early Iraqi and Lebanese Islamists. The roots of Fadlallah's Islamism can be sought primarily in the sociopolitical and intellectual milieu of Najaf, where he lived for three decades, and secondarily in the South, which he visited intermittently in the 1950s, and in Beirut, to where he moved permanently in 1966.

Fadlallah was born in Najaf in 1936 to a Lebanese Shi'ite family from the village of 'Aynatha in the South that cultivated the Islamic legal-religious sciences.[81] Around the age of fifteen or sixteen, Fadlallah was reading Marxist works and participating in discussions about colonialism, secularism, and Islamic tradition with Iraqi intellectuals. He was also introduced to diverse Arab nationalist ideas through the Iraqi newspaper *al-Ahali*.[82] His preliminary readings on dialectical materialism and historical materialism shaped a particular view of Islamic history.[83] Indeed, his public conversations reveal his use of Hegelian dialectic as well as Marxist concepts, not the least through his explanation that to transform society one has to move "against the current where reality flows."[84] Marx discussed the "radical negation of social reality" by the proletariat, who breach this reality and try to substitute another for it.[85] Marx's idea that change is an inevitable part of reality is expressed in Fadlallah's reference to *"harakiyyat al-waqi'"* (perpetual transformation of reality) and the necessity of reshaping Islamic legal and doctrinal positions accordingly.[86] For Fadlallah, however, changing reality happens primarily at the level of ideas, as in Hegel's "power of thought," before change occurs at the economic and political levels. Yet one can also argue that Fadlallah's commitment to providing critical economic and educational services for the poor reveals the importance he and other early Islamists placed on converting the lower classes to political Islam.

In a visit to southern Lebanon in 1952, Fadlallah met a host of nationalist and leftist thinkers, but he singled out Husayn Muroeh, an acquaintance from Najaf of whom he had a high opinion. Muroeh's Marxist study of Islamic traditions possibly provided Fadlallah with a postcolonial leftist line of reasoning and a linguistic arsenal to speak about revolutionary Islam. Fadlallah considered himself "an Islamist" at heart, but he continued to engage with Arab secular ideological currents.[87] The breadth of his intellectual inquiries and political concerns were nurtured within and outside Najaf's seminary. Discussions about Arab poetic and literary transformation shaped his thinking about modernity, as they had done to Communist thinkers. During his days as a seminary student, he wrote poems under the pen name "Najaf's Son" and "Abu 'Ali," lest the seminary scholars consider him a flimsy student unfit for clerical life.[88] He excelled, however, in his legal studies, receiving solid training at the hands of prominent jurists such as Muhsin al-Hakim (d. 1970) and Abu al-Qasim al-Khu'i (d. 1992).

Fadlallah was closely mentored by Muhammad Baqir al-Sadr and eventually joined the Da'wa Party.[89] He shared al-Sadr's view that the clerical hierarchy needed radical restructuring to create an organic link between the seminary as the site of legal expertise and the marja'iyya as a public spiritual-political post. Like the early founders of Hizbullah, Fadlallah denounced the indifference of the conventional maraji' to the social concerns of common believers and the political turmoil in Shi'ite society.[90] The 'ulama's aversion to political activism, Fadlallah argued, forced the Shi'ites to succumb to the political and cultural arrangements of Western imperialism.[91] To counteract these historical forces, the marja'iyya must organize multiple tasks of juridical leadership, political negotiation, and administration of the seminaries at the national and international levels.[92] Fadlallah accepted the theoretical link between the marja'iyya and the seat of executive political power, the wilaya or niyaba (deputy of the Imam). Yet he rejected any coercive role for the Iranian state in joining the two together.[93]

Fadlallah moved from Najaf to al-Nab'a in Beirut's suburbs in 1966 after an invitation from the founders of the Islamist organization

Fraternity Home (Usrat al-Ta'akhi). Shortly thereafter he established the Legal Islamic Seminary (al-Ma'had al-Shar'i al-Islami) in Beirut, in Harat Hurayk, which featured a short but condensed program of religious-legal studies and political instruction. The teacher-student bond was a decisive factor in shaping the students' Islamist orientation. Fadlallah's lectures about the revolutionary capacity of Shi'ism caught the attention of young displaced Shi'ites, in particular southerners radicalized by economic grievances, political instability, and marginality. His reputation rapidly grew among lower-class Shi'ites through the founding of Jam'iyyat al-Mabarrat al-Khayriyya, which included nine orphanages, fifteen schools, six vocational academies, four hospital centers and clinics, a school for the handicapped, and around forty cultural and religious centers.[94]

In 1976, a year after the outbreak of the civil war, Fadlallah was forced to leave al-Nab'a, first to al-Ghubayri and later to Bir al-'Abd in Beirut. In Bir al-'Abd, he built the University of al-Imam al-Rida and a mosque connected to it.[95] A number of students who came to study with Fadlallah had insecure livelihoods and changed homes a few times owing to the devastations of the civil war and Israeli attacks on the South. To these students and early followers, Fadlallah expressed his dismay that Islam had turned into a set of customary rituals devoid of inner meaning. Rituals must be consciously performed and charged with spiritual intent and salvific experience.[96] Despite the weight the Islamists gave to religious-legal knowledge, Fadlallah also stressed the import of secular knowledge in fields such as modern education, psychology, science, and technology.

Whereas Sayyid Musa al-Sadr's movement was critical to Nasrallah's formation as an Islamist, Fadlallah saw it as an impediment to Islamic revolutionary change. He contested the role of the Supreme Islamic Shi'ite Council established through Sayyid Musa's efforts and questioned its ability to fulfill modern-day Shi'ites' aspirations. After Sayyid Musa's disappearance, Fadlallah strove to convert AMAL's members to Islamism in coordination with the Da'wa Party.[97] Meanwhile, a group of Fadlallah's students who formed the organization Muslim Student Union (Ittihad al-Talaba al-Muslimin) became the nucleus of the Lebanese branch of the Da'wa Party and participated in the *muqawama* against Israel. In order to preserve Islamist unity in Lebanon and buttress the struggle against

Israel, however, Fadlallah dissolved the Muslim Student Union and asked its members to join Hizbullah.[98]

Fadlallah had originally admired Khomeini's struggle against the shah in Iran and welcomed his doctrinal modifications to classical Imamate theory through the post of *wilayat al-faqih*. A few years after Khomeini's death, however, Fadlallah raised doubts about the adequacy of the comprehensive political authority extended to the jurist.[99] He denied that it could be supported by textual or rational legal proofs. He also argued that the assertions made by Khamenei and a few others about the deputy-jurist's comprehensive authority were also illegitimate.[100] He insisted that the jurist can act as the deputy of the Imam only in a specific legal capacity, such as in controlling the affairs of children under the legal age or the mentally impaired. Therefore, a specific and more limited type of deputyship is well supported by reference to the Shi'ite scriptural sources. At the same time, Fadlallah argued that the political system under which Muslim believers live should not be "un-Islamic." The jurists are consequently expected to shape a wider sphere of political relations and ideas.[101] Indeed, the centrality of the jurist for the spiritual and sociopolitical management of Shi'ite society is unmistakable in Fadlallah's legal works.[102] The deputy-jurist is thus designated by the hidden Imam to guide the believers through the performance of worship rituals and fulfillment of certain political obligations.

Like several members of the Da'wa Party who fled Iraq to Iran following the assassination of Baqir al-Sadr in 1980, Fadlallah became increasingly estranged from the Iranian government.[103] In his exchanges with Iranian officials, he maintained a particular understanding of public religion as a modernizing force that needs to be fitted to the Lebanese context.[104] In 1995, following Fadlallah's official designation as a *marja'* and Khamenei's objection to it, Fadlallah attacked the Iranian government openly, which in turn strained his relationship with Hizbullah.[105] Fadlallah occasionally cautioned Hizbullah's leaders against losing sight of the intricacies of Lebanese politics in their support of Iranian policies.[106] Despite their differences on theoretical and practical questions, however, Fadlallah and Hizbullah remained allies through their shared responsibility in defending public religion and the *muqawama* against Israel. Like

Hizbullah, Fadlallah declared that the historical conditions for the establishment of an Islamic state were lacking, in particular because Lebanon's multireligious composition.[107]

As a jurist and an activist, Fadlallah was thoroughly concerned with power and spoke relentlessly about the capacity of shari'a to produce modern law and organize society efficiently. Fadlallah suggested that the just rule (al-hukm al-'adil) of the Imam was lacking in the modern nation-state and contrasted a just (Islamic) government with the Lebanese sectarian one. A fair representation of Christians and Jews, Fadlallah argued, is naturally built into the structure of an Islamic society governed by shari'a. By having to acknowledge the earlier two monotheistic religions, Christianity and Judaism, Islamic legislation addressed the rights of non-Muslims and organized the Muslims' relations with them.[108] Fadlallah placed much hope in a "modern democratic" Islam whose advocates would accept diversity and adversity in the public sphere.[109] He thus drew the boundaries of an Islamic society widely, including secularists and heterodox Muslims as members of this society.[110] In his view, a modern Islamic system with renewed laws and practices is superior to the Lebanese state because it guarantees respect for all groups and their faiths. At the same time, Fadlallah feared that an Islamic state might flounder and fail owing to dissension among Islamist leaders or to a "Salafi mindset," which he explained as a tendency to resist cultural renewal and follow time-honored legal practices.[111] He accused a number of "Iranian jurists" in Qom of "Salafism". Fadlallah's disillusionment with the Iranian government may have led him to propose multiple models for an Islamic "state" or "project" instead of just one. Islamist goals can be more realistically fulfilled under diverse rubrics, he argued.[112] He also welcomed the formation of an international Islamic council whose decisions can be accepted and implemented by various Muslim constituencies.[113]

The Palestinian question played a far greater role in Fadlallah's Islamist thought than in Baqir al-Sadr's.[114] Fadlallah was in this respect much like Nasrallah, whose advocacy of public religion was intertwined with the muqawama against Israel and Western ideological justification for its establishment.[115] Fadlallah maintained confidently that armed struggle against Israel is a process of self-liberation that at times involved attacks on Jews who occupy Arab land or houses unlawfully.[116] The Palestinian crisis caused by the alliance between Zionist colonialism and Western imperialism, he proclaimed, threatened the integrity and development of Islamic society.[117] He urged Shi'ite and Sunnite leaders to unite against the alliance between Israel and Western powers: "Palestine forced us [Shi'ites and Sunnites] to stand behind it in Islamic unity. [I ask you to] be objective, to be Qur'anian. Are we going to reckon to the enemy rather than to each other in order to save the Muslim situation? Or are we going to provoke Shi'ite mistrust and instruct Shi'ites about the blasphemy of the Sunnites or raise Sunnite mistrust and instruct the Sunnites about the blasphemy of Shi'ites? [If we do so,] the hegemonic imperial order will laugh [at us]."[118] All peace treaties with Israel, he said, must be rejected given the humiliating conditions of such treaties for the Palestinians.[119]

Fadlallah firmly believed that radical Islamic action was essential in an international space dominated by American hegemonic policies.[120] "The downtrodden" appear to be those Muslims subdued by the "West" and forced to live without control over their livelihood or culture.[121] In the last decade of his life, Fadlallah revisited the Islam-West binarism that had distinguished his previous political discussions. He revisited the "clash of civilizations" discourse, which several Islamist and Western thinkers evoked to account for the adversarial relationship between modern Muslims and the "West." The West, however, cannot be reduced to the totality of its governments and their policies in the Middle East, he declared plainly. Many people in Western countries have protested against their leaders and denounced their foreign policies at political and intellectual forums.[122] In a curious twist, Fadlallah cautioned against arousing unnecessarily the Muslims' hostility toward the West and stressed the "West"'s interconnections with the "East."

With respect to his legal authority and juridical leadership, Fadlallah was known to give rational proofs based on *ijtihad* a greater weight in furnishing his rulings than Imami reports (*riwayat*).[123] He incurred both anger and admiration for a range of bold legal injunctions.[124] For instance, he argued that the *marja'* does not have to be the most learned jurist and that the believer can emulate more than one jurist on any matter she or he chooses. Fadlallah also argued that a woman can become a *marjaʿ* and that humans are in general pure whether they are believers or infidels, Muslims or non-Muslims.[125] Two broad groups of ʿulama, one Wahhabi Salafi and another Shiʿite, have written refutations of Fadlallah's legal fatwas or accused him of outright heresy.[126] The Wahhabi clerics rarely engaged in serious legal debate with Fadlallah, reverting instead to their customary denial of the legitimacy of Imami beliefs.[127] They simply declared "un-Islamic" all of Fadlallah's legal opinions on questions such as purity (*tahara*) and marital relations. The second group of polemicists made up of Iranian clerics were outraged by Fadlallah's assertion that the hadiths describing the violence inflicted by the Caliph ʿUmar on Fatima are weak. These clerics furnished multiple refutations of Fadlallah's position, supporting them with scriptural texts. Shaykh Yasir al-Habib, a contentious Shiʿite cleric from Kuwait, directed yet another criticism at Fadlallah. He counted him among the Batriyya Shiʿites, a group of Zaydis who combined loyalty to Imam ʿAli with clemency toward his enemies, the first two caliphs and ʿAʾisha.[128] The intraclerical controversy surrounding Fadlallah made his role as a *marjaʿ* and leader for thousands of Lebanese Shiʿites all the more significant. Today he is remembered as an unrivaled thinker, a broad-minded politician, and an affable discussant, striving to resolve discord in Islamic society through public discussion and compromise.[129]

Summary

This chapter investigated the interconnection between public religion and political power in Hizbullah's movement and its reservations toward the Lebanese nation-state and its secular apparatus.[130] Islamists saw secularism as a by-product of Western historical processes alien to Islamic society but assimilated by that society through colonialism. The Islamists "readmit" God into society as the One who creates and develops history and insist that humans be loyal first to Him.[131] Faith, however, is not abstract, and God is to be served through the shariʿa—that is, through public rites of worship and legal obligations. Without performing the rites and fulfilling these obligations, the Muslim's struggle against Israel and the imperial order would be impaired. Hizbullah's followers speak of rejoining human agency to God and giving religious morality a central role in the organization of modern life.

Applying and arranging the shari'a locally and privileging certain models of Islamic governance over the nation-state have significant implications for Shi'ite modern citizenry. Hizbullah's ideal vision of Islamic governance competes with that of the nation-state. Given the latter's centrality (with its secular origins) to modernism, Hizbullah's ambivalence toward the nation-state undermines its modernist assertions. Islamist theory deems the separation between religion and political authority artificial for Muslim society, especially since the shari'a in its premodern rubric embodies their unity. At the same time, the renewal of family law through *ijtihad*, a creative and multifaceted endeavor, pervades spheres of state legislation and the economy. This ultimately undermines the legitimacy and permanency of the nation-state in Islamist thought.

Neither studies that vilify Hizbullah for its lack of national loyalty nor those that ascertain its core nationalism have captured the complex nature of its performance as a civil *and* jihadist movement. On the one hand, tensions that the Islamists hold toward the modern nation-state do not cancel out their Lebanese patriotism or the way they reshaped national symbolisms. They have also stressed the importance of the homeland's security, sovereignty, and dignity. On the other hand, the Islamists are preoccupied with transforming the structure of power, of which the nation-state is a critical element. Hizbullah's statements relinquishing an Islamic state project do not agree with its principal interest in power. Whether Hizbullah revises its support for *wilayat al-faqih* or forfeits it completely does not change its aspiration for an Islamic system of governance (with a Shi'ite basis) and its view that this system alone is legitimate. In the meantime, Hizbullah continues to draw certain transactions with the state to maximize its control over decision making in the Parliament and the cabinet to protect the *muqawama*. Yet to abandon the idea of an Islamic state altogether or the jurist's role in shaping the state would negate the foundations of Hizbullah's thought.

The chapter also shed light on Hizbullah's theoretical and practical approaches toward sectarianism. In theory, Islamist ideology is antithetical to political sectarianism, which Islamists denounce as a Western neocolonial practice. Hizbullah has protested primarily against Maronite political hegemony and Shi'ite marginality as a function and malfunction of political sectarian "balance." In practice, it has inevitably used the sectarian rubric of parliamentary and national politics to empower itself. In a curious way, it took part in both the production and the repudiation of certain sectarian practices. Its emphasis on Islamist commitments created an important pull against political sectarianism, particularly during its confrontation with AMAL. Islamist ideology and the *muqawama* also enhanced new forms of Sunnite-Shi'ite unity in the South. Yet the strengthening of the alliance between Hizbullah and AMAL in 2005 was symptomatic of its increasing sectarian performance. The declarations made by Hizbullah against sectarianism in its second manifesto in 2009 were not accompanied by plans for political reform, such as the modification of electoral laws or the elimination of the sectarian distribution of jobs and administrative-political posts. Moreover, one area of sectarian performance—namely, the personal-status courts—overlapped with public religion and hence need to be preserved. The Islamists did not view the personal-status courts that presided over the regulation of family law as "sectarian" institutions but rather as religious ones. For the Islamists, the personal-status courts were the outcome of subjecting shari'a to the secular operation of the modern state. They thus hoped to expand shari'a's jurisdiction over society even beyond the courts' framework, an approach evident in public life, where Islamists were turning to their own clerics for guidance on religious observances and economic transactions.

Any account of the Islamists in Lebanon would be incomplete without a close look at their approach to modernity and the universalistic values of Western modernism. Fadlallah and Hizbullah's thinkers perceive *ijtihad* as the engine of legal modernity and socioeconomic progress achieved through Islamic traditions rather than through Western secular models. The *mujtahid*s on the whole, the Islamists argue, modernize society through new and diverse legal opinions on questions such as gender relations, women, labor, and religious plurality. Muslims applying *ijtihad* and applying themselves to jihad achieve a modern "moral" society—that is, one that lives by God's law. Fadlallah refashioned jihad as a modernizing force aiming to fulfill the human's "right" to freedom and equality, without which Muslim "progress" cannot be achieved. Islamists from different walks of life are conversant with the universalizing themes of Western modernity, both analyzing and critiquing them. Hizbullah's reinterpretation of Shi'ite doctrine and legal traditions became part of controlling disruptive forms of Western modernity and advancing a local one. In their espousal of modernism, Islamists place confidence in a distinct category of reason, one which is derived from Islamic legal and theological traditions. In Islamist epistemology, reason ascertains and is ascertained by metaphysical reality. Islamist intellectuals see the workings of a practical juridical rationality only within the boundaries of the Qur'an, the hadith, and consensus. The ability to reach certainty is always probabilistic and the Shi'ite jurist simply aims to get as close as possible to God's law through the use of reason. This practical rationality is capable of resolving the believers' needs and helping them fulfill their duties toward God.

In investigating Hizbullah's claims to modernity, this chapter argued that its modernity can be best described as a local modernity that creates its social aims and cultural themes by redefining modernist ideas of "progress" and "freedom." Yet because the secular features of the nation-state are integral to modernism, Hizbullah's predicament with modernity is not totally resolved. To make things more complicated, this subtle anti-modern element is coupled with a postmodern one—for instance, Hizbullah's militant struggle against systems of domination and its critique of the foundations of Western modernity. Yet neither of these elements is substantial or coherent enough to override Hizbullah's overall modernist character. To be sure, Hizbullah's Islamist project clings steadfastly to a narrative of certainty and universal truths that make it a stranger to postmodernism.

Finally, the chapter highlighted some of the complex questions surrounding Fadlallah's Islamist modernism and militancy. Like a host of southern Lebanese *talaba*, Fadlallah denounced the academic isolation of Najaf's seminary and joined intellectual arenas shaped by nationalist and Communist ideas. He adapted Marxist ideas of historical change and the Iraqi Communists' methods of argumentation even as he developed his Islamist critique of communism. He took part in organized political action against the Communists through Najaf's clerical movement and the Daʻwa Party. Equally important for Fadlallah's ideological formation was the Palestinian crisis and Israel's episodic attacks and occupation of South Lebanon. All these experiences played a major role in Fadlallah's radicalism and his view that physical and cultural struggle against Zionism is incumbent upon all Muslims. Although his approach to Israeli society and the Jews remained formulaic, his ideas about "the West" grew more nuanced over time. He revisited expressions of blind hostility to the "West" and came to state that its conflict with Islam is not "civilizational," stressing the interconnections and exchanges between them.

In Lebanon, Fadlallah emerged as a major benefactor and institutional leader through the foundation of welfare, educational, and civil institutions. He devoted much effort to legal-religious instruction and Islamist socialization at his own madrasas and seminaries. Even though he rejected *wilayat al-faqih*, he continued to stress the "organic" features of an Islamic system or systems of governance. Fadlallah discussed more openly than Hizbullah's thinkers the basis for the illegitimacy of the Lebanese state and underlined the ideal "democratic" features of an Islamic state or "project," as he referred to it. An Islamic political system, he proposed, is superior to the Lebanese state system because it safeguards the interests of all its subjects, including Christians. Fadlallah did not consider it essential for the jurist to assume political authority or for Muslims to conform to one model of Islamic rule. Notwithstanding these views, he did not rule out the possibility that an Islamic system of governance may fail if it were to become prey to rigid legal practices or enshrined customs that have lost their relevance to modern society. Fadlallah's Lebanese legacy is his ability to shape civil society and furnish a basis for shared public discourse on revolutionary Islam. He is also remembered for his moral reasoning in defending public Islam and upholding the *muqawama* against Israel. Even as he summoned Shiʻites and Sunnites to cast off their differences and embrace a basic "Qurʼanian" identity, he also created a civic Islamist rubric in which sectarian and doctrinal differences could be negotiated.

Conclusion

Of all the social groups and communities that formed Grand Liban, the colonial state created by the French in 1920, the Shi'ites, especially in the South, expressed the most persistent and militant rejection of this state. Southern peasants and workers suffered from the colonial parceling of Greater Syria between the British and the French, which impeded the flow of peoples, commodities, and social traditions between northern Palestine, Grand Liban, and Syrian cities. Militant Zionist activities also were felt more directly by the southerners than the rest of the Lebanese population. The French preferential treatment of the peoples of Mount Lebanon and Beirut was compounded by the establishment of a military administration in the south that enforced punitive taxes and coercive measures following the first revolt in 1920. With the reinstitution of the Régie tobacco monopoly, the southerners were again in open arms against the French in 1936.

This period witnessed the rise of a "youth culture" in the South that identified with peasants and advanced a local modernism against a good part of the nationalist elites whose interests were interdependent with French ones. The peasants, though forced to end Bint Jubayl's revolt in 1936, did not in fact "recognize" Grand Liban as their new homeland. The ambivalent end to the revolt and the pragmatic reasons for accepting Grand Liban only sparked a long and agonizing dispute over the place of the Shi'ites in Lebanon and the resources of their citizenry. Neither the Lebanese constitution nor its ideological justification at the hands of Libanist Maronite entrepreneurs created a commitment to the Lebanese state by the Shi'ite working and middle classes. Libanism was disconnected from 'Amili (southern) and Biqa'i experiences not only because it excluded the Shiʿites from its vision of Lebanon, but, more important, because it recapitulated neocolonial perceptions of Christian versus Muslim contributions to modernism. Among these perceptions were Muslim Shiʿites backwardness and Maronite civilizing agency in the Arab-Islamic region. To counteract these perceptions, the Shiʿite nationalist elites embraced modernism and laid claims to state leadership in the young Lebanese secular-sectarian state.

Colonialism, the modern state (national politics), social class, and provincial politics did not merely shape southern revolts but also debates over religious modernism and Islamic "reform." Since the late nineteenth century, the ʿulama had entered into a competitive relationship—unforeseen by them—with European educational models and legal codes, which deprived the shariʿa of efficacy and autonomous development. European cultural domination sanctioned universalizing ideas about modern progress that led southern thinkers to question the value of religious learning at the Shiʿite madrasas and seminaries. At the same time, they resisted the evolutionism inhering in the Enlightenment project, proposing a distinct temporality that validated renewal and conservation of tradition simultaneously. Islamic legal and philosophical traditions, they insisted, also hold secular knowledge and have a propensity for modernism through their emphasis on reason, scientific inquiry, and free will.

Out of this "indigenous" modernism emerged also religious Marxism. Localized readings of Marxism in southern Lebanon promised to resolve problems of labor, land, and agricultural deterioration attributed largely to the exploitative practices of the landed elites, capitalist processes, and governmental discrimination. Marxism evidently did not entail a formulaic adherence to Marxist theory or severance of ties with religious traditions. Communism in turn appeared to its broad public of sympathizers not merely as a program for economic equity and secular political reform, but also as a moral system—a system that reinforced Shiʿite notions of social justice, righteous governance, and revolutionary change. In this respect, local communism generated its particular forms of enchantment that competed with the metaphysical and ritualistic dimensions of the shariʿa that the ʿulama upheld. For this and later periods of Shiʿite Lebanese history, the complex interface between the sacred and the secular and their shared spaces challenges studies that continue to treat secular experiences and processes as simply the reverse of "the religious."

Rural disintegration in the South and the Biqaʿ during the 1950s and the 1960s led to antistate movements and leftist protests demanding political and economic change. The subsequent radicalization of the Shiʿites was further shaped by Palestinian activism in the South following the 1967 Arab-Israeli War. Many Shiʿites turned to secular ideologies—in particular, communism, Syrian nationalism, and Baʿthism—to resolve questions of state and society. A small group of Lebanese *talaba* and clerics, however, began challenging these ideologies, drawing inspiration from the Iraqi clerical movement led by the *marjaʿ*, Sayyid Muhsin al-Hakim in Najaf and Islamist thinkers. The clerical movement tried to renew the jurists' moral resources by diminishing the Communists' power inside Najaf's *hawza* and replenishing the *hawza*'s revenues, which the *ʿulama* depended on for producing and controlling religious-legal knowledge. Al-Hakim's combative *marjaʿiyya* became the nexus of sociolegal and spiritual authority, protecting aspects of public Islam from being eroded or taken over by the state.

Islamist jurists such as Baqir al-Sadr and Fadlallah aimed to go further than the clerical movement of al-Hakim. Their ideas had particular uses for a generation of Lebanese Islamists. These jurists sought to modernize Najaf's *hawza* and cast away its detachment from the political struggles of common Shiʿites. Juridical rationalism or *usulism*, the tradition from which Baqir al-Sadr emerged provided him with a legal methodology and resources for a local Islamic modernity that would compete with secular modernities. The shariʿa, in Baqir al-Sadr's view, allowed Muslims to reconcile economic needs with salvation and fulfill their duties toward God, whose worship is presented as the final source of happiness. Marxism was another force through and against which Baqir al-Sadr furnished public Islam and its revolutionary vision. His advocacy of Islamic "economics" bore the mark of a dialectical (and adversarial) relationship with Iraqi communism. The modernist Islamist arguments leveled against the Communists in Iraq, particularly Baqir al-Sadr's, had distinct uses for young Lebanese students and scholars experiencing a political-economic crisis at home. At the same time, these students and scholars drew upon Khomeinist revolutionary ideals to combat Israeli occupation in the South.

The Communists in Iraq strove to secularize economic relations, education, family law, and politics, which Najaf's jurists felt entitled to regulate through the shari'a. The Communist support for the issuance of the 1959 Code of Personal Status under Qasim fueled the anger of powerful jurists. This Code not only privatized religion further but threatened to make *ijtihad* marginal to the application and expansion of Shi'ite law. Najaf's powerful clerics who were allied to the large landholders also found Communist support for land redistribution threatening to their financial interests. An additional factor, however, turned these threats into a well-organized and militant clerical attack on Communist "atheism." This factor was Communist advocacy of a moral-social system that competed with the shari'a and spread out in the heart of Najaf. Shi'ite Communists embellished themes of revolt against tyranny, exploitation, and colonial domination by turning to local religious culture and Imami traditions. Broad leftist ideals were also affirmed through the veneration of Imam 'Ali, Imam Husayn, and exemplary pious Muslims. Some Communist intellectuals renewed their ties to Sufi and philosophical traditions as a counterforce to clericalism and the shari'a. Others turned to Western intellectual traditions for inspiration. Al-Hakim's and the Da'wa Party's campaigns against the Communists transformed the discourse of heresy into a militant program to remove communism from Iraqi society by force.

In southern Lebanon at the time, radicalization of thought and action was taking place in response to the specific conditions of political-economic crisis. Episodic Israeli attacks against the Palestinian-Lebanese resistance jeopardized southern security and impinged on the workers and peasants' economic stability. Unskilled and destitute Shi'ite migrants swarmed the eastern and southern suburbs of Beirut, forming with other disadvantaged groups the "belt of misery." During this period, the Shi'ite Communists attacked state apathy, and held Libanism and sectarianism responsible for the crisis. Their thrust to rationalize state bureaucracy and electoral laws was expressed in the public sphere's cultural, artistic, and political arenas. Religion was not ephemeral to these arenas but its shades and shadows were fitted to the secular framework of local leftism. For one, Imam Husayn's revolt against Yazid provided the richest and most fluid religious material for embellishing revolutionary struggle against Israeli oppression and American injustice. The looming victory of political Islam was hardly the outcome of reestablishing religious faith after an absence of such faith. Local leftist culture did not chase God and the spirits out of the life of common Shiʿites. Rather, it produced alternative sources of enchantment to public religion.

It is in this context that Sayyid Musa al-Sadr made his forceful appearance on the Lebanese scene in the early 1970s. He forged new links between Shiʿite clerical leadership and the state's semisecular apparatus. He facilitated the privatization of religion demanded by the state and gave the cleric the role, however ineffective, of turning the Shiʿites into loyal citizens. This modernist project as Sayyid Musa saw it was tied to the expansion of the Shiʿite business bourgeoisie whose ability to adopt the language of the state was undermined by state discrimination, Maronite hegemony, and the Shiʿite radical Left. Speaking the language of the state meant, among other things, justifying the sectarian system and fighting against the Left's proposition to replace it with a secularized one based on social equity and merit. Through the Supreme Islamic Shiʿite Council, Sayyid Musa excluded nonsectarian ways in which Shiʿites had already represented themselves—for instance, as civil activists, laborers, peasants, antistate clerics, and Arab nationalists. When Sayyid Musa realized that the Lebanese state was unwilling or incapable of rewarding Shiʿite national loyalty, he co-opted the Left's demands, launching his *mahrumin* (dispossessed) movement against the government in 1974. He also found himself organizing a militia for the security of the South against Israeli attacks. Given the rich history of Shiʿite anticolonial, nationalist, and leftist activism before this point, Sayyid Musa's *mahrumin* movement was hardly an "awakening" for the Shiʿites. The *mahrumin* movement came to have a life of its own that Sayyid Musa could not have predicted or controlled. It became a vehicle for promoting contradictory and overlapping streams: Lebanese nationalism, accommodation of the state, state reformism, Islamic leftism, and political Islam. These developments seem ironic given the fact that the *mahrumin* movement aimed initially at bargaining with the state to achieve concrete sectarian gains for the Shiʿites. The AMAL Party, which emerged from Sayyid Musa's militia, harnessed the aspirations of the middle-class entrepreneurial and commercial sectors, which demanded greater power in the state. With Sayyid Musa, then, we see a new modernist discourse centered on citizenry and conformity to the national state and its main secular-sectarian features. Therefore, it is crucial not to envision Sayyid Musa merely as the man of the shari'a and the Communists as antireligious secularists. Each side supported a distinct arrangement for religion and its place in civil society. In the postcolonial public sphere shaped by the leftists, the secular meant something specific and had to be derived from local conditions. The secular has always been connected to other forms of communal ideologies and religious experiences but it was a real option, not an illusion.

The outbreak of the Lebanese Civil War in 1975, a year after the *mahrumin* movement was launched, brought into sharper focus the crisis of the sectarian-secular state and its national justification. The Islamists of today's Hizbullah did not make their appearance, however, until the late 1980s, having adapted selective modernist and leftist revolutionary elements. The Islamists were fully prepared to refute the foundations of Western modernity, secularism, and communism. More importantly, they advocated a renewed commitment to the shari'a, reformulated the liberation movement in the South on Islamist grounds, and instituted a formidable network of social and economic services primarily for the benefit of the Shi'ite poor. Iranian funding was crucial for the establishment of this network.

The political calamity in the South entered a new phase with Israel's invasion of Lebanon in 1982. By 1985, and with U.S. complicity, Israel consolidated its occupation of a region stretching from southern Lebanon to western Biqa'. Israeli officers imprisoned, tortured, and killed resistance fighters with the aid of the Lebanese Southern Army. From the *husayni-yya*s, Islamist preachers marshaled the civil and militant resources of Shi'ite society, declaring that the Islamic resistance against Israel was a sacred duty incumbent upon all believers. Looking to resolve this crisis, young Shi'ites found Ayatollah Khomeini's defeat of the pro-American Iranian government of Reza Shah inspiring. They also drew new ties between the Palestinian tragedy and the displacement of southerners, stressing the spiritual value of revolt against the Israeli occupier and the collective rewards of self-sacrifice. Martyrdom elevated the status of the martyr, whose grace redeemed society and delivered justice. The Communists had their share of martyrs too, but they were slowly losing ground to the Islamists in civil arenas and political organizations. This resulted from the Communists' shortcomings, sectarian violence, and Syrian intervention against the Left. By the early 1990s, the Communists were discouraged from maintaining their role in the national liberation movement against the occupation.

The Shi'ite poor defined broadly as the politically subordinate Muslims formed the early base for Hizbullah. As the latter's representatives seized several parliamentary seats in 1992, the business and entrepreneurial Shi'ite classes saw an opportunity for greater political power through membership in Hizbullah. Meanwhile, men and women of Hizbullah's and Fadlallah's civil arenas emerged as pious, self-reliant believers who made sacrifices for the benefit of the "resisting society." Piety and sacrifice were confirmed by Qur'anic verses and Imami traditions, drawing the ethical boundaries of the resisting society. Experiences of loss, displacement, political subordination, and death grounded women's active piety during the struggle against Israeli occupation. Among women, acts of ritual ablution and public prayer ensured that norms of sexual purity were not transgressed and that the resisting society was collectively safe. Embracing death and its emblems was expected to bring rewards in the natural and social worlds. These realities reveal the subtle and complex ways in which political and economic forces have shaped public piety.

Hizbullah's ability to attract substantial Shi'ite following over the past two decades was in part a function of its adaptation to the democratic forces of the public sphere, its military successes against the occupation, and its efforts in social and economic aid. In many contexts, coercion and conflict are necessary for admission into the public sphere. Between the late 1980s and 2000, Islamist civil arenas brought a greater inclusion of marginal groups—in particular, displaced rural Shi'ites and lower-class advocates of public Islam. The Islamists drew links to groups both secular and religious that supported the Palestinian cause and the elimination of state corruption. The enthusiasm for Hizbullah in the public sphere was overwhelming at the eve of the liberation in 2000. This picture, however, began to change after 2005 with the onset of new social processes. Hizbullah's political agenda became more centered on the protection of the *muqa-wama* against mounting national and American-Israeli demands for the organization's dissolution. Hizbullah and AMAL agreed to a long-term alliance and with it a sectarian partnership in parliamentary elections that soon dominated Shi'ite representation and civil life. Major historical incidents, central to which was the assassination of Rafiq al-Hariri in 2005 and the use of armed force against civilian neighborhoods in 2008, alienated many of Hizbullah's enthusiasts.[1]

The defense of the *muqawama*, despite its importance, also diminished the hopes of civil activists that the Islamists want or are capable of reforming the government system, modifying electoral laws, and restructuring the economy. Hizbullah's interest in sociopolitical reform seemed largely rhetorical at this stage. In its second manifesto (2009), it restated its recognition of the Ta'if Accord, even evoking Libanist arguments in support of pluralism and consensual democracy based on a balance of sectarian representation. Hizbullah thus ultimately seeks to abide by the state's modus operandi as long as the state will accommodate the *muqawama*. The Islamists as such may continue to develop and change their transactions with the Lebanese state depending on the demands of the *muqa-wama* and their allies—namely, AMAL and the Free Patriotic Movement.

A final chapter in this book was devoted to the relationship of public Islam to modernism among Hizbullah's and Fadlallah's followers. Islamist thinkers challenged universalizing ideas of Western modernity as they defined and shaped their local modernity. They considered the use of *ijti-had* a vital medium for societal renewal and cultural advancement. Jihad, as a militant defense against Israel and a struggle against Western domination, also fulfills modern demands for human "freedom" and "progress." Despite the unique facets of Islamist modernism, it holds unresolved theoretical elements. For one thing, the Islamists' unease with the secular apparatus of the modern nation-state carries an antimodern element. The shari'a to which the Islamists resort for organizing this life and the hereafter contradicts the secular legal processes instituted by the modern state relating to family, education, defense, the economy, leisure and others. For another thing, the Islamists' critique of Western modernity converges partially with postmodern positions. On the one hand, the Islamists, much like postmodernists, confront a local system of domination and challenge the foundations of secular democracy and the alleged "triumph of reason" in human history. But inasmuch as the Islamists insist on final truths, that God and religious morality are ultimate sources of meaning and human happiness, they remain strangers to postmodernism. Islamist modernism therefore carries tensions and irreconcilable features that continue to develop in relationship to new historical conditions. There will undoubtedly be further experimentation with ideas derived from Shi'ite legal and doctrinal traditions and attempts to reconcile them with societal demands and secular procedures known to the modern state. Another historical stage will probably be shaped by future Shi'ite graduates from Hizbullah's schools and seminaries, who will produce yet another Islamic understanding of relations between power, modernism, and the shari'a.

Notes

Bibliography

Index

Notes

Prologue: Landscapes of Shi'ite Protest

1. The term *Shi'ite* as used in this book refers to the Twelver Shi'ites, whose origins and early history are briefly introduced in chapter 1.

2. Peter Gran, "Islamic Marxism in Comparative History: The Case of Lebanon, Reflection on the Recent Book of Husayn Muruwah," in *The Islamic Impulse*, ed. Barbara Freyer Stowasser (Washington, DC: Center for Contemporary Arab Studies, 1987), 109.

3. See Zaynab Isma'il, "Min al-Najaf ila Shaqra' tariq shi'r wa-thaqafa wa-din: kayfa kana al-intiqal wa-al-'awda min al-hawza al-diniyya ila al-hawza al-mariksiyya?" *al-Safir*, October 29, 2004.

4. Quoted in ibid.; all translations are ours unless otherwise noted.

5. See Faleh Abd al-Jabbar, *The Shi'ite Movement in Iraq* (London: Saqi, 2003), 133.

6. Hadi Fadlallah, *Muhammad Jawad: Fikr wa-islah* (Beirut: Dar al-Hadi, 1993), 381.

7. Al-Jabbar, *The Shi'ite Movement in Iraq*, 70–75.

8. Hanna Batatu, *The Old Social Classes and the Revolutionary Movements of Iraq: A Study of Iraq's Old Landed and Commercial Classes and of Its Communists, Ba'thists, and Free Officers* (Princeton, NJ: Princeton University Press, 1978), 694–95; al-Jabbar, *The Shi'ite Movement in Iraq*, 75–76, 79. See also 'Ali al-Kawrani al-'Amili, "*Al-Mawja al-shuyu'iyya allati 'asarnaha*," Mawqi' Samahat al-Shaykh 'Ali al-Kawrani al-'Amili, http://www.alameli.net/books/?id=3403; Hani Fahs, "Tullab al-Najaf al-lubnaniyyun," *al-Safir*, July 16, 1999.

9. Fahs, "Tullab al-Najaf al-lubnaniyyun."

10. Muhammad Husayn Fadlallah, *Al-Haraka al-islamiyya: Humum wa-qadaya* (Beirut: Dar al-Malak, 1990); Craig J. Calhoun and Joseph Gerteis, *Classical Sociological Theory*, 2nd ed. (Malden, MA: Blackwell, 2007), 77–78.

11. Muhammad Husayn Fadlallah, "Al-Shahid al-Sadr: Naqla naw'iyya fi 'alam al-fikr," *Muntadayat al-Adwa'*, August 4, 2009, http://184.172.176.53/~adwgtrh/showthread.php?p=156296.

12. Quoted in 'Ali al-Ibrahimi, "Hadi al-'Alawi wa-'Ali Shari'ati: Man minhuma fahima al-tarikh?" *al-Mitro*, July 27, 2009, http://www.almitro.com/09/2868.html.

219

13. 'Abbas Baydun, "Shadhra min sira siyasiyya: Aqni'at Lenin," *Bahithat* 4 (1997–98): 367.

14. In a conversation with Karim Baqradoni, Sayyid Musa noted this point. See Karim Baqradoni, *Al-Salam al-mafqud: 'Ahd Ilyas Sarkis, 1976–1982* (Beirut: Dar 'Abr al-Sharq li-al-Manshurat, 1984), 118.

15. Quoted in ibid., 424–25.

16. Talal Asad, *Formations of the Secular: Christianity, Islam, and Modernity* (Palo Alto, CA: Stanford University Press, 2003), 135.

17. Majed Halawi, *A Lebanon Defied: Musa al-Sadr and the Shi'a Community* (Boulder, CO: Westview Press, 1992), 144. For a more detailed account of Sayyid Musa's relationship to the Palestinians and the Iranian government, see Roschanack Shaery-Eisenlohr, *Shi'ite Lebanon: Transnational Religion and the Making of National Identities* (New York: Columbia University Press, 2008). See also Houchang E. Chehabi, "The Anti-shah Opposition and Lebanon," in *Distant Relations: Iran and Lebanon in the Last 500 Years*, ed. Houchang E. Chehabi (London: Centre for Lebanese Studies and I. B. Tauris, 2006), 182–85; and Houchang E. Chehabi, "Iran and Lebanon in the Revolutionary Decade," in Chehabi, ed., *Distant Relations*, 205–7.

18. Halawi, *A Lebanon Defied*, 89.

19. Ibid.

20. Hani Fahs, *Al-Shi'a wa-al-dawla fi Lubnan: Malamih fi al-ru'ya wa-al-dhakira* (Beirut: Dar al-Andalus, 1996), 36.

21. See Mahdi 'Amil, *Bahth fi asbab al-harb al-ahliyya fi Lubnan* (Beirut: Dar al-Farabi, 1979), 303–13.

22. See Mahdi 'Amil, *Fi al-dawla al-ta'ifiyya* (Beirut: Dar al-Farabi, 1986), 264–67.

23. Fahs, *Al-Shi'a wa-al-dawla fi Lubnan*, 36.

24. Ibid., 345.

25. Speech by Sayyid Hassan Nasrallah, October 18, 2006, at http://www.shiaweb.org/hizbullah. On martyrdom and "symbolic capital," see Joseph Alagha, "Hizbullah and Martyrdom," *Orient* 45, nos. 1–4 (2004): 54–55.

26. On the intensification of sectarianism, see Sayyid Muhammad Hassan al-Amin, "Hizbullah lam yastati' tahqiq tawazun al-ru'b ma'a Isra'il," *Al-Sharq Al-Awsat*, September 16, 2006, http://www.aawsat.com/details.asp?section=4&article=382997&issueno=10154.

27. Quoted in Najib Nur al-Din, *Al-Sayyid Muhammad Husayn Fadlallah: Umara' wa-qaba'il: khafaya wa-haqa'iq lubnaniyya* (Beirut: Riad El Rayess Books, 2001), 123.

28. Kais M. Firro, "Lebanese Nationalism versus Arabism: From Bulus Nujaym to Michel Chiha," *Middle Eastern Studies* 40, no. 5 (September 2004): 20–21; Michelle Hartman and Alessandro Olsaretti, "'The First Boat and the First Oar': Inventions of Lebanon in the Writings of Michel Chiha," *Radical History Review* 86, no. 1 (Spring 2003): 37–65. On early nationalist narratives, see Malek Abisaab, *Militant Women of a Fragile Nation* (Syracuse, NY: Syracuse University Press, 2010), 107–11.

29. Toufic K. Gaspar, *A Political Economy of Lebanon, 1948–2002: The Limits of Laissez-faire* (Leiden: Brill, 2004), 183–86.

30. Under the 1943 Lebanese Pact, the Maronites came to control the presidency and the military, the central bank, the judiciary, the Ministry of Information, the civil service, and the post of chair at the Lebanese University. The Sunnite bourgeoisie controlled the prime ministry. Legislative power was given to the Shi'ite landed bourgeoisie through the post of Parliament president. See Albert Mansur, *Al-Inqilab 'ala al-Ta'if* (Beirut: Dar al-Jadid, 1993), 46–47.

31. Leading Maronite thinkers stressed their cultural separation from the Near East and their natural ties to western Europe. See Muhammad Shuman, "Qira'a fi fikr Charles Malik wa-al-Kaslik: Al-'Unsuriyya bayna zuhurat al-kiyan wa-al-intihar," *Al-Tariq* 44, no. 3 (July 1985): 104–5. On the Shi'ites, see Rula Jurdi Abisaab, "Shi'ite Beginnings and Scholastic Tradition in Jabal 'Amil in Lebanon," *The Muslim World* 89, no. 1 (January 1999): 1–21; Shaery-Eisenlohr examines the function of certain ethnonationalist constructs in *Shi'ite Lebanon*, 11–13, 21–23.

32. Peter Gran, "The Failure of Social Theory to Keep Up with Our Times: The Study of Women and Structural Adjustment Programs in the Middle East as an Example." Paper presented at the 34th annual conference of the Association of Muslim Social Scientists, Temple University, September 30, 2005, 7–8.

33. Peter Gran, *Beyond Eurocentrism: A New View of Modern World History* (Syracuse, NY: Syracuse University Press, 1996), 193–94.

34. Ibid.

35. Suad Joseph discusses the nature and implications of kinship politics in Lebanon and its use by the state. The "kin contract," she writes, has been "the hidden civic myth in the gentlemen's agreement" underlying the Lebanese National Pact of 1943. Suad Joseph, "Civic Myths, Citizenship, and Gender in Lebanon," in *Gender and Citizenship in the Middle East*, ed. Suad Joseph (Syracuse, NY: Syracuse University Press, 2000), 135; see also 107–36.

36. Ussama Makdisi, *The Culture of Sectarianism: Community, History, and Violence in Nineteenth-Century Ottoman Lebanon* (Berkeley: University of California Press, 2000), 163–65; Ussama Makdisi, "Moving beyond Orientalist Fantasy, Sectarian Polemic, and Nationalist Denial," *International Journal of Middle Eastern Studies* 40, no. 4 (November 2008): 559–60.

37. Gran, *Beyond Eurocentrism*, 195.

38. Michael Young, *The Ghosts of Martyrs Square: An Eyewitness Account of Lebanon's Life Struggle* (New York: Simon & Schuster, 2010), 12. Young contrasted this liberalism with Hizbullah's "hegemony over Shiite minds and lives"; see also 113, 115. Nubar Hovespian argued that the culture of sectarianism "is the historically contingent moment when religious difference becomes accepted and imagined as the bedrock of a modern politics of equal representation." Nubar Hovespian, *The War on Lebanon: A Reader* (Charles City, VA: Olive Branch Press, 2008), 24.

39. See Max Weiss, *In the Shadow of Sectarianism: Law, Shi'ism, and the Making of Modern Lebanon* (Cambridge: Cambridge University Press, 2010), 17–19,124–25, 228–36.

40. Ibid., 15.

41. Ibid., 71, 120, 159, 204, 235.

42. The Ja'fari courts were established under the modern Iraqi state, which shared little if any of the sectarian makeup of the Lebanese state. Nonetheless, in the eyes of the Shi'ite religious leaders, the Personal Status Laws applied in these courts were hardly a victory. See J. N. D. Anderson, "A Draft Code of Personal Law for 'Iraq," *Bulletin of the School of Oriental and African Studies* 15, no. 1 (1953): 43. Following the state's drafting of the Code of Personal Law in 1947, the Ja'fari Court of Cassation argued that the provisions of the Code do "not conform to the correct precepts of the shari'a." Anderson noted that "the still more vehement opposition of the Ja'faris [to the Code] can be traced to the fact that they regard the Code as a direct infringement upon the prerogatives of those mujtahids whom their school still recognizes" (43). The fact that the Ja'fari *qadis* at the courts were not themselves *mujtahids* comprised another dimension of the conflict.

43. For example, these studies include Samir Khalaf, *Civil and Uncivil Violence: A History of the Internalization of Communal Conflict* (New York: Columbia University Press, 2002), esp. 262–63; Hovespian, *The War on Lebanon*; and Young, *The Ghosts of Martyrs Square*. For nuanced approaches to sectarianism, see Makdisi, *The Culture of Sectarianism*; Shaery-Eisenlohr, *Shi'ite Lebanon*; Lucia Volk, *Memorials and Martyrs in Modern Lebanon* (Bloomington: Indiana University Press, 2010), 20–24.

44. See Wael Hallaq, *An Introduction to Islamic Law* (Cambridge: Cambridge University Press, 2009), 115–16; Asad, *Formations of the Secular*, chapters 5 and 6; Ussama Makdisi, "Reconstructing the Nation-State: The Modernity of Sectarianism in Lebanon," *Middle East Report*, no. 200 (July–September 1996): 23, 26–30.

45. Malek Abisaab, "Syrian-Lebanese Communism and the National Question, 1924–1968" (Master's thesis, City College, City University of New York, 1992); Rony Gabbay, *Communism and Agrarian Reform in Iraq* (London: Croom Helm, 1978), 53–54.

46. Ibrahim al-Haydari, *Trajidiya Karbala': Sociolojiya al-khitab al-sha'bi li-al-'aza' al-husayni* (Beirut: Dar al-Saqi, 1999), 376; al-Jabbar, *The Shi'ite Movement*, 75–80; al-Amin Ahmad Gharbiyya, "Ahmad Gharbiyya," in *Min daftar al-dhikrayat al-janubiyya*, part 2, ed. al-Majlis al-Thaqafi li-Lubnan al-Janubi (Beirut: Al-Majlis al-Thaqafi li-Lubnan al-Janubi, 1984), 119–20; Fuad Kahil, "Fuad Kahil," in *Min daftar al-dhikrayat al-janubiyya*, part 2, 141–42, 158; Rashid Karmih, "Ila al-shuyu'iyyin al-karbala'iyyin," *Al-Hiwar Al-Mutamaddin*, January 3, 2007, http://www.ahewar.org/debat/show.art.asp?aid=89988; Rashid Karmih, "'Ashura' al-Husayn": Min wahi karnaval al-karbala'iyyin," part 1, *Al-Hiwar Al-Mutamaddin*, December 23, 2009, http://www.ahewar.org/debat/show.art.asp?aid=196458; 'Abd al-Shahid al-Thawr, "Al-Layla al-yatima fi al-dahr," in *Tajarib mawkibiyya fi sirat radud*, Muntada al-Sahil al-Sharqi, April 24, 2008, http://enjazat.maktoobblog.com/977248/22-.

47. Asad, *Formations of the Secular*, 15.

48. Ibid., 25–27, 84–85, 121–24.

49. Fadil Hassan, "Mawkib mahallat al-'Abbasiyya wa-sha'iruhu al-Shahid 'Abd al-Zahra al-Sa'di," *Iraqi Communist Party*, November 30, 2011, http://iraqicp.com/2010-11-21-17-19-16/10183-2011-11-30-20-03-36.html; Fadil Hassan, "Karbala': Al-Raddat al-husayniyya tatajawaz al-janib al-dini ila al-siyasi," *Wakalat Kurdistan li-al-Anba'*, March 12, 2011, http://www.aknews.com/ar/aknews/3/275945/; Sa'id al-'Udhari, "Baqat ward wa-qubulat li-al-shuyu'iyyin fi 'id tajammu'ihim; Min islamiyy mutashaddid," *Al-Nur* (Syrian Communist weekly), March 29, 2011, http://www.alnoor.se/article.asp?id=109775.

50. See Jose Casanova, "The Secular, Secularizations, Secularisms," in *Rethinking Secularism*, ed. Craig J. Calhoun, Mark Juergensmeyer, and Jonathan Van Antwerpen (Oxford: Oxford University Press, 2011), 55, 72–73; Charles Taylor, "Western Secularity," in *Rethinking Secularism*, ed. Calhoun, Juergensmeyer, and Van Antwerpen, 38–43, 51.

51. Some Communist intellectuals drew upon philosophical and Sufi traditions as alternative sources of spiritual authority. See 'Abd al-Razzaq Dahnun, "Thamani sanawat 'ijaf 'ala rahil Hadi al-'Alawi al-Baghdadi," *Al-Nur*, September 27, 2006.

52. Chibli Mallat, "Shi'ism and Sunnism in Iraq: Revisiting the Codes," in *Islamic Family Law*, ed. Chibli Mallat and Jane Frances Connors (London: Graham & Trotman, 1990), 71–92.

53. Georg Hegel, *Philosophy of History*, trans. J. Sibree (New York: Dover, 1956), 9–10.

54. Ibid., v, xiii, 56, 68–69, 103. Hegel writes that the "History of the World travels from East to West, for Europe is absolutely the end of History, Asia the beginning" (103). Despite the presence of several competing experiences of modernity in the West, the Hegelian discourse embodied for many the universalistic values of Western modernity. This discourse dominated Arab (including Lebanese) discussions of modernism, the state, and civil society.

55. Ibid., 104.

56. Ibid., 360.

57. See Teshale Tibebu, *Hegel and the Third World: The Making of Eurocentrism in World History* (Syracuse, NY: Syracuse University Press, 2011); Zachary Lockman, *Contending Visions of the Middle East: The History and Politics of Orientalism* (Cambridge: Cambridge University Press, 2004), 75–76; Gran, *Beyond Eurocentrism*, 2. For discussions of the "clash of civilizations" thesis, see Samuel Huntington, *The Clash of Civilizations and Remaking of World Order* (New York: Simon & Schuster, 1997); Dominique Moïsi, "The Clash of Emotions," in *The Clash of Civilizations? The Debate*, ed. James F. Hoge Jr. (New York: Council on Foreign Relations, 2010), 120. Moïsi sees Islamic "fundamentalism as unique, driven by a "dual sense of revenge: by the Shiite minority against the Sunni majority and by the fundamentalists against the West at large" (124).

58. The Lebanese literature covering this question is vast. Representative studies are Mushir Basil Aoun, *Bayna al-din wa-al-siyasa: Al-fikr al-siyasi al-masihi fi bina'ihi*

al-nazari wa-waqi'ihi al-lubnani (Beirut: Dar al-Nahar li-al-Nashr, 2008), and Jad al-Qasifi, ed., *Lubnan: Al-Mafhum wa-al-tahaddiyat* (Markaz Finiks li-al-Dirasat al-Lubnaniyya, 2011). For a criticism of Hegelian Arab thought, see Mahdi 'Amil, *Azamat al-hadara al-'arabiyya am azamat al-burjuwaziyyat al-'arabiyya?* (Beirut: Dar al-Farabi, 1978), 12–18. 'Amil argued that Arab intellectuals treated Arab "civilization" or "culture" as the primary site for historical "progress," declaring in the late 1970s that it was stagnant and incapable of "modernizing" itself. 'Amil shifted the focus to social class and relations of production tied to the crisis of the Arab bourgeoisie. Notwithstanding this shift, he stopped short of scrutinizing the Hegelian features of Arab leftist thought. See George Corm, "Fi fikr Mahdi 'Amil: Li-tatahalaf kul manahij al-fikr al-naqdi," April 2011, http://mehdiamel.wordpress.com/2011/04/21/. Corm laments the failure of Arab culture to embrace the "Enlightenment" model of modernism.

59. Muhammad Muru, *Hizbullah: Al-Nash'a, al-'amaliyyat, al-jihad wa-al-intisar* (N.p.: Dar al-Nasr li-al-Tiba'a al-Islamiyya, n.d.), 95, http://www.Kotobarabia.com. He writes elsewhere that the "struggle is one between the Islamic and the Western Civilizations. The former civilization represents truth, freedom, and justice," and the second represents "oppression, violence and injustice." Muhammad Muru, "Fadlallah: Al-Fahm al-khati' li-al-din wa-al-anzima," *Bayynat*, July 23, 2002, http://arabic.bayynat.org.lb/nachatat/ahd23072002.htm. Fadlallah argued that Islam "made a civilization for the world in earlier centuries and is the mother of modern civilizations." Quoted in Amal Saad-Ghorayeb, *Hizbu'llah: Politics and Religion* (London: Pluto Press, 2002), 81–82. For a revisionist Islamist approach to this question see 'Ali Fayyad, "Ayyu Hiwar ma'a al-Gharb?" *Qadaya Islamiyya Mu'asira*, no. 5 (1999): 208–13.

60. Hegel, *Philosophy of History*, 107. Subjective freedom "is the reflection of the Individual in his own conscience" (104); see also 13–14, 460.

61. Craig J. Calhoun, ed. *Habermas and the Public Sphere* (Cambridge, MA: MIT Press, 1992); Michel Foucault, *The Foucault Reader*, ed. Paul Rabinow (New York: Random House, 1984); Bent Flyvbjerg, "Habermas and Foucault: Thinkers for Civil Society?" *British Journal of Sociology* 49, no. 2 (June 1998): 210–33.

62. See Robert W. Hefner, *Muslims and Democratization in Civil Islam* (Princeton, NJ: Princeton University Press, 2000); David Herbert, *Religion and Civil Society: Rethinking Public Religion in the Contemporary World* (Brookfield, VT: Ashgate, 2003), esp. chapters 2, 3, and 4. See also Augustus Richard Norton ed., *Civil Society in the Middle East* (Leiden: Brill, 2001), x–xiv, 5–16.

63. Georg Hegel, *Philosophy of Right*, trans. T. M. Knox (London: Oxford University Press, 1952), 286, cited in Jürgen Habermas, *The Philosophical Discourse of Modernity: Twelve Lectures*, trans. Frederick G. Lawrence (Cambridge, MA: MIT Press, 1990), 16. Hegel, *Philosophy of History*, 104. Subjective freedom, according to Hegel, liberates the subject from "servitude" toward the laws and thus the individual becomes "a law to himself." (104)

64. Hegel, *Philosophy of History,* 9.

65. Among these scholars are Sa'ud al-Mawla, "'An al-muwatana wa-al-mujtama' al-madani wa-al-tajruba al-lubnaniyya: Mulahazat hiwariyya," *Middle East Transparent,* October 23, 2005, http://www.metransparent.com/old/texts/saud_mawla_on_citizenship_and_civl_society.htm. Al-Mawla insisted on the exclusive semantics of "civil society" and its historical ties to Western liberal democracy, where the nation-state is a precondition. See also Michael D. Dawahare, *Civil Society and Lebanon: Toward a Hermeneutic Theory of the Public Sphere* (Parkland, FL: Brown Walker Press, 2000), 9–10. Dawahare, guided by the Hegelian model, doubted that a public sphere could emerge in a multiconfessional state "where *asabiya* [tribal solidarity] is a principal source of the self."

66. See Fadia Kiwan, "Consolidation ou recomposition de la société civile d'après-guerre," in *Liban état et société: la reconstruction difficile,* ed. Ghassan El-Ezzi, special issue of *Confluences Méditerranée,* no. 47 (Autumn 2003): 67–77; Kamil Muhanna, "Al-Mujtama' al-madani fi Lubnan: Halat al-haql al-ma'rifi fi al-buhuth wa-al-dirasat allati tamma ijra'uha fi al-sanawat al-madiya," *Amel Association* (Beirut, n.d.), 29.

67. On Max Weber and civil society, see Sung Ho Kim, *Max Weber's Politics of Civil Society* (Cambridge: Cambridge University Press, 2004).

68. Wajih Kawtharani, "Al-Mujtama' al-madani wa-al-dawla fi al-tarikh al-'arabi," in *Al-Mujtama' al-madani fi al-watan al-'arabi wa-dawruhu fi tahqiq al-dimuqratiyya,* ed. Sa'id Bin Sa'id 'Alawi (Beirut: Markaz Dirasat al-Wahda al-'Arabiyya, 1992), 120, 123–29.

69. Ibid. See also Michaelle Browers, *Democracy and Civil Society in Arab Political Thought: Transcultural Possibilities* (Syracuse, NY: Syracuse University Press, 2006), 99–106. Browers noted that despite Kawtharani's significant contribution to the debate on civil society, he does not resolve the polarization between *ahli* and *madani* found in the prevalent scholarship.

70. Kawtharani, "'Al-Mujtama' al-madani': su'al sa'b fi zil hukm al-hizb al-wahid li-al-dawla kama li-al-ta'ifa," *al-Hayat,* February 23, 2008.

71. See Dale F. Eickelman and Jon W. Anderson, eds., *New Media in the Muslim World: The Emerging Public Sphere* (Bloomington: Indiana University Press, 1999); John L. Esposito, "Islam and Civil Society," in *Modernizing Islam: Religion in the Public Sphere in Europe and the Middle East,* ed. John L. Esposito and Francois Burgat, (New Brunswick, NJ: Rutgers University Press, 2003); Hefner, *Muslims and Democratization in Civil Islam*; Herbert, *Religion and Civil Society*; Mitsuo Nakamura, Sharon Siddique, and Omar Farouk Bajunid, eds., *Islam and Civil Society in Southeast Asia* (Tokyo: Sasakawa Peace Foundation, 2001); Amyn Sajoo, ed., *Civil Society in the Muslim World: Contemporary Perspectives* (London: I. B. Tauris, 2002).

72. Geoff Eley, "Nations, Publics, and Political Cultures: Placing Habermas in the Nineteenth Century," in Calhoun, ed., *Habermas and the Public Sphere,* 292. See also Flyvbjerg, "Habermas and Foucault," 210–11, 229; David Zaret, "Religion, Science, and

Printing in the Public Spheres of England," in Calhoun, ed., *Habermas and the Public Sphere*, 213–14, 221, 229.

73. Flyvbjerg, "Habermas and Foucault," 226; Eley, "Nations, Publics, and Political Cultures," 307. See also Asad, *Formations of the Secular*, 184–85.

74. See Dalal al-Bizri, *Akhawat al-zil wa-al-yaqin* (Beirut: Al-Nahar, 1996). Al-Bizri considers modernism an artificial feature of Hizbullah's movement. Against this position, see Lara Deeb, *An Enchanted Modern: Gender and Public Piety in Shi'i Lebanon* (Princeton, NJ: Princeton University Press, 2006).

75. See Deeb, *An Enchanted Modern*, 23–28.

76. Asad, *Formations of the Secular*, 182, 193; Jose Casanova, *Public Religions in the Modern World* (Chicago: University of Chicago Press, 1994).

77. Asad, *Formations of the Secular*, chapter 6.

78. Wael Hallaq, "What Is Shari'a?" in *Yearbook of Islamic and Middle Eastern Law, 2005–2006*, vol. 12 (Leiden: Brill, 2007), 155–56.

79. Wael Hallaq, *The Impossible State: Islam, Politics, and Modernity's Moral Predicament* (New York: Columbia University Press, 2012), chapter 3.

1. The Shi'ites and Grand Liban

1. Greater Syria or historical Syria is the area located to the east of the Mediterranean Sea that includes modern-day Syria, Lebanon, Jordan, Israel, the Palestinian Occupied Territories, parts of Iraq, Alexandretta, and the city of Antioch.

2. The "South" or "South Lebanon" is the region of Jabal 'Amil following the formation of Grand Liban in 1920.

3. Maronites are Eastern Catholic Christians and form a principal religious group in Lebanon.

4. For more on Shi'ite doctrine and political thought see Moojan Momen, *Introduction to Shi'i Islam* (New Haven, CT: Yale University Press, 1985); Said A. Arjomand, *Authority and Political Culture in Shiism* (Albany: State University of New York Press, 1988); Juan Cole, *Sacred Space and Holy War: The Politics and History of Shiite Islam* (London: I. B. Tauris, 2002).

5. See W. Montgomery Watt, *Muhammad: Prophet and Statesman* (Oxford: Oxford University Press, 1961); Momen, *Introduction to Shi'i Islam*; Wilfred Madelung, *The Succession to Muhammad* (Cambridge: Cambridge University Press, 1997).

6. On Sunna, see Wael Hallaq, *The Origins and Evolution of Islamic Law* (Cambridge: Cambridge University Press, 2005), 46–52.

7. On the life of Imam Husayn, see Wilfred Madelung, in *Encyclopaedia Iranica*, s.v. Hosayn b. 'Ali: Life and Significance in Shi'ism.

8. Momen, *Introduction to Shi'i*, 28–29; Heinz Halm, *Shi'a Islam: From Religion to Revolution* (Princeton, NJ: Markus Wiener, 1997), 16–20.

9. Halm, *Shi'a Islam*, 20.

10. Marshall G. S. Hodgson, "How Did the Early Shi'a Become Sectarian?" *Journal of the American Oriental Society* 75, no. 1 (January–March 1955): 11–13.

11. Cole, *Sacred Space and Holy War*, 21.

12. See Ron Buckley, "The Imam Ja'far al-Sadiq, Abu'l-Khattab, and the 'Abbasids," *Der Islam* 79, no. 1 (2002): 137.

13. Muhib Hamada, *Tarikh 'alaqat al-biqa'iyyin bi-al-suriyyin wa-istiratijiyyat al-Biqa' fi al-muwajaha al-suriyya al-isra'iliyya, 1918–1936* (Beirut: Dar al-Nahar, 1983), 79.

14. Ibid., 252.

15. Ibid., 80.

16. Ibid., 252. In al-Hirmil, Sabri Hamada assisted the French politically and militarily against pro-unity Shi'ites, in 1926 providing them with almost "fifty thousand soldiers." For more on the Hamadas, see Stefan Winter, *The Shiites of Lebanon under Ottoman Rule, 1516–1788* (New York: Cambridge University Press, 2010), chapters 3 and 6.

17. See Situation in Lebanon, Ministère des Affaires Ètranger (MAE), Syrie-Liban, 1930–40, vol. 500.

18. Hamada, *Tarikh 'alaqat al-biqa'iyyin*, 80–81. The Haydars negotiated social influence and political sway with another Shi'i family, the Yaghi.

19. For more on Biqa'i scholars, see Faysal al-Athath, *Al-Shu'a' fi 'ulama' Ba'labak wa-al-Biqa'* (Beirut: Mu'assassat al-Nu'man, 1993).

20. Rifa'at Abou-El-Haj, *Formation of the Modern State: The Ottoman Empire, Sixteenth to Eighteenth Centuries*, 2nd ed. (Syracuse, NY: Syracuse University Press, 2005), 64.

21. Tarif Khalidi, "Shaykh Ahmad 'Arif al-Zayn and *al-'Irfan*," in *Intellectual Life in the Arab East, 1890–1939*, ed. Marwan Buheiry (Beirut: American University of Beirut Press, 1981), 122.

22. The sources refer to the *a'shar* tax, which is the plural of *'ushr* or one-tenth.

23. Akram Ja'far Al-Amin, *Ja'far Muhsin Al-Amin: Sira wa-'amiliyyat* (Beirut: Al-Farabi, 2004), 125. This amount was usually estimated by a village committee appointed by the tax collector, who was normally a provincial leader (*za'im*, pl. *zu'ama*) presiding over the political affairs of the whole region.

24. Ibid.

25. Mustafa Bazzi, *Jabal 'Amil wa-tawabi'uhu fi shamal Filastin* (Beirut: Dar al-Mawasim, 2002), 40–43, 67–8, 82–83.

26. For more on land reform in the South see ibid., 82–98.

27. See Malek Abisaab, *Militant Women of a Fragile Nation* (Syracuse, NY: Syracuse University Press, 2010), chapter 1.

28. Etude sommaire de la region du Djebel Amel, Ministère des Affaires Ètrangere (MAE), Syrie-Liban, 1930-40, Juin 20, 1930, vol. 2200.

29. Al-Amin, *Ja'far Muhsin*, 131. They did not own the means of production and were temporarily hired by large landowners for diverse tasks. Even peasants of a modest background avoided marrying their daughters to *falati* men.

30. Musa al-Zayn Sharara, "Min dhikrayat al-sha'ir Musa al-Zayn Sharara," in *Min daftar al-dhikrayat al-janubiyya*, ed. al-Majlis al-Thaqafi li-Lubnan al-Janubi, (Beirut: Dar al-Kitab al-Lubnani, 1981), 61.

31. Ja'far al-Amin referred to this payment as the "*badal*"—that is, substitute for service in the Ottoman army. See al-Amin, *Ja'far Muhsin*, 27.

32. 'Ali Hijazi, "Sha'ir al-tahhaddi: Al-Shaykh 'Ali Mahdi Shams al-Din," in *Wujuh thaqafiyya min al-Janub*, part 2, ed. al-Majlis al-Thaqafi li-Lubnan al-Janubi (Beirut: Dar Ibn Khaldun, 1984), 39.

33. Sharara, "Min dhikrayat al-sha'ir Musa al-Zayn Sharara," 63.

34. Al-Amin, *Ja'far Muhsin*, 26.

35. Ibid., 26–27.

36. The chief of the Battalion of Rangers, Roumel, had written this report in June 20, 1930, and sent it to his superiors. See Ètude sommaire de la region du Djebel Amel, MAE, Syrie-Liban, 1930-40, Juin (June) 20, 1930, vol. 2200.

37. Al-Amin, *Ja'far Muhsin*, 25.

38. Ibid. Several households of the al-Amin *'ulama* family moved out of their town, Shaqra', to Siddiqqin or moved to a farm in Niha (in the Biqa') and away from populated areas.

39. Ètude sommaire de la region du Djebel Amel, MAE, Syrie-Liban, 1930-40, Juin (June) 20, 1930, vol. 2200.

40. See al-Amin, *Ja'far Muhsin*, 25.

41. The French divided the 'Amilis arbitrarily into two social groups, the first including the notables, beys, *sayyids*, and religious shaykhs, and the second included all the peasants, "the fellahs." See Etude sommaire de la region du Djebel Amel, MAE, Syrie-Liban, 1930-40, Juin (June) 20, 1930, vol. 2200.

42. Khalidi, "Shaykh Ahmad 'Arif al-Zayn and *al-'Irfan*," 118.

43. Ibid. See also al-Amin, *Ja'far Muhsin al-Amin*, 131.

44. Ibid.

45. Khalidi, "Shaykh Ahmad 'Arif al-Zayn and *al-'Irfan*," 121.

46. For more on this question, see Martha Mundy and Richard Saumarez Smith, eds., *Governing Property, Making the Modern State: Law, Administration, and Production in Ottoman Syria* (London: I. B. Tauris, 2007), 44. The Ottoman reforms, as Mundy and Smith noted, aimed "to unify practice" and gave regional and provincial leaders "a considerable place within the context of a centralizing regime."

47. Khalidi, "Shaykh Ahmad 'Arif al-Zayn and *al-'Irfan*," 122.

48. Not all members of the Mughniyya family, however, were affluent. Moreover, a number of the *'ulama* families were *sayyids*—that is, claimed descent from the house of the Prophet.

49. On the exemplar, see Linda S. Walbridge, ed., *The Most Learned of the Shi'a: The Institution of Marja' al-Taqlid* (Oxford: Oxford University Press, 2001); Rula Jurdi Abisaab, "Lebanese Shi'ites and the *Marja'iyya*: Polemic in the Late 20th Century," *British Journal of Middle Eastern Studies* 36, no. 2 (August 2009): 215–39.

50. Hasan Al-Amin, *A'yan al-Shi'a*, vol. 10 (Beirut: Dar al-Ta'aruf, 1986), 362.

51. For more on Ottoman approaches toward Syrian Shi'ites, see Rula Jurdi Abisaab, "The *'Ulama* of Jabal 'Amil in Safavid Iran, 1501–1736: Marginality, Migration, and Social Change," *Iranian Studies* 27, nos. 1–4 (1994): 103–22; Rula Jurdi Abisaab, "The Shi'ite 'Ulama', the Madrasas, and Educational Reform in the Late Ottoman Period," *Ottoman Studies*, no. 36 (2010): 155–83; Winter, *The Shiites of Lebanon under Ottoman Rule.*

52. The prosecution usually takes the form of accusing the Shi'ite scholar in question of defaming the first three caliphs and 'A'isha, who signify Sunnite "orthodoxy."

53. Winter, *The Shiites of Lebanon*, 14, 21–24.

54. Hijazi, "Sha'ir al-tahaddi," 41; Zaynab Isma'il, "Min al-Najaf ila Shaqra' tariq shi'r wa-thaqafa wa-din, kayfa kana al-intiqal wa-al-'awda min al-hawza al-diniyya ila al-hawza al-mariksiyya?" *al-Safir*, October 29, 2004.

55. Ibid., 2. The observations in this essay are based on 'Abdullah al-Amin's statements. See also Muhammad Jabir Al Safa, *Tarikh Jabal 'Amil* (Beirut: Dar al-Nahar, 1992), 245–46. Musa Amin Sharara (d. 1886) reorganized the 'Ashura' funereal councils in harmony with their counterparts in Iraq and held them regularly in the South.

56. See Al Safa, *Tarikh Jabal 'Amil*, 245–46.

57. Khalidi, "Shaykh Ahmad 'Arif al-Zayn and *al-'Irfan*," 120.

58. Ibid., 119.

59. A *dunam* is around one-tenth of a hectare.

60. Khalidi, "Shaykh Ahmad 'Arif al-Zayn and *al-'Irfan*," 120.

61. Winter, *The Shiites of Lebanon*, 32.

62. Ibid., 33.

63. For a closer look at these developments, see Engin Deniz Akarli, *The Long Peace: Ottoman Lebanon, 1861–1920* (Berkeley: University of California Press, 1993); Ussama Makdisi, "After 1860: Debating Religion, Reform, and Nationalism in the Ottoman Empire," *International Journal of Middle Eastern Studies* 34, no. 4 (November 2002): 601–17; and Ussama Makdisi, *The Culture of Sectarianism: Community, History, and Violence in Nineteenth-Century Ottoman Lebanon* (Berkeley: University of California Press, 2000).

64. Akarli, *The Long Peace*, 51–52.

65. See Evelyn Early, "The 'Amiliyya Society of Beirut: A Case Study of an Emerging Urban Za'im" (Master's thesis, American University of Beirut, 1971), 18–19.

66. Ibid., 180–81.

67. William Cleveland, *A History of the Modern Middle East* (Boulder, CO: Westview Press, 2000), 213.

68. Philip S. Khoury, "Continuity and Change in Syrian Political Life: The Nineteenth and Twentieth Centuries," *American Historical Review* 96, no. 5 (December 1991): 1387.

69. Vahe Karyergatian, "Monopoly in the Lebanese Tobacco Industry" (Master's thesis, American University of Beirut, 1965), 19–23.

70. Situation Politique au Liban-Sud et son évolution, MAE, Mandat Syrie-Liban, 1918–40, April 6, 1936, vol. 944.

71. Al-Amin, *Khitat Jabal 'Amil* (Beirut: Dar al-'Amiliya, 1983), 146.

72. "Li-Hadrat mustashar al-awqaf fi al-mufawwadiyya al-'ulya," MAE, Mandat Syrie-Liban, September 25, 1932, vol. 607. See also Hamada, *Tarikh 'alaqat al-biqa'iyyin bi-al-suriyyin*, 268.

73. See Elizabeth Thompson, *Colonial Citizens: Republican Rights, Paternal Privileges, and Gender in French Syria and Lebanon* (New York: Columbia University Press, 2000), 19–38; Michael Gilsenan, *Lords of the Lebanese Marches: Violence and Narrative in Arab Society* (London: I. B. Tauris, 1996), 115–39.

74. Note Pour Monsieur Le Commandant Dantz, MAE, Mandat Syrie-Liban, 1918–40, Août (August) 12, 1924, vol. 931.

75. Joseph Eid, Maronite patriarch of the Syro-Lebanese immigrants in the United States, noted in his address to the French government that the French had been the protectors of his people, "Les Français de L'Orient," the French of the Orient, since the time of Charlemagne and Saint Louis. "A Son Excellence Monsieur de Laboulaye, Ambassadeur de France a Washington DC (États-Unis)," MAE, Levant 1918–40, April 21, 1935, vol. 551.

76. Christian tobacco farmers in northern Lebanon and Muslim tobacco farmers from the South sent petitions to the French protesting against the tobacco monopoly. "Li-Fakhamat al-mufawwad al-sami," MAE, Mandat Syrie-Liban, 1930–40, Janvier 10, 1935, carton 718.

77. Promulgation of the San Remo Agreement.

78. Hamada, *Tarikh 'alaqat*, 108–9.

79. Ibid., 81.

80. Many Shi'ites assisted the Syrian rebels against the French from 1925 to 1927.

81. Hamada, *Tarikh 'alaqat*, 269.

82. Ibid., 268.

83. In terms of their organization and ties to the elite, these groups offer a different example of Ottoman banditry from the one that Karen Barkey describes for the seventeenth century. See Karen Barkey, *Bandits and Bureaucrats: The Ottoman Route to State Centralization* (Ithaca, NY: Cornell University, 1994), x, 8, 13, 21.

84. Al-Amin, *Ja'far Muhsin*, 33.

85. This was the case in 1920. See "Historique Du Poste De Merdjeyoun," MAE, Mandat Syrie-Liban 1918–40, Juin 9, 1928, vol. 2200.

86. Ibid.

87. As Barkey notes, the Ottoman state had found a useful function for the bandits and resorted to "negotiation by inclusion" whenever they threatened it. Barkey, *Bandits and Bureaucrats*, 13, 141–42. See also Winter, *The Shiites of Lebanon*, 221–23.

88. "Le Secteur Sud, Notables," MAE, Mandat Syrie-Liban 1918–40, n.d., vol. 2200.

89. Sabrina Mervin and Tamara Chalabi highlight only the disruptive features of banditry. See Sabrina Mervin, *Harakat al-islah al-Shi'i* (Beirut: Dar al-Nahar, 2000), 433–38; Tamara Chalabi, *The Shi'is of Jabal 'Amil and the New Lebanon: Community and Nation-State 1918–1943* (New York: Palgrave Macmillan, 2006), 120, 130–31. See also Mundhir Jabir, "Al-Kiyan al-siyasi li-Jabal 'Amil qabla 1920," *Safahat min tarikh Jabal 'Amil*, ed. al-Majlis al-Thaqafi li-Lubnan al-Janubi (Beirut: Al-Majlis al-Thaqafi li-Lubnan al-Janubi, 1979), http://www.tibneen.com/index.php?option=com_content&view=article&id=98:-1920&catid=7:2010-12-28-09-50-37&Itemid=21. On the anticolonial dimension of banditry, see Jihad Bannut, *Harakat al-nidal fi Jabal 'Amil* (Beirut: Dar al-Mizan, 1993), 223–29, 254–55.

90. Mervin, *Harakat al-islah al-Shi'i*, 422.

91. Hasan al-Amin, "Min dhikrayat Hasan al-Amin," in *Min daftar al-dhikrayat al-janubiyya*, ed. al-Majlis al-Thaqafi li-Lubnan al-Janubi (Beirut: Dar al-Kitab al-Lubnani, 1981), 17–18.

92. See Tom Segev, *One Palestine Complete: Jews and Arabs under the British Mandate* (New York: Henry Holt, 2000), 122–26, and Henry Laurens, *La question de Palestine, vol. 1: 1922–1947* (Paris: Fayard, 1999), 502.

93. See Jihad al-Zayn, "Min dhikrayat al-Shaykh 'Ali," *Min daftar al-dhikrayat al-janubiyya*, 32, 33.

94. Fuad Kahil, "Fu'ad Kahil," in *Min daftar al-dhikrayat al-janubiyya*, part 2, ed. al-Majlis al-Thaqafi li-Lubnan al-Janubi (Beirut: Dar al-Kitab al-Lubnani,1984), 145; Al-Amin, *Ja'far Muhsin*, 44.

95. Al-Zayn, "Min dhikrayat al-Shaykh 'Ali," 30–31.

96. Al-Amin, *A'yan al-Shi'a*, 10:360.

97. "Requête adressée a Son Excellence le Comte De Martel, Haut-commissaire," MAE, Mandat-Syrie-Liban 1930–49, Janvier 29, 1936, vol. 607.

98. The French sources traced the bandits' activities to the machinations of one person, Sayyid Sharaf al-Din. "Historique du Poste De Merdjeyoun," MAE, Mandat Syrie-Liban, 1918–40, Juin 9, 1928, vol. 2200.

99. See al-Shaykh Ahmad Rida, *Mudhakkarat li-al-tarikh: Hawadith Jabal 'Amil, 1914–1922* (Beirut: Dar al-Nahar, 2009), 236, 239.

100. "Historique du Poste de Merdjeyoun," MAE, Mandat Syrie-Liban 1918–40, Juin, 1928, vol. 2200.

101. Most of the 'Amili accounts assumed that the bandits acted solely upon the directives of Sharaf al-Din. See Al-Amin, *A'yan al-Shia*, 10:360. Mervin, *Harakat al-islah*, 425–27; Chalabi, *The Shi'is of Jabal 'Amil*, 138–41.

102. See Mervin, *Harakat al-islah*, 448–49.

103. Nawal Fayyad, *Safahat min tarikh Jabal 'Amil fi al-'ahdayn al-'uthmani wa-al-faransi* (Beirut: Dar al-Jadid, 1998), 65–66.

104. Mervin, *Harakat al-islah*, 435, 436.

105. Sulayman Taqi al-Din, "Al-Janub al-lubnani bi-ri'ayat al-istiqlal," in *Safahat min tarikh Jabal 'Amil*, ed. al-Majlis al-Thaqafi li-Lubnan al-Janubi (Beirut: Dar al-Farabi, 1979), 135. Several Christians from the South also demanded unity with Syria. See Ja'far Sharaf al-Din, "Sayyid Ja'far Sharaf al-Din," in *Min daftar al-dhikrayat*, part 2, 30.

106. Mervin, *Harakat al-islah*, 431–32.

107. Ibid., 432.

108. Fayyad, *Safahat*, 75 n. 93.

109. Taqi al-Din, "Al-Janub al-lubnani," 135–37.

110. L'occasion des événements de Bint-Jbail, MAE, Syrie-Liban, 1930-1940, Avril 11, 1936, Box 411. Pechkoff's reports to the French Foreign Ministry aimed to convey to the French government, first, that he was ruling the South effectively; second, that members of the elite had been co-opted and forced to distance themselves from the rebels; and, third, that economic and political policies in the South need to be changed to appease the locals.

111. Winter, *The Shiites of Lebanon*, 176–79.

112. The Lebanese Christians expressed different political views on the French Mandate. The creation of an independent Lebanese homeland (Grand Liban), however, received most Christians' support. See Fawwaz Traboulsi, *A History of Modern Lebanon* (London: Pluto Press, 2007), 82–83.

113. Fayyad, *Safahat*, 74–75.

114. Quoted in ibid.

115. Bannut, *Harakat al-nidal*, 292.

116. Mustafa Bazzi, *Bint Jubayl: Hadirat Jabal 'Amil* (Beirut: Dar al-Amir li-al-Thaqafa wa-al-'Ulum, 1998), 569–77.

117. For more on the notables who were allied to the French, see Tamara Chalabi, *The Shi'is of Jabal 'Amil*, 101–2.

118. When we refer to Libanism here, we distinguish it from the trend that overlapped with Syrian nationalism for some time, stressing the ancient cultural traits of Greater Syria.

119. Bazzi, *Jabal 'Amil wa-tawabi'uhu*, 330–31. Patriarch al-Huwayyik wrote a petition to the French with such requests in 1919.

120. Ghanim, Moutran, and Tabet are cited in Kais M. Firro, "Lebanese Nationalism versus Arabism: From Bulus Nujaym to Michel Chiha," *Middle Eastern Studies* 40, no. 5 (September 2004): 1–3, 8, 10, 13. Firro notes the overlap between Libanism and Syrianism, both of which shared an opposition to Arabism.

121. Michelle Hartman and Alessandro Olsaretti, "'The First Boat and the First Oar': Inventions of Lebanon in the Writings of Michel Chiha," *Radical History Review* 86, no. 1 (Spring 2003): 37–38.

122. Michel Chiha, *Politique Interieure* (Beirut: Editions du Trident, 1964), 261–63, 324.

123. Firro, "Lebanese Nationalism versus Arabism," 20–21. Hartman and Olsaretti, "'The First Boat and the First Oar,'" 37–65.

124. In 1935, the Maronite Church under Patriarch Antoine 'Arida and a group of tobacco industrialists opposed the French fiscal policies and protested against the French commissioner Damian de Martel. Then in November 1943, Maronite leaders like Patriarch 'Arida and Archbishop Ignatius Mubarak of Beirut supported the parliamentary protests against the French. See Abisaab, *Militant Women of a Fragile Nation*, 22–25. See also Raghid al-Solh, *Lebanon and Arabism: National Identity and State Formation* (London: Centre for Lebanese Studies in association with I. B.Tauris, 2004), 35, 215–16.

125. Al-Solh, *Lebanon and Arabism*, 6.

126. Quoted in ibid. A group of Maronite thinkers supported the formation of an independent Lebanese state but rejected Libanist attempts to privilege French politics and culture. Among these thinkers were Communist leaders such as Yusuf Ibrahim Yazbik, Fuad al-Shimali, and Farajallah al-Helou. Others were Syrian nationalists such as Salah Labaki. Many more Greek Orthodox Christians opposed French hegemony over Grand Liban. See Wajih Kawtharni, *Al-Ittijahat al-ijtima'iyya wa-al-siyasiyya fi Jabal Lubnan wa-al-Mashriq al-'arabi: 1860–1920* (Beirut: Ma'had al-Inma' al-'Arabi, 1978), 318, 345, 346.

127. Matti Moosa, *The Maronites in History* (Syracuse, NY: Syracuse University Press, 1986), 290.

128. Al-Solh, *Lebanon and Arabism*, 6; Asher Kaufman, *Reviving Phoenicia: In Search of Identity in Lebanon* (London: I. B.Tauris, 2004), 26. Kaufman notes that from 1860 until 1920, French colonial administrators saw the Maronites as possessing a more "civilized and noble culture" than other Orientals.

129. Chief of the Battalion of Rangers Roumel wrote this report on June 20, 1930, and sent it to his superiors. See Ètude sommaire de la region du Djebel Amel, June 20, 1930, MAE, Syrie-Liban, vol. 2200. See also Rula Jurdi Abisaab, *"From the Shi'ite Hawza to Marxism: 'Amili Interpretations of Anti-colonial 'Modernism,' 1920–1950,"* paper presented at the annual conference of the Middle East Studies Association, Boston, November 20, 2006.

130. See Roschanack Shaery-Eisenlohr, *Shi'ite Lebanon: Transnational Religion and the Making of National Identities* (New York: Columbia University Press, 2008), 21–23.

131. The discourse on Shi'ite modernism is illuminated through the debates between Sayyid Muhsin al-Amin and 'Abd al-Husayn Sadiq. See Muhsin al-Amin, *Thawrat al-tanzih: "Risalat al-tanzih,"* ed. Muhammad al-Qasim al-Husayni al-Najafi (Beirut: Dar al-Jadid, n.d.), 24, 27–28; 'Abd al-Husayn Sadiq, *Sima' al-sulaha'* (Sidon,

Lebanon: Matba'at al-'Irfan, 1927), 14; al-Amin, *A'yan al-Shi'a*, 10:374. See also Fayyad, *Safahat*, 63, 64, 93.

132. Bazzi, *Bint Jubayl*, 412–18.

133. Fayyad, *Safahat*, 90.

134. "Liban-Sud, Note D'Information," MAE, Mandat Syrie-Liban, 1930–40, note no. 271, Juin 1936, carton 944.

135. See al Safa, *Tarikh Jabal 'Amil*, 114–21, 213–24.

136. Taqi al-Din, "Al-Janub al-lubnani," 139.

137. Ibid., 140.

138. On immigration and loss of employment, see al Safa, *Tarikh Jabal 'Amil*, 301–2; Early, "The 'Amiliyya Society," 17–18.

139. Taqi al-Din, "Al-Janub al-Lubnani," 141.

140. See Bazzi, *Jabal 'Amil wa-tawabi'uhu*, 406–21; Fayyad, *Safahat*, 94–96.

141. Sulayman Zahir, "Poem," quoted in Fayyad, *Safahat*, 96.

142. Taqi al-Din, "Al-Janub al-lubnani," 137; Bannut, *Harakat al-nidal*, 288–90.

143. Al-Din, "Al-Sayyid Ja'far Sharaf al-Din," 25.

144. Kahil, "Fu'ad Kahil," 143–44.

145. "Liban-Sud, Note D'Information," Juin 6, 1936.

146. Bazzi, *Bint Jubayl*, 502–5, and *al-Nahar*, May 17, 1936.

147. Bazzi, *Bint Jubayl*, 504; Mustafa Bazzi, *Jabal 'Amil fi muhitihi al-arabi, 1864–1948* (Beirut: Markaz al-Dirasat li-al-Tawthiq wa-al-Nashr, 1993), 367–72. See also Shafiq al-Arna'ut, *Ma'ruf Sa'd: Nidal wa-thawra* (Beirut: Al-Mu'assasa al-Lubnaniyya li-al-Nashr wa-al-Khadamat al-Tiba'iyya, 1981), 104–13.

148. Al-Din, "Al-Sayyid Ja'far Sharaf al-Din," 31.

149. "Liban-Sud, number 266, Note D'information," MAE, Mandat Syrie-Liban, 1930–40, Mai (May) 30, 1936, vol. 944. See also, Fayyad, *Safahat*, 92–93, 146.

150. These fighters were Muhammad 'Ali Zahir, 'Abd al-Husayn 'Abdullah, and 'Ali Jabir.

151. Bannut, *Harakat al-nidal*, 295–96; al-Arna'ut, *Ma'ruf Sa'd*, 104–13.

152. Bannut, *Harakat al-nidal*, 296; Taqi al-Din, "Al-Janub al-lubnani," 140.

153. Jabir, *Safahat min tarikh Jabal 'Amil*, 92–93.

2. Education, Modernism, and Anticolonial Struggle

1. The conventional leaders of the al-As'ad family supported the revolt.

2. Liban Sud, no. 191, Saida," MAE, Syrie-Liban, 1930–40, Avril 11, 1936, Box 411.

3. Ibid.

4. On tobacco cultivation and monopoly see Malek Abisaab, *Militant Women of a Fragile Nation* (Syracuse, NY: Syracuse University Press, 2010), chapter 2.

5. *L'indicateur*, Libano-Syrien, 1928–29, Per 356, Nantes, 15–16.

6. Abisaab, *Militant Women*, 16–19.

7. George Hakim, "Industry," in *Economic Organization of Syria*, ed. Sa'id Himadeh (Beirut: American Press, 1936), 137; Isma'il Haqqi Bey, *Lubnan mabahith 'ilmiyya wa ijtima'iyya* (Beirut: n.p., 1969), 365.

8. "Ya alf sawm wa sala 'ala al-Regie," *Lisan al-Hal*, May 23, 1930.

9. Situation au Liban, MAE, Syrie-Liban, 1930-40, Avril 9, 1935, vol. 500.

10. Ja'far Sharaf al-Din, "Al-Sayyid Ja'far Sharaf al-Din," in *Min daftar al-dhikrayat al-janubiyya*, part 2, 30–31. See also Liban-Sud, no. 191, MAE, Syrie-Liban, 1930-40, Avril 11, 1936, Box 411.

11. Jihad Bannut, *Harakat al-nidal fi Jabal 'Amil* (Beirut: Dar al-Mizan, 1993), 286.

12. Ibid.

13. Fouad Kahil, "Fuad Kahil," in *Min daftar al-dhikrayat al-janubiyya*, part 2, 151.

14. Ibid., 152.

15. Ibid., 153, 137.

16. L'occasion des événements de Bint-Jbail, MAE, Syrie-Liban, 1930-40, Liban-Sud, Avril 11, 1936, Box 411.

17. Réunion du 12 Avril a Taybe, MAE, Liban-Syrie, 1918-140, Avril 17, 1936, Box 411.

18. Al-Zayn, "Min dhikrayat al-Shaykh 'Ali al-Zayn," 30–31.

19. For more on the candidates, see Tamara Chalabi, *The Shi'is of Jabal 'Amil and the New Lebanon: Community and Nation-State, 1918–1943* (New York: Palgrave Macmillan, 2006), 218–27, 240–42.

20. Mustafa Bazzi, *Bint Jubayl: Hadirat Jabal 'Amil* (Beirut: Dar al-Amir li-al-Thaqafa wa-al-'Ulum, 1998), 277. On Pechkoff, see Mervin, *Harakat al-islah*, 532. Pechkoff was the adopted son of Maxim Gorky, the Russian novelist. When World War I erupted, he joined the French army battalion in Nis. In South Lebanon, he worked as an intelligence officer for the French and became a military governor.

21. Sharara, "Min dhikrayat Musa al-Zayn Sharara," 70.

22. Kahil, "Fuad Kahil," 61–63; Nawal Fayyad, *Safahat min tarikh Jabal 'Amil fi al-'ahdayn al-'uthmani wa-al-faransi* (Beirut: Dar al-Jadid, 1998), 75.

23. 'Abbas Bazzi, "Intifadat Bint Jubayl wa-Jabal 'Amil, April 1st, 1936," *Dirasat 'Arabiyya*, 29, nos. 1–2 (November–December 1992): 62, 63, 64. See also *al-Nahar*, April 3, 1936.

24. Cabinet Politique, "The Development of the Political Situation in South Lebanon," April 6, 1936, MAE, Mandat, Syrie-Liban, vol. 944. The Syrian Unity Party appeared in early 1921, reflecting both Christian and Muslim aspirations for Syria's independence from colonial rule. It was eclipsed, however, by the People's Party (Hizb al-Sha'b) founded in 1925, which called for Syria's full sovereignty and unity. See Stephen Hemsley Longrigg, *Syria and Lebanon under French Mandate* (London: Oxford University Press, 1958), 143, 151.

25. Situation Politique au Liban-Sud et son évolution, MAE, Mandat Syrie-Liban, 1918-140, Avril 8, 1936, vol. 944.

26. Ibid.

27. Agitation pro-unitaire dans le Liban Sud, MAE, Mandat, Syrie-Liban 1918–40, Avril 2, 1936, carton 411, p. 2.

28. Ibid.

29. Interview with Jacques Dagher, January 28, 1997, Ba'bda, Lebanon. See also *al-Hurriyya*, September 7, 1970, 9.

30. Interview with Hassan al-Amir and Adnan Salameh, June 16, 2002, Detroit.

31. See Salam al-Rasi, *Al-A'mal al-kamila: Li'alla tadi'*, vol.1 (Beirut: Dar Nawfal, 2000), 89–90; Bazzi, *Intifadat Bint Jubayl*, 83.

32. Bazzi, "Intifadat Bint Jubayl 1936," 82.

33. Al Safa, *Tarikh Jabal 'Amil*, 301–2; see also Evelyn Early, "The 'Amiliyya Society of Beirut: A Case Study of an Emerging Urban Za'im" (Master's thesis, American University of Beirut, 1971), 17–18.

34. Réunion du 12 Avril a Taybe, MAE, Mandat, Liban-Syrie, 1918–40, Avril 17, 1936, vol. 944; Réunion du 12 Avril a Taybe, MAE, Liban-Syrie, 1918–40, Avril 17, 1936, Box 411.

35. Ibid. On the *aghnam* tax, see Mas'ud Dahir, *Tarikh Lubnan al-ijtima'i, 1926–1914* (Beirut: Dar al-Matbu'at al-Sharqiyya, 1984), 123 n. 26.

36. Réunion du 12 Avril a Taybe, MAE, Liban-Syrie, 1918–40, Avril 17, 1936, Box 411, 2.

37. *The Lebanese Constitution*, trans. Gabriel M. Bustros (London: Bureau of Lebanese and Arab Documentation, 1973).

38. Hani Fahs, *Al-Shi'a wa-al-dawla fi Lubnan: Malamih fi al-ru'ya wa-al-dhakira* (Beirut: Dar al-Andalus, 1996), 72–73.

39. Hans Kohn, *Nationalism and Imperialism in the Hither East* (London: George Routledge and Sons, 1932), 304, n. 87.

40. Shafiq Juha, *Ma'rakat masir Lubnan fi 'ahd al-intidab al-faransi, 1918–1946*, vol.1 (Beirut: Maktabat Ra's Beirut, 1995), 245, 255.

41. Rania Maktabi, "The Lebanese Census of 1932 Revisited: Who Are the Lebanese?" *British Journal of Middle Eastern Studies* 26, no. 2 (November 1999): 219.

42. Ibid., 233, 239.

43. See Albert Mansur, *Al-Inqilab 'ala al-Ta'if* (Beirut: Dar al-Jadid, 1993), 46–47.

44. Peter Gran, "The Failure of Social Theory to Keep Up with Our Times: The Study of Women and Structural Adjustment Programs in the Middle East as an Example," paper presented at the 34th annual conference of the Association of Muslim Social Scientists, Temple University, September 30, 2005, 7–8.

45. See Mahdi 'Amil, *Madkhal ila naqd al-fikr al-ta'ifi* (Beirut: Al-Farabi, 1989), 141.

46. The Parliament chair was Habib Abu Chahla.

47. Shafiq Rayyis, *Al-Tahadi al-lubnani* (Beirut: Dar al-Masira, 1978), 33–34.

48. Kahil, "Fuad Kahil," 137.

49. Ibid.

50. Juan Cole, *Sacred Space and Holy War: The Politics, Culture, and History of Shi'ite Islam* (London: I. B. Tauris, 2002), 176.

51. Jihad al-Zayn, "Min dhikrayat al-Shaykh 'Ali," 26.

52. Al-Amin, *Khitat Jabal 'Amil*, 186.

53. Ibid., 186, 188.

54. Muhammad Jabir al Safa, *Tarikh Jabal 'Amil* (Beirut: Dar Matn al-Lugha, n.d.), 168.

55. Benjamin C. Fortna, *Imperial Classroom: Islam, the State, and Education in the Late Ottoman Empire* (Oxford: Oxford University Press, 2002), 72; Selçuk Akşin Somel, *The Modernization of Public Education in the Ottoman Empire, 1839–1908* (Leiden: Brill, 2001), 65.

56. Al Safa, *Tarikh*, 171–72; Hani Farhat, *Al-Thulathi al-'amili fi 'asr al-nahda* (Beirut: Al-Dar al-'Alamiyya, 1981), 31.

57. Farhat, *Al-Thulathi al-'amili*, 115. In Ba'labak, a Shi'ite madrasa was founded in 1854. See Fouad Khalil, *Al-Harafisha: Imarat al-musawama, 1530–1850* (Beirut: Al-Farabi, 1997), 127.

58. See the case of Muhammad 'Izz al-Din (d. 1886 or 1887) in al Safa, *Tarikh*, 244.

59. Al-Amin, *Khitat Jabal 'Amil*, 191.

60. For more on Shi'ite *fiqh* (law), see Hossein Modarressi, *Introduction to Shi'i Law* (London: Ithaca Press, 1994), chapter 1.

61. Legal monies came from Shi'ite believers' payment of *khums* (a one-fifth tax) and the Imam's share (*sahm al-Imam*) to their jurists.

62. Muhammad Hassan al-Suri, "Hayat al-talib fi al-Najaf," *Al-'Irfan* 25, no. 3 (1934): 235.

63. Najaf's chief seminary (*hawza*) consists of several schools referred to as madrasas or *hawzat* seminaries.

64. Ahmad Mughniyya, "Al-Shaykh Ahmad Mughniyya," *Min daftar al-dhikrayat al-janubiyya*, part 2, 85, 88–89. Mughniyya's family was originally from Tayr Dibba. See 'Ali al-Zayn, "Bawadir al-islah fi al-Najaf aw nahdat Kashif al-Ghita," *Al-'Irfan* 29, (1939): 181–83.

65. Al-Suri, "Hayat al-talib fi al-Najaf," 236.

66. See al-Amin, *Khitat Jabal 'Amil*, 188–89.

67. Ibid.; al-Zayn, "Bawadir al-islah," 179–81.

68. Agha Buzurg Tehrani, *Al-Dhari'a ila tasanif al-Shi'a*, vol.18 (Beirut: Dar al-Adwa', 1983), 45; 'Ali al-Khaqani, *Shu'ara' al-Ghuri*, vol. 4 (Qom, Iran: Matba'at Behman, 1987), 296–97. For more on the question of reform, see 'Ali al-Bahadili, *Al-Hawza al-'ilmiyya fi al-Najaf* (Beirut: Dar al-Zahra', 1993).

69. Al-Zayn, "Bawadir al-islah," 185. For more on the developments in Najaf during the nineteenth century, see Meir Litvak, *Shi'i Scholars of Nineteenth Century Iraq: The 'Ulama of Najaf and Karbala* (Cambridge: Cambridge University Press, 2002).

70. Al-Khaqani, *Shu'ara' al-Ghuri,* 300.

71. Musa al-Zayn Sharara, "Min dhikrayat al-sha'ir Musa al-Zayn," 75.

72. J. M., "Siyar al-'ilm fi al-Najaf," *Al-'Irfan* 21, nos. 4–5 (1931): 498–99.

73. Immanuel Wallerstein, "Eurocentrism and Its Avatars: The Dilemmas of Social Science," *New Left Review* 26, no. 1 (November–December 1997): 96, 106.

74. Mustafa Bazzi, *Muhammad Sharara: Al-Adib wa-al-insan* (Lebanon: Hay'at Inma' al-Mintaqa al-Hududiyya, 1994), 46–47.

75. Al-Zayn, "Bawadir al-islah," 181–83. See also Rainer Brunner, *Islamic Ecumenism in the 20th Century: Al-Azhar and Shiism Between Rapproachment and Restraint* (Leiden: Brill, 2004), 49–50.

76. Hassan al-Amin, ed., *A'yan al-Shia,* vol. 9 (Beirut: Dar al-Ta'aruf, 1986), 48–50; Sabrina Mervin, *Harakat al-islah al-shi'i* (Beirut: Dar al-Nahar, 2000), 261–62.

77. Indeed, the madrasas, depending on their character and location, have nurtured these sciences to different degrees.

78. See Kamran Rastegar, *Literary Modernity Between the Middle East and Europe: Textual Transactions in Nineteenth-Century Arabic, English, and Persian Literatures* (New York: Routledge, 2007), 4–5, 12–13. A comparison between the writings of Zaynab Fawwaz and Musa al-Zayn Sharara or Zahra al-Hurr reveals these diverse engagements with literary modernity. See Fawziyya Fawwaz, "Al-Adiba al-ra'ida: Zaynab Fawwaz, siratuha, adabuha," in *Wujuh thaqafiyya min al-Janub,* part 2, ed. al-Majlis al-Thaqafi li-Lubnan al-Janubi (Beirut: Dar Ibn Khaldun, 1984), 9–34.

79. Al-Zayn, "Min dhikrayat al-Shaykh 'Ali," 26.

80. Husayn Muroeh, "Muhammad Sharara," in *Wujuh thaqafiyya min al-Janub,* 11–12. See also al-Khaqani, *Shu'ara' al-Ghuri,* 8:219–28.

81. Al-Zayn, "Min dhikrayat al-Shaykh 'Ali," 29.

82. For more on *al-'Irfan* see Mervin, *Harakat al-islah,* 450–51.

83. Al-Zayn, "Min dhikrayat al-Shaykh 'Ali," 28, 30–32. See also Sayyid 'Ali Ibrahim, "Sayyid 'Ali Ibrahim," in *Min daftar al-dhikrayat al-janubiyya,* 46.

84. Sharara, "Min dhikrayat al-Sha'ir Musa al-Zayn," 64–65. See also Shafiq al-Arna'ut, "Adib mujahid wa-majalla ra'ida," in *Wujuh thaqafiyya min al-Janub,* 39.

85. Quoted by Jihad al-Zayn, "Min dhikrayat al-Shaykh 'Ali," 28–29.

86. Ibid., 29.

87. These seminarians were Muhammad 'Ali al-Humani, Sayyid 'Ali Ibrahim, Husayn Muroeh, Muhammad Sharara, Hashim al-Amin, Sadr al-Din Sharaf al-Din, and Muhammad Ja'far Hamdar. Tarif Khalidi, "Shaykh Ahmad 'Arif al-Zayn and *al-'Irfan,*" in *Intellectual Life in the Arab East, 1890–1939,* ed. Marwan Buheiry (Beirut: American University of Beirut Press, 1981), 117 n. 19; Ibrahim, "Sayyid 'Ali Ibrahim," 45.

88. Quoted in Zaynab Isma'il, "Min al-Najaf ila Shaqra' tariq shi'r wa-thaqafa wa-din: Kayfa kana al-intiqal wa-al-'awda min al-hawza al-diniyya ila al-hawza al-marik-siyya?" *Al-Safir*, October 29, 2004. Mundhir Jabir, a Lebanese scholar, argued that the "religious intellectual and the Marxist intellectual did not acknowledge each other's existence" in the South. This observation, however, applies to the 1960s and thereafter. See Mundhir Jabir, "Al-Kiyan al-siyasi li-Jabal 'Amil qabla 1920," in *Safahat min tarikh Jabal 'Amil*, ed. al-Majlis al-Thaqafi li-Lubnan al-Janubi (Beirut: Al-Majlis al-Thaqafi li-Lubnan al-Janubi, 1979), 83.

89. See Robert Nisbet, "Idea of Progress: A Bibliographical Essay," *The Forum, Online Library of Liberty*, 26. The article first appeared in *Literature of Liberty: A Review of Contemporary Liberal Thought* 2, no. 1 (January–March 1979).

90. Ibid., 27. Nisbet points to Marx's English article "The British Rule in India," published in the *New York Tribune* in 1853.

91. Quoted in "Jabal 'Amil fi al-'Iraq," *Al-'Irfan* 24, no. 625 (1934): 528.

92. Quoted in Bazzi, *Muhammad Sharara*, 45. For more on Sharara, see Balqis Sharara, *Min al-iman ila hurriyyat al-fikr* (Damascus: Dar al-Mada, 2009).

93. An illuminating analysis of this question is offered in Samira Haj, *Reconfiguring Islamic Tradition: Reform, Rationality, and Modernity* (Palo Alto, CA: Stanford University Press, 2009), 67–77.

94. Husayn Muroeh, *Al-Naza'at al-maddiyya fi al-falsafa al-'arabiyya al-islamiyya*, 2 vols. (Beirut: Dar al-Farabi, 1988) 1: 28, 29–30, 42. See also Rula Jurdi Abisaab, "Deconstructing the Modular and the Authentic: Husayn Muroeh's Early Islamic History," *Critique: Critical Middle Eastern Studies* 17, no. 3 (Fall 2008): 239–59.

95. Peter Gran, "Islamic Marxism in Comparative History: The Case of Lebanon, Reflections on the Recent Work of Husayn Muruwah," in *The Islamic Impulse*, ed. Barbara Stowasser (Washington, DC: Croom Helm and Georgetown University, 1987), 117, 118.

96. Ibid., 115.

97. Wallerstein, "Eurocentrism," 101–2.

98. Gran, "Islamic Marxism in Comparative History," 109.

99. Talal Asad's approach to this question is useful here. He dispels the idea that "cultural borrowing must lead to total homogeneity," yet he also insists that the "specific forms of power and subjection" are shared by Western and non-Western societies. See Talal Asad, *Genealogies of Religion: Discipline and Reasons of Power in Christianity and Islam* (Baltimore: John Hopkins University Press, 1993), 11–13.

3. Communists in the 'Ulama's Homes:
Economic Shifts, Religious Culture, and the State

1. By "the Left," we mean the Lebanese Communist Party, the Popular Front for the Liberation of Palestine, the Organization of Socialist Lebanon, the Organization of

Communist Action, the Party of Arab Socialist Action, the Popular Democratic Party, the Iraqi and Syrian branches of the Ba'th Party, the leftist wing of the Syrian Nationalist Party, the Progressive Socialist Party under Kamal Junblat's leadership, the Party of Arab Socialist Action, Maoist and Trotskyite Communist groups, labor unions affiliated with the National Trade Unions Federation, women's organizations associated with leftist parties, leftist newspapers and journals, and student organizations. Indeed, a number of these groups show an overlap between nationalist and Marxist leanings.

2. Communists were present in Ba'labak and al-Hirmil, but in smaller numbers and mostly from the 1960s onward.

3. Fouad S. Khoury, "Continuity and Change in Syrian Political Life: The Nineteenth and Twentieth Centuries," *American Historical Review* 96, no. 5 (December 1991): 1388.

4. Liban-Sud, no. 191, Saida, MAE, Syrie-Liban, 1930-40, Avril 11, 1936, Box 411.

5. See Ja'far al-Amin, "Sayyid Ja'far al-Amin," in *Min daftar al-dhikrayat al-janubiyya*, part 2, 110, 114; Ahmad Gharbiyya, "Al-Amin Ahmad Gharbiyya," in *Min daftar al-dhikrayat al-janubiyya*, part 2, 120–121. See also Malek Abisaab, "Shi'ite Peasants and a New Nation in Colonial Lebanon: The *Intifada* (Uprising) of Bint Jubayl, 1936," *Comparative Studies of South Asia, Africa, and the Middle East* 29, no. 3 (November 2009): 483–501.

6. Muhammad Dakrub, *Judhur al-sindiyana al-hamra'* (Beirut: Dar al-Farabi, 1985), 110–11.

7. 'Abdullah Hanna, *Al-Qadiyya al-zira'iyya wa-al-harkat al-fallahiyya fi Suriyya wa-Lubnan: 1920–1945*, vol. 2 (Beirut: Dar al-Farabi, 1978), 291–93, and al-Hakam Darwaza, *Al-Shuyu'iyya al-mahalliyya wa-ma'rakat al-'Arab al-qawmiyya* (N.p.: n.p., 1961), 266.

8. Ahmad Mughniyya, "Al-Shaykh Ahmad Mughniyya," *Min daftar al-dhikrayat al-janubiyya*, part 2, 90–92.

9. See al-Amin Ahmad Gharbiyya, "Ahmad Gharbiyya," in *Min daftar al-dhikrayat al-janubiyya*, part 2, 130–32; "Jabal 'Amil fi al-Iraq," *al-'Irfan* 24, no. 625 (1934): 529; Husayn Muroeh, "Dhikra 9 sha'ban: Mithaq muqaddas fi a'naq al-'Arab," *al-Hatif* 4, no. 141 (October 7, 1938): 3–4.

10. Quoted in Yusuf Khattar al-Hilu, *Awraq min tarikhina*, vol. 2 (Beirut: Dar al-Farabi, 1988), 36, 47–48; Darwaza, *Al-Shuyu'iyya al-mahalliyya*, 239. See also Alexander Flores, "The Arab CPs and the Palestinian Problem," *Khamsin*, no. 7 (1980): 9.

11. Darwaza, *Al-Shuyu'iyya al-mahalliyya*, 266.

12. Gharbiyya, "Ahmad Gharbiyya," 124–25; Akram al-Amin, ed., *Ja'far Muhsin al-Amin: Sira wa 'amiliyyat* (Beirut: Al-Farabi, 2004), 110.

13. See also Artin Madoyan, *Hayat 'ala al-mitras* (Beirut: Dar al-Farabi, 1986), 106–7; Dakrub, *Judhur al-sindiyana al-hamra'*, 374, 375; Michael Suleiman, "The Lebanese Communist Party," *Middle Eastern Studies* 3, no. 2 (January 1967): 115–16.

14. For more on the question of reason and Marxism in Europe and "the nonwhite world" see Eric J. Hobsbawm, *The Age of Empire: 1875–1914* (New York: Pantheon Books, 1987), 262–66.

15. At the same time, French communism provided much inspiration to the Lebanese Communists in Grand Liban during the 1930s. See Ilyas Murqus, *Tarikh al-ahzab al-shuyu'iyya fi al-watan al-'arabi* (Beirut: Dar al-Tali'a, 1964), 30–31.

16. Yitzhak Nakash, *The Shi'is of Iraq* (Princeton, NJ: Princeton University Press, 1994), 118.

17. 'Abd al-Halim al-Ruhaymi, *Ta'rikh al-haraka al-islamiyya fi al-Iraq: Al-Judhur al-fikriyya wa-al-waqi' al-tarikhi, 1900–1924* (Beirut: Al-Dar al-'Alamiyya li-al-Tiba'a, 1985), 163–65, 173, 219–23.

18. Nakash, *The Shi'is of Iraq*, 132.

19. Faleh 'Abd al-Jabbar, *The Shi'ite Movement in Iraq* (London: Dar al-Saqi, 2003), 66.

20. Nakash, *The Shi'is of Iraq*, 134. Around that time, Mahdi al-Khalisi returned to Iraq from exile with British blessings to help in new initiatives against the Communists.

21. See Rula Jurdi Abisaab, *From the Shi'ite Hawza to Marxism: 'Amili Interpretations of Anti-colonial "Modernism," 1920–1950*, paper present at the annual conference for Middle East Studies Association, Boston, 2006. It should be noted that the use of the term *affinity* is not based on a Weberian notion of "elective affinity." It simply delineates a connection and likeness between two seemingly different social phenomena. This connection occurs under particular sociopolitical and economic circumstances. See Michael Löwy's use of the term *elective affinity* in connection to Jewish messianism and libertarian socialism in *Redemption and Utopia: Jewish libertarian Thought in Central Europe: A Study in Elective Affinity*, trans. Hope Heaney (Palo Alto, CA: Stanford University Press, 1992), 3, 9, 11, 17. Löwy examines the neoromanticism and premodern nostalgic elements of Marxism in the writings of Jewish intellectuals. We thank Gabriel Piterberg for bringing this work to our attention and its notion of *affinity*.

22. On Mahdism and Shi'ite political thought, see Wilfred Madelung, "Authority in Twelver Shiism in the Absence of the Imam," in *La notion d'autorité au Moyen Age: Islam, Byzance, Occident*, ed. George Makdisi, D. Sourdel, and J. Sourdel-Thomme (Paris: Presses Universitaires de France, 1982), 163–73; Said Amir Arjomand, *The Shadow of God and the Hidden Imam: Religion, Political Order, and Societal Change in Shi'ite Iran from the Beginning to 1890* (Chicago: University of Chicago Press, 1984), chapter 1.

23. Juan Cole does not view communism as millennial, noting that it is grounded in specific causal actions. See Juan Cole, "Millennialism in Modern Iranian History," in *Imagining the End: Visions of Apocalypse from the Ancient Middle East to Modern America*, ed. Abbas Amanat and Magnus Thorkel Bernhardsson (London: I. B. Tauris, 2002), 304–5.

24. See Gharbiyya, "Ahmad Gharbiyya," 119–20; Fuad Kahil, "Fuad Kahil," in *Min daftar al-dhikrayat al-janubiyya*, part 2, 141–42, 158. Gharbiyya's and Kahil's accounts reflect the meshing of Communist activism and anticolonialism with 'Ashura's symbolisms.

25. Interview with Muhammad Hashishu, July 4, 2005, July 24, 2007, Sidon, Lebanon; interview with Bashir Osmat, June 29, 2008, Beirut. Bashir Osmat served as the head of the archive office of the Lebanese Communist Party from 1977 to 1993. Hashishu is

a civil activist in the South and a leading member of the Popular Democratic Party in Lebanon, a Communist organization.

26. Osmat interview. In July 2007 we also interviewed three Communists from the South who preferred to remain anonymous. Similar features appeared in Iraq, where clandestine Communist groups competed over the organization of the 'Ashura' rituals. See Jabbar, *The Shiʻi Movement in Iraq*, 75–80.

27. Hashishu and Osmat interviews.

28. Osmat interview. See also Hamid al-Harizi, "Al-Zahira al-taʻifiyya wa-ishkali-yyat al-dawla al-madaniyya," *al-Hiwar al-mutamaddin*, June 6 2011, http://www.ahewar.org/debat/show.art.asp?aid=264958. Al-Harizi advances a Marxist analysis of Imam 'Ali's role as a defender of the lower classes that Muslims such as Abu Dharr al-Ghifari supported. See also the article by an anonymous Communist, "In Defense of the Communists," *Shabakat Akhbar al-Nasiriyya*, December 24, 2009, http://www.ahewar.org/

29. Reza Shah-Kazemi, *Justice and Remembrance: Introducing the Spirituality of Imam 'Ali* (London: I. B. Tauris, 2007), 220, 226, 229.

30. There is a rich literature in Egypt and Syria by Arab socialists, including Nasserites, that presents the Prophet and the Rightly Guided Caliphs as having "socialist" leanings. See Mahmud Shalabi, *Ishtirakiyyat Muhammad* (Cairo: Maktabat al-Qahira al-Haditha, 1962). See Yvonne Yazbeck Haddad, *Contemporary Islam and the Challenge of History* (Albany: State University of New York Press, 1982), 31–32, 212–13, notes how some religious scholars in Egypt tried to find "socialist" elements in Islam and others emphasized its revolutionary character.

31. Osmat interview. See also Abdurrahman Badawi, "A Pioneer of Socialism in Islam: Abu Dharr al-Ghifari," *Minbar al-Islam* 2, no. 1 (January 1962): 49–51.

32. Hashim al-Amin experienced a crisis that drove him away from the Syrian–Lebanese Communist Party. He stated: "[Muslim] believers drove me to the path of Marxism and those who brought me back to religion and Islam were the Communists themselves." Quoted in Zaynab Ismaʻil, "Min al-Najaf ila Shaqra' tariq shiʻr wa-thaqafa wa-din: kayfa kana al-intiqal wa-al-ʻawda min al-hawza al-diniyya ila al-hawza al-marik-siyya?" *al-Safir*, October 29, 2004.

33. Muhammad 'Ali Muqallid, "Al-Shaʻir 'Abd al-Muttalib al-Amin," in *Wujuh thaqafiyya min al-janub*, 87–88. 'Abd al-Muttalib left the seminary to pursue a university degree in law from Damascus and graduated in 1939.

34. Sayyid Jaʻfar wrote in his memoirs: "My mother was a black African, stolen by an Arab Muslim along with female and male children from northern Africa. To Mecca he dragged them in a gloomy caravan like cattle." From A. al-Amin, ed. *Jaʻfar Muhsin al-Amin*, 7. For more on his early life, see 18–26 in the same source.

35. Ibid.

36. See Jaʻfar al-Amin, "Jaʻfar al-Amin," *Min daftar al-dhikrayat al-janubiyya*, part 2, 99–102.

37. Al-Amin, ed., *Ja'far Muhsin*, 35.

38. Ibid., 40.

39. Al-Amin, "Sayyid Ja'far," 103–4.

40. Ibid., 36 n. 1.

41. Ibid., 43.

42. Ibid., 36 n. 1.

43. A. al-Amin, ed., *Ja'far Muhsin al-Amin*, 74.

44. J. al-Amin, "Sayyid Ja'far al-Amin," 109.

45. Ibid., 110. The Bint Jubayl branch was founded eight years earlier. Kahil, "Fuad Kahil," 154; Mustafa Bazzi, *Bint Jubayl: Hadirat Jabal 'Amil* (Beirut: Dar al-Amir li-al-Thaqafa wa-al-'Ulum, 1998), 581.

46. Ibid., 109–10.

47. Ibid., 109.

48. J. al-Amin, "Sayyid Ja'far al-Amin," 110.

49. A. al-Amin, ed., *Ja'far Muhsin al-Amin*, 50; J. al-Amin, "Sayyid Ja'far al-Amin," 110. Other party branches emerged in Marji'yun and Hula. The branch in Bint Jubayl was popular and drew in men of the Bazzi and Sharara families. See Bazzi, *Bint Jubayl*, 583.

50. J. al-Amin, "Sayyid Ja'far al-Amin," 109, 114–15.

51. A. al-Amin, *Ja'far Muhsin al-Amin*, 585.

52. Gharbiyya, "Ahmad Gharbiyya," 119–20.

53. Ibid., 158.

54. See the issues of Ja'far al-Amin's magazine *Abu al-Kashakish* in A. al-Amin, ed., *Ja'far Muhsin al-Amin*. The magazine used satire to express views about the contemporary economic and social conditions in Jabal 'Amil.

55. J. al-Amin, "Sayyid Ja'far al-Amin," 114.

56. Ibid.

57. Kahil, "Fuad Kahil," 154.

58. J. al-Amin, "Sayyid Ja'far al-Amin," 114.

59. A. al-Amin, *Ja'far Muhsin al-Amin*, 75. See also Hashim al-Amin's statement (page 79) that the self-proclaimed "progressive" Communists coalesced with the *zu'ama* against his brother Ja'far to protect the existing conventions and "the law."

60. Ibid., 75.

61. Ibid.

62. See Nabil Khalifa, *Al-Shi'a fi Lubnan: Thawrat al-dimughrafiya wa-al-hirman* (Beirut: Markaz Byblos li-al-Dirasat wa-al-Abhath, 1984), 48–50; *Al-Qadiyya al-zira'iyya fi Lubnan fi daw' al-mariksiyya* (Beirut: Manshurat al-Hizb al-Shuyu'i al-Lubnani, c. 1970), 214–21.

63. Sulayman Taqi al-Din, "Al-Janub al-Lubnani bi-ri'ayat al-istiqlal," in *Safahat min tarikh Jabal 'Amil*, ed. al-Majlis al-Thaqafi li-Lubnan al-Janubi (Beirut: Dar al-Farabi, 1979), 151–52.

64. See Abisaab, "Shiite Peasants and a New Nation in Colonial Lebanon," and Ja'far Sharaf al-Din, "Sayyid Ja'far Sharaf al-Din," in *Min daftar al-dhikrayat al-janubiyya*, part 2, 46–47.

65. See Charles Issawi, *The Fertile Crescent, 1800–1914: A Documentary Economic History* (New York: Oxford University Press, 1988), 309.

66. Salim Nasr, "Backdrop to Civil War: The Crisis of Lebanese Capitalism," *MERIP Reports*, no. 73 (December 1978): 8–9; Claude Dubar and Salim Nasr, *Al-Tabaqat al-ijtima'iyya fi Lubnan: Muqaraba susiyulujiyya tatbiqiyya* (Beirut: Mu'assat al-Abhath al-'Arabiyya, 1982), 110.

67. Majed Halawi, *A Lebanon Defied: Musa al-Sadr and the Shi'a Community* (Boulder, CO: Westview Press, 1992), 52–53.

68. Nasr, "Backdrop to Civil War," 6.

69. Chehab's economic policies remained in effect during the administration of Charles Helou (1964–1970).

70. William Persen, "Lebanese Economic Development since 1950," *Middle East Journal* 12, no. 3 (Summer 1958): 277–78.

71. See Allan Richards and John Waterbury, *A Political Economy of the Middle East: State, Class, and Economic Development* (Boulder, CO: Westview Press, 1990), 74.

72. Charles Issawi, "Economic Development and Liberalism in Lebanon," *Middle East Journal* 18, no. 3 (Summer 1964): 285. Despite Issawi's admiration for "economic liberalism," the figures he provided underscored the economic hardships of the working-class.

73. During the first three months of 1960 alone, about twenty labor strikes erupted in Lebanon. See ibid., 285.

74. Edmund Y. Asfour, "Industrial Development in Lebanon," *Middle East Economic Papers* (1959): 2.

75. Nasr, "Backdrop to Civil War," 3, 6, 9.

76. Adnan A. Fahs, *Al-Zuruf al-iqtisadiyya li-al-harb al-ta'ifiyya al-lubnaniyya* (Beirut: Dar al-Nahar, 1979), 35–41.

77. Nasr, "Backdrop to Civil War," 8.

78. Ibid., 4.

79. Ibid.

80. Sharaf al-Din, "Sayyid Ja'far Sharaf al-Din," 70.

81. August R. Norton examines the Israeli military activities and aims in South Lebanon in "Making Enemies in South Lebanon: Harakat Amal, the IDF, and South Lebanon," *Middle East Insight* 3, no. 3 (1984): 13–20.

82. See Charles Churchill, "Village Life of the Central Beqa' Valley of Lebanon," *Middle East Economic Papers* (1959): 8.

83. *Al-Qadiyya al-zira'iyya fi Lubnan fi daw' al-mariksiyya*, 166–70. In 1970, two public hospitals and one private were properly functioning.

84. Ibid., 104–5, 166–67, 223.

85. Richards and Waterbury, *A Political Economy of the Middle East*, 150.

86. Ibid., 21, 104; Fahs, *Al-Zuruf*, 33.

87. For more on these activities, see *Al-Qadiyya al-zira'iyya fi Lubnan fi daw' al-mariksiyya*, 48–50, 214–21.

88. Asfour, "Industrial Development in Lebanon," 1. See also Richards and Waterbury, *A Political Economy of the Middle East*, 97.

89. Richards and Waterbury, *A Political Economy of the Middle East*, 264. Rural–urban migration accounted for 65 percent of Lebanese urban growth, the second-highest proportion in the Middle East after that of the Yemen Arab Republic.

90. Although there were no official censuses for the Lebanese population from 1932 until 1970, a few scholars attempted to come up with approximate estimates of the size of sectarian groups. See Richards and Waterbury, *A Political Economy of the Middle East*, 97; Michael Hudson, *The Precarious Republic: Political Modernization in Lebanon* (New York: Random House, 1968), 22; Shafiq al-Rayyis, *Al-Tahhadi al-lubnani: 1975–1976* (Beirut: Dar al-Masira, 1978), 184.

91. Basim al-Jisr, *Fouad Chehab: Dhalika al-majhul* (Beirut: Sharikat al-Matbu'at li-al-Tawzi' wa-al-Nashr, 1988), 84–85.

92. See Fawwaz Traboulsi, *A History of Modern Lebanon* (London: Pluto Press, 2007), 141. See also the annual reports of the Régie's Board of Directors and Budget Commission presented to the General Assembly between 1962 and 1970, private collection of Jacques Dagher, Beirut.

93. Taqi al-Din, "Al-Janub," 148.

94. Ibid.

95. *Al-Nahar*, October 31, 1963.

96. Traboulsi, *A History of Modern Lebanon*, 139.

97. Ibid., 147–52. See also Bernard Reich, *Political Leaders of the Contemporary Middle East and North Africa: A Biographical Dictionary* (New York: Greenwood, 1990), 141.

98. Augustus Richard Norton, "Hizbullah: From Radicalism to Pragmatism?" *Middle East Policy* 5, no. 4 (January 1998): 4.

99. Nabil Khalifa, *Al-Shi'a fi Lubnan: Thawrat al-dimughrafiya wa-al-hirman* (Beirut: Nabil Khalifa, 1984), 47; Halawi, *A Lebanon Defied*, 65. Maronites ranked at the opposite end (i.e., the top) of the occupational and income chart.

100. *Al-'Irfan*, nos. 9–10 (January–February 1971): 1208. By 1971, around four million Lebanese, including Shi'ite émigrés, lived in African countries such as Egypt, Senegal, Ivory Coast, Nigeria, Liberia, Ghana, and Guinea. See Nabil Harfush, "Awda' al-mughtaribin fi al-'alam," *Al-'Irfan*, nos. 9–10 (January–February, 1971): 1182–93.

101. Hadi Fadlallah, *Muhammad Jawad: Fikr wa islah* (Beirut: Dar al-Hadi, 1993), 381. Mughniyya's enemies accused him of Communist affiliations and argued that he should not remain in his clerical post.

102. Muhammad Jawad Mughniyya, "Al-'Aql wa-'alam ma ba'd al-mawt," *Al-Mawsu'a al-Islamiyya* (2000), http://www.dahsha.com/old/viewarticle.php?id=5737.

103. Fadlallah, *Muhammad Jawad*, 381.

104. Ibid.

105. Al-Hizb al-Shuyu'i al-Lubnani, *Sittun 'aman min al-nidal min ajli Lubnan afdal* (Beirut: Manshurat al-Hizb al-Shuyu'i al-Lubnani, 1988), 64–65.

106. Al-Hizb al-Shuyu'i al-Lubnani, *Al-Shuyu'iyyun al-lubnaniyyun wa-muhimmat al-marhala al-muqbila* (Beirut: Matabi' al-Amal, n.d.), 86.

107. Mahdi 'Amil, *Al-Nazariyya fi al-mumarasa al-siyasiyya: Bahth fi asbab al-harb al-ahliyya fi Lubnan*, part 1 (Beirut: Dar al-Farabi, 1979), 309, 310, 233–34, 311. See also Shuman, "Qira'a fi fikr Charles Malik wa-al-Kaslik," 104–5.

108. Ilyas al-Buwari, *Tarikh al-haraka al-'ummaliyya wa-al-naqabiyya fi Lubnan: 1947–1970*, vol. 2 (Beirut: Dar al-Farabi, 1986), 115, 118,169–78.

109. Ibid., 169–78. See "Mustafa al-'Aris' Parliamentary Electoral Program," Beirut, March 15, 1951, in ibid., document no. 8, 389–92.

110. Ibid., 183–90, 215–20, 288–91. See also "A Memorandum by the Trade Unions to the Ministry of Labor Regarding the Reduction of Rents," in ibid., document no. 14, 398–401.

111. Marwan Amin, "Al-Mas'ala al-ta'ifiyya fi idiyulujiyyat al-haraka al-wataniyya," *al-Tariq* 37, no. 6 (December 1978): 76–77.

112. A few among these activists were Mahdi 'Amil, Husayn Muroeh, Karim Muroeh, Husayn Hamdan, Muhsin Ibrahim, 'Ali al-'Abd, and Habib Sadiq.

113. Subscriptions to the Communist daily *al-Nida'* among workingwomen and men at the Régie increased markedly in the 1960s. Interview with Ahmad 'Abdallah, January 1997, Wadi al-Zinni, Lebanon.

114. Régie Co-Intéressée Libanaise des Tabacs et Tombac, Personnel Department, "Development in the Size of the Régie Working Force, 1959–1972," n.d., Régie archives, Beirut.

115. "Vente Annuelle de Produits Manufactures," Record Group 2, Private Collection of Jacques Dagher, Beirut.

116. *Al-Nahar*, July 11, 1963.

117. See *al-Hayat*, March 9, 1965; March 14, 1965.

118. *Al-Hayat*, March 30, 1965.

119. *Al-Nahar*, March 7, 1965. Well-known Shi'ite Communist activists at the Régie included Hasan Hamid, 'Ali Subayti, Ahmad 'Abdallah, and 'Abdul 'Aziz Harfush, all of whom played a critical role in organizing the 1963 and 1965 strikes.

120. Ibid.

121. *Al-Nahar*, March 7, 1965; March 13, 1965; March 26, 1965.

122. Malek Abisaab, *Women of a Fragile Nation* (Syracuse, NY: Syracuse University Press, 2010), chapter 6.

123. *Al-Thaqafa al-Wataniyya*, April 1, 1965; interview with George al-Batal, February 1997, Beirut; interview with 'Ali Subayti, January 1997, Kafarsir, Lebanon.

124. *Al-Nahar*, March 28, 1965, and *Al-Anba'*, March 26, 1965.

125. Egyptian Communists of the Democratic Movement for National Liberation described Israel as an "advanced capitalist state" compared to the Arab "feudal states." See Ilyas Murqus, *Tarikh al-ahzab al-shuyu'iyya fi al-watan al-'arabi* (Beirut: Dar al-Tali'a, 1964), 63–66; Dakrub, *Judhur al-sindiyana al-hamra'*, 298–99.

126. Ibid.

127. 'Amil, *Al-nazariyya fi al-mumarasa al-siyasiyya*, 291.

128. Ibid., 289–91, 297.

129. A good example of these critiques can be found in the writings of Ilyas Murqus, Yasin al-Hafiz, and the Munir Shafiq. See Murqus, *Tarikh al-ahzab al-shuyu'iyya*, 13–22, 67–76.

130. 'Amil, *Al-Nazariyya fi al-mumarasa al-siyasiyya*, 290.

131. Mahdi 'Amil argues that in 1936, 1948, and 1959 the Communist Party (Syrian-Lebanese and later Lebanese) failed to put into practice the principles it had proclaimed. As a consequence, the workers turned to bourgeois nationalist chauvinism to achieve their aims. See 'Amil, *Al-Nazariyya fi al-mumarasa al-siyasiyya*, 293.

132. The Soviet Union's approach to Israel also changed over time and became more amenable to Arab and Palestinian concerns in the 1960s.

133. Madoyan, *Hayat 'ala al-mitras*, 201.

134. See Husayn Muroeh, "Min al-Najaf dakhala hayati Marx," in *Husayn Muroeh fi masiratihi al-nidaliyya fikran wa mumarasa* (Beirut: Dar al-Farabi, 1997), 89–91. See also Husayn Muroeh, *Wulidtu shaykhan wa 'amutu tiflan* (Beirut: Dar al-Farabi, 1990).

135. For more on Muroeh's relationship to his father, see Silvia Naef, "Shi-i-Shuyu'i or How to Become a Communist in a Holy City," in *The Twelver Shia in Modern Times: Religious Culture & Political History*, ed. Rainer Burnner and Werner Ende (Leiden: Brill, 2001), 255–67; Silvia Naef, "La presse en tant que moteur du renouveau culturel et littéraire: la revue chiite libanaise al-'Irfan," *Études asiatiques, revue de la société Suisse-Asie* L2 (1996): 385–97.

136. 'Abd al-Muhsin al-Qassab, "Husayn Muroeh," *Al-Hatif* 4, no. 136 (September 2 1938): 12–15. Muroeh took off his turban and *jubba*, vest, to put on "modern" clothes on the train in al-Nasiriyya on his way from Najaf to Baghdad.

137. Husayn Muroeh, "Muhammad Sharara," *Wujuh thaqafiyya min al-janub*, 9.

138. Ibid., 7, 9.

139. "Jabal 'Amil fi al-Iraq," 529. These essays and speeches were published in *al-'Irfan* and *al-Hatif*.

140. Husayn Muroeh, "Al-Taj al-Hashimi: Shu'a' risala wa daw' 'aqida," *al-Hatif* 4, no. 137 (September 8 1938): 4–5.

141. Husayn Muroeh, "Thawrat 14 Tammuz al-'Iraqiyya: Thawra wataniyya dimuqratiyya 'amiqat al-judhur," al-Thaqafa al-Wataniyya 7, no. 7 (January 1958): 19.

142. Muroeh, "Dhikra 9 Sha'ban," 3–4. He also expressed support for the 1925 Great Arab Revolt in Syria against the French. See Husayn Muroeh, "Qissa qawmiyya: Shahid," al-Hatif 5, no. 164 (April 28 1939): 19.

143. Husayn Muroeh, "Bayna al-'aql al-qadim wa-al-'aql al-hadith," al-Hatif 5, no. 170 (1939): 7, 9–10.

144. Husayn Muroeh, "Sa'a fi zilal al-butula: Hakadha tughras al-karama al-wataniyya fi al-nufus," al-Hatif, June 3, 1938, 3–4.

145. Husayn Muroeh, "Al-Jundiyya wa-al-islah al-ijtima'i," al-Hatif, January 24 1938, 24–25.

146. Husayn Muroeh, "Adab al-jil al-'iraqi al-hadir yaftaqir ila thaqafa adabiyya dhat wajhayn," al-Hatif, August 28, 1939, 13.

147. Muroeh, "Muhammad Sharara," 7, 9, 19.

148. Muroeh, Wulidutu shaykhan, 56.

149. Shibli Shumayyil translated Charles Darwin's Origin of the Species into Arabic. See also Albert Hourani, Arabic Thought in the Liberal Age: 1798–1939 (New York: Cambridge University Press, 1983), 248–53.

150. Muroeh, Wulidutu shaykhan, 39.

151. Ibid., 61.

152. Saqr Abu Fakhr, Karim Muroeh yatadhakkar fi ma yushbih al-sira (Beirut: Maktabat Bustan, 2002), 292–93.

153. Peter Gran, "Islamic Marxism in Comparative History: The Case of Lebanon, Reflections on the Recent Work of Husayn Muruwah," in The Islamic Impulse, ed. Barbara Stowasser (Washington, DC: Croom Helm and Georgetown University, 1987), 106.

154. Husayn Muroeh, Al-Naza'at al-maddiyya fi al-falsafa al-'arabiyya al-islamiyya, vol. 1 (Beirut: Dar al-Farabi, 1985), 29.

155. Husayn Muroeh, "Harakat al-thaqafa al-'Arabiyya fi muwajahat harb khamsa Huzayran," in Husayn Muroeh, Dirasat fi al-fikr wa-al-adab (Beirut: Dar al-Farabi, 1993), 123.

156. Ibid., 116.

157. Muroeh, Al-Naza'at al-maddiyya, 1:5–6, 28, 13. Muroeh excludes from this scholarship the work of another southern Communist, Mahdi 'Amil's Azamat al-hadara al-'arabiyya am azamat al-burjuwaziyyat al-'arabiyya (Beirut: Dar al-Farabi, 1974).

158. Asfour, "Industrial Development in Lebanon," 3. See also Fahs, Al-Zuruf, 44–46, 47.

159. Peter Gran, "Modern Middle East History beyond Oriental Despotism, World History Beyond Hegel: An Agenda Article," in New Frontiers in the Social History of the Middle East, ed. Enid Hill, Cairo Papers in Social Science 23, no. 2 (Cairo: American University in Cairo Press, 2001), 195; Peter Gran, "The Failure of Social Theory to Keep

Up with Our Times: The Study of Women and Structural Adjustment Programs in the Middle East as an Example," paper presented at the 34th annual conference of the Association of Muslim Social Scientist, Temple University, September 30, 2005, 7–8.

160. 'Amil, *Al-Nazariyya fi al-mumarasa al-siyasiyya*, 235.

4. The "Shi'ite Communist," the Clerical Movement, and the Islamists in Iraq

1. For a discussion of these terms, see Hamid Dabashi, *Theology of Discontent: The Ideological Foundations of the Islamic Revolution in Iran* (New York: New York University Press, 1993).

2. See Zaki Khayri, *Kitabat al-rafiq Husayn Muhammad al-Shabibi* (Baghdad: Matba'at al-Sha'b, 1974), 90–97.

3. Yitzhak Nakash, *The Shi'is of Iraq* (Princeton, NJ: Princeton University Press, 1994), 134. Around that time, Mahdi al-Khalisi returned to Iraq from exile with British blessings to help in new initiatives against the Communists.

4. Ibid.

5. Hanna Batatu, *The Old Social Classes and the Revolutionary Movements of Iraq: A Study of Iraq's Old Landed and Commercial Classes and of Its Communists, Ba'thists, and Free Officers* (Princeton, NJ.: Princeton University Press, 1978), 49, 58–62.

6. See Khayri, *Kitabat al-rafiq Husayn Muhammad al-Shabibi*, 6–7, 25, 78–81; "Mahdar ijtima' mu'tamar al-hizb al-awwal," *Al-Qa'ida*, March 16, 1944, http://www.iraqicp.com/2010-12-30-11-08-49/99-2010-12-01-13-08-13.html. The reports of the conference were published in *Al-Qa'ida*, March 16, 1944. See also Tareq Y. Ismael, *The Rise and Fall of the Communist Party of Iraq* (Cambridge: Cambridge University Press, 2008), 39.

7. "Mahdar ijtima' mu'tamar"

8. Faleh A. Jabbar, *The Shi'ite Movement in Iraq* (London: Saqi, 2003), 65–66. See also Khayri, *Kitabat al-rafiq Husayn Muhammad al-Shabibi*, 34, 40–41.

9. "Mahdar ijtima' mu'tamar"

10. Ibid.

11. Ibid. On deteriorating peasant conditions, see 'Abd al-Sahib al-'Alwan, *Dirasat fi al-islah al-zira'i* (Baghdad: Matba'at al-Aswaq al-Tijariyya, 1961), 163–64.

12. Samira Haj, *The Making of Iraq, 1900–1963: Capital, Power, and Ideology* (Albany: State University of New York Press, 1997), 34. For more background on this question see al-'Alwan, *Dirasat fi al-islah al-zira'i*, 133–47.

13. Batatu, *The Old Social Classes*, 664–65.

14. Khayri, *Kitabat al-rafiq Husayn Muhammad al-Shabibi*, 104–5. See Iraqi Communist Party documents at http://www.iraqicp.com/index.php.

15. Rony Gabbay, *Communism and Agrarian Reform in Iraq* (London: Croom Helm, 1978), 83. It is also possible that some peasants preferred to own land privately instead of working freely on it for the state. See ibid., 96–97.

16. Muhammad Baqir al-Husayni, "Al-Sayyid ʿAbd al-Karim Qasim (qaddasa sirrahu) and al-zaʿim Muhsin al-Hakim: Al-Shuyuʿiyya kufr wa-ilhad," part 3, *al-Hiwar al-Mutamaddin*, May 31, 2007, http://www.ahewar.org/debat/show.art.asp?aid=98257.

17. Jabbar, *The Shiʿite Movement in Iraq*, 123.

18. Muhammad Baqir al-Husayni, "Al-Sayyid ʿAbd al-Karim Qasim (qaddasa sirrahu) and al-zaʿim Muhsin al-Hakim: Al-Shuyuʿiyya kufr wa-ilhad," part 1, *Al-Hiwar al-Mutamaddin*, April 27, 2007, http://www.ahewar.org/debat/show.art.asp?aid=95108.

19. Jabbar, *The Shiʿite Movement in Iraq*, 123.

20. Muhammad Baqir al-Husayni, "Al-Sayyid ʿAbd al-Karim Qasim," part 2, *al-Hiwar al-Mutamaddin*, April 30, 2007, http://www.ahewar.org/debat/show.art.asp?aid=95238; Muhammad Baqir al-Husayni, "Al-Sayyid ʿAbd al-Karim Qasim (qaddasa sirrahu)," part 3. See also Jabbar, *The Shiʿite Movement in Iraq*, 123; Khayri, *Kitabat al-rafiq*, 66, 123.

21. Batatu, *The Old Social Classes*, 699. The Kurds occupied critical posts in the ICP, too. On the ICP's theoretical developments and political program see Haj, *The Making of Iraq*, 92–119.

22. Eric Davis, *Memories of State: Politics, History, and Collective Identity in Modern Iraq* (Berkeley: University of California Press, 2005), 96–98, 116–19; Batatu, *The Old Social Classes*, 615. The president of the executive committee of the National Student Congress was Jaʿfar al-Labban, a Shiʿite Communist from Hilla.

23. Davis, *Memories of State*, 96–97; Ismael, *The Rise and Fall of the Communist Party of Iraq*, 91.

24. Batatu, *The Old Social Classes*, 751. On the programs and activities of the labor movement and the Communists in Iraq during this period, see Ilario Salucci, *A People's History of Iraq: The Iraqi Communist Party, Workers' Movements, and the Left, 1924–2004* (Chicago: Haymarket Books, 2005), chapter 3.

25. Batatu, *The Old Social Classes*, 751.

26. Ibid., 754.

27. Ibid., 752; Khayri, *Kitabat al-Rafiq Husayn Muhammad al-Shabibi*, 40–41.

28. Batatu, *The Old Social Classes*, 752, 754. See also S. Seyyed Vali Reza Nasr, *The Shia Revival: How Conflicts within Islam Will Shape the Future* (New York: W. W. Norton, 2006), 115–16. Nasr stresses the deep roots that the Left had in Iraq, among the Shiʿites in particular.

29. M. Ismail Marcinkowski and Hamid Algar, *Religion and Politics in Iraq: Muslim Shia Clerics Between Quietism and Resistance* (Singapore: Pustaka Nasional, 2004), 44, 64.

30. See Davis, *Memories of State*, 129; Haj, *The Making of Iraq*, 189 n. 54.

31. See Davis, *Memories of State*, 129.

32. Orit Bashkin, *The Other Iraq: Pluralism and Culture in Hashimite Iraq* (Palo Alto, CA: Stanford University Press, 2009), 136.

33. Ibid., 135.

34. Batatu, *The Old Social Classes*, 694–95. See also 'Ali al-Kawrani al-'Amili and al-Wahid al-Khurasani, *Al-Haqq al-mubin fi ma'rifat al-ma'sumin 'alayhim al-salam: buhuth mustafada min muhadarat al-marja' al-dini Ayatullah al-'uzma al-Wahid al-Khurasani madda zillahu*, 2nd ed., (Qom, Iran: Dar al-Huda, 2003), introduction; Hani Fahs, "Tullab al-Najaf al-lubnaniyyun," *al-Safir*, July 16, 1999.

35. Jabbar, *The Shi'ite Movement in Iraq*, 65–66. Jabbar discusses the factors that encouraged Shi'ites to adopt communism. See also Marion Farouk-Sluglett and Peter Sluglett, *Iraq since 1958: From Revolution to Dictatorship* (New York: Routledge, 1987), 191–92.

36. The ICP attracted many students, but its efforts were focused on organizing railway and port workers. See Batatu, *The Old Social Classes*, 616–21, 639–42.

37. See al-Kawrani al-'Amili and al-Wahid al-Khurasani, *Al-Haqq al-mubin fi ma'rifat al-ma'sumin 'alayhim al-salam*, 2nd ed., introduction. In this introduction, al-Kawrani removed sections, which appeared in the first edition depicting Baqir al-Sadr and his modernist arguments in a negative light.

38. See ICP documents at http://www.iraqicp.com/index.php.

39. Chibli Mallat, "Shi'ism and Sunnism in Iraq: Revisiting the Codes," in *Islamic Family Law*, ed. Chibli Mallat and Jane Frances Connors (London: Graham & Trotman, 1990), 71–92.

40. Jabbar, *The Shi'ite Movement in Iraq*, 177.

41. Mallat, "Shi'ism and Sunnism in Iraq," 80.

42. Ibid., 83–86, 90.

43. Interview with Shaykh Subhi al-Tufayli, July 2005, 'Ayn Burday, Lebanon

44. See Salucci, *A People's History of* Iraq, 10–11; Karim Muroeh, "'An al-din wa-al-turath, wa-al-thawra," in *Hiwarat: Mufakkirun 'Arab yunaqishun Karim Muroeh fi al-qawmiyya wa-al-ishtirakiyya wa-al-dimuqratiyya wa-al-din wa-al-thawra*, ed. Karim Muroeh and 'Adil Ahmad (Beirut: Dar al-Farabi, 1990), 32–35.

45. See "Mahdar ijtima' mu'tamar"; Gabbay, *Communism and Agrarian Reform in Iraq*, 51–52. Gabbay notes that the large landholders attacked Communist land reformists by "playing heavily on the religious sentiments of the masses with the pretext of the Reformist 'irreligious ideology.'" See also Malik Sayf, *Li-al-tarikh lisan: Dhikrayat wa-qadaya khassa bi-al-hizb al-shuyu'i al-'iraqi mundhu ta'sisihi hatta al-yawm* (Baghdad: Dar al-Huriyya li-al-Tiba'a, 1983), 130–32, 142–48, 211–14, 236–38.

46. See Vladimir Ilyich Lenin, *Religion* (Bristol, UK: Burleigh Press, 2007), 5–6, 11–15; Sheila Fitzpatrick, *Education and Social Mobility in the Soviet Union, 1921–1934* (Cambridge: Cambridge University Press, 2002), 18–19, 162.

47. Harold Joseph Berman, *Faith and Order: The Reconciliation of Law and Religion* (Grand Rapids, MI: Eerdmans, 2000), 394.

48. For the questions that preoccupied the Communists in the 1940s and the 1950s, see Gabbay, *Communism and Agrarian Reform in Iraq*, 51–59. On religion, see Ismael, *The Rise and Fall of the Communist Party of Iraq*, 22–23.

49. See statements made by Communists in periodicals between 1944 and 1958 in Gabbay, *Communism and Agrarian Reform in Iraq*, 65–68. On Marxism and religion, see Nikolaus Lobkowicz, "Karl Marx's Attitude toward Religion," in *Marxism: The Inner Dialogues*, ed. Michael Curtis (New Brunswick, NJ: Transaction, 1997), 155–56; Berman, *Faith and Order*, 356.

50. Gabbay, *Communism and Agrarian Reform in Iraq*, 65, 73.

51. Ismael, *The Rise and Fall of the Communist Party of Iraq*, 70.

52. Batatu, *The Old Social Classes*, 449–50.

53. Al-Husayni, "Al-Sayyid 'Abd al-Karim Qasim," part 2.

54. Khayri, *Kitabat al-rafiq Husayn Muhammad al-Shabibi*, introduction, a.

55. Batatu, *The Old Social Classes*, 696.

56. Quoted in ibid., 696–97.

57. Jabbar, *The Shi'ite Movement in Iraq*, 75–80. Jabbar notes that when the Islamists came to dominate Najaf later on, disguised Communists vied with them in organizing the *'Ashura'* ceremonies.

58. Ibrahim al-Haydari, *Trajidya Karbala': Sociolojya al-khitab al-sha'bi li-al-'aza' al-husayni* (Beirut: Dar al-Saqi, 1999), 376.

59. Batatu, *The Old Social Classes*, 698.

60. This composition is clearly reflected in the statements of the anti-Communist Lebanese cleric 'Ali al-Kawrani al-'Amili, who lived in Najaf in the 1950s. See his chapter "Al-Mawja al-shuyu'iyya allati 'asarnaha," in *Ila talib al-'ilm*, ed. 'Ali al-Kawrani al-'Amili (Qom, Iran: N.p., 2010).

61. One essay accuses the Shi'ite Communists of hypocrisy for accepting historical materialism while endorsing the imamate of 'Ali b. Abi Talib. See 'Abdallah al-Faqir, "Fidiraliyyat al-shinat al-thalatha 'Shi'i shuyu'i shuruki,'" *Al-Jazeera Talk*, June 6, 2006, http://www.aljazeeratalk.net/forum/archive/index . . . /t-134500.html.

62. Al-Husayni, "Al-Sayyid 'Abd al-Karim Qasim," parts 1 and 2.

63. The martyrdom of Imam Husayn and the sacrifices of *ahl al-bayt* were also central themes in poems written by Badr Shakir al-Sayyab, a Sunnite Communist. See Jasim al-Mutir, "'An al-shi'r wa al-shuyu'iyin wa dhikra al-Husayn," *Jaridat Babil*, February 1, 2010, http://www.babil.info/printVersion.php?mid=24185.

64. Muzaffar al-Nawwab, "Watariyyat Layliyya," *al-Hiwar al-Mutamaddin*, February 27, 2003, http://www.ahewar.org/debat/show.art.asp?aid=413#.

65. Muzaffar al-Nawwab, "Min al-daftar al-sirri al-khususi li-Imam al-mughannin," *al-Mawsu'a al-'alamiyya li-al al-shi'r al-'arabi*, April 12, 2005, http://www.adab.com/modules.php?name=Sh3er&doWhat=shqas&qid=64132&r=&rc=1.

66. Psychoanalytic studies have treated the head as a phallic symbol and thus beheading as a castration anxiety. Martyrdom is seen in this context as a form of castration.

67. Talal Asad, *Formations of the Secular: Christianity, Islam, Modernity* (Palo Alto, CA: Stanford University Press, 2003), 26, 35, 54–56, 189. When discussing the use of

"redemptive myth" by liberal Arab intellectuals such as Adonis, Asad suggests that it aimed to achieve poetic modernity and did not produce a "religious" experience per se. Rather, it culminates in profaning and undermining a religious tradition. Adonis, however, is concerned with the non-Islamic myth and its supernatural elements, which allow him to expand its secular facets. This is not the case with Islamic symbolism already shared and renewed by a living society.

68. An example is the appearance of al-Husayn in the early poetry of Badr Shakir al-Sayyab. See Terri de Young, *Placing the Poet: Badr Shakir al-Sayyab and Postcolonial Iraq* (Albany: State University of New York Press, 1998), 121.

69. On 'Ashura' and *ahl al-bayt*, see also the poems of the leftist scholar Muhammad Mahdi al-Jawahiri from Najaf in *Diwan al-Jawahiri*, vol. 2 (Najaf, Iraq: Matba'at al-Ghuri, 1935), 111–12, 286–89. Al-Husayn emerges not merely a tragic hero bemoaned by his partisans but a source of illumination, fortitude, and knowledge. See Muhammad Mahdi al-Jawahiri, "Amantu bi-al-Husayn," *al-Bayyina*, 2005, http://www.al-bayyna.com/modules.php?name=News&file=article&sid=45046.

70. Muzaffar al-Nawwab, "Al-Wuquf bayna al-samawat wa-al-Imam al-Husayn," *Muntadayat Ya Husayn*, 2000, http://www.yahosein.org/vb/showthread.php?t=112601.

71. Ibid.

72. Some scholars have noted that anticlericalism does not aim to transform the epistemological foundations of Islamic faith or its metaphysical constructs. See Richard Rorty, "Anti-clericalism and Atheism," in *Religion after Metaphysics*, ed. Mark A. Wrathal (Cambridge: Cambridge University Press, 2003), 39–40.

73. Muhammad Salih Bahr al-'Ulum, "Ayna Haqqi," *Muntadayat Ya Husayn*, 2000, http://www.yahosein.org/vb/showthread.php?t=105870. The poem was composed in 1955. On Bahr al-'Ulum, see Silvia Naef, "Shi'i-Shuyu'i, or How to become a Communist in a Holy City?" in *The Twelver Shia in Modern Times: Religious, Culture, and Political History*, ed. Rainer Brunner and Werner Ende (Leiden: Brill, 2001), 255–67.

74. See 'Abd al-Razzaq Dahnun, "Thamani sanawat 'ijaf 'ala rahil Hadi al-'Alawi al-baghdadi," *al-Nur*, September 27, 2006, 4.

75. Ibid., 4–5.

76. Hadi al-'Alawi, *Fusul min tarikh al-Islam al-siyasi*, 2nd ed. (Nicosia, Cyprus: Center for Socialist Studies and Research in the Arab World, F.K.A. Publishing, 1999), 17–20.

77. 'Ali al-Ibrahimi, "Hadi al-'Alawi wa-'Ali Shari'ati: Man minhuma fahima al-tarikh?" July 27, 2009, http://www.almitro.com/09/2868.html.

78. See Ismael, *The Rise and Fall of the Communist Party of Iraq*, 241–45. The ICP leaders proposed a "new agenda" based on the integration of Islamic heritage and scientific socialism. On communism and atheism, see Muhammad Mahdi Shamseddine, *Dirasat wa-mawaqif fi al-fikr wa-al-siyasa wa-al-mujtama': Abhath fikriyya wa-islamiyya 'amma* (Beirut: Al-Mu'assassa al-Dawliyya li-al-Dirasat wa-al-Nashr, 1990), 131–34.

79. Muhammad Jawad Mughniyya, *Abu Dharr: Ramz al-yaqza fi al-damir al-insani: 'Ard wa-tahlil* (Beirut: Dar al-Ta'aruf, 1990), 52–56, 70–78, 345.

80. Hadi Fadlallah, *Muhammad Jawad Mughniyya: Fikr wa-islah* (Beirut: Dar al-Hadi, 1993), 227, 180, 182, 184.

81. One example is *Ru'a al-hayat fi nahj al-balagha* (Beirut: Dar al-Safwa, 1998) by Hasan al-Saffar, a religious scholar who highlights Imam 'Ali's opposition to class divisions and support for the redistribution of wealth, issues emphasized by the Communists. At the same time, however, he challenges the Communist view that private ownership is not embedded in human nature.

82. See 'Adil Ra'uf, *Muhammad Baqir al-Sadr bayna diktaturiyyatayn*, 6th ed. (Damascus: Al-Markaz al-'Iraqi li-al-I'lam wa-al-Dirasat, 2001), 281–83; Gabbay, *Communism and Agrarian Reform in Iraq*, 51–52.

83. Laurence Louer, *Transnational Shia Politics: Religious and Political Networks in the Gulf* (New York: Columbia University Press, 2008), 90–91.

84. Ra'uf, *Muhammad Baqir al-Sadr*, 256–57.

85. 'Abd al-Jabbar al-'Itabi, "Hadi al-'Alawi . . . kana fi ittihad al-udaba'," *Elaph*, November 26, 2008, http://www.elaph.com/Web/Culture/2008/11/385553.htm.

86. Hani Fahs, "Hunaka man yumaris al-naqd al-'am ba'da fawat al-awan," *al-Mustaqbal*, December 12, 2010, http://www.almustaqbal.com/Nawafez.aspx?pageid=66050.

87. Dahnun, "Thamani sanawat 'ijaf," 263.

88. See Hadi al-'Alawi, *Fi al-din wa-al-turath* (Beirut: Dar al-Tali'a, 1973); Hadi al-'Alawi, *Fi al-siyasa al-islamiyya* (Beirut: Dar al-Tali'a, 1974); Hadi al-'Alawi, *Fusul min tarikh al-Islam al-siyasi* (Nicosia, Cyprus: Markaz al-Abhath wa al-Dirasat al-Ishtirakiya fi al-'Alam al-'Arabi, 1999); As'ad Abu Khalil, "Against the Taboos of Islam: Anti-conformist Tendencies in Contemporary Arab/Islamic Thought," in *Between the State and Islam*, ed. Charles E. Butterworth and I. William Zartman (Cambridge: Cambridge University Press, 2001), 130–31.

89. Today the original texts of the *'ulama*'s fatwas on heresy are difficult to obtain because they have created controversy and divisions in Iraqi Shi'ite society. Sections and statements from these fatwas were available in accounts by contemporary clerics and scholars; see Fadlallah, *Muhammad Jawad Mughniyya*, 227.

90. Ra'uf, *Muhammad Baqir al-Sadr*, 256–57.

91. Al-Husayni, "Al-Sayyid 'Abd al-Karim Qasim," parts 1, 2, and 3; 'Ali al-Kawrani al-'Amili, "*Al-Mawja al-shuyu'iyya allati 'asarnaha*."

92. Al-Husayni, "Al-Sayyid 'Abd al-Karim Qasim," parts 2 and 3; Ra'uf, *Muhammad Baqir al-Sadr*, 256; Jabbar, *The Shi'ite Movement in Iraq*, 133–34.

93. Isam al-Khafaji, *Tormented Births: Passages to Modernity in Europe and the Middle East* (London: I. B. Tauris, 2004), 142 n. 27.

94. Gabbay, *Communism and Agrarian Reform in Iraq*, 51–52. Gabbay notes that the large landholders attacked Communist land reformists by "playing heavily on the religious sentiments of the masses with the pretext of the Reformist 'irreligious ideology.'"

See also Nakash, *The Shi'is of Iraq*, 98–100. On land reform see Haj, *The Making of Iraq*, 97, 122, 189 n49.

95. Al-Husayni, "Al-Sayyid 'Abd al-Karim Qasim," part 3.

96. Dhiyab Mahdi Muhsin, "Min dhakirat al-sinin al-najafiyya. . . . : Al-Shaykh al-rahil Muhammad al-Shabibi," *al-Hiwar al-Mutamaddin*, October 29, 2005, http://www.ahewar.org/debat/show.art.asp?aid=49152.

97. Ibid.; Ra'uf, *Muhamad Baqir al-Sadr*, 305.

98. See Ra'uf, *Muhammad Baqir al-Sadr*, 284; Ra'd al-Jabburi, "Hal hum aqlam li-al-ijar?: Muthaqqafun shuyu'iyyun bayna khiwa' al-thaqafa wa-inhiraf al-tatbiq: Rashid al-Khayyun namuzajan," *al-Sharq*, March 3, 2010, http://oreint.arabblogs.com/archive/2010/3/1023840.html.

99. Al-Husayni, "Al-Sayyid 'Abd al-Karim Qasim," part 1. The jurists 'Abd al-Karim Zanjani and Muhammad Fadil Qa'ini refused to issue fatwas similar to al-Hakim's.

100. Al-Husayni, "Al-Sayyid 'Abd al-Karim Qasim," part 2.

101. See Ra'uf, *Muhammad Baqir al-Sadr*, 256. Al-Hakim seemed to have forced an Ayatullah, al-Hasani al-Baghdadi, to write a fatwa condemning communism, which he did, but it had a more cautious tone than al-Hakim's.

102. Al-Husayni, "Al-Sayyid 'Abd al-Karim Qasim," part 2; Jabbar, *The Shi'ite Movement in Iraq*, 133–34; Nakash, *The Shi'is of Iraq*, 98–100. On land reform, see Haj, *The Making of Iraq*, 97, 122, 189 n. 49.

103. Al-Husayni, "Al-Sayyid 'Abd al-Karim Qasim," part 2.

104. Arif was an observant Muslim but his government was "secularist" in attempting to privatize religion and protect the secular legal and administrative processes of the state.

105. On the cooperation between the Shi'ite *'ulama'* and the Ba'th regime, see Talib M. Aziz, "The Role of Muhammad Baqir al-Sadr in Shi'i Political Activism in Iraq from 1958- 1980," *International Journal of Middle East Studies* 25 no.2 (1993): 209–19.

106. See 'Ali al-Wardi, *Lamahat ijtima'iyya min tarikh al-Iraq al-hadith*, part 5, (London: Al-Warrak, 2007), 54–57; Nakash, *The Shi'is of Iraq*, 60–65; Jabbar, *The Shi'ite Movement in Iraq*, 75–76.

107. Nakash, *The Shi'is of Iraq*, 88.

108. For more on the Shi'ite *maraji'*, see the section on it in al-Jabbar, *The Shi'ite Movement in Iraq*, 171–84.

109. Marcinkowski and Algar, *Religion and Politics in Iraq*, 104.

110. Ismael, *The Rise and Fall of the Communist Party of Iraq*, 91.

111. Farouk-Sluglett and Sluglett, *Iraq since 1958*, 64–65.

112. See Aziz, "The Role of Muhammad Baqir al-Sadr in Shi'i Political Activism," 209–19.

113. Ali A. Allawi, *The Occupation of Iraq: Winning the War, Losing the Peace* (New Haven, CT: Yale University Press, 2007), 27. See also al-Husayni, "Al-Sayyid 'Abd al-Karim

Qasim," part 1. Al-Hakim tried to form a political group named "Al-Hizb al-Ja'fari," but it did not see the light for reasons that remain unclear.

114. Aziz, "The Role of Muhammad Baqir al-Sadr," 209-19.

115. Al-Kawrani al-'Amili, *Al-Mawja al-shuyui'yya allati 'asarnaha.*

116. Al-Husayni, "Al-Sayyid 'Abd al-Karim Qasim," part 1.

117. See al-Husayni, "Al-Sayyid 'Abd al-Karim Qasim," part 3; Jabbar, *The Shi'ite Movement in Iraq,* 100.

118. 'Abdul-Halim al-Ruhaimi, "The Da'wa Islamic Party: Origins, Actors, and Ideology," in *Ayatollahs, Sufis, and Ideologues: State, Religion, and Social Movements in Iraq,* ed. Falih Abd al-Jabbar (London: Saqi Books, 2002), 151–52.

119. See Jabbar, *The Shi'ite Movement,* 129–30. The ICP secretary-general, Salam 'Adil, was a Shi'ite sayyid from Najaf.

120. Aziz, "The Role of Muhammad Baqir al-Sadr," 209-19.

121. Talib Aziz, "Baqr al-Sadr's Quest for the Marja'iyya," in *The Most Learned of the Shi'a: The Institution of Marja' al-Taqlid,* ed. Linda S. Walbridge (New York: Oxford University Press, 2001), 141; Aziz, "The Role of Muhammad Baqir al-Sadr," 209–19.

122. This adaptation led al-Kawrani to declare that communism "left its imprint on trends in religious practice in our seminaries and societies." He disparaged Islamist thinkers such as Baqir al-Sadr and Fadlallah for drawing upon Marxist and Sunnite political concepts. See al-Kawrani al-'Amili and al-Wahid al-Khurasani, *Al-Haqq al-mubin fi ma'rifat al-ma'sumin 'alayhim al-salam,* introduction.

123. Al-Husayni, "Al-Sayyid 'Abd al-Karim Qasim," part 3.

124. A. 'Ali 'Allawi, *The Occupation of Iraq: Winning the War, Losing the Peace* (New Haven, CT: Yale University Press, 2007), 27–28.

125. Aziz, "The Role of Muhammad Baqir al-Sadr," 209-19.

126. Jean-Pierre Luizard's depiction of al-Hakim's *marja'iyya* as "apolitical" or "quietist" contradicts his statements about al-Hakim's political involvement in fighting communism. See Jean-Pierre Luizard, "The Nature of the Confrontation Between the State and Marja'ism: Grand Ayatollah Muhsin al-Hakim and the Ba'th," in Abd al-Jabbar, ed., *Ayatollahs, Sufis, and Ideologues,* 92–93, 94–95. In comparison, Jawdat al-Qazwini provides evidence for the political activism of Muhsin al-Hakim in "The School of Najaf," in *Ayatollahs, Sufis, and Ideologues,* ed. Abd al-Jabbar, 252–54. See also al-Kawrani's account in *Al-Mawja al-shuyu'iyya allati 'asarnaha.*

127. Al-Husayni, "Al-Sayyid 'Abd al-Karim Qasim," parts 1 and 3.

128. See al-Qazwini, "The School of Najaf," 251–52. Luizard's observation that the Communist and Ba'thist dealings with the jurists in Najaf "did not differ greatly" from each other can hardly be supported by historical evidence. See Luizard, "The Nature of the Confrontation," 91.

129. Baqir al-Sadr established the Usul al-Din College in Baghdad in 1964.

130. Al-Husayni, "Al-Sayyid 'Abd al-Karim Qasim," parts 1 and 3; al-Kawrani, *Al-Mawja al-shuyu'iyya allati 'asarnaha.*

131. See Davis, *Memories of State,* 118; Aziz, "The Role of Muhammad Baqir al-Sadr," 209-19.

132. Ra'uf, *Muhammad Baqir al-Sadr,* 282; al-Husayni, "Al-Sayyid 'Abd al-Karim Qasim," part 1.

133. Al-Husayni, "Al-Sayyid 'Abd al-Karim Qasim," part 3. See also al-Hizb al-Shuyu'i al-'Iraqi, *Kitab shuhada' al-hizb, shuhada' al-watan,* 2nd ed. (Osby, Sweden: Media Vision, 2009), 305.

134. Ra'uf, *Muhammad Baqir al-Sadr,* 275.

135. On the introduction to al-Kawrani al-'Amili and al-Wahid al-Kurasani, *Al-Haqq al-mubin fi ma'rifat al-ma'sumin 'alayhim al-salam,* introduction. See also Rula Jurdi Abisaab, "Lebanese Shi'ites and the Marja'iyya: Polemic in the Late Twentieth Century," *British Journal of Middle Eastern Studies* 36, no. 2 (August 2009): 222, 234.

136. Hamid Ruhani, *Nehzat-e Imam Khomeini,* vol. 2 (Tehran, Iran: N.p., 1985), 150–51, 392–93. Chibli Mallat dismisses such accounts, claiming that Khomeini's isolation in Najaf was caused by his fear of being deported by the Ba'thist regime. See Chibli Mallat, *The Renewal of Islamic Law: Muhammad Baqer as-Sadr, Najaf, and the Shi'i International* (Cambridge: Cambridge University Press, 1993), 51.

137. Quoted in al-Husayni, "Al-Sayyid 'Abd al-Karim Qasim," part 3.

138. See Hamid Algar, *Islam and Revolution: Writings and Declarations of Imam Khomeini* (Berkeley, CA: Mizan Press, 1981), for an English translation of Khomeini's lectures.

139. Jabbar, *The Shi'ite Movement in Iraq,* 106.

140. Charles Tripp, *A History of Iraq* (Cambridge: Cambridge University Press, 2000), 202–3.

141. For an overview on Baqir al-Sadr's life and thought, see Muhammad Baqir al-Sadr, "The General Framework of the Islamic Economy," in *Princeton Readings in Islamist Thought,* ed. Roxanne Leslie Euben and Muhammad Qasim Zaman (Princeton: Princeton University Press, 2009), 181–86.

142. See Mallat, *The Renewal of Islamic Law,* 9–10. The works intended as seminary texts were Muhammad Baqir al-Sadir, *Al-Ma'alim al-jadida fi al-usul* (Tehran: Maktabat al-Najah, 1975), first published in 1964, and Muhammad Baqir al-Sadr, *Durus fi 'ilm al-usul,* 4 vols. (Qom, Iran: Mu'assasat al-Nashr al-Islami al-Tabi'a li-Jama'at al-Mudarrisin bi-Qum al-Muqaddas, 1994–95), with the first volume published in 1977. See also Muhammad Baqir al-Sadr, *Lessons in Islamic Jurisprudence,* trans. Roy P. Mottahedeh (Oxford: Oneworld, 2003).

143. Mallat, *The Renewal of Islamic Law,* 51–53.

144. Aziz, "The Role of Muhammad Baqir al-Sadr," 215.

145. See Joyce Wiley, "'Alima bint al-Huda, Women's Advocate," in *The Most Learned of the Shi'a*, 149–160; Aziz, "The Role of Muhammad Baqir al-Sadr," 216. Ba'thist attacks on Iran in connection to Islamism are highlighted in Eric James Hoogland, *Twenty Years of Islamic Revolution: Political and Social Transition in Iran* (Syracuse, NY: Syracuse University Press, 2002), 159–61.

146. These themes appear in Bint al-Huda's short stories, *Imra'atan wa-rajul* (Beirut: Dar al-Ta'aruf li-al-Matbu'at, 1979), and Bint al-Huda, "Butulat al-mar'a al-muslima," in *Al-Majmu'a al-qasasiyya al-kamila* (Beirut: Dar al-Ta'aruf li-al-Matbu'at, 1981).

147. Farouk-Sluglett and Sluglett, *Iraq since 1958*, 196–97.

148. For more on Baqir al-Sadr, see Kazim Husayn al-Ha'iri, *Mabahith al-usul: Taqriran li-abhath samahat Ayatullah al-'uzma al-shahid al-sayyid Muhammad Baqir al-Sadr* (Qom, Iran: Maktab al-I'lam al-Islami, 1987), 11–68.

149. For more on Marxism and Shi'ite scholars, see Daniel Brumberg, *Reinventing Khomeini: The Struggle for Reform in Iran* (Chicago: University of Chicago Press, 2001), 75–79; Aziz, "The Role of Muhammad Baqir al-Sadr," 209–210.

150. Brumberg, *Reinventing Khomeini*, 4, 17.

151. Baqir al-Sadir, *Falsafatuna:Dirasa mawdu'iyya fi mu'tarak al-sira' al-fikri al-qa'im bayna mukhtalaf al-tayyarat al-falsafiyya wa-khassatan al-falsafa al-islamiyya wa-al-maddiyya al-diyaliktikiyya al-mariksiyya* (Beirut: Manshurat 'Uwaydat, 1962), 4, 11, 12, 75; see also pages 12–17, 70–73, 93, 140–46. For a useful account of Baqir al-Sadr's philosophical precepts and approach to logic, see John Walbridge, "Muhammad-Baqir al-Sadr: The Search for New Foundations," in *The Most Learned of the Shi'a*, ed. Walbridge, 133–36.

152. Walbridge, "Muhammad-Baqir al-Sadr," 135–36.

153. For a detailed study of Baqir al-Sadr's Islamic economics, see Mallat, *The Renewal of Islamic Law*, 113–57.

154. Al-'Alawi, *Fusul min tarikh al-Islam al-siyasi*, 397–98, 403, 396–408, 6–11.

155. Muhammad Baqir al-Sadr, *Iqtisaduna: Dirasa mawdu'iyya tatanawalu bi-al-naqd wa-al-bahth al-madhahib al-iqtisadiyya li-al-mariksiyya wa-al-ra'smaliyya fi ususiha al-fikriyya wa-tafasiliha* (Beirut: Dar al-Ta'arf li-al-Matbu'at, 1981), 21, 212–14.

156. See Charles Tripp, *Islam and the Moral Economy: The Challenge to Capitalism* (Cambridge: Cambridge University Press, 2006), 134–36, 141–43.

157. For more on the Islamic Revolution, see Mallat, *The Renewal of Islamic Law*, 69–72.

158. Juan Cole, *The Ayatollahs and Democracy in Iraq*, ISIM Papers (Leiden: Amsterdam University Press, 2005), 7.

159. Mallat, *The Renewal of Islamic Law*, 67. One of the main essays in the collection *Islam Directs Life* is "Manabi' al-qudra fi al-dawla al-islamiyya." See Muhammad Baqir al-Sadr, *Al-Islam yaqud al-hayat: Khilafat al-insan wa-shahadat al-anbiya'*, vol. 4 (Tehran: Wizarat al-Irshad al-Islami, 1982).

160. Baqir al-Sadr, *Al-Islam yaqud al-hayat*, 5–7, 24–27,45–46.

161. Abisaab, "Lebanese Shi'ites and the Marja'iyya," 217, 220.

162. Salim al-Hasani, *Al-Ma'alim al-jadida li-al-marja'iyya al-shi'iyya: Dirasa wa-hiwar ma'a al-sayyid Muhammad Husayn Fadlallah* (Beirut: Dar al-Malak, 1993), 169, 171.

163. Ahmad Nizar Hamzeh, *In the Path of Hizbullah* (Syracuse, NY: Syracuse University Press, 2004), 18, 23; Nicholas Noe and Nicholas Blanford, eds., *Voice of Hezbollah: The Statements of Sayed Hassan Nasrallah*, trans. Ellen Khouri (London: Verso, 2007), 4, 118.

164. Johan Franzén, "Education and the Radicalization of Iraqi Politics: Britain, the Iraqi Communist Party, and the 'Russian Link,' 1941–49," *International Journal of Contemporary Iraqi Studies* 2, no. 1 (2008): 99–113.

165. See Muhsin Ibrahim, "Mufid al-Jaza'iri: al-Husayn aththara fi tawajjuhi ila al-hizb al-shuyu'i," *al-Shabaka al-'iraqiyya*, January 30, 2011, http://magazine.imn.iq/articles/view.13956/.

166. Marcinkowski and Algar, *Religion and Politics in Iraq*, 43–44; Farouk-Sluglett and Sluglett, *Iraq since 1958*; A. R. Kelidar, "Aziz al-Haj: A Communist Radical," in *The Integration of Modern Iraq*, ed. Abbas Kelidar (London: Croom Helm, 1979), 191.

167. Asad, *Formations of the Secular*, 191.

5. Shi'ite Discontent: Sayyid Musa al-Sadr and the Left

1. Representative works include Samir Khalaf, *Civil and Uncivil Violence in Lebanon: A History of the Internationalization of Communal Conflict* (New York: Columbia University Press, 2002); Ussama Makdisi, "Reconstructing the Nation-State: The Modernity of Sectarianism in Lebanon," 23–26; Max Weiss, *In the Shadow of Sectarianism*.

2. Karim Muroeh, *Al-Muqawama: Afkar li-al-niqash 'an al-judhur wa-al-tajriba wa-al-afaq* (Beirut: Dar al-Farabi, 1985), 38; Mustafa al-'Aris, *Mustafa al-'Aris yatadhakkar* (Beirut: Dar al-Farabi, 1982), 177–82.

3. William Cleveland, *A History of the Modern Middle East* (Boulder, CO: Westview Press, 2000), 346–49. On the earlier wave of Palestinian refugees, see Ilan Pappe, *Britain and the Arab-Israeli Conflict, 1948–51* (Basingstoke, UK: Macmillan, 1988), 130, 155, 159–60, and Ilan Pappe, *The Ethnic Cleansing of Palestine* (Oxford: Oneworld, 2006).

4. See Ilyas al-Buwari, *Tarikh al-haraka al-'ummaliyya wa-al-naqabiyya fi Lubnan: 1947–1970*, part 2, (Beirut: Dar al-Farabi, 1986), 273–74.

5. See Samih Farsoun, "Student Protests and the Coming Crisis in Lebanon," *MERIP Reports*, no. 19 (1973): 11–12.

6. To give but one example, Habib Sadiq, a southern Communist elegized Nasser in 1971: "When Egypt's sun collapsed, oh bird of Lebanon, the night tore its bosom and lingered. With one wing over the martyr, it fell, and another was over the wounds." See

"Al-Saha al-jarih," *Al-'Irfan*, nos. 9–10 (January–February 1971): 1108; Walid Khalidi, *Conflict and Violence in Lebanon: Confrontation in the Middle East* (Cambridge, MA: Center for International Affairs, Harvard University, 1979).

7. *Al-'Irfan* 85, nos. 3–4 (July–August 1970): 259.

8. Quoted in ibid., 231–32.

9. One should add to this coalition the presence of leftist Iranian groups with the Palestinians in Beirut. See Houchang Chehabi, "The Anti-Shah Opposition and Lebanon," in *Distant Relations: Iran and Lebanon in the Last 500 Years*, ed. Houchang Chehabi (London: I. B. Tauris, 2006), 189–90. The Israeli military activities and aims in South Lebanon were examined by Augustus R. Norton in his "Making Enemies in South Lebanon: Harakat Amal, the IDF, and South Lebanon," *Middle East Insight* 3, no. 3 (1984): 13–20.

10. Sulayman Taqi al-Din, "Al-Janub al-lubnani bi-ri'ayat al-istiqlal," in *Safahat min Tarikh Jabal 'Amil*, ed. al-Majlis al-Thaqafi li-Lubnan al-Janubi (Beirut: Dar al-Farabi, 1979), 152.

11. Son of the South, "Al-'Asal al-hazin aw ma'sat al-nuzuh," *Al-'Irfan*, nos. 9–10 (January–February 1971): 840–43.

12. Al-Buwari, *Tarikh al-haraka al-'ummaliyya wa-al-naqabiyya fi Lubnan*, 297–98.

13. Dorothée Klaus, *Palestinian Refugees in Lebanon: Where to Belong?* (Berlin: Schwarz, 2003), 96–100.

14. Ja'far Sharaf al-Din, "Al-Sayyid Ja'far Sharaf al-Din," in *Min daftar al-dhikrayat al-janubiyya*, part 2, 74.

15. Waddah Sharara, *Dawlat Hizbullah: Lubnan mujtama'an islamiyyan* (Beirut: Dar al-Nahar, 1996), 74–75.

16. Ibid., 73–74.

17. Ibid., 76.

18. Examples of studies that treat sectarianism as an independent category of analysis with little ties to economic and sociopolitical forces are Fuad I. Khuri, "The Changing Class Structure in Lebanon," *Middle East Journal* 23, no. 1 (Winter 1969): 29–44; Samir Khalaf, *Lebanon's Predicament* (New York: Columbia University Press, 1987). Revisionist studies have provided new insights into sectarianism, modernism, and colonialism. See Ussama Makdisi, *The Culture of Sectarianism: Community, History, and Violence in Nineteenth-Century Ottoman Lebanon* (Berkeley: University of California Press, 2000).

19. Khuri, "The Changing Class Structure in Lebanon," 29.

20. Ibid., 29–30, 38. See also Augustus Richard Norton, *Hezbollah: A Short History* (Princeton, NJ: Princeton University Press, 2007), 14–16.

21. Majed Halawi, *A Lebanon Defied: Musa al-Sadr and the Shi'a Community* (Boulder, CO: Westview Press, 1992), 71–72.

22. Ibid.

23. Emile F. Sahliyeh, *Religious Resurgence and Politics in the Contemporary World* (Albany: State University of New York Press, 1990), 233.

24. This picture hardly supports Fouad Ajami's view that southern Shi'ites embraced "a tradition of lament and submission." See Fouad Ajami, *The Vanished Imam: Musa al-Sadr and the Shi'a of Lebanon* (Ithaca, NY: Cornell University Press, 1986), 51, 73.

25. Halawi, *A Lebanon Defied*, 68.

26. Ibid., 52–55.

27. The population of the southern suburb, an area that did not exceed twenty-five square kilometers, had multiplied 166 times in forty-seven years (1928–75). See Ilyas 'Abbud, "Dahiyat al-muhajjarin," *Al-Safir*, August 4 and 5, 1980.

28. Halawi, *A Lebanon Defied*, 68; see also 69–74 on proletarianization and immigration.

29. Ibid.

30. Sharaf al-Din, "Al-Sayyid Ja'far Sharaf al-Din," 70.

31. Halawi, *A Lebanon Defied*, 5–6, 9.

32. Malek Abisaab, *Militant Women of a Fragile Nation* (Syracuse, NY: Syracuse University Press, 2010), 95.

33. Taqi al-Din, "Al-Janub," 153. On the multifaceted uses of sectarianism, see Suad Joseph, "The Politicization of Religious Sects in Borj Hammoud, Lebanon" (PhD diss., Columbia University, 1975).

34. See Malek Abisaab, "Contesting Space: Gendered Discourse and Labor among Lebanese Women," in *Geographies of Muslim Women*, ed. Ghazi Falah and Caroline Nagel (New York: Guilford, 2005), 249–74.

35. *Al-Hayat*, June 24, 1970.

36. Halawi, *A Lebanon Defied*, 178.

37. On marital and kinship ties between al-Sadr and Sharaf al-Din's families, see Sabrina Mervin, *Harakat al-islah al-shi'i* (Beirut: Dar al-Nahar, 2000), 533.

38. Seyyed Vali Nasr, *The Shia Revival: How Conflicts within Islam Will Shape the Future* (New York: W. W. Norton, 2006), 110.

39. Houchang Chehabi and Majid Tafreshi, "Musa Sadr and Iran," in *Distant Relations*, ed. Chehabi, 156.

40. Nizar al-Zayn, "Editorial," *Al-'Irfan*, nos. 9–10 (January–February 1971): 999–1000.

41. Kais Firro, *Inventing Lebanon: Nationalism and the State under the Mandate* (London: I. B.Tauris, 2003), 89.

42. See 'Ali Shariati, *Tashayyu'-i Alavi va Tashayyu'-i Safavi* (Tehran: Intisharat-i Chapakhsh, 1998), 73–82. Mughniyya supported Arab unity and the Palestinian cause. See Hadi Fadlallah, *Muhammad Jawad Mughniyya: Fikr wa-islah* (Beirut: Dar al-Hadi, 1993), 316, 323, 329. At the same time, though, he stressed Lebanon's "cultural uniqueness."

43. Imam Musa al-Sadr, "Ya abna' Ba'labak wa-al-Hirmil," *Al-'Irfan* 85, nos. 3–4 (July–August 1970): 423–25.

44. Ibid., 425.

45. Ibid., 424–25.

46. Ibid., 425.

47. Salim Nasr and Diane James, "Roots of the Shi'i Movement," *MERIP Reports*, June 1985, 13; Roschanack Shaery-Eisenlohr, *Shi'ite Lebanon: Transnational Religion and the Making of National Identities* (New York: Columbia University Press, 2008), xiv, 23, 30, 83–84.

48. For a discussion of AMAL's sectarian politics as a negotiation of the "nation," see Shaery-Eisenlohr, *Shi'ite Lebanon*, 33–35, 81–86, 121.

49. Sayyid Musa noted that he wanted to free the Shi'ites from their inferiority complex toward Palestinians. See Karim Baqradoni, *Al-Salam al-mafqud: 'Ahd Ilyas Sarkis, 1976–1982* (Beirut: Dar 'Abr al-Sharq li-al-Manshurat, 1984), 118.

50. Halawi, *A Lebanon Defied*, 144.

51. Hani Fahs, *Al-Shi'a wa-al-dawla fi Lubnan: Malamih fi al-ru'ya wa-al-dhakira* (Beirut: Dar al-Andalus, 1996), 36.

52. An Israeli attack on Beirut International Airport in December 1968 created nationwide condemnation. It was followed by a general strike in the major cities called for by workers' unions and student organizations, demanding military training for citizens to defend the country. For more on these labor and nationalist protests, see al-Buwari, *Tarikh al-haraka al-'ummaliyya wa-al-naqabiyya fi Lubnan*, 321–47.

53. Ibid., 89.

54. Ibid.

55. See Halawi, *A Lebanon Defied*, 71–72.

56. Ibid., 149.

57. Fahs, *Al-Shi'a wa-al-dawla fi Lubnan*, 36.

58. Abisaab, "Contesting Space," 249.

59. Ibid., 259.

60. The GFW, however, did not accord the Ghaziyya workingwomen serious consideration, after which the women mobilized civil activists and laborers at major national institutions such as the central branch of the Régie in al-Hadath and the nearby campus of the Lebanese University.

61. Abisaab, "Contesting Space," 267.

62. On Sayyid Musa and Lebanese Shi'ite identity, see Shaery-Eisenlohr, *Shi'ite Lebanon*, 24–32. On Sayyid Musa and Iran see Chehabi, "The Anti-Shah Opposition and Lebanon," 182–85, and Houchang Chehabi, "Iran and Lebanon in the Revolutionary Decade," in *Distant Relations*, ed. Chehabi, 205–7.

63. Fahs, *Al-Shi'a wa-al-dawla fi Lubnan*, 35; Olivier Moos, "Lebanon: Hizbullah, a Progressive Islamic Party? Interview with Joseph Alagha," *Religioscope*, May 17, 2007, 2–3, http://religion.info/english/interviews/article_317.shtml.

64. Sayyid Musa's leadership was not fundamentally committed to the betterment of the Shi'ite poor, as Majed Halawi otherwise argues. See Halawi, *A Lebanon Defied*, 132.

65. Sharara, *Dawlat Hizbullah*, 76.

66. Quoted in Halawi, *A Lebanon Defied*, 149.

67. Authors' interview with Fadi Hammoud, Montreal, May 11, 2009.

68. For more on Sayyid Musa and communism, see Augustus Richard Norton, *Amal and the Shiʻa: Struggle for the Soul of Lebanon* (Austin: University of Texas Press, 1987), 42–43.

69. Authors' interview with Bashir Osmat, Beirut, June 29, 2010.

70. Sharara, *Dawlat Hizbullah*, 91.

71. As a young Islamist, Shaykh Subhi al-Tufayli had criticized Sayyid Musa and the Supreme Islamic Shiʻite Council for their reconciliatory position toward the Lebanese government and the Christian Right from 1969 until 1973. He welcomed, however, the Mahrumin movement in 1974–75. Authors' interview with Subhi al-Tufayli, ʻAyn Burday-Biqaʻ, Lebanon, 2007.

72. On the relationship of Sayyid Musa to Mostafa Chamran, see Houchang Chehabi, *Iranian Politics and Religious Modernism: The Liberation Movement of Iran under the Shah and Khomeini* (London: I. B.Tauris, 1990), 190–202.

73. Fahs, *Al-Shiʻa wa-al-dawla fi Lubnan*, 53.

74. Shaery-Eisenlohr, *Shiʻite Lebanon*, 29.

75. For a close look at these processes following the formation of Grand Liban, one can turn to the efforts of the mujtahid Yusuf al-Faqih (d. 1957) in producing his work on the personal-status law when he acted as counselor at the Jaʻfari Court of Cassation in Beirut.

76. This runs counter to Makdisi's view that the Lebanese state is principally non-secular. See Ussama Makdisi, "Reconstructing the Nation-State: The Modernity of Sectarianism in Lebanon." On the question of the shariʻa and the modern state, see Talal Asad, *Formations of the Secular: Christianity, Islam, Modernity* (Palo Alto, CA: Stanford University Press, 2003), chapters 5 and 6.

77. See Asad, *Formations of the Secular*, 227–31.

78. Quoted in ʻAdil Jamil Amin, *Maʻrakat al-sanatayn fi al-harb al-lubnaniyya* (Beirut: Maktabat al-Afwaj al-ʻArabiyya, 1976), 125.

79. Ibid.

80. Ibid.

81. See Fahs, *Al-Shiʻa wa-al-dawla fi Lubnan*, 9.

82. Ibid., 20.

83. See Mahdi ʻAmil, *Bahth fi asbab al-harb al-ahliyya fi Lubnan* (Beirut: Dar al-Farabi, 1979), 303–13.

84. See Augustus Richard Norton, "Making Enemies in South Lebanon," *Middle East Insight* 3, no. 3 (1984): 13–20.

85. Norton, *Amal and the Shiʻa*, 62–63. For more on the relationship of AMAL to the Palestinian armed movement and Syria, see 66–68.

86. On AMAL's position, see Augustus Richard Norton, "The Shiites and the MNF," in *The Multinational Force in Beirut, 1982–1984*, ed. Anthony McDermott and Kill

Skjelsbaek (Gainesville: University Press of Florida, 1991), 227–30, and Norton, *Amal and the Shiʻa*, 68.

87. Norton, *Amal and the Shiʻa*, 42, 43. In 1976, Syria sided with the Maronite right-wing militias against the Palestinian-leftist coalition. Sayyid Musa supported the Syrian position.

88. Norton, *Hezbollah*, 23; Sharara, *Dawlat Hizbullah fi Lubnan*, 119.

89. Norton, *Amal and the Shiʻa*, 62–63.

90. Magnus Ranstorp, *Hizbʼallah in Lebanon: The Politics of the Western Hostage Crisis* (New York: St. Martin's Press, 2002), 31–33.

91. Muroeh, *Al-Muqawama*, 22.

92. Augustus Richard Norton, "Changing Actors and Leadership among the Shiites of Lebanon," *Annals of the American Academy of Political and Social Science* 482, no. 1 (November 1985): 109–21.

93. See Moureh, *Al-Muqawama*, 88–91.

94. Shaery-Eisenlohr, *Shiʻite Lebanon*, 38.

95. Norton, *Amal and the Shiʻa*, 11.

96. See Asad, *Formations of the Secular*, 191–92.

97. Norton, "The Shiites and the MNF," 227–30.

98. Saqr Abu Fakhr, *Karim Muroeh yatadhakkar: Fi ma yushbih al-sira* (Damascus: Dar al-Mada li-al-Thaqafa wa-al-Nashr, 2002), 289–93.

6. Political Islam and the Formation of Hizbullah

1. This does not imply that Iranian funding solved the problem of poverty among the Shiʻites. Rather, it improved some of the conditions of the poor through socioeconomic aid and welfare programs. This is discussed at length in the following chapter.

2. See Ahmad Nizar Hamzeh, *In the Path of Hizbullah* (Syracuse, NY: Syracuse University Press, 2004); Judith Harik, *Hezbollah: The Changing Face of Terrorism* (London: I. B. Tauris, 2004); Augustus Richard Norton, *Hezbollah: A Short History* (Princeton, NJ: Princeton University Press, 2009). Hala Jaber, *Hezbollah: Born with a Vengeance* (New York: Columbia University Press, 1997). Norton also wrote several articles on Hizbullah and AMAL, including "Hizbullah: From Radicalism to Pragmatism?" *Middle East Policy* 5, no. 4 (January 1998): 147–58.

3. Hizbullah and its allies insist on the further liberation of the Shibʻa Farms in South Lebanon area, which continues to be under Israeli occupation.

4. Some of the key informants preferred to remain anonymous. In such cases, only their first names are provided.

5. Irene Gendzier, "Exporting Death as Democracy: An Essay on U.S. Foreign Policy in Lebanon," *MIT Electronic Journal of Middle East Studies*, 6 (Summer 2006): 177.

6. Ibid.

7. Norton, *Hezbollah*, 34.

8. Ibid.

9. Rami Hukayma, "Hizbullah min al-mansha' ila al-barlaman," in *Mustqabal al-usuliyya fi al-'alam al-'arabi* (Beirut: Al-Markaz al-'Arabi li al-Ma'lumat, 1993), 21.

10. Waddah Sharara, *Dawlat Hizbullah: Lubnan mujtama'an islamiyyan* (Beirut: Dar al-Nahar, 1996), 85; Houchang Chehabi, "Iran and Lebanon after Khomeini," in *Distant Relations: Iran and Lebanon in the Last 500 Years*, ed. Houchang Chehabi (London: I. B. Tauris, 2006), 290–93.

11. Jaber, *Hezbollah*, 32–37.

12. Sharara, *Dawlat Hizbullah*, 355–57.

13. Norton, *Hezbollah*, 35–36.

14. M. H. Shakir, *The Qur'an: Hardcover Arabic and English*, 9th ed. (N.p.: Tahrike Tarsile Qur'an Inc., 2002). The translation of verse 5:56 was slightly changed from that provided by Shakir.

15. Norton, *Hezbollah*, 37–38.

16. Said Amir Arjomand, "Authority in Shi'ism and Constitutional Developments in the Islamic Republic of Iran," in *The Twelver Shia in Modern Times*, ed. Rainer Brunner and Werner Ende (Boston: Brill, 2001), 301.

17. Khomeini's lectures on Islamic government and *wilayat al-faqih* are trans. Hamid Algar in *Islam and Revolution: Writings and Declarations of Imam Khomeini* (Berkeley, CA: Mizan Press, 1981).

18. Arjomand, "Authority in Shi'ism," 301.

19. "Al-Wathiqa al-siyasiyya li-hizbullah," *Al-Intiqad*, November 2009, http://www.moqawama.org/essaydetailsf.php?eid=16245&fid=47.

20. Hamzeh, *In the Path of Hizbullah*, 45.

21. Ibid., 47–48.

22. Jaber, *Hezbollah*, 62–66.

23. "Nasrallah aminan 'amman li-al-hizb li-al-marra al-sadisa . . . wa-la taghyiran fi majlis al-shura,"*Al-Shariq al-Awsat*, November 20, 2009, http://www.aawsat.com/details.asp?issueno=10992&article=545001.

24. Hamzeh, *In the Path of Hizbullah*, 45.

25. A similar pattern existed within the Da'wa Party. See Abdul-Halim al-Ruhaimi, "The Da'wa Islamic Party: Origins, Actors, and Ideology," in *Ayatollahs, Sufis, and Ideologues: State, Religion, and Social Movements in Iraq*, ed. Falih Abdul-Jabbar (London: Saqi, 2002), 158. On the Da'wa Party's early period, see Hanna Batatu, "Shi'i Organizations in Iraq: Al-Da'wah al-Islamiyah and al-Mujahidin," in *Shi'ism and Social Protest*, ed. Juan Cole and Nikki Keddie, 179–200 (New Haven, CT: Yale University Press, 1986).

26. In Sidon, Hizbullah struck alliances with Sunnite Islamist organizations such as the Popular Nasserite Organization (Al-Tanzim al-Sha'bi al-Nasiri) and Islamic Unification Movement (Harakat al-Tawhid al-Islami).

27. Hukayma, "Hizbullah min al-Mansha'," 21.

28. Sharara, *Dawlat Hizbullah*, 238–39. Among the early preachers were Afif al-Nabulsi, Raghib Harb, Abbas al-Musawi, and Subhi al-Tufayli.

29. Authors' interview with Bashir Osmat, Beirut, July 9, 2009.

30. Hukayma, "Hizbullah min al-Mansha'," 22.

31. The Syrian president and top military officers are mostly 'Alawi Shi'i Muslims who express a range of mainstream and heterodox beliefs.

32. Norton, *Hezbollah*, 34–35.

33. For more on Hizbullah's relationship to Syria and Iran, see Chehabi, "Iran and Lebanon after Khomeini," 296–97.

34. Hukayma, "Hizbullah min al-Mansha'," 22.

35. For more on the seminaries, see Rula Jurdi Abisaab, "The Cleric as Organic Intellectual: Revolutionary Shi'ism in the Lebanese *Hawzas*," in *Distant Relations*, ed. Chehabi, 231–58.

36. Mona Harb and Reinoud Leenders, "Know Thy Enemy: Hizbullah, 'Terrorism,' and the Politics of Perception," *Third World Quarterly* 26, no.1 (2005): 182–83.

37. See Kinda Chaib, "Le Hezbollah libanais a travers ses images: La représentation du martyr," in *Les mondes chiites et l'Iran*, ed. Sabrina Mervin, 113–31 (Paris: Karthala, 2007).

38. Observations made to the authors while they were on research visits to Lebanon.

39. Augustus Richard Norton, "Hizbullah: From Radicalism to Pragmatism?" *Middle East Policy* 5, no. 4 (2004): 4.

40. Michael C. Hudson, "Trying Again: Power-Sharing in Post–Civil War Lebanon," *International Negotiation* 2, no. 1 (1997): 113, 117.

41. Ibid.

42. Jaber, *Hezbollah*, 71.

43. Amal Saad-Ghorayeb argues that the Ta'if Accord preserved Christians' hegemonic role. This view is difficult to sustain even if the seat of presidency continued to be reserved to Maronite Christians. See Amal Saad-Ghorayeb, *Hizbu'llah: Politics and Religion* (Sterling, VA.: Pluto Press, 2002), 26–27.

44. Ibid., 114, 117–18.

45. Najib Nur al-Din, *Al-Sayyid Muhammad Husayn: Al-'aqlaniyya wa-al-hiwar min ajli al-taghyir wa-al-nahda* (Beirut: Markaz al-Hadara li-Tanmiyat al-Fikr al-Islami, 2010), 68.

46. Chehabi, "Iran and Lebanon after Khomeini," 296–97; Saad-Ghorayeb, *Hizbu'llah*, 26–27.

47. Jaber, *Hezbollah*, 71.

48. Hukayma, "Hizbullah min al-Mansha'," 24.

49. For more on the dismissal and realignment, see Hamzeh, *In the Path of Hizbullah*, 117–35.

50. Jaber, *Hezbollah*, 71.

51. Authors' interview with 'Ali Fayyad, Beirut, July 30, 2005, and August 5, 2007. At the time of both interviews, Dr. 'Ali Fayyad was the chair of the Center for Information and Documentation, bringing together a group of experts affiliated with Hizbullah. Since 2009, he has been a deputy in the Lebanese Parliament.

52. Fayyad interview; Chehabi, "Iran and Lebanon after Khomeini," 305.

53. Fayyad interview.

54. Ibid.

55. Ibid.

56. "Al-Tufayli hamala 'ala al-nuwwab," *al-Nahar*, July 3, 1997.

57. "Al-Tufayli: Najahna fi Ba'labak," *al-Nahar*, July 7, 1997.

58. "Al-Tufayli hamala 'ala al-nuwwab," *al-Nahar*, July 3, 1997.

59. Na'um Sarkis, "Al-Mawqif hadha al-nahar," *al-Nahar*, July 5, 1997.

60. Subhi Mundhir Yaghi, ed., "Wahdahu Qansu kana mutahhaffizan 'an thawrat al-jiya'," *al-Nahar*, July 3, 1997, 7–8. Tulays, al-Tufayli's son-in-law, was killed in 1998 when the Lebanese army, with Syrian support, tried to clamp down on al-Tufayli's movement.

61. Authors' interview with A. B., Biqa', July 2, 2005. A. B. is a member in the People's Movement (Harakat al-Sha'b), a secular Arab nationalist organization led by the Greek Orthodox leader and past deputy, Najah Wakim.

62. Na'um Sarkis, "Al-Mawqif hadha al-nahar," *al-Nahar*, July 5, 1997.

63. Saad-Ghorayeb, *Hizbu'llah*, 31.

64. *Inma' al-Biqa' al-shamali: Al-Itar al-'am wa-al-siyasat al-iqta'iyya* (Beirut: al-Markaz al-Istishari li-al-Dirasat wa-al-Tawthiq, 2002), 73, 130.

65. The Shi'ite *'ulama* and believers consider the Sunnite caliphates to have also deviated from the authoritative teachings of the Prophet and his family, the *ahl al-bayt*, the progeny of 'Ali and Fatima.

66. Quoted in Talal Jaber, "Le discours Shi'ite sur le pouvoir," *Peuples Méditer-ranéens* 78, no. 20 (July–September 1982): 78. Jaber quotes here from Waddah Sharara's *Transformation d'une manifestation religieuse dans un village du Liban Sud* (Beirut: Centre de recherche' de L'Institut des sciences sociales de l'université libanaise, 1968), 111.

67. Quoted in Hadi Fadlallah, *Muhammad Jawad Mughniyya: Fikr wa islah* (Beirut: Dar al-Hadi, 1993), 330.

68. Quoted in Muhammad 'Ali Mouqalled, "Al-Sha'ir 'Abd al-Muttalib al-Amin," in *Wujuh thaqafiyya min al-janub*, part 1, 96–97.

69. Augustus Richard Norton, *Amal and the Shi'a: Struggle for the Soul of Lebanon* (Austin: University of Texas Press, 1987), 62–63.

70. Jaber, *Hezbollah*, 23.

71. Nadine Picaudou, *Territoires palestiniens de mémoire*, (Beirut: Institut français de Proche-Orient, 2006), 214–15. See also Laleh Khalili, *Heroes and Martyrs of Palestine: The Politics of National Commemoration* (Cambridge: Cambridge University Press, 2007).

72. See Sharara, *Dawlat Hizbullah*, 353–54.

73. Jaber, *Hezbollah*, 21–22.

74. *Al-Shahid Shaykh Raghib Harb*, http://www.wa3ad.org/index.php?show=sounds &action=play&id=441.

75. Norton, "Hizbullah," 6.

76. Jaber, *Hezbollah*, 168.

77. Norton, "Hizbullah," 6.

78. Ibrahim Mousawi, "Fadlallah Explains Religious Basis for Suicide Attacks," *Daily Star*, June 8, 2002, http://www.lebanonwire.com/0206/02060802DS.asp.

79. Elias, "Hizbullah Fighting under the Leadership of Imam Khamene'i: Interview with Sayyid Hasan Nasrallah, Secretary General of Hizbullah in Lebanon," *Hamburg Der Spiegel*, October 20, 1997, http://www.khamenei.de/others/others1997.htm.

80. In a Shi'ite hadith transmitted by the Imams, the Prophet said: "Three groups of people can intercede with Allah, the Great and Almighty and their intercession is accepted: the prophets then the scholars and then the martyrs." Al-Shaykh al-Saduq, *Al-khisal*, ed. 'Ali Akbar al-Ghifari (Qom, Iran: Jama'at al-Mudarrisin, 1983) 156.

81. 'Abdullah Yusuf 'Ali, The *Holy Qur'an: Text, Translation, and Commentary* (New York: Tahrike Tarsile Qur'an, 1998).

82. See Yusuf al-Bahrani, *Al-Hada'iq al-nadira fi ahkam al-'itra al-tahira*, vol. 3 (Qom, Iran: Mu'assassat al-Nashr al-Islami, 1984), 413–16. Prayers must be performed for the martyr, but he is buried without washing. If one reaches the martyr before he takes his last breath, his body is washed and buried.

83. Al-Shaykh Na'im Qasim, *Hizbullah: Al-Manhaj, al-tajriba, al-mustaqbal* (Beirut: Dar al-Hadi, 2002), 162.

84. Ibid., 163.

85. The second manifesto (2009) provided by Muhammad Abdullah in "Wathiqat Hizbullah: Tashdid 'ala mawqi' al-muqawama fi al-sigha al-difa'iyya 'an Lubnan," November 29, 2009, http://almanar.com.lb/NewsSite/NewsDetails.aspx?id=113293&language=ar.

86. Ibid.

87. Ibid.

88. "Junblat li-al-Quds al-'arabi: Tabqa ma'rakat al-tamalluk," *Al-Quds al-'Arabi*, August 18, 2010.

89. Hizbullah denounced the army's bombardment of the Palestinian camps in Nahr al-Barid in Tripoli during 2007, but it did not intervene. For more on Hizbullah's approach to the Palestinians, see Laleh Khalili, "'Standing with My Brother': Hizbullah, Palestinians, and the Limits of Solidarity," *Comparative Studies in Society and History* 49, no. 2 (April 2007): 276–303.

90. Abisaab, "The Cleric as Organic Intellectual," 245, 251–52.

91. Norton discusses AMAL' s loss of popularity as it faced the same accusations it once directed against the Shi'ite landed elites. See Norton, *Hezbollah*, 23–24, 72–73.

92. Chehabi, "Iran and Lebanon in the Revolutionary Decade," 225–26.

93. Roschanack Shaery-Eisenlohr, *Shi'ite Lebanon Transnational Religion and the Making of National Identities* (New York: Columbia University Press, 2008), 200–201.

94. This pro-government coalition is known as the March 14 Bloc. It lost Junblat as an ally in 2009 when the latter unexpectedly resolved its differences with Hizbullah, albeit temporarily.

95. See Ahmad Beydoun, *Al-Jumhuriyya al-mutaqatti'a: Masa'ir al-sigha al-lubnaniyya ba'da ittifaq al-Ta'if* (Beirut: Dar al-Nahar, 1999), 264–66.

96. On the approach of the Saudi Arabian state toward the Shi'ites and Iran, see Vali Reza Seyyed Nasr, *The Shia Revival: How Conflicts within Islam Will Shape the Future* (New York: W. W. Norton, 2006), 150–51, 241–42, 246–47.

97. See Chehabi, "Iran and Lebanon after Khomeini," 300–301.

98. Hamzeh, *In the Path of Hizbullah*, 33.

99. Ayman Muhammad, "Sectarian Tension: From Extremists to Moderates," *Conflicts Forum*, October 15, 2008, http://conflictsforum.org/2008/sectarian-tension-from-extremists-to-moderates/.

100. In 2004, Hizbullah negotiated the release of twenty-three Lebanese and Arab prisoners and four hundred Palestinians from Israeli prisons.

101. Abd Ilah Balkaziz, *Hizbullah: Min al-tahrir ila al-rad', 1982–2006* (Beirut: Markaz Dirasat al-Wahda al-Arabiyya, 2006), 62–64.

102. Gendzier, "Exporting Death as Democracy," 177–78; Seymour M. Hersh, "Watching Lebanon: Washington's Interests in Israel's War," *New Yorker*, August 21, 2006, 1.

103. Human Rights Watch, "Israeli Cluster Munitions Hit Civilians in Lebanon," July 23, 2006, http://www.hrw.org/en/news/2006/07/23/israeli-cluster-munitions-hit-civilians-lebanon.

104. Hersh, "Watching Lebanon," 5.

105. Jean Shaoul, "Israel Used Chemical Weapons in Lebanon and Gaza," *World Socialist*, October 24, 2006, http://www.wsws.org/articles/2006/oct2006/isra-o24.shtml. The United Nations estimated "that Israel used up to 4 million submunitions" against Lebanon in 2006. See the information released by Cluster Munition Coalition accessed through http://www.stopclustermunitions.org/en-gb/cluster-bombs/use-of-cluster-bombs/a-timeline-of-cluster-bomb-use.aspx.

106. Ibid.

107. Balkaziz, *Hizbullah*, 88–96; Abbas Baydun, "Al-'awd al-abadi li-al-ahlam al-muta'akhkhira," *al-Safir*, August 25, 2006, http://www.assafir.com/iso/today/weekly_culture/7833.html.

108. Muhammad 'Ali Muqallad, "Kitab Maftuh ila al-Sayyid Hasan Nasrallah," *al-Hiwar al-Mutamaddin*, December 18, 2007, http://www.ahewar.org/debat/show.art.asp?aid=118763.

109. Authors' interview with Husayn S. and Rafiq S., Beirut, July 2008.

110. "Kalimat Samahat al-Sayyid Hasan Nasrallah li-al-daʻwa ila al-musharaka fi al-iʻtisam al-maftuh," *al-Muntada al-akhbari*, December 1, 2006. http://www.n3omy.com/vb/archive/index.php/t-33692.html.

111. Authors' observations, Beirut, May–August 2006.

112. The press, loyal to March 14 Bloc, blamed the sit-in and the Syrian–Iranian policies for the systemic destruction of the downtown area and consequently for the economic and political crisis. See ʻUmar Harqus, "Hina yaʻtasim al-muʻtasam ʻalayhim," *Al-Mustaqbal*, May 26, 2007, http://www.almustaqbal.com/storiesv4.aspx?storyid=223550; Yusuf Bazzi, "Ila al-wara'... ila jiwar Gazza... taqriban," *Al-Mustaqbal*, August 26, 2007; and Shadi ʻAla' al-Din, "Yawmiyyat multabisa tufrighu al-sahat ... lakinna ʻal-iʻtisam' mustamir," *Al-Mustaqbal*, June 17, 2007. This view is also supported by the authors' observations in Beirut in May–August 2007.

113. "Mufti al-Amin: Amal Gunmen Are Still Occupying my House and Offices," *Now Lebanon*, May 16, 2008, http://www.nowlebanon.com/NewsArchiveDetails.aspx?ID=43180.

114. "Junblat Accuses Hizbullah of Creating Parallel State," *naharnet* (Beirut), January 21, 2008, http://www.naharnet.com/domino/tn/NewsDesk.nsf/getstory?openform&AEAB4AF089F34ECAC22573D7005DBA55.

115. See Paige Kollock, "The Shiʻa Political Elite: Talking to Ziad Majed," *Now Lebanon*, January 30, 211, http://www.nowlebanon.com/NewsArchiveDetails.aspx?ID=235613.

116. Authors' interviews with ʻAli Fayyad, Beirut, July 30, 2005, and August 2007; Mundhir Jabir, "Sanat al-tahrir al-'ula wa-al-sunan al-lubnaniyya: Al-Janub 'ib' al-watan al-awwal," *al-Safir*, May 24, 2001, http://khiyam.com/tammouz/tam_articles_details.php?articleID=845.

117. See Mona Fayad, *Maʻna an takuna lubnaniyyan: Maqalat fi hal al-watan . . . wa ahwal al-muwatin* (Beirut: Arab Scientific Publishers, 2009), 160–64. A few writers attributed the crisis of the state to one or more of the following factors: foreign interference in Lebanese affairs, lack of civil consciousness as part of a lack of national loyalty, and citizens' unrealistic expectations about the state. See Ghassan Tueni, *Une Guerre pour les autres* (Paris: J. C. Lattès, 1985); Ayman al-Safadi, "Dawlat Hizbullah," *Al-ʻArabiyya*, April 13, 2007, http://www.alarabiya.net/save_print.php?print=1&cont_id=33440. See also Wajih Kawtharani, "Al-Sulta al-madaniyya wa-al-iʻtiqad bi-wilayat al-faqih al-mutlaqa," *al-Nahar*, November 3, 2006.

118. Adib Talib, "Hizbullah: Dawlat wilayat al-faqih mu'ajjala," *al-Hiwar al-Mutamaddin*, October 22, 2008, http://www.ahewar.org/debat/show.art.asp?aid=150960.

119. Tony Badran, "Hizbullah is Being Elusive on Wilayat al-Faqih," *Now Lebanon*, June 24, 2009, http://www.nowlebanon.com/NewsArchiveDetails.aspx?ID=100216.

120. Abbas Baydun, "Shiʻat Hizbullah. .daqiqat taʼkhir hasima ʻan al-waqiʻ," *al-Safir*, March 25, 2005, http://www.assafir.com/iso/oldissues/2005032/weekly_culture/9.html, and Baydun, "Al-ʻawd al-abadi li-al-ahlam," 3–4.

121. Baydun, "Al-ʻawd al-abadi li-al-ahlam," 3–4.

122. See ʿIsam al-Jurdi, "Privatization and Hizbullah's Approach to It." Private Papers of ʿIsam al-Jurdi, Beirut, June 2011.

123. Ibid.

124. "Lebanon's Mobile Phone Boycott," *Daily Star*, July 16, 2004.

125. Al-Jurdi, "Privatization and Hizbullah's Approach to It."

126. Osama Habib, "Fneish Wants to Spark Electric Revival," *Daily Star*, June 12, 2006, http://www.dailystar.com.lb/Business/Lebanon/Jun/12/Fneish-wants-to-spark -electric-revival.

127. "The Ministerial Statement as Read by PM Mikati at Parliament Today," July 5, 2011, http://www.najib-mikati.net/EN/LatestNews/3962/.

128. Al-Jurdi, "Privatization and Hizbullah's Approach to It."

129. "Al-Sayyid Hasan Nasrallah," in *Maʿlumat Mustaqbal al-Usuliyya fi al-ʿAlam al-ʿArabi*, May 1993, 107.

130. *Mawsuʿat Nasrallah: Al-Rajul alladhi yakhtasiru umma*, vol. 1 (Beirut: Manshurat al-Fajr, 2006), 13. *Mawsuʿat* offers a fragmentary biographical account of Nasrallah.

131. Ibid.

132. Ibid., 14.

133. "Al-Sayyid Hasan Nasrallah," 107.

134. "Biography of His Eminence, the Secretary General, Sayyid Hassan Nasrallah," http://www.english.moqawama.org/siteindex.php. .

135. At least around 1979, these lectures were in print in the form of small booklets.

136. Muhammad Baqir al-Sadr, *Al-Islam yaqud al-hayat: Lamha fiqhiyya tamhidi-yya ʿan mashruʿ dustur al-jumhuriyya al-islamiyya fi Iran*, vol. 1 (Qom, Iran: Matbaʿat al-Khayyam, 1979), 16–18, 20–37.

137. Muhammad Baqir al-Sadr, *Khilafat al-insan wa-shahadat al-anbiya'* (Beirut: Dar al-Taʿaruf li-al-Matbuʿat, 1979), 40–41; Muhammad Baqir al-Sadr, *Manabiʿ al-qudra fi al-dawla al-islamiyya*, vol. 5 (Beirut: Dar al-Taʿaruf li-al-Matbuʿat, 1979), 7–25.

138. "Biography of His Eminence."

139. Ibid., 20.

140. Muhammad Taqi al-Mudarrissi, *Kayfa tantasiru al-thawra al-islamiyya fi Lubnan?* (N.p.: Al-Markaz al-Thaqafi al-Islami, 1985).

141. *Mawsuʿat Nasrallah*, 1:37–38.

142. "Biography of His Eminence."

143. Ibid.

144. Hamzeh, *In the Path of Hizbullah*, 48; "Biography of His Eminence."

145. During these raids, Israel targeted a United Nations shelter in Qana, killing 118 Lebanese women, men, and children.

146. "Al-Shahid Sayyid Hadi Hasan Nasrallah," http://www.youtube.com/watch ?v=ioVQAOpAEt8. On martyrdom and "symbolic capital," see Joseph Alagha, "Hizbullah and Martyrdom," *Orient* 45, nos. 1–4 (2004): 54.

147. Speech by Sayyid Hasan Nasrallah, October 18, 2006, http://www.debianhelp
.org/node/1463.

148. Norton, *Hezbollah*, 88–89. See also Mas'ud Asadullahi, *Az Muqavamat ta Piruzi: Tarikhchah-yi Hizbullah-i Lubnan, 1361–1379* (Tehran: Mu'assasa-yi Mutali'at va-Tahqiqat-i Andishah Sazan-i Nur, 2000); *Junbish-i Hizbullah-i Lubnan: Ghuzashtah va-Hal* (Tehran: Pazhuhashkadah-yi Mutali'at-i Rahburdi, 2004).

149. See Rabi' Ya'qub, "Hakadha yurabbi Hizbullah al-atfal 'ala thaqafat al-mawt," *al-Naqid*, July 17, 2007, 1–4, http://www.annaqed.com/ar/content/show; Yusuf Bazzi, "Bint Jubayl, Michigan, and Hizbullah," May 29, 2005, http://www.bintjbeil.com.

150. "Hizbullah's Successful Prisoner Swap Promotes Armed Struggle," July 22, 2008, http://www.irinnews.org/lebanon. In the exchange and in addition to Samir al-Quntar and four other prisoners, the bodies of seven dead Hizbullah fighters and the remains of Dalal al-Mughrabi, a Palestinian woman fighter, along with those of four members of her group were returned to Lebanon. Moreover, 200 bodies of Arab fighters killed between the 1970s and 2000 were also returned to Lebanon.

151. "Sayyid Hassan Nasrallah Speaking on the Martyr's Day, November 14, 2009," http://www.youtube.com/watch?v=mUbLdpwpwI8.

152. "Nasrallah fi khutbat 'Ashura'," *Nawaret*, December 15, 2010 http://news.nawaret .com/al-'alam-al-'arabi/nasr-Allah-al-hukuma-al-lubnaniyya-wa-al-mahkama-a.

153. Ibid.

154. Authors' interview with Fawwaz Traboulsi, Beirut, July 11, 2010.

155. Nasrallah, speech delivered during 'Ashura', December 15, 2010.

7. The Islamists and Civil Society

1. On late-twentieth-century debates surrounding civil society in the American and European contexts, see J. A. Hall, *Powers and Liberties: The Causes and Consequences of the Rise of the West* (Harmondsworth, UK: Penguin, 1985); Krishan Kumar, "Civil Society: An Inquiry into the Usefulness of a Historical Term," *British Journal of Sociology* 44, no. 3 (September 1993): 375–95; Ernest Gellner, *Conditions of Liberty: Civil Society and Its Revivals* (London: Penguin, 1994); Peter L. Berger and Richard John Neuhaus, "To Empower People: From State to Civil Society," in *The Essential Civil Society Reader*, ed. Don E. Eberly, 143–82 (Lanham, MD: Rowman & Littlefield, 2000). On the public sphere, see Jürgen Habermas, *The Structural Transformation of the Public Sphere: An Inquiry into a Category of Bourgeois Society*, trans. Thomas Berger with the assistance of Frederick Lawrence (Cambridge, MA: MIT Press, 1991).

2. See Patricia Crone, *God's Rule: Government and Islam* (New York: Columbia University Press, 2005); Bryan S. Turner, ed., *Islam: Critical Concepts in Sociology* (London: Routledge, 2004); Ernest Gellner, *Muslim Society* (Cambridge, New York: Cambridge

University Press, 1983), 1–2, 84–85, and Ernest Gellner, *Postmodernism, Reason, and Religion* (London: Routledge, 1992), xi–xiv.

3. See Ernest Gellner, "Islam and Marxism: Some Comparisons," in *Islam: Critical Concepts in Sociology*, ed. Bryan S. Turner, 24–30 (London: Routledge, 2004). Gellner argues that Islam has an inherent antipathy to civil society, defined as a purely secularized and individualized sphere. For other arguments about the lack of civility in Islamic societies, see Youssef Mouawad, "Civil Society, God, and Cousins: The Case of the Middle East," in *A New Euro-Mediterranean Cultural Identity*, ed. Stefania Panebianco (London: Frank Cass, 2003), 112–18. In these studies, Islam is treated as a religious culture authoring all levels of change in Islamic society—namely, economic, social, and intellectual.

4. For critiques of the Orientalist conceptions in Gellner's work, see Talal Asad, "The Idea of an Anthropology of Islam," in *The Social Philoslophy of Ernest Gellner*, ed. John A. Hall and Ian Jarvie, 381–404 (Amsterdam: Rodolpi, 1996); Robert W. Hefner, *Civil Islam: Muslims and Democratization in Indonesia* (Princeton, NJ: Princeton University Press, 2000), 21–22; Sami Zubaida, "Is There a Muslim Society? Ernest Gellner's Sociology of Islam," in *Islam*, ed. Turner, 37–54; Masoud Kamali, "Civil Society and Islam: A Sociological Perspective," in *Islam*, ed. Turner, 95–118.

5. Craig Calhoun, ed., *Habermas and the Public Sphere* (Cambridge, MA: MIT Press, 1992); Michel Foucault, *The Foucault Reader* (New York: Random House, 1984); Bent Flyvbjerg, "Habermas and Foucault: Thinkers for Civil Society?" *British Journal of Sociology* 49, no. 2 (June 1998): 210–33; Talal Asad, *Formations of the Secular: Christianity, Islam, Modernity* (Palo Alto, CA: Stanford University Press, 2003).

6. See Hefner, *Civil Islam*; David Herbert, *Religion and Civil Society: Rethinking Public Religion in the Contemporary World* (Aldershot, UK: Ashgate, 2003), esp. chapters 2, 3, and 4. See also Augustus Richard Norton, "Preface" and "Introduction," in *Civil Society in the Middle East*, ed. Augustus Richard Norton (Leiden: Brill, 2001), x–xiv, and 5–16, respectively.

7. Geoff Eley, "Nations, Publics, and Political Cultures: Placing Habermas in the Nineteenth Century," in *Habermas and the Public Sphere*, ed. Calhoun, 292. See also Flyvbjerg, "Habermas and Foucault," 210–11, 229; Asad, *Formations of the Secular*, 183–87. On Max Weber and civil society, see Sung Ho Kim, *Max Weber's Politics of Civil Society* (Cambridge: Cambridge University Press, 2004).

8. See Jose Casanova, *Public Religions in the Modern World* (Chicago: University of Chicago Press, 1994), where Casanova identifies a set of criteria for those public religions that can enhance civil society (accept the rules of public engagement in a secularized modern sphere). See also David Zaret, "Religion, Science, and Printing in the Public Spheres of England," in *Habermas and the Public Sphere*, ed. Calhoun, 213–14, 221, 229.

9. Talal Asad agrees in principle with critics of the secularization theory that underlies Weberian and neo-Marxist conceptions of civil society. Yet he finds it problematic to

neglect the critical link between civil society and power relations, particularly in connection to the nation-state. See Asad, *Formations of the Secular*, chapter 6.

10. See Dale F. Eickelman and Jon W. Anderson, eds., *New Media in the Muslim World: The Emerging Public Sphere* (Bloomington: Indiana University Press, 1999); John L. Esposito, "Islam and Civil Society," in *Modernizing Islam: Religion in the Public Sphere in Europe and the Middle East*, ed. John L. Esposito and Francois Burgat (New Brunswick, NJ: Rutgers University Press, 2003), 69–91; Hefner, *Civil Islam*; Herbert, *Religion and Civil Society*, Mitsuo Nakamura, Sharon Siddique, and Omar Farouk Bajunid, eds., *Islam and Civil Society in Southeast Asia* (Tokyo: Sasakawa Peace Foundation, 2001); Amyn Sajoo, ed., *Civil Society in the Muslim World: Contemporary Perspectives* (London: I. B. Tauris, 2002).

11. A host of theorists about civil society argues for multiple spheres and ones overlapping or competing against each other. See Nancy Fraser, "Rethinking the Public Sphere: A Contribution to the Critique of Actually Existing Democracy," in *Habermas and the Public Sphere*, ed. Calhoun, 111–15; Mary P. Ryan, "Gender and Public Access: Women's Politics in Nineteenth-Century America," in *Habermas and the Public Sphere*, ed. Calhoun, 259–88.

12. This differs from Antonio Gramsci's assertion that one cannot separate between the state (modern European) and civil society because the former permeates institutionally many aspects of civil society. See Antonio Gramsci, *Prison Notebooks* (New York: Columbia University Press, 1992), 233–38; Kai Neilsen, "Reconceptualizing Civil Society for Now: Some Somewhat Gramscian Turnings," in *Toward a Global Civil Society*, ed. Michael Walzer (Providence, RI: Berghahn, 1995), 46–53.

13. Flyvbjerg, "Habermas and Foucault," 226; Eley, "Nations, Publics, and Political Cultures," 307. Eley notes that the public sphere was constituted "from a field of conflict, contested meanings, and exclusion." See also Asad, *Formations of the Secular*, 184–85.

14. Craig J. Calhoun, "Introduction: Habermas and the Public Sphere," in *Habermas and the Public Sphere*, ed. Calhoun, 37.

15. Thomas McCarthy, "Practical Discourse: On the Relation of Morality to Politics," in *Habermas and the Public Sphere*, ed. Calhoun, 51–72; Craig J. Calhoun, "Concluding Remarks," in *Habermas and the Public Sphere*, ed. Calhoun, 475, 479; Jeffrey C. Alexander, *The Civil Sphere* (Oxford: Oxford University Press, 2006), 5, 311, 551–53.

16. See Hazim Saghiyya, "Fusul min qissat 'Hizbullah' al-lubnani," part 2, *Al-Hayat*, May 1, 2005, http://www.daralhayat.com/special/features/o1-2005/20050104-05p15-01. Michel Wakid, a Christian Communist living in the southern suburb, tried to prevent the selling of Christian lands to affluent Shi'ite immigrants connected to Hizbullah. He was assassinated under obscure circumstances, after which many Christians in Hart Hurayk and al-Murayja sold their lands to Shi'ites.

17. Casanova, *Public Religions*, 234.

18. Asad, *Formations of the Secular*, 182, 193.

19. Authors' interview with Subhi al-Tufayli, 'Ayn Burday- Biqa', July 9, 2005.

20. For more on this question, see Asad, *Formations of the Secular*, 187–94.

21. Authors' interview with Muhammad Hashishu, Sidon, Lebanon, July 24, 2007.

22. Authors' interview with Bashir Osmat, Beirut, Lebanon, June 29, 2008.

23. One should also add the conflicts between the Iraqi Ba'th and AMAL in addition to those between AMAL and the PLO.

24. Authors' interview with Muhammad Hashishu, Sidon, Lebanon, July 24, 2007.

25. Habermas considers "communicative rationality" universal in human beings, deriving from an inevitable thrust for reciprocal understanding and consensus. See Flyvbjerg, "Habermas and Foucault," 212, 215, 226. Flyvbjerg challenges Habermas's assumption that access to the public sphere is linked to the inherent realization of and engagement in rational discourse. Michel Foucault argues that communication is infused with power. See Gilles Deleuze, *Foucault*, trans. Sean Hand (London: Athlone, 1988), 23–27.

26. In 2000, Shi'ite Islamists talked about how they felt they had formed an "empire" both in connection to the liberation of the South and the civil institutions.

27. Abbas Baydun, "Al-'awd al-abadi li-al-ahlam al-muta'akhkhira," *al-Safir*, August 25, 2006, http://www.assafir.com/iso/today/weekly_culture/7833.html. See also Maher Abi Samra, *Shuyu'iyyun Kunna* (Lebanon: Orjouane Productions et Les Films, 2010). We thank Miriam Younes for providing us with this film.

28. See As'ad Abu Khalil, "Hizbullah in Lebanon: Islamisation of Leninist Organizational Principles," *Middle Eastern Studies* 27, no. 3 (July 1991): 390–403; authors' interview with Rita Hamdan and Ghazi Abi Saab, Communists who lent their support to Hizbullah, Beirut, July 7, 2010. See also Ibrahim al-Amin's reflections in the film *We Were Communists*.

29. For an overview of the transformation at which the Communists aimed, see Karim Muroeh, *Nahwa jumhuriyya thalitha* (Lebanon: Dar al-Farabi, 2007), 103–20. On the complexity of political reform initiated by civil society, see Norton, "Introduction," 15–16.

30. Dalal al-Bizri, *Akhawat al-zil wa-al-yaqin (Beirut: Al-Nahar, 1996)*; Waddah Sharara, *Dawlat Hizbullah: Lubnan mujtama'an islamiyyan* (Beirut: Dar al-Nahar, 1996).

31. Fuad I. Khuri, "The Changing Class Structure in Lebanon," *Middle East Journal* 23, no. 1 (1969): 29. Khuri argues unconvincingly that the Shi'ites expressed a stronger sectarian "consciousness" than the Maronites or Sunnite Muslims during the late 1960s. He fails to investigate sects' disparate ability to have access to social services and economic relief through state agencies.

32. See Mona Harb and Reinoud Leenders, "Know thy enemy: Hizbullah, 'Terrorism,' and the Politics of Perception," *Third World Quarterly* 26, no.1 (2005): 189–90.

33. The Committee for Supporting the Islamic Resistance, founded in 1990, took these initiatives. See Marlene Khalifa, "Man huwa Hizbullah? Wa ma ahdafuhu?" *Al-Nahar*, August 13, 2006.

34. "Nadi al-Kashshaf," http://www.mabarrat.org.lb/arabic/ali/nawadi.php. The Scout's Club at al-Mabarrat develops children's physical and social skills as part of building self-reliance.

35. Mirvat Talib, "Nur al-mas'uliyya," Madaris al-Mahdi, Bint Jubayl, http://www.almahdischools.org/newsite/, June 28, 2008.

36. 'Ali Yusuf, former director of educational training and literacy at Al-Mu'assassa al-Islamiyya li-al-Tarbiya wa-al-Ta'lim (The Islamic Institute for Culture and Education) for Hizbullah, expressed these views in his article, "Kayfa naqi al-tifl min al-isaba bi-al-ittikaliyya," September 2008, Madaris al-Mahdi, http://www.almahdischools.org/newsite/.

37. Al-Shaykh Mustafa Qasir, "Al-Istiqlal al-haqiqi wa-thaqafat al-muqawama," September 2008, http://www.almahdischools.org/newsite/_makalat.php?filename=2007 08070903420. Al-Shaykh Mustafa Qasir is the general director of the Islamic Institute for Culture and Education, the educational board of Hizbullah.

38. See "Lamha Tarikhiyya," 2006, http://www.daralaytam.org/historical.htm.

39. On al-Mabarrat's global networks, see its website at http://www.mabarrat.org.lb/arabic/default.php; Annabelle Böttcher, "Ayatollah Fadlallah und seine Wohltaetigkeits Organisation al-Mabarrat," in Islamstudien Ohne Ende, Festschrift für Werner Ende zum 65 Geburtstag, ed. Rainer Brunner, M. Gronka, J. P. Laut, and U. Rebstock (Würzburg, Germany: Ergon 2002), 41–47.There are also religious and intellectual centers and subsidiary associations.

40. See "Markaz al-'Abbas al-Suhhi al-Thaqafi," http://www.mabarrat.org.lb/arabic/sahiya4.php. It can also be accessed through the main website of al-mabarrat.

41. See Böttcher, "Ayatollah Fadlallah und seine Wohltaetigkeitsorganisation al-Mabarrat," 41–47; Annabelle Böttcher, "Sunni and Shi'i Networking in the Middle East," in Shaping the Current Islamic Reformation, ed. Barbara Allen Roberson (London: Frank Cass, 2003), 44–45.

42. Hala Jaber, Hezbollah: Born with a Vengeance (New York: Columbia University Press, 1997), 157–59; Augustus Richard Norton, Hezbollah: A Short History (Princeton, NJ: Princeton University Press, 2007), 107–12.

43. Jaber, Hezbollah, 147–48.

44. Authors' interviews with 'Ali Fayyad, Beirut, July 30, 2005, and August 5, 2007.

45. Jaber, Hezbollah, 155. See also Judith Harik, Hezbollah: The Changing Face of Terrorism (London: I. B. Tauris, 2004), 85.

46. August Richard Norton, "Hizbullah: From Radicalism to Pragmatism?" Middle East Policy 5, no. 4 (January 1998): 2.

47. Rami Hukayma, "Hizbullah min al-mansha' ila al-barlaman," in Mustqabal al-usuliyya fi al-'alam al-'arabi (Beirut: Al-Markaz al-'Arabi li al-Ma'lumat, 1993), 23. After the war in 2006, the Good Loan Organization provided an estimated $200 million in loans to those who suffered from the destruction. It increased its outreach into

non-Muslim areas in late 2007. International Finance Corporation, World Bank, and Grameen Jameel Pan-Arab Microfinance Limited, *A Diagnostic Study on the Demand for Financial Services by Micro and Small Entrepreneurs* (Washington, DC: World Bank, July 2008), 35–36.

48. On the "resisting society," see 'Abd al-Halim Fadlallah, "Al-Mantiq al-ijtima'i li-al-muqawama," in *Al-Intisar al-muqawim min al-mujtama' al-muqawim*, introduction by Shaykh Na'im Qasim (Beirut: n.p., 2007). Qasim also gave a lecture in Beirut on May 23, 2007, titled "Kayfa nabni mujtama' al-muqawama?" http://www.alamin-sy.com/vb /archive/index.php/t-24884.html.

49. Authors' interviews with 'Ali Fayyad.

50. Ibid.

51. Ibid.

52. Hukayma, "Hizbullah min al-mansha' ila al-barlaman," 23.

53. Jaber, *Hezbollah*, 147–48.

54. Ibid., 150.

55. Ibid., 152.

56. *Inma' al-Biqa' al-shamali: Al-Itar al-'am wa-al-siyasat al-iqta'iyya* (Beirut: Al-Markaz al-Istishari li-al-Dirasat wa-al-Tawthiq, 2002), 64.

57. Ibid., 38. Around 70 to 75 percent of the people in Ba'labak-al-Hirmil were involved in agriculture.

58. Ibid., 55–57.

59. Isam Jurdi, "Al-Islah al-iqtisadi fi al-qayd al-ta'ifi," *al-Nahar*, November 1, 2007, 1–2.

60. Ibid., 73, 130; authors' interview with A. B., Beirut, July 2009.

61. *Inma' al-Biqa' al-shamali*, 168–69.

62. Authors' interview with 'Ali Fayyad, Beirut, August 2007.

63. Guido Bertucci and Adriana Alberti, "Globalization and the Role of the State: Challenges and Perspectives," in *United Nations World Public Sector Report 2001*, 1–25 (New York: United Nations, 2001), http://unpan1.un.org/intradoc/groups/public /documents/UN/UNPAN006225.pdf. The authors insist that adaptation to globalization succeeds under a strong state and effective welfare programs. But given the unequal circulation of commodities and peoples characteristic of globalization, the latter tends to weaken democratic practices and eliminate social-welfare programs.

64. Ibid., 7. See also Mustafa Kamal Pasha, "Globalization, Islam, and Resistance," in *The Globalization Reader*, ed. Frank J. Lechner and John Boli (Oxford: Blackwell, 2004), 330–34.

65. On the relationship between economic changes caused by globalization (technology, labor, finance) and cultural politics, see Arjun Appadurai, "Disjuncture and Difference in the Global Cultural Economy," in *The Globalization Reader*, ed. Lechner and Boli, 106.

66. See Jonathan Xavier Inda and Renato Rosaldo, *The Anthropology of Globalization* (Oxford: Blackwell, 2008), 7–12, 15. Inda and Rosaldo suggest that Third World subjects translate and reinterpret the global flow of commodities and culture differently (see 17–18).

67. Ibid., 11.

68. "Arabs Boycott U.S. Goods Against American Mideast Policies," Associated Press, July 28, 2002, http://www.inminds.com/boycott-news-0252.html.

69. Inda and Rosaldo, *The Anthropology of Globalization*, 13.

70. See Yves Gonzalez-Quijano, "The Birth of a Media Ecosystem: Lebanon in the Internet Age," in *New Media in the Muslim World*, ed. Eickelman and Anderson, 74. See Jenine Abboushi Dallal, "Hizballah's Virtual Civil Society," in *Internationalizing Cultural Studies: An Anthology*, ed. M. Ackbar Abbas, John Nguyet Erni, and Wimal Dissanayake (Malden, MA: Blackwell, 2005), 232–33.

71. See the website of *Al-Muqawama al-Islamiyya fi Lubnan* at http://www.moqawama.org/siteindex.php. See also the website of al-Manar, Hizbullah's TV, at http://www4.almanar.com.lb/main.php.

72. Dallal, "Hizballah's Virtual Civil Society," 233–34.

73. Ibid., 235.

74. See Batul Shuman, "Talawwuth al-hawa'," Madaris al-Mahdi, *al-Majadil*, February 5, 2008, http://www.almahdischools.org/newsite/; Shuman is a student of the secondary school, discussing.

75. See Harik, *Hezbollah*, 90–92.

76. "The Electoral Program of Hizbullah, 1996," Al-Manar TV, June 20, 1997, http://www.freedrive.com/file/431445,the-electoral-program-of-hizbullah---199.

77. Rania Masri, "The Human Impact of the Environment in Lebanon," November 1995, http://almashriq.hiof.no/lebanon/300/360/363/363.7/humanimp2.html.

78. "Arab International Anti-golablization Forum," http://www.hic-mena.org/documents/AAGG.doc. The Gathering warned against the implications of the Middle Eastern project and the Euro-Mediterranean partnership (in which Israel is an integral member).

79. See website of Euro-Mediterranean Partnership (EUROMED) at http://ec.europa.eu/external_relations/euromed/index_en.htm.

80. "Arab International Anti-globalization Forum," http://www.hic-mena.org/documents/AAGG.doc.

81. Ibid.

82. Raed Rafei, "Hezbollah Finds Friends Abroad," *Los Angeles Times*, August 30, 2008.

83. Hassan Nasrallah, Hizbullah's secretary-general, initiated a campaign to plant one million trees in Lebanon. See Bassam Kuntar, "10/10/10: Hal yunqiz sihr al-arqam kawkabana?" *al-Akhbar*, October 9, 2010.

84. See Mona Harb, "Pious Entertainment in Beirut: Al-Saha Traditional Village," *ISIM Review*, no. 17 (Spring 2006): 10–11. The Courtyard Village received an award in 2005.

85. 'Adnan al-Ghul, "Qaryat al-saha al-turathiyya," 46–47.

86. Harb, "Pious Entertainment in Beirut," 10.

87. In the Biqa', several women—in particular, single older women—undertook these trips.

88. Fatat Zurayq, a kindergarten teacher at Madaris al-Mahdi, Bir Hasan, stressed the importance of "repeating God's words" and Qur'anic verses to one's child, having her or him distinguish between *halal* (what is licit) and *haram* (what is prohibited), and urging her or him to pray. See Fatat Zurayq, "Risala ila kull 'um," Madaris al-Mahdi, Bi'r Hasan, October 2008, http://www.almahdischools.org.newsite/.

89. See Al-Shaykh al-Mufid, *Al-Amali*, ed. Husayn al-Ustadh Wali and 'Ali Akbar al-Ghifari (Beirut: Dar al-Mufid li-al-Tiba'a wa-al-Nashr wa-al-Tawzi', 1993), 193–95, 201–5.

90. See al-Shaykh Mustafa Qasir, "Al-Bu'd al-tarbawi fi shakhsiyyat al-fard al-mu'min," *al-Mahdi Schools*, August 7, 2007, http://www.almahdischools.org.newsite/.

91. Ibid.

92. Hizbullah's followers and sympathizers observe the party prohibition on the public selling and consuming alcohol in the areas where they are dominant.

93. The Office for Soliciting Legal Opinions abridged the three volumes of Muhammad Fadlallah's *Fiqh al-Shari'a* under the title *Ahkam al-Shari'a* (Beirut: Dar al-Malak, 2003). This work included a chapter titled "Al-Amr bi-al-ma'ruf wa-al-nahi 'an al-munkar."

94. Amal Saad-Ghorayeb, *Hizbu'llah: Politics and Religion* (Sterling, VA: Pluto Press, 2002), 17–18.

95. Authors' interviews with Rita Hamdan and Ghazi Abi Saab, Mount Lebanon, July 7, 2010.

96. Lysandra Ohrstrom, "Some of Fneish's Reforms Left When He Stepped Down," *Daily Star*, March 12, 2007. When acting minister Muhammad al-Safadi took over Fneish's post (after the latter's resignation in November 2007), these reforms were cancelled.

97. Ibrahim al-Amin, "Al-Radd 'ala "aqidat al-dahiyya': Matar min nar 'ala Gush Dan," *al-Akhbar*, August 17, 2009.

98. They took part in labor demonstrations by the General Labor Union on February 28 and 29, 1996, which were met by an army clampdown.

99. Saad-Ghorayeb, *Hizbu'llah*, 17–18, 89–90.

100. Najib Nur al-Din, *Al-Sayyid Muhammad Husayn Fadlallah: Al-'aqlaniyya wa-al-hiwar min ajl al-taghyir wa-al-nahda* (Beirut: Markaz al-Hadara li-Tanmiyat al-Fikr al-Islami, 2010), 336–37.

101. For more on al-Hariri's project see Richard Becherer, "A Matter of Life and Debt: The Untold Costs of Rafiq Hariri's New Beirut," *Journal of Architecture* 10, no. 1 (February 2005): 1–42.

102. Quoted in Nur al-Din, *Al-Sayyid Muhammad Husayn Fadlallah: Al-'aqlaniyya wa-al-hiwar*, 336–37.

103. See Norton, *Hizbullah*, 90–94.

104. 'Abd al-Rahim Shalha, "Al-Tufayli yad'u li-rahil Lahhud al-yawm qabla al-ghad," *al-Safir*, February 28, 2006, http://www.assafir.com/iso/today/local/128.html.

105. We based our observations on interviews and unstructured conversations with six Islamists, three women and three men, in July 2005 and July–August 2007. Most of them preferred to remain anonymous, so we gave them fictional names here.

106. See Mary Douglas, *Purity and Danger: An Analysis of Concepts of Pollution and Taboo* (London: Routledge, 2002), xi–xii, xviii–xx, 63–64.

107. Ibid., 131.

108. Muhammad Jawad Mugniyya, *Fiqh al-Imam Ja'far al-Sadiq: 'Ard wa-istidlal*, vol. 1 (Qom, Iran: Mu'assassat Ansariyan li-al-Tiba'a wa-al-Nashr, 2000), 56, 84–85, 100–101.

109. Harik, *Hezbollah*, 88.

110. On volunteer work see Lara Deeb, *Enchanted Modern: Gender and Public Piety in Shi'i Lebanon* (Princeton, NJ: Princeton University Press, 2006), 90–91.

111. Ibid., 91–92.

112. Jaber, *Hezbollah*, 22.

113. See Rabi' Ya'qub, "Hakadha yurabbi Hizbullah al-atfal 'ala thaqafat al-mawt," *al-Naqid*, July 17, 2007, http://www.annaqed.com/ar/content/show.

114. Jaber, *Hezbollah*, 22.

115. On the early martyrs and their missions see Norton, *Hizbullah*, 80–81.

116. Deeb, *Enchanted Modern*, 210–11.

117. See Dalal al-Bizri, *Akhawat al-zil wa al-yaqin: Islamiyat bayna al-hadatha wa-al-taqlid* (Beirut: Dar al-Nahar, 1996), 86–89, 132–33; Zeina Zaatari, "The Culture of Motherhood: An Avenue for Women's Civil Participation in South Lebanon," *Journal of Middle Eastern Women's Studies* 2, no. 1 (Winter 2006): 48.

118. Malek Abisaab, *Militant Women of a Fragile Nation* (Syracuse, NY: Syracuse University Press, 2010), 6, 43–46.

119. Ibid.

120. See Farhad Daftary, *The Isma'ilis: Their History and Doctrines* (Cambridge: Cambridge University Press, 2007), 50–52.

121. Douglas, *Purity and Danger*, 2–3; see also 175–77.

122. Maher Abi-Samra, *The Women of Hizbullah* (New York: Icarus Films, 2000).

123. Numerous essays and poems are devoted to mothers of martyrs and posted on the Madaris al-Mahdi website and published elsewhere. See, for instance, Zahra' Fahs, "Qum ayyuha al-shahid, " *Ajyal al-Mustafa*, no. 10, 1998, 29; Batul Karnib, "Ila um al-shahid," *Ajyal al-Mustafa*, no. 10, 1998, 31; Fatima al-Halbawi, "Dami ilayki hadi-yyati," *'Ajyal al-Mustafa*, no. 13, 2000, 33; Zaynab al-Qarsifi, "Li 'amirat al-dar," Madaris

al-Mahdi, Shmustar, July 13, 2007, http://www.almahdischools.org/newsite. Mothers are described as "heavenly plants" placed "on the throne of eternity and offerings," having "a sacred responsibility" and imparting great values in a "society where true men are rare."

124. Mother of Wasim Sharaf, "Al-Tadhiya," Madaris al-Mahdi, al-Bazzaliyya, July 3, 2008, http://www.almahdischools.org/newsite.

125. No exact hadith matches her account, but she seemed to be combining two or three different traditions together.

126. Al-Kulayni, *Al-Kafi*, 2:142. Other versions of it can be found—for example, *Bihar al-Anwar* 74, 49.

127. Zaatari, "The Culture of Motherhood," 34, 39, 40–41.

128. See al-Sayyid Muhammad al-Husayni al-Shirazi, *Fatima al-Zahra': Afdal 'uswat al-nisa* (Karbala: Dar al-'Alqami, 2008).

129. On other symbolic dimensions of Fatima, see Todd Lawson, "Fatima's Religious Authority in an Early Work by the Bab," in *The Most Learned of the Shi'a: The Institution of the Marja' Taqlid* (New York: Oxford University Press, 2001), 102–4; Abbas Amanat, "Meadow of the Martyrs: Kashifi's Persianization of Shi'i Martyrdom in Late Timurid Herat," in *Culture and Memory in Medieval Islam: Essays in Honor of Wilfred Madelung*, ed. Farhad Daftari and Joseph W. Meri (London: I. B.Tauris, 2003), 265–66.

130. Muahmmad Husayn Fadlallah, *Al-Zahra' al-qudwa* (Beirut: Dar al-Malak, 2000); see also Rola el-Hosseini, "Women, Work, and Political Participation in Lebanese Shi'a Contemporary Thought: The Writings of Ayatollahs Fadlallah and Shams al-Din," *Comparative Studies of South Africa and the Middle East* 28, no. 2 (2008): 276–77.

131. Al-Shaykh al-Mufid, *Al-Amali*, 130.

132. *Mawsu'at Nasrallah: al-Rajul alladhi yakhtasir umma*, vol. 1 (Beirut: Manshurat al-Fajr, 2006), 119–23, 150–51, 110, 125, 140, 144.

133. Sana' Abu Zayd, "Nisa' khalidat," Madaris al-Mahdi, Tyre, July 12, 2007, http://www.almahdischools.org/newsite/.

134. Al-Mufid, *Al-Amali*, 321.

135. Authors' interview with F. Samar, Beirut, July 11, 2005.

136. Flyvbjerg, "Habermas and Foucault," 226; Eley, "Nations, Publics, and Political Cultures," 307; Asad, *Formations of the Secular*, 184–85.

137. See McCarthy, "Practical Discourse," 51-72; Alexander, *The Civil Sphere*, 5, 311, 551–53.

8. The Islamists: Modernity and Predicament of the Nation-State

1. The words *jihad* and *ijtihad* have the same Arabic root, J-H-D.

2. Amal Saad-Ghorayeb, *Hizbu'llah: Politics and Religion*, 36.

3. Nizar Hamzeh, "Lebanon's Hizballah: From Islamic Revolution to Parliamentary Accommodation," *Third World Quarterly* 14, no. 2 (1993): 323.

4. Saad-Ghorayeb, *Hizbu'llah*, 34–35.

5. Muhammad 'Abdullah, "Wathiqat Hizbullah," November 29, 2009, http://alma nar.com.lb/NewsSite/NewsDetails.aspx?id=113293&language=ar.

6. Najib Nur al-Din, *Al-Sayyid Muhammad Husayn Fadlallah: Umara' wa-qaba'il, khafaya wa-haqa'iq lubnaniyya* (Beirut: Riyad al-Rayyis Books, 2001), 68.

7. Lara Deeb, "Deconstructing a 'Hizbullah Stronghold,'" *MIT Electronic Journal of Middle East Studies*, no. 6 (Summer 2006): 118; Joseph al-Agha, "Hizbullah's Conception of the Islamic State," in *Les mondes chiites et l'Iran*, ed. Sabrina Mervin (Paris: Karthala, 2007), 90–91, 105.

8. Al-Agha, "Hizbullah's Conception of the Islamic State," 105.

9. Deeb, "Deconstructing a 'Hizbullah Stronghold,'" 118.

10. Waddah Sharara, *Dawlat Hizbullah: Lubnan mujtama'an islamiyyan* (Beirut: Dar al-Nahar, 2006), 119, 336; Saud al-Mawla, "Qira'a susiyu-tarikhiyya fi masar 'Hiz-bullah' wa-masirihi," May 16, 2009, http://www.10452lccc.com/special%20studies/saou-dalmula.hezbollah16.4.09.htm; Ilyas Khuri, "Tehran wa-al-thaqafa al-'arabiyya," *al-Quds al-'Arabi*, June 23, 2009.

11. See Abdallah Qubrusi, *Abdullah Qubrusi yatadhakkar*, vol. 1 (Beirut: Mu'assasat Fikr li-al-Abhath wa-al-Nashr, 1982); Michel 'Aflaq, *Fi sabil al-ba'th* (Beirut: Dar al-Tali'a, 1959); Mahdi 'Amil, *Fi al-dawla al-ta'ifiyya* (Beirut: Dar al-Farabi, 1986).

12. See Shafiq al-Rayyis, "Al-Birnamij al-marhali li-al-ahzab wa-al-qiwa al-watani-yya wa-al-taqaddumiyya fi Lubnan: Min ajli islah dimuqrati li-al-nizam al-siyasi," in his book *Al-Tahaddi al-lubnani, 1975–1976* (Beirut: Dar al-Masira, 1978), 94–107; al-Hizb al-Dimuqrati al-Sha'bi, *Mudhakkara ila al-rifaq wa-al-ikhwa fi al-haraka al-wataniyya al-lubnaniyya wa-al-muqawama al-filastiniyya* (Beirut: n.p., 1980); Hay'at tahrir al-tariq, *Hiwar fikri siyasi sarih ma'a George Hawi: Madha jara? Wa-li-madha? Wa-ma al-'amal?* (Beirut: n.p., 1982).

13. On Islamist approaches to shari'a and the dilemma posed to it by modernity, see Wael Hallaq, "What Is Shari'a?" in *Yearbook of Islamic and Middle Eastern Law, 2005–2006*, vol. 12 (Leiden: Brill, 2007), 154.

14. Saad-Ghorayeb, *Hizbu'llah*, 22. Saad-Ghorayeb argues that Hizbullah considered the Lebanese government legitimate.

15. See August Richard Norton, "Hizbullah: From Radicalism to Pragmatism?" *Mid-dle East Policy* 5, no. 4 (January 1998): 1–6; Augustus Richard Norton, *Hezbollah: A Short History* (Princeton, NJ: Princeton University Press, 2007), 99, 158. See also Mats Warn, "Staying the Course: The 'Lebanonization' of Hizbollah—the Integration of an Islamist Movement into a Pluralist Political System" (Master's thesis, Stockholm University, 1999), esp. chapter 4 and the conclusion.

16. See Roschanack Shaery-Eisenlohr, *Shi'ite Lebanon: Transnational Religion and the Making of National Identity* (New York: Columbia University Press, 2008), 23–25, 49.

17. 'Abdullah, "Wathiqat Hizbullah."

18. See Talal Asad, *The Formations of the Secular: Christianity, Islam, and Modernity*, last two chapters.

19. Authors' interview with 'Ali Fayyad, Beirut, August 5, 2007.

20. Fadil Abu al-Nasr, *Hizbullah: Haqa'iq wa-ab'ad* (Beirut: Al-Sharika al-'Alamiyya li-al-Kitab, 2003), 24–25.

21. Saad-Ghorayeb, *Hizbu'llah*, 34–35. Authors' interview with 'Ali Fayyad, Beirut, July 2007.

22. Rula Jurdi Abisaab, "Lebanese Shi'ites and the Marja'iyya: Polemic in Late Twentieth Century Lebanon," *British Journal of Middle East Studies* 36, no. 2 (August 2009): 217, 220–21, 231–34.

23. Authors' interview with Subhi al-Tufayli, 'Ayn Burday-Biqa', July 9, 2005.

24. Norton, *Hezbollah*, 35, 46.

25. Hallaq, "What is Shari'a?" 155–56. See also Sami Zubaida, *Law and Power in the Islamic World* (London: I. B. Tauris, 2005), 220–21.

26. On the question of modern citizenry under an Islamic government, see 'Abd al-Rahman al-Hajj, "Mafhum al-dawla al-haditha wa-ishkalatuha fi al-fikr al-islami al-siyasi al-mu'asir," May 7, 2008, Hizb al-Wasat al-Jadid, http://www.alwasatparty.com/modules .php?name=News&file=article&sid=8800.

27. Zubaida, *Law and Power*, 197–210.

28. Said Amir Arjomand, "Authority in Shi'ism and Constitutional Developments in the Islamic Republic of Iran," in *The Twelver Shia in Modern Times*, ed. Rainer Brunner and Werner Ende (Boston: Brill, 2001), 322.

29. H. Varulkar, "Radicalization in Hizbullah's Positions Following the Gaza War: Hizbullah Must Be Independent of All State Institutions," *Memri*, March 11, 2009, 1–4.

30. Ibid.

31. Ibid.

32. 'Abdullah, "Wathiqat Hizbullah."

33. Varulkar, "Radicalization in Hizbullah's Positions," 3.

34. Saad-Ghorayeb, *Hizbu'llah*, 26.

35. Ibid. In its rejection of political sectarianism, Hizbullah seemed to have adapted secular notions of democracy.

36. Ibid., 26.

37. On the reform of the electoral system, see Ahmad Baydun, *Al-Jumhuriyya al-mutaqatti'a* (Beirut: Dar al-Nahar, 1999), 225–46.

38. Karim Muroeh, *Nahwa jumhuriyya thalitha* (Beirut: Dar al-Farabi, 2007), 104. Muroeh accepted the Ta'if's recognition of a council of elders in preserving sectarian balance, but only as long as the council did not play a legislative role. This proposition, however, is hardly realistic in the Lebanese context.

39. Violette Daghir, "Al-Zawaj al-madani fi Lubnan: Haqq wa-darura," *al-Lajna al-'Arabiyya li-Huquq al-Insan*, April 1998, at http://www.achr.nu/rep4.htm. Hizbullah,

like Sunnite Islamist groups, rejected the project for legitimizing civil marriages in Lebanon.

40. Wael Hallaq, *An Introduction to Islamic Law* (Cambridge: Cambridge University Press, 2009), 115–16.

41. The Islamists are in theory hostile to the implementation of secularism at the state level. See Saad-Ghorayeb, *Hizbu'llah*, 20.

42. Muroeh, *Nahwa jumhuriyya thalitha*, 110–11.

43. Abbas Baydun, "Shi'at Hizbullah . . . daqiqat ta'khir hasima 'an al-waqi'," *al-Safir*, March 25, 2005, http://www.assafir.com/iso/oldissues/2005032/weekly_culture/9 .html. Ibrahim al-Amin, a leftist journalist supportive of Hizbullah, urged the party to nominate women to Parliament and launch a radical political program to remove the dysfunctional governmental system and establish electoral laws on a nonsectarian basis. See Ibrahim al-Amin, "Al-Sayyid Hasan," *al-Akhbar*, November 11, 2008.

44. Authors' interview with 'Abd al-Halim Fadlallah, Beirut, Lebanon, July 29, 2010.

45. 'Abdullah, "Wathiqat Hizbullah." The second manifesto introduced changes to Hizbullah's political program but not to its "doctrinal or ideological" foundations.

46. These changes in Hizbullah's national performance can also be gleaned from its support for the Orthodox Electoral Law, drafted by the Lebanese Orthodox Assembly in 1997, reflecting the aspirations of a main Christian parliamentary bloc. The law stipulates that each Lebanese sect must vote for its own representatives, hence, Shi'ite voters can only vote for Shi'ite candidates, Maronite voters for Maronite candidates and so forth. The law was not adopted by Parliament in 1997 but it was proposed again in February 2013 by the Free Patriotic Movement led by General Michel Aoun. The structure of the current Lebanese electoral law forces Christian candidates to depend on non-Christian votes to get elected to parliament. The Free Patriotic Movement aimed to "free" the Christian vote from the hegemony of its opponents mainly, the Druze led by Walid Junblat, and the Sunni-based political group, al-Mustaqbal. Hizbullah's support for the law would allow its allies in the Free Patriotic Movement to maintain the majority Christian vote. It would also nurture Christian sectarian autonomy from Saudi persuasions and interests. Secular supporters of the *muqawama* including leftists and feminists, however, criticized Hizbullah harshly for supporting this law. See "The Unintended Consequences of the Orthodox Election Law," http://www.karlremarks.com/2013/01/the-unintended-consequences-of-orthodox.html.

47. On progress, see Saad-Ghorayeb, *Hizbu'llah*.

48. Ali Fayyad, interview, August 5, 2007.

49. See Muhammad Husayn Fadlallah, *Al-Ijtihad bayna 'asr al-madi wa-'afaq al-mustaqbal* (Beirut: Al-Markaz al-Thaqafi al-'Arabi, 2009).

50. Shaykh Mustafa Qasir, "Al-Huriyya bayna al-nazariyya al-diniyya wa-al-nazariyya al-'ilmaniyya," Al-Mahdi Schools, September 2008, http://www.almahdischools.org /newsite/; Shaykh Mustafa Qasir, "Al-Wahda al-islamiyya," Al-Mahdi Schools, October 2008, http://www.almahdischools.org.newsite/.

51. Muhammad Husayn Fadlallah, *Fiqh al-Shari'a*, vol. 1 (Beirut: Dar al-Malak, 1999), 7–8. Like Sistani, Fadlallah initially permitted the believer to emulate a deceased mujtahid at the outset of his emulation, but he changed this fatwa later.

52. Authors' interview with Sayyid Hasan al-Amin, Beirut, March 3, 1994.

53. Nur al-Din, *Al-Sayyid Muhammad Husayn Fadlallah: Umara' wa-qaba'il*, 230.

54. Ibid., 231.

55. Ibid., 422; Isma'il Faqih, "Al-Marja' al-islami Muhammad Husayn Fadlallah li-'al-Bayan': La atawaqqa'u fitna sunniyya-shi'iyya musallaha fi-al-Iraq," *Majallat al-Bayan Imaratiyya*, April 28, 2005, http://arabic.bayynat.org.lb/mbayynat/nachatat/albaya 28042005.htm.

56. For more on Hizbullah's approach to jihad and its ramifications see Ahmad Nizar Hamzeh, *In the Path of Hizbullah* (Syracuse, NY: Syracuse University Press, 2004), 36–39.

57. Saad-Ghorayeb, *Hizbu'llah*, 73–74, 140–41.

58. Said Amir Arjomand, *The Turban for the Crown: The Islamic Revolution in Iran* (New York: Oxford University Press, 1988), 97; Hamid Dabashi, *Islamic Liberation Theology: Resisting the Empire* (London: Routledge, 2008), 92–93; Daniel Brumberg, *Reinventing Khomeini: The Struggle for Reform in Iran* (Chicago: University of Chicago Press, 2001), 56, 71, 97–100. See also As'ad Abu Khalil, "Ideology and Practice of Hizballah in Lebanon: Islamization of Lennist Organizational Principles," *Middle Eastern Studies* 27, no. (July 1991): 390–403.

59. Quoted in Faqih, "Al-Marja' al-Islami Muhammad Husayn Fadlallah."

60. Nur al-Din, *Al-Sayyid Muhammad Husayn Fadlallah: Umara' wa-qaba'il*, 422. Majmu'a min al-'Ulama', *Fatawa 'ulama al-Islam fi masa'il jihadiyya wa-hukm al-'amaliyyat al-istishhadiyya* (Beirut: Dar al-Mahajja al-Bayda', 2002), chapter 6.

61. For a range of approaches to jihad see, al-Muhaqqiq al-Hilli, *Shara'i' al-Islam*, vol.1, (Iran, Qom: Matba'at Amir, 1988) 232-60; Abu al-Qasim al-Khu'i, *Minhaj al-Salihin*, vol.1, (Beirut: Dar al-Zahra', 1990), 360-403 and the full work of Muhammad Taqi al-Mudarrissi, *Al-Wajiz fi al-fiqh al-islami: Fiqh al-jihad wa-ahkam al-qital* (Iran, n.c.: Dar Muhibbi al-Husayn, n.d.).

62. See Sayyid Ali Khamenei's *Ajwibat al-istifta'at* is available on his web page, http://www.leader.ir/. For more on government and the jurist's deputyship see Sayyid 'Ali Khamenei, *Al-Hukuma fi al-Islam: Majmu'at muhadarat* (Beirut: Dar al-Rawda, 1995), and Sayyid 'Ali Khamenei, *Wilaya* (Beirut: Dar al-Hadi, 2000).

63. Lara Deeb, *An Enchanted Modern: Gender and Public Piety in Shi'i Lebanon* (Princeton, NJ: Princeton University Press, 2006), 14–16, 229. Compare Deeb's view with Dalal al-Bizri's view on the Islamization of modernity in *Akhawat al-zil wa-al-yaqin* (Beirut: Al-Nahar, 1996), based on her work *L'ombre et son double: Femmes islamistes libanaises et modernes* (Beirut: CERMOC, 1995).

64. Saad-Ghorayeb, *Hizbu'llah*, 88–90, 106–11; Rula Jurdi Abisaab, "The Cleric as Organic Intellectual: Revolutionary Shi'ism in the Lebanese *Hawzas*," in *Distant Relations:*

Iran and Lebanon in the Last 500 Years, ed. Houchang E. Chehabi (London: Center for Lebanese Studies and I. B. Taurus, 2006), 255-57. Some Islamists are aware of Western scholars' attempts to unearth multiple experiences of modernity repressed in the hegemonic narrative of Western modernity that confronts colonial and postcolonial subjects.

65. Faqih, "Al-Marja' al-islami Muhammad Husayn Fadlallah."

66. Ibid.

67. Jose Casanova, *Public Religions in the Modern World* (Chicago: University of Chicago Press, 1994), 43, 57–58, 17–39. Lara Deeb argues for the "modern-ness" of public religion. She discusses the dual material and spiritual "progress" embodied in the type of modernity advocated by Hizbullah's Shi'ites and its democratizing features. The notion of "progress," though, is integral to Western universalistic values. See Deeb, *An Enchanted Modern*, 228–29.

68. Talal Asad, *The Formations of the Secular: Christianity, Islam, Modernity* (Palo Alto, CA: Stanford University Press, 2003), 193, 182.

69. Abbas Baydun, "Al-'awd al-abadi li-al-ahlam al-muta'akhkhira," *Al-Safir*, August 25, 2006, http://www.assafir.com/iso/today/weekly_culture/7833.html.

70. David Harvey, *The Condition of Postmodernity: An Inquiry into the Origins of Cultural Change* (Oxford: Blackwell, 1990), 42.

71. See Michael Hardt and Antonio Negri, *Empire* (Cambridge, MA: Harvard University Press, 2000), 147–49; Saad-Ghorayeb, *Hizbu'llah*, 93–05,102–4.

72. Philip Sampson, "The Rise of Postmodernity," in *Faith and Modernity*, ed. Philip Sampson, Vinay Samuel, and Chris Sugden (Oxford: Regnum Books International, 1994), 34–35; Saad-Ghorayeb, *Hizbu'llah*, 102–6.

73. Harvey, *The condition of Postmodernity*, 41.

74. Sampson, "The Rise of Postmodernity," 29– 34.

75. Ali Fayyad interview, August 5, 2007.

76. Qasir, "Al-Wahda al-islamiyya." See also Qasir, "Al-Huriyya bayna al-nazariyya."

77. On late capitalism see Harvey, *The Condition of Postmodernity*, 46. See also Varulkar, "Radicalization in Hizbullah's Positions," 3. Varulkar stated that Mahmoud Qamati, Hizbullah politburo deputy, resisted the integration of the *muqawama* with the Lebanese army, noting that "if we become part of the establishment, we will be forced to abide by decisions of the state that are dictated by international power balances."

78. Varulkar, "Radicalization in Hizbullah's Positions," 3.

79. Harvey, *The Condition of Postmodernity*, 46.

80. Saad-Ghorayeb, *Hizbu'llah* 35–36, 88; Sampson, "The Rise of Postmodernity," 38; Harvey, *The Condition of Postmodernity*, 43–45.

81. Hasan Yusuf, "Muhammad Husayn Fadlallah," in *Mustaqbal al-usuliyya if al-'alam al-'arabi* (Beirut: Al-Markaz al-'Arab li-al-Ma'lumat, 1993), 95.

82. On *al-Ahali* see Charles Tripp, *A History of Iraq* (Cambridge: Cambridge University Press, 2002), 84–86.

83. Ziad Itani, "Tajribat hayat al-Sayyid Muhammad Husayn Fadlallah 'al-shaykh' alladhi qara'a Kutub 'Marx'," *'Ukaz*, November 2003, http://arabic.bayynat.org.lb/nach atat_archieve/tajribat_7ayat.htm.

84. Muhammad 'Ali al-Zayn, "Interview-Rawafid: Ma'a al-Sayyid Muhammad Husayn Fadlallah," parts 1 and 2, July 9, 2004, http://www.sawtakonline.com/forum /showthread.php/1257; "Al-Sayyid Fadlallah: Al-Iltizam ya'ni al-infitah fima al-ta'assub ya'ni al-in'izal," *al-Tanawu' al-Islami*, April 30, 2010, http://www.alwihdah.com/news /interviews/2010-04-26-225.htm#;

85. Craig J. Calhoun and Joseph Gerteis, *Classical Sociological Theory*, 2nd ed. (Malden, MA: Blackwell, 2007), 77–78.

86. "Al-Sira al-dhatiyya: Kalimat takhtasir al-hayat," *Bayynat*, n.d., at http://arabic .bayynat.org.lb/sira/al-soukoun.htm. On Imam Husayn's martyrdom and social change see "Archival Information on al-'Allama al-Marja' al-Sayyid Muhammad Husayn Fadlallah," http://arabic.bayynat.org/nachatat_archieve/bahrein.htm. On Marxism see John Rees, *The Algebra of Revolution: The Dialectic and the Classical Marxist Tradition* (New York: Routledge, 1998), 33; see also 23 and 27.

87. 'Itani, "Tajribat hayat al-Sayyid Muhammad Husayn Fadlallah."

88. Najib Nur al-Din, *Al-Sayyid Muhammad Husayn Fadlallah: Umara' wa-qaba'il*, 456.

89. See Jamal Sankari, *Fadlallah: The Making of a Radical Shi'ite Leader* (London: Saqi, 2005), 75, and Falih Abd al-Jabbar, *The Shi'ite Movement in Iraq* (London: Saqi, 2003), 114–22.

90. Abisaab, "Lebanese Shi'ites and the Marja'iyya," 233–34.

91. Salim al-Hasani, *Al-Ma'alim al-jadida li-al-marja'iyya al-shi'iyya: Dirasa wa-hiwar ma'a al-sayyid Muhammad Husayn Fadlallah* (Beirut: Dar al-Malak, 1993), 8, 47–50.

92. Abisaab, "Lebanese Shi'ites and the Marja'iyya," 215–39.

93. Ibid., 217.

94. Wassim Mroueh, "Fadlallah's Charity for Orphans Still Giving Despite Top Cleric's Death," *Daily Star*, August 13, 2010, http://www.dailystar.com.lb/article.asp?edition _id=1&categ_id=1&article_id=118164#axzz1AaA8HdKY.

95. Sankari, *Fadlallah*, 76–77.

96. Abisaab, "Lebanese Shi'ites and the Marja'iyya," 231.

97. Diya' al-Shakarji, "Muhammad Husayn Fadlallah," *Minbar al-Katib al-'Iraqi*, July 8, 2010, http://www.iraqwriters.com/iNP/view.asp?ID=2396. Al-Shakarji (or Shakar-chi) was a member of the Da'wa Party and Fadlallah's agent (*wakil*) in Germany before he embraced secularism and thrust aside his commitments to political Islam.

98. Ibid.

99. Ilhami al-Miliji, "Al-Marja' al-shi'i Ayatullah Fadlallah," *al-Quwwa al-Thalitha*, July 29, 2009, http://www.thirdpower.org/read-37985.html.

100. ʿAbd al-ʿAziz Qasim, "Fadlallah: Wilayat al-faqih nazariyya la yaraha akthar al-Shiʿa," *Madarik*, August 31, 2008, http://mdarik.islamonline.net.servle..ik2FMDALayout.

101. Ibid.

102. See Muhammad Husayn Fadlallah's work *Ahkam al-shariʿa*.

103. Sankari, *Fadlallah*, 76–77; Jabbar, *The Shiʿite Movement in Iraq*, 114–22.

104. Nur al-Din, *Al-Sayyid Muhammad Husayn Fadlallah: Umaraʾ wa-qabaʾil*, 41–42, 156.

105. Al-Shakarji, "Muhammad Husayn Fadlallah." Al-Mashriq, http://almashriq .hiof.no/lebanon/300/320/324/324.2/hizballah/Fadlallah-Muhammad.html.

106. See also Rami Hukayma, "Hizbullah min al-manshaʾ ila al-barlaman," in *Mustqabal al-usuliyya fi al-ʿAlam al-ʿarabi* (Beirut: Al-Markaz al-ʿArabi li-al-Maʿlumat, 1993), 21.

107. Nur al-Din, *Al-Sayyid Muhammad Husayn: Umaraʾ wa-qabaʾil*, 68–69, 282–83.

108. Ibid., 61, 66–68, 257–59, 76–77.

109. Ibid., 264–65, 454.

110. Muhammad Husayn Fadlallah, "Mahmud Darwish: Shaʿir Filastin wa-al-insaniyya," *Al-Hayat*, July 11, 2008, http://www.tanwer.org/tanwer/news/379.html.

111. Qasim Qasir, "Al-Salafiyya al-shiʿiyya: Muʾashshirat rahina wa-mustaqbaliyya," *Muntada Manar li-al-Hiwar*, May 13, 2009, http://www.manaar.com/vb/showthread. php?t=20358.

112. Nur al-Din, *Al-Sayyid Muhammad Husayn Fadlallah: Umaraʾ wa-qabaʾil*, 70.

113. Ibid., 114.

114. Ibid., 73.

115. Ibid., 239–43.

116. Al-Sayyid Muhammad Husayn Fadlallah, *Al-Haraka al-islamiyya: Humum wa-qadaya* (Beirut; Dar al-Malak, 1990), 280–81. See also "Sheik Muhammad Husayn Fadlallah," *al-Mashriq*, March 13, 1996, http://almashriq.hiof.no/lebanon/300/320/324/324.2 /hizballah/Fadlallah-Muhammad.html.

117. See Warn, "Staying the Course," sections 3.5 and 4.1.

118. Muhammad Husayn Fadlallah, speech delivered during the Conference of the Muslim ʿUlama. See Tajammuʿ al-ʿUlamaʾ al-Muslimin fi Lubnan, *Muʾtamar ʿulamaʾ al-Islam: Inqadh al-Quds wa-nusrat al-shaʿb al-filastini taklif sharʿi wa-wajib jihadi* (Beirut: Tajammuʿ al-ʿUlamaʾ al-Muslimin fi Lubnan, 2003).

119. "Sheik Muhammad Husayn Fadlallah."

120. Nur al-Din, *Al-Sayyid Muhammad Husayn Fadlallah: Umaraʾ wa-qabaʾil*, 211–12.

121. "Sheik Muhammad Husayn Fadlallah."

122. Nur al-Din, *Al-Sayyid Muhammad Husayn Fadlallah: Umaraʾ wa-qabaʾil*, 285.

123. Al-Shakarji, "Muhammad Husayn Fadlallah."

124. See Talib Aziz, "Fadlallah and the Remaking of the Marja'iyya," in *The Most Learned of the Shi'a: The Institution of Marja' Taqlid*, ed. Linda S. Walbridge (New York: Oxford University Press, 2001), 208–11.

125. Ibid.; Fadlallah, *Fiqh al-shari'a*, 1:31–32.

126. See Shaery-Eisenlohr, *Shi'ite Lebanon*, 150–53.

127. See Aziz, "Fadlallah and the Remaking of the Marja'iyya," 208–11; Ahmad al-Katib, "Al-Marja'iyya al-shi'iyya dawla fi-al-dawla?" *al-Wasat*, February 5, 2001, 19.

128. Interview with the Kuwaiti Shi'ite cleric, Shaykh Yasir al-Habib, http://www.youtube.com/watch?v=lyHtOjzUs98.

129. Al-Shakarji, "Muhammad Husayn Fadlallah."

130. See Asad, *Formations of the Secular*, 182. For more on Islamist discourse, legal regulation and the modern state, see 252–56.

131. "Divine Victory" invoked in Sayyid Hassan Nasrallah's speech when he attributed Israel's military failures in the 2006 war to God first and to organized struggle second. Speech by Sayyid Hassan Nasrallah, October 18, 2006, http://www.debianhelp.org/node/1463.

Conclusion

1. "Nasrallah fi khitab Nari: Sanastakhdim al-Silah li-al-Difa' 'an Silah al-Muqawama wa Shabakat al-Ittisalat," August 5, 2008, http://www.syria-news.com/readnews.php?sy_seq=76184.

Bibliography

Primary Sources

Archives

L'indicateur, Nantes.
Ministère des Affaires Ètranger (MAE), Paris.

Interviews

A. B. Interview. July 2, 2005, Biqaʻ.
ʻAbdallah, Ahmad. Interview. January 28, 1997, Wadi al-Zinni, Lebanon.
Al-Amin, Hassan Sayyid. Interview. March 3, 1994, Beirut.
Al-Batal, George. Interview. February 5, 1997, Beirut.
Dagher, Jacques. Interview. January 28, 1997, Baʻbda.
Elmir, Hassan. Interview. June 16, 2002, Detroit.
Fadlallah, ʻAbd al-Halim. Interview. July 29, 2010, Beirut.
Fayyad, Ali. Interview. July 30, 2005, and August 5, 2007, Beirut.
Hamdan, Rita, and Ghazi Abi Saab. Interview. July 7, 2010, Beirut.
Gharbiyya, Rayyan. Interview. August 17, 2008, Montreal.
Hashishu, Muhammad. Interview. July 4, 2005, and July 24, 2007, Sidon, Lebanon.
Osmat, Bashir. Interview. June 29, 2008, and July 9, 2009, Beirut.
Samar, F. Interview. July 11, 2005, Beirut.
Salameh, Adnan and Hassan al-Amir. Interview. June 16, 2002, Detroit.
Subayti , ʻAli. Interview. January 5, 1997, Kafarsir, Lebanon.
Subayti, H., and R. Subayti. Interview. July 12, 2008, Beirut.
Traboulsi, Fawwaz, Interview. July 11, 2010, Beirut.
Al-Tufayli, Shaykh Subhi. Interview. July 9, 2005, ʻAyn Burday, Lebanon.

Periodicals

Al-Ahram Weekly. 2006.
Al-Akhbar. 2008, 2009, 2010.
Al-Anba'. 1965.
Daily Star. 2002, 2004, 2006, 2007, 2010.
Hamburg Der Spiegel. 1997.
Al-Hatif. 1938, 1939.
Al-Hayat. 1965, 1970, 2005, 2008.
Al-'Irfan. 1931, 1970, 1971.
Lisan al-Hal. 1930.
Los Angeles Times. 2008.
Al-Mustaqbal. 2006, 2007, 2010.
Al-Nahar. 1936, 1963, 1965, 1997, 2006.
New Yorker. 2006.
Al-Quds al-'Arabi. 2010.
Al-Safir. 1980, 1999, 2004, 2006.
Al-Sharq al-Awsat. 2006, 2009.
Al-Thaqafa al-Wataniyya. 1958, 1965.

Films and Video Clips

Abi Samra, Maher. *Shuyu'iyyun Kunna.* Orjouane Productions et Les Films. 2010.
"Al-Shahid Shaykh Raghib Harb." http://www.wa3ad.org/index.php?show=sounds &action=play&id=441.
"Interview with Shaykh Yasir al-Habib." April 11, 2009. http://www.youtube .com/watch?v=lyHtOjzUs98.
"Sayyid Hassan Nasrallah Speaking on the Martyrs' Day." November 14, 2009. http://www.youtube.com/watch?v=mUbLdpwpwI8.
"Sayyid Hassan Nasrallah Speaking on the Martyrdom of His Son." http://www .metacafe.com/watch/yt-BoF6NdWs9PI/sayed_hasan_nasrallah_speaking _on_the_martyrdom_of_his_son/.
"Speech by Sayyid Hassan Nasrallah." September 22 2006. http://somod.shiaweb .org/index.php?show=sounds&action=viewcat&id=78.

Unpublished Documentary Sources

Jurdi, 'Isam. "Privatization and Hizbullah's Approach to it." June 2011. Private papers, Beirut.

Régie, Board of Directors and Budget Commission. Annual reports presented to the General Assembly between 1962 and 1970. Private collection of Jacques Dagher, Beirut.

Régie, Personnel Department. "Development in the size of the Régie working force, 1959–1972." No date.

Vente Annuelle De Produits Manufactures, Record Group 2, Private Collection of Jacques Dagher, Beirut.

Arabic Secondary Sources

'Abbud, Ilyas. "Dahiyat al-muhajjarin." *Al-Safir*, August 4–5, 1980.

'Abdullah, Muhammad. "Wathiqat Hizbullah: Tashdid 'ala mawqi' al-muqawama fi al-sigha al-difa'iyya 'an Lubnan." *Al-Manar*, November 29, 2009.

Abu Fakhr, Saqr. *Karim Muroeh yatadhakkar fi ma yushbih al-sira*. Beirut: Maktabat Bustan, 2002.

Abu al-Nasr, Fadil. *Hizbullah: Haqa'iq wa-ab'ad*. Beirut: Al-Sharika al-'Alamiyya li-al-Kitab, 2003.

Aflaq, Michel. *Fi sabil al-ba'th*. Beirut: Dar al-Tali'a, 1959.

'Ala' al-Din, Shadi. "Yawmiyyat multabisa tufrighu al-sahat . . . lakinna 'al-i'tisam' mustammir." *Al-Mustaqbal*, June 17, 2007.

Al-'Alawi, Hadi. *Fi al-din wa-al-turath*. Beirut: Dar al-Tali'a, 1973.

———. *Fusul min tarikh al-Islam al-siyasi*. 2nd ed. Nicosia: Center for Socialist Studies and Research in the Arab World, 1999.

Al-'Alwan, 'Abd al-Sahib. *Dirasat fi al-islah al-zira'i*. Baghdad: Matba'at al-Aswaq al-Tijariyya, 1961.

'Amil, Mahdi. *Azamat al-hadara al-'arabiyya am azamat al-burjuwaziyyat al-'arabiyya?* Beirut: Dar al-Farabi, 1978.

———. *Bahth fi asbab al-harb al-ahliyya fi Lubnan*. Beirut: Dar al-Farabi, 1979.

———. *Fi al-dawla al-ta'ifiyya*. Beirut: Dar al-Farabi, 1986.

———. *Madkhal ila naqd al-fikr al-ta'ifi*. Beirut: Al-Farabi, 1989.

———. *Al-Nazariyya fi al-mumarasa al-siyasiyya: Bahth fi asbab al-harb al-ahliyya fi Lubnan*. Part 1. Beirut: Dar al-Farabi, 1979.

Al-Amin, Hassan, ed. *A'yan al-Shi'a*. Volumes. 9 and 10. Beirut: Dar al-Ta'aruf, 1986.

———. "Min dhikrayat Hassan al-Amin." In *Min daftar al-dhikrayat al-janubiyya*, edited by al-Majlis al-Thaqafi li-Lubnan al-Janubi, 9–21. Beirut: Dar al-Kitab al-Lubnani, 1981.

Al-Amin, Ibrahim. "Al-Radd 'ala "aqidat al-dahiyya': Matar min nar 'ala Gush Dan." *Al-Akhbar*, August 17, 2009.

———. "Al-Sayyid Hasan." *Al-Akhbar*, November 11, 2008.

Al-Amin, Akram Ja'far, ed. *Ja'far Muhsin Al-Amin: Sira wa-'amiliyyat*. Beirut: Al-Farabi, 2004.

Al-Amin, Ja'far. "Sayyid Ja'far al-Amin." In *Min daftar al-dhikrayat al-janubiyya*, part 2, edited by al-Majlis al-Thaqafi li-Lubnan al-Janubi, 97–115. Beirut: Dar al-Kitab al-Lubnani, 1984.

Amin, Jamil 'Adil. *Ma'rakat al-sanatayn fi al-harb al-lubnaniyya*. Beirut: Maktabat al-Afwaj al-'Arabiyya, 1976.

Amin, Marwan. "Al-Mas'ala al-ta'ifiyya fi idiyulujiyyat al-haraka al-wataniyya." *Al-Tariq* 37, no. 6 (December 1978): 69–77.

Al-Amin, Muhammad Hassan. "Hizbullah lam yastati' tahqiq tawazun al-ru'b ma'a Isra'il." *Al-Sharq al-Awsat*, September 16, 2006.

Al-Amin, Muhsin. *Khitat Jabal 'Amil*. Beirut: Dar al-'Amiliya, 1983.

———. *Thawrat al-tanzih: "Risalat al-tanzih."* Edited by Muhammad al-Qasim al-Husayni al-Najafi. Beirut: Dar al-Jadid, n.d.

'Awn, Basil Mushir. *Bayna al-din wa-al-siyasa: Al-fikr al-siyasi al-masihi fi bina'ihi al-nazari wa-waqi'ihi al-lubnani*. Beirut: Dar al-Nahar li-al-Nashr, 2008.

Al-'Aris, Mustafa. *Mustafa al-'Aris yatadhakkar*. Beirut: Dar al-Farabi, 1982.

Al-Arna'ut, Shafiq. "Adib mujahid wa majalla ra'ida." In *Wujuh thaqafiyya min al-Janub*, edited by al-Majlis al-Thaqafi li-Lubnan al-Janubi, 37–52. Beirut: Dar Ibn Khaldun, 1981.

———. *Ma'ruf Sa'd: Nidal wa-thawra*. Beirut: Al-Mu'assasa al-Lubaniyya li-al-Nashr wa-al-Khadamat al-Tiba'iyya, 1981.

"Al-'Asal al-hazin aw ma'sat al-nuzuh." *Al-'Irfan*, nos. 9–10 (January–February 1971): 840–43.

Al-Athath, Faysal. *Al-Shu'a' fi 'ulama' Ba'labak wa-al-Biqa'*. Beirut: Mu'assasat al-Nu'man, 1993.

Al-Bahadili, 'Ali. *Al-Hawza al-'ilmiyya fi al-Najaf*. Beirut: Dar al-Zahra', 1993.

Bahr al-'Ulum, Salih Muhammad. "Ayna Haqqi." Muntadayat Ya Husayn.

Al-Bahrani, Yusuf. *Al-Hada'iq al-nadira fi ahkam al-'itra al-tahira.* Volume 3. Qom, Iran: Mu'assassat al-Nashr al-Islami, 1985.

Bannut, Jihad. *Harakat al-nidal fi Jabal 'Amil.* Beirut: Dar al-Mizan, 1993.

Baqradoni, Karim. *Al-Salam al-mafqud: 'Ahd Ilyas Sarkis, 1976–1982.* Beirut: Dar 'Abr al-Sharq li-al-Manshurat, 1984.

Baydun, 'Abbas. "Al-'awd al-abadi li-al-ahlam al-muta'akhkhira," *Al-Safir,* August 25, 2006.

———. "Shadhara min sira siyasiyya: Aqni'at Lenin." *Bahithat* 4 (1997–98): 365–76.

———. "Shi'at Hizbullah . . . daqiqat ta'khir hasima 'an al-waqi'." *Al-Safir,* March 25, 2005.

Baydun, Ahmad. *Al-Jumhuriyya al-mutaqatti'a: Masa'ir al-sigha al-lubnaniyya ba'da ittifaq al-Ta'if.* Beirut: Dar al-Nahar, 1999.

Bazzi, 'Abbas. "Intifadat Bint Jubayl wa-Jabal 'Amil, April 1, 1936." *Dirasat 'Arabiyya* 29, nos. 1–2 (November–December 1992): 72–88.

Bazzi, Mustafa. *Bint Jubayl: Hadirat Jabal 'Amil.* Beirut: Dar al-Amir li-al-Thaqafa wa-al-'Ulum, 1998.

———. *Jabal 'Amil fi muhitihi al-'arabi, 1864–1948.* Beirut: Markaz al-Dirasat li-al-Tawthiq wa-al-Nashr, 1993.

———. *Jabal 'Amil wa-tawabi'uhu fi shamal Filastin.* Beirut: Dar al-Mawasim, 2002.

———. *Muhammad Sharara: Al-Adib wa-al-insan.* Lebanon: Hay'at Inma' al-Mintaqa al-Hududiyya, 1994.

Bazzi, Yusuf. "Bint Jubayl, Michigan, and Hizbullah." May 29, 2005.

———. "Ila al-wara' . . . ila jiwar Gaza . . . taqriban." *Al-Mustaqbal,* August 26, 2007.

Balkaziz, 'Abd Ilah. *Hizbullah: Min al-tahrir ila al-rad', 1982–2006.* Beirut: Markaz Dirasat al-Wahda al-'Arabiyya, 2006.

"Al-Barnamaj al-marhali li-al-ahzab wa-al-qiwa al-wataniyya wa-al-taqaddumiyya fi Lubnan: Min ajli islah dimuqrati li-al-nizam al-siyasi." In *Al-Tahaddi al-lubnani, 1975–1976,* edited by Shafiq al-Rayyis. Beirut: Dar al-Masira, 1978.

Al-Bizri, Dalal. *Akhawat al-zill wa-al-yaqin.* Beirut: Al-Nahar, 1996.

Al-Buwari, Ilyas. *Tarikh al-haraka al-'ummaliyya wa-al-naqabiyya fi Lubnan: 1947–1970.* Volume 2. Beirut: Dar al-Farabi, 1986.

Corm, George. "Fi fikr Mahdi 'Amil: Li-tatahalaf kul manahij al-Fikr al-Naqdi."

Daghir, Violette. "Al-Zawaj al-madani fi Lubnan: Haqq wa-darura." *Al-Lajna al-'Arabiyya li-huquq al-insan*, April 1998.

Dahir, Mas'ud. *Tarikh Lubnan al-ijtima'i, 1926–1914*. Beirut: Dar al-Matbu'at al-Sharqiyya, 1984.

Dahnun, 'Abd al-Razzaq. "Thamani thanawat 'ijaf 'ala rahil Hadi al-'Alawi al-Baghdadi." *Al-Nur*, September 27, 2006, 1–5.

Dakrub, Muhammad. *Judhur al-sindiyana al-hamra'*. Beirut: Dar al-Farabi, 1985.

Darwaza, Al-Hakam. *Al-Shuyu'iyya al-mahalliyya wa-ma'rakat al-'Arab al-qawmiyya*. N.p.: n.p., 1961.

Dubar, Claude, and Salim Nasr. *Al-Tabaqat al-ijtima'iyya fi Lubnan: Muqaraba susiyulujiyya tatbiqiyya*. Beirut: Mu'assasat al-abhath al-'Arabiyya, 1982.

Fadlallah, 'Abd al-Halim. "Al-Mantiq al-ijtima'i li-al-muqawama." In *Al-Intisar al-muqawim min al-mujtama' al-muqawim*. Beirut: n.p., 2007.

Fadlallah, Hadi. *Muhammad Jawad Mughniyya: Fikr wa-islah*. Beirut: Dar al-Hadi, 1993.

Fadlallah, Muhammad Husayn. *Ahkam al-shari'a*, 3 volumes. Beirut: Dar al-Malak, 2003.

———. *Fiqh al-Shari'a*. Volume 1. Beirut: Dar al-Malak, 1419H/2003.

———. *Al-Haraka al-islamiyya: Humum wa-qadaya*. Beirut: Dar al-Malak, 1990.

———. *Al-Ijtihad bayna 'asr al-madi wa-afaq al-mustaqbal*. Beirut: Al-Markaz al-Thaqafi al-'Arabi, 2009.

———. "Mahmud Darwish: Sha'ir Filastin wa-al-insaniyya." *Al-Hayat*, July 11, 2008.

———. "Al-Shahid al-Sadr: Naqla naw'iyya fi 'alam al-fikr." *Muntadayat al-Adwa'*, August 4, 2009.

———. *Al-Zahra' al-qudwa*. Beirut: Dar al-Malak, 2000.

Fahs, A. Adnana. *Al-Zuruf al-iqtisadiyya li-al-harb al-ta'ifiyya al-lubnaniyya*. Beirut: Dar al-Nahar, 1979.

Fahs, Hani. "Hunaka man yumaris al-naqd al-'am ba'da fawat al-awan." *Al-Mustaqbal*, December 12, 2010.

———. *Al-Shi'a wa-al-dawla fi Lubnan: Malamih fi al-ru'ya wa-al-dhakira*. Beirut: Dar al-Andalus, 1996.

———. "Tullab al-Najaf al-lubnaniyyun." *Al-Safir*, July 16, 1999.

Fahs, Zahra'. "Qum ayyuha al-shahid." *Ajyal al-Mustafa*, no. 10 (1998).

Faqih, Isma'il. "Al-Marja' al-islami Muhammad Husayn Fadlallah li-'al-Bayan': La atawaqqa' fitna sunniyya-shi'iyya musallaha fi al-Iraq." *Majallat al-Bayan al-Imaratiyya*, April 28, 2005.

Al-Faqir, 'Abdullah. "Fidiraliyyat al-shinat al-thalatha 'Shi'i Shuyu'i shuruki.'" *Al-Jazeera Talk*, September 18, 2007.

Farhat, Hani. *Al-Thulathi al-'amili fi 'asr al-nahda*. Beirut: Al-Dar al-'Alamiyya, 1981.

Fawwaz, Fawziyya. "Al-Adiba al-ra'ida: Zaynab Fawwaz, siratuha, adabuha." In *Wujuh thaqafiyya min al-Janub*, part 2, edited by al-Majlis al-Thaqafi li-Lubnan al-Janubi, 7-34. Beirut: Al-Majlis al-Thaqafi li-Lubnan al-Janubi, 1984.

Fayyad, 'Ali. "Ayyu hiwar ma'a al-gharb?" *Qadaya Islamiyya Mu'asira*, no. 5 (1999): 208–13.

Fayyad, Mona. *Ma'na an takuna lubnaniyyan: Maqalat fi hal al-watan . . . wa ahwal al-muwatin*. Beirut: Arab Scientific Publishers, 2009.

Fayyad, Nawal. *Safahat min tarikh Jabal 'Amil fi al-'ahdayn al-'uthmani wa-al-faransi*. Beirut: Dar al-Jadid, 1998.

Gharbiyya, al-Amin Ahmad. "Ahmad Gharbiyya." In *Min daftar al-dhikrayat al-janubiyya*, part 2, edited by al-Majlis al-Thaqafi li-Lubnan al-Janubi, 117–32. Beirut: Al-Majlis al-Thaqafi li-Lubnan al-Janubi, 1984.

Al-Ghul, 'Adnan. "Qaryat al-saha al-turathiyya." *Al-Birr Journal*, July 27, 2005.

Al-Ha'iri, Husayn Kazim. "Tarjumat hayat al-sayyid al-shahid." In *Mabahith al-usul: Taqriran li-abhath samahat Ayatullah al-'uzma al-shahid al-sayyid Muhammad Baqir al-Sadr*, edited by Kazim Husayn al-Ha'iri and Muhammad Baqir al-Sadir. Qom, Iran: K. al-Ha'iri, 1987.

Al-Haj, Sana'. "Al-Sayyid Fadlallah: Al-Iltizam ya'ni al-infitah fima al-ta'assub ya'ni al-in'izal." *Al-Tanawwu' al-Islami*, April 30, 2010.

Al-Hajj, Abd al-Rahman. "Mafhum al-dawla al-haditha wa-ishkalatuha fi al-fikr al-islami al-siyasi al-mu'asir." *Hizb al-Wasat al-Jadid*, May 7, 2008.

Al-Halbawi, Fatima. "Dami ilayki hadiyyati." *Ajyal al-Mustafa*, no. 13 (2000).

Hamada, Muhib. *Tarikh 'alaqat al-biqa'iyyin bi-al-suriyyin wa-istiratijiyyat al-Biqa' fi al-muwajaha al-suriyya al-isra'iliyya, 1918–1936*. Beirut: Dar Al-Nahar, 1983.

Hanna, 'Abdullah. *Al-Qadiyya al-zira'iyya wa-al-harkat al-fallahiyya fi Suriyya wa-Lubnan: 1920–1945*. Volume 2. Beirut: Dar al-Farabi, 1978.

Haqqi, Bey Isma'il. *Lubnan mabahith 'ilmiyya wa-ijtima'iyya*. Beirut: n.p., 1969.

Harfush, Nabil. "Adwa' 'ala al-mughtaribin fi al-'alam." *Al-'Irfan*, nos. 9–10 (January–February, 1971): 1182–93.

Al-Harizi, Hamid."Al-Zahira al-ta'ifiyya wa-ishkaliyyat al-dawla al-madaniyya." *Al-Hiwar al-mutamaddin*, June 6, 2011.

Harqus, 'Umar. "Hina ya'tasim al-mu'tasam 'alayhim." *Al-Mustaqbal*, May 26, 2007.

Hassan, Fadil. "Karbala': Al-Raddat al-husayniyya tatajawaz al-janib al-dini ila al-siyasi." *Wakalat Kurdistan li-al-Anba'*, March 12, 2011.

———. "Mawkib mahallat al-ʿabbasiyya wa-shaʿiruhu al-shahid ʿAbd al-Zahra' al-Saʿdi." *Iraqi Communist Party*, November 30, 2011.

Al-Hasani, Salim. *Al-Maʿalim al-jadida li-al-marjaʿiyya al-shiʿiyya: Dirasa wa-hiwar maʿa al-sayyid Muhammad Husayn Fadlallah.* Beirut: Dar al-Malak, 1993.

Hay'at tahrir al-Tariq. *Hiwar fikri siyasi sarih maʿa George Hawi: Madha jara? Wa limadha? Wa-ma al-ʿamal?* Beirut: n.p., 1982.

Al-Haydari, Ibrahim. *Trajidiya Karbala': Sociolojiya al-khitab al-shaʿbi li-al-ʿaza' al-husayni.* Beirut: Dar al-Saqi, 1999.

Hijazi, ʿAli. "Shaʿir al-tahhaddi: Al-Shaykh ʿAli Mahdi Shams al-Din." In *Wujuh thaqafiyya min al-Janub*, part 2, edited by al-Majlis al-Thaqafi li-Lubnan al-Janubi, 35-62. Beirut: Al-Majlis al-Thaqafi li-Lubnan al-Janubi, 1984.

Al-Hilu, Khattar Yusuf. *Awraq min tarikhina.* Volume 2. Beirut: Dar al-Farabi, 1988.

Al-Hizb al-Shuyuʿi al-ʿIraqi. *Kitab shuhada' al-hizb, shuhada' al-watan.* 2nd ed. Stockholm: Media Vision, 2009.

Al-Hizb al-Shuyuʿi al-Lubnani. *Al-Shuyuʿiyyun al-lubnaniyyun wa-muhimmat al-marhala al-muqbila.* Beirut: Matabiʿ al-Amal, n.d.

———. *Sittun ʿaman min al-nidal min ajli Lubnan afdal.* Beirut: Manshurat al-Hizb al-Shuyuʿi al-Lubnani, 1988.

Al-Huda, Bint. *Imra'atan wa-rajul.* Beirut: Dar al-Taʿaruf li-al-Matbuʿat, 1979.

———. *Al-Majmuʿa al-qasasiyya al-kamila.* Beirut: Dar al-Taʿaruf li-al-Matbuʿat, 1981.

Hukayma, Rami. "Hizbullah min al-mansha' ila al-barlaman." In *Mustqabal al-usuliyya fi al-ʿalam al-arabi.* Beirut: Al-Markaz al-ʿArabi li al-Maʿlumat, 1993.

Al-Husayni, Baqir Muhammad. "Al-Sayyid ʿAbd al-Karim Qasim (qaddasa sirrahu) and al-zaʿim Muhsin al-Hakim: Al-Shuyuʿiyya kufr wa-ilhad." Part 1. *Al-Hiwar al-Mutamaddin*, no. 1898. April 27, 2007.

———. "Al-Sayyid ʿAbd al-Karim." Part 2. *Al-Hiwar al-Mutamaddin*, no. 1901. April 30, 2007.

———. "Al-Sayyid ʿAbd al-Karim Qasim (qaddasa sirrahu) and al-zaʿim Muhsin al-Hakim: Al-Shuyuʿiyya kufr wa-ilhad." Part 3. *Al-Hiwar al-Mutamaddin*, no. 1932. May 31, 2007.

Ibrahim, Muhsin. "Mufid al-Jaza'iri: al-Husayn aththara fi tawajjuhi ila al-hizb al-shuyuʿi." *Al-Shabaka al-ʿIraqiyya.* No. 141, January 30, 2011.

Ibrahim, Sayyid ʿAli. "Sayyid ʿAli Ibrahim." In *Min daftar al-dhikrayat al-janu-biyya*, edited by al-Majlis al-Thaqafi li-Lubnan al-Janubi, 39–56. Beirut: Dar al-Kitab al-Lubnani, 1981.

Al-Ibrahimi, ʿAli. "Hadi al-ʿAlawi wa-ʿAli Shariʿati: Man minhuma fahima al-tarikh?" July 27, 2009.

Inmaʾ al-Biqaʿ al-shamali: Al-Itar al-ʿam wa-al-siyasa al-iqtaʿiyya. Beirut: Al-Markaz al-Istishari li-al-Dirasat wa-al-Tawthiq, 2002.

Ismaʿil, Zaynab. "Min al-Najaf ila Shaqraʾ tariq shiʿr wa-thaqafa wa-din, kayfa kana al-intiqal wa-al-ʿawda min al-hawza al-diniyya ila al-hawza al-mariksiyya?" *Al-Safir*, October 29, 2004.

Al-ʿItabi, ʿAbd al-Jabbar. "Hadi al-ʿAlawi . . . kana fi ittihad al-udabaʾ." *Elaph*, November 26, 2008.

ʿItani, Ziad. "Tajribat hayat al-Sayyid Muhammad Husayn Fadlallah ʿal-shaykhʾ alladhi qaraʾa Kutub ʿMarx.ʾ" *Bayynat*, November 2003.

"Jabal ʿAmil fi al-ʿIraq." *Al-ʿIrfan* 24, no. 625 (1934): 529.

Al-Jabburi, Raʿd. "Hal hum aqlam li-al-ijar? Muthaqqafun shuyuʿiyyun bayna khiwaʾ al-thaqafa wa-inhiraf al-tatbiq: Rashid al-Khayyun namuzajan" *Al-Sharq*, March 3, 2010.

Jabir, Mundhir. "Al-Kiyan al-siyasi li-Jabal ʿAmil qabla 1920." In *Safahat min tarikh Jabal ʿAmil*, edited by al-Majlis al-Thaqafi li-Lubnan al-Janubi. Beirut: Al-Majlis al-Thaqafi li-Lubnan al-Janubi, 1979. At

———. "Sanat al-tahrir al-ula wa-al-sunan al-lubnaniyya: Al-Janub ʿibʾ al-watan al-awwal." *Al-Safir*, May 24, 2001.

Al-Jawahiri, Muhammad Mahdi. *Diwan al-Jawahiri*. Volume 2. Najaf, Iraq: Matbaʿat al-Ghuri, 1935.

———. "Amantu bi-al-Husayn." *Al-Bayyina*, 2005.

Al-Jisr, Basim. *Fouad Chehab: Dhalika al-majhul*. Beirut: Sharikat al-Matbuʿat li-al-Tawziʿ wa-al-Nashr, 1988.

J. M. "Siyar al-ʿilm fi al-Najaf." *Al-ʿIrfan* 21, nos. 4–5 (1931) : 498–99.

Juha, Shafiq. *Maʿrakat masir Lubnan fi ʿahd al-intidab al-faransi, 1918–1946.* Beirut: Maktabat Raʾs Beirut, 1995.

Kahil, Fuad. "Fuad Kahil." In *Min daftar al-dhikrayat al-janubiyya*, part 2, edited by al-Majlis al-Thaqafi li-Lubnan al-Janubi, 133-59. Beirut: Al-Majlis al-Thaqafi li-Lubnan al-Janubi, 1984.

"Kalimat takhtasir al-hayat." *Bayyinat*, n.d.

Karmih, Rashid. "ʿAshuraʾ Al-Husayn": Min wahi karnaval al-karbalaʾiyyin." Part 1. *Al-Hiwar Al-Mutamaddin*, December 23, 2009.

———. "Ila al-shuyu'iyyin al-karbala'iyyin." *Al-Hiwar Al-Mutamaddin*, January 3, 2007.

Karnib, Batul. "Ila um al-shahid." *Ajyal al-Mustafa*, no. 10 (1998).

Al-Kawrani al-'Amili, 'Ali. *Ila Talib al-'Ilm*. Qom, Iran: N.p., 2010.

Al-Kawrani al-'Amili, 'Ali. *"Al-Mawja al-shuyu'iyya allati 'asarnaha,"* Mawqi' Samahat al-Shaykh 'Ali al-Kawrani al-'Amili.

Al-Kawrani al-'Amili, 'Ali and al-Wahid al-Khurasani, eds. *Al-Haqq al-mubin fi ma'rifat al-ma'sumin 'alayhim al-salam: Buhuth mustafada min muhadarat al-marja' al-dini al-wahid al-Khurasani madda zillahu*. 2nd ed. Qom, Iram: Dar al-Huda, 2003.

Kawtharani, Wajih. *Al-Ittijahat al-ijtima'iyya wa-al-siyasiyya fi Jabal Lubnan wa-al-Mashriq al-'arabi: 1860–1920*. Beirut: Ma'had al-Inma' al-'Arabi, 1978.

———. "Al-Mujtama' al-madani wa-al-dawla fi al-tarikh al-'arabi." In *Al-Mujtama' al-madani fi al-watan al-'arabi wa-dawruhu fi tahqiq al-dimuqrati-yya*, edited by Sa'id Bin Sa'id 'Alawi. Beirut: Markaz Dirasat al-Wahda al-'Arabiyya, 1992.

———. "'Al-Mujtama' al-madani' su'al sa'b fi zil hukm al-hizb al-wahid li-al-dawla kama li-al-ta'ifa." *Al-Hayat*, February 23, 2008.

———. "Al-Sulta al-madaniyya wa-al-i'tiqad bi-wilayat al-faqih al-mutlaqa," *al-Nahar*, November 3, 2006.

Khalifa, Marlene. "Man huwa Hizbullah? Wa-ma ahdafuhu?" *Al-Nahar*, August 13, 2006.

Khalifa, Nabil. *Al-Shi'a fi Lubnan: Thawrat al-dimughrafiyya wa-al-hirman*. Beirut: Markaz Byblos li-al-Dirasat wa-al-Abhath, 1984.

Khalil, Fouad. *Al-Harafisha: Imarat al-musawama, 1530–1850*. Beirut: Al-Farabi, 1997.

Khamenei, 'Ali Sayyid. *Al-Hukuma fi al-Islam: Majmu'at muhadarat*. Beirut: Dar al-Rawda, 1995.

———. *Wilaya*. Beirut: Dar al-Hadi, 2000.

Al-Khaqani, 'Ali. *Shu'ara' al-Ghuri*. Volume 4. Qom, Iran: Matba'at Behman, 1987.

Al-Katib, Ahmad. "Al-Marja'iyya al-shi'iyya dawla fi al-dawla?" *Al-Wasat*, February 5, 2001, 19–20.

Khayri, Zaki. *Kitabat al-rafiq Husayn Muhammad al-Shabibi*. Baghdad: Matba'at al-Sha'b, 1974.

Khuri, Ilyas. "Tehran wa-al-thaqafa al-'arabiyya." *Al-Quds al-'Arabi*, June 23, 2009.

Kuntar, Bassam. "10/10/10: Hal yunqidh sihr al-arqam kawkabuna?" *Al-Akhbar*, October 9, 2010.

Madoyan, Artin. *Hayat 'ala al-mitras.* Beirut: Dar al-Farabi, 1986.

Mahdar ijtima' mu'tamar al-hizb al-awwal. Al-Qa'ida 2, no. 3 (March 1944).

Majmu'a mina al-'Ulama'. *Fatawa 'ulama' al-Islam fi masa'il jihadiyya wa-hukm al-'amaliyyat al-istishhadiyya.* Beirut: Dar al-Mahajja al-Bayda', 2002.

Mansur, Albert. *Al-Inqilab 'ala al-Ta'if.* Beirut: Dar al-Jadid, 1993.

Al-Mawla, Sa'ud. "'An al-muwatana wa-al-mujtama' al-madani wa-al-tajriba al-lubnaniyya: Mulahazat hiwariyya." *Middle East Transparent*, October 23, 2005.

———. "Qira'a susiyo-tarikhiyya fi masar 'Hizbullah' wa-masirihi." May 16, 2009.

Mawsu'at Nasrallah. *Al-Rajul alladhi yakhtasir umma.* 2 vols. Beirut: Manshurat al-Fajr, 2006.

Mervin, Sabrina. *Harakat al-islah al-Shi'i.* Beirut: Dar al-Nahar, 2000.

Al-Miliji Ilhami. "Al-Marja' al-shi'i Ayatullah Fadlallah." *Arabiya*, March 19, 2009.

Muqallid, Muhammad 'Ali. "Kitab Maftuh ila al-Sayyid Hasan Nasrallah." *Al-Hiwar al-Mutamaddin*, December 18, 2007.

———. "Al-Sha'ir 'Abd al-Muttalib al-Amin." In *Wujuh thaqafiyya min al-Janub*, edited by al-Majlis al-Thaqafi li-Lubnan al-Janubi, 87–102. Beirut: Dar Ibn Khaldun, 1984.

Mroueh, Wassim. "Fadlallah's Charity for Orphans Still giving Despite Top Cleric's Death." *Daily Star*, August 13, 2010.

Al-Mudarrissi, Muhammad Taqi. *Kayfa tantasir al-thawra al-islamiyya fi Lubnan?* N.p.: Al-Markaz al-Thaqafi al-Islami, 1405 H.

Mughniyya, Ahmad. "Al-Shaykh Ahmad Mughniyya." In *Min daftar al-dhikrayat al-janubiyya*, part 2, edited by al-Majlis al-Thaqafi li-Lubnan al-Janubi, 81–96. Beirut: Dar al-Kitab al-Lubnani, 1984.

Mughniyya, Jawad Muhammad. *Abu Dharr: Ramz al-yaqza fi al-damir al-insani: 'Ard wa-tahlil.* Beirut: Dar al-Ta'aruf, 1990.

———. "Al-'Aql wa-'alam ma ba'd al-mawt." *Al-Mawsu'a al-Islamiyya.* 2000.

———. *Fiqh al-Imam Ja'far al-Sadiq: 'Ard wa-istidlal.* Volume 1. Qom, Iran: Mu'assassat Ansariyan li-al-Tiba'a wa-al-Nashr, 1379q/2000.

Muhanna, Kamil. "Al-Mujtama' al-madani fi Lubnan: Halat al-haql al-ma'rifi fi al-buhuth wa-al-dirasat allati tamma ijra'uha fi al-sanawat al-madiya." *Amel Association*, Beirut, n.d.

Muhsin, Mahdi Dhiyab. "Min dhakirat al-sinin al-najafiyya . . . : Al-Shaykh al-rahil Muhammad al-Shabibi." *Al-Hiwar al-Mutamaddin*, October 29, 2005.

Muroeh, Husayn. "Adab al-jil al-'iraqi al-hadir yaftaqir ila thaqafa adabiyya dhat wajhayn." *Al-Hatif*, August 28, 1939, 10–15.

———. "Bayna al-'aql al-qadim wa-al-'aql al-hadith." *Al-Hatif* 5, no. 170 (1939), 1, 8–10.

———. "Dhikra 9 sha'ban: mithaq muqaddas fi a'naq al-'Arab." *Al-Hatif*, October 7, 1938, 3–4.

———. "Harakat al-thaqafa al-'Arabiyya fi muwajahat harb khamsa Huzayran," 119–39. In *Dirasat fi al-fikr wa-al-adab*, edited by Husayn Muroeh. Beirut: Dar al-Farabi, 1993.

———. "Al-Jundiyya wa-al-islah al-ijtima'i." *Al-Hatif*, January 24, 1938, 24–25.

———. "Min al-Najaf dakhala hayati Marx." In *Husayn Muroeh fi masiratihi al-nidaliyya fikran wa-mumarasa*, edited by 'Abbas Baydun. Beirut: Dar al-Farabi, 1997.

———. "Muhammad Sharara." In *Wujuh thaqafiyya min al-Janub*, edited by al-Majlis al-Thaqafi li-Lubnan al-Janubi, 7–24. Beirut: Dar Ibn Khaldun, 1981.

———. *Al-Naza'at al-maddiyya fi al-falsafa al-'arabiyya al-islamiyya*. 2 vols. Beirut: Dar al-Farabi, 1988.

———. "Qissa qawmiyya: Shahid." *Al-Hatif*, April 28, 1939, 18–21.

———. "Sa'a fi zilal al-butula: Hakadha tughras al-karama al-wataniyya fi al-nufus." *Al-Hatif*, June 3, 1938, 3–5.

———. "Al-Taj al-Hashimi: Shu'a' risala wa-daw' 'aqida." *Al-Hatif*, September 8, 1938, 4–5.

———. "Thawrat 14 Tammuz al-'iraqiyya: Thawra wataniyya dimuqratiyya 'amiqat al-judhur." *Al-Thaqafa al-Wataniyya* 7, no. 7 (January 1958): 11–78.

———. *Wulidtu shaykhan wa-'amutu tiflan*. Beirut: Dar al-Farabi, 1990.

Muroeh, Karim. "'An al-din wa-al-turath, wa-al-thawra." In *Majmu'a mina al-Bahithin wa-al-mufakkirin al-'arab, hiwarat: Mufakkirun 'arab yunaqishun Karim Muroeh fi al-qawmiyya wa-al-ishtirakiyya wa-al-dimuqratiyya wa-al-din wa-al-thawra*, edited by Karim Muroeh and 'Adil Ahmad. Beirut: Dar al-Farabi, 1990.

———. *Al-Muqawama: Afkar li-al-niqash 'an al-judhur wa-al-tajriba wa-al-afaq*. Beirut: Dar al-Farabi, 1985.

———. *Nahwa jumhuriyya thalitha*. Beirut: Dar al-Farabi, 2007.

Murqus, Ilyas. *Tarikh al-ahzab al-shuyu'iyya fi al-watan al-'arabi*. Beirut: Dar al-Tali'a, 1964.

Muru, Muhammad. "Fadlallah: Al-Fahm al-khati' li-al-din wa-al-anzima." *Bayynat*, July 23, 2002.

———. *Hizbullah: Al-Nash'a, al-'amaliyyat, al-jihad wa-al-intisar*. N.p.: Dar al-Nasr li-al-Tiba'a al-Islamiyya, n.d.

Al-Mutir, Jasim. "'An al-shi'r wa al-shuyu'iyin wa-dhikra al-Husayn." *Jaridat Babil*, February 1, 2010.

"Nasrallah fi khitab nari: Sanastakhdim al-silah li-al-difa' 'an silah al-muqawama wa-shabakat al-ittisalat." *Syria News*, August 5, 2008.

Al-Nawwab, Muzaffar. "Min al-daftar al-sirri al-khususi li-Imam al-mughannin." *Al-Mawsu'a al-'Alamiyya li-al-Shi'r al-Arabi*, April 12, 2005.

———. "Watariyyat layliyya." *Al-Hiwar al-Mutamaddin*, February 27, 2003.

———. "Al-Wuquf bayna al-samawat wa-al-Imam al-Husayn." *Muntadayat Ya Husayn*, 2000.

Nur al-Din, Najib. *Al-Sayyid Muhammad Husayn Fadlallah: Al-'aqlaniyya wa-al-hiwar min ajli al-taghyir wa-al-nahda*. Beirut: Markaz al-Hadara li-Tanmiyat al-Fikr al-Islami, 2010.

———. *Al-Sayyid Muhammad Husayn Fadlallah: Umara' wa-qaba'il, khafaya wa-haqa'iq lubnaniyya*. Beirut: Riad al-Rayess Books, 2001.

Al-Qadiyya al-zira'iyya fi Lubnan fi daw' al-mariksiyya. Beirut: Manshurat al-Hizb al-Shuyu'i al-Lubnani, c.1970.

Al-Qasifi, Jad, ed. *Lubnan: Al-Mafhum wa-al-tahaddiyat*. Lebanon, Al-Kaslik: Markaz Finiks li-al-Dirasat al-Lubnaniyya, 2011.

Qasim, Abd al-'Aziz. "Fadlallah: Wilayat al-faqih nazariyya la yaraha akthar al-Shi'a." *onislam*, August 31, 2008.

Qasim, Na'im. *Hizbullah: Al-Manhaj, al-tajriba, al-mustaqbal*. Beirut: Dar al-Hadi, 2002.

———. "Kayfa nabni mujtama' al-muqawama?" *Muntada al-Amin*, May 23, 2007.

Qasir, Mustafa al-Shaykh. "Al-Bu'd al-tarbawi fi shakhsiyyat al-fard al-mu'min." *Al-Mahdi Schools*, August 2007.

———. "Al-Hurriyya bayna al-nazariyya al-diniyya wa-al-nazariyya al-'ilmaniyya." *Al-Mahdi Schools*, September 2008.

———. "Al-Istiqlal al-haqiqi wa-thaqafat al-muqawama." *Al-Mahdi Schools*, September 2008.

———. "Al-Wahda al-islamiyya." *Al-Mahdi Schools*, October 2008.

Al-Qassab, 'Abd al-Muhsin. "Husayn Muroeh." *Al-Hatif*, September 2, 1938, 12–15.

Qsir, Qasim. "Al-Salafiyya al-shi'iyya: Mu'ashshirat rahina wa-mustaqbaliyya." *Muntada Manar li-al-Hiwar*, May 13, 2009.

Qubrusi, Abdullah. *Abdullah Qubrusi yatadhakkar.* Volume 1. Beirut: Mu'assasat Fikr li-al-Abhath wa-al-Nashr, 1982.

Al-Rasi, Salam. *"Li-'alla tadi'."* In Salam al-Rasi, *Al-A'mal al-kamila.* Beirut: Dar Nawfal, 2000.

Ra'uf, 'Adil. *Muhammad Baqir al-Sadr bayna diktaturiyyatayn.* 6th ed. Damascus: Al-Markaz al-'Iraqi li-al-I'lam wa-al-Dirasat, 2001.

Al-Rayyis, Shafiq. *Al-Tahaddi al-lubnani.* Beirut: Dar al-Masira, 1978.

Rida, al-Shaykh Ahmad. *Mudhakkarat li-al-tarikh: Hawadith Jabal 'Amil, 1914–1922.* Beirut: Dar al-Nahar, 2009.

Al-Ruhaymi, 'Abd al-Halim. *Ta'rikh al-haraka al-islamiyya fi al-'Iraq: al-Judhur al-fikriyya wa-al-waqi' al-tarikhi, 1900–1924.* Beirut: Al-Dar al-'Alamiyya li-al-Tiba'a, 1985.

Sadiq, 'Abd al-Husayn. *Sima' al-Sulaha'.* Sidon, Lebanon: Matba'at al-'Irfan, 1927.

Sadiq, Habib. "Al-Saha al-jarih." *Al-'Irfan,* nos. 9–10 (January–February 1971): 1106–8.

Al-Sadr, Muhammad Baqir. *Durus fi 'ilm al-usul.* Qom, Iran: Mu'assasat al-Nashr al-Islami al-Tabi'a li-Jama'at al-Mudarrisin bi-Qum al-Muqaddas, 1994–95.

———. *Falsafatuna: Dirasa mawdu'iyya fi mu'tarak al-sira' al-fikri al-qa'im bayna mukhtalaf al-tayyarat al-falsafiyya wa-khassatan al-falsafa al-islamiyya wa-al-madiyya al-diyaliktikiyya al-mariksiyya.* Beirut: Manshurat 'Uwaydat, 1962.

———. *Iqtisaduna: Dirasa mawdu'iyya tatanawalu bi-al-naqd wa-al-bahth al-madhahib al-iqtisadiyya li-al-mariksiyya wa-al-ra'ismaliyya fi ususiha al-fikriyya wa-tafasiliha.* Beirut: Dar al-Ta'aruf li-al-Matbu'at, 1981.

———. *Al-Islam yaqud al-hayat: Khilafat al-insan wa-shahadat al-anbiya'.* Volume 4. Tehran: Wizarat al-Irshad al-Islami, 1982.

———. *Khilafat al-insan wa-shahadat al-anbiya'.* Beirut: Dar al-Ta'aruf li-al-Matbu'at, 1979.

———. *Manabi' al-qudra fi al-dawla al-islamiyya.* Volume 5. Beirut: Dar al-Ta'aruf li-al-Matbu'at, 1979.

Al-Sadr, Imam Musa. "Ya abna' Ba'labak wa-al-Hirmil," *Al-'Irfan,* July–August 1970, 423–25.

Al-Saduq, Al-Shaykh. *Al-khisal.* Edited by 'Ali Akbar al-Ghifari. Qom, Iran: Jama'at al-Mudarrisin, 1983.

Al Safa, Jabir Muhammad. *Tarikh Jabal 'Amil.* Beirut: Dar al-Nahar, 1992.

Al-Saffar, Hassan. *Ru'a al-hayat fi nahj al-balagha.* Beirut: Dar al-Safwa, 1998.

Saghiyya, Hazim. "Fusul min qissat 'Hizbullah' al-lubnani. Part 2." *Al-Hayat,* May 1, 2005.

Sayf, Malik. *Li-al-Ta'rikh lisan: Dhikrayat wa-qadaya khassa bi-al-hizb al-shuyu'i al-'iraqi mundhu ta'sisihi hatta al-yawm.* Baghdad: Dar al-Huriyya li-al-Tiba'a, 1983.

Al-Shakarji, Diya'. "Muhammad Husayn Fadlallah." *Minbar al-Katib al-'Iraqi,* July 8, 2010.

Shalabi, Mahmud. *Ishtirakiyyat Muhammad.* Cairo: Maktabat al-Qahira al-Haditha, 1962.

Shalha, 'Abd al-Rahim. "Al-Tufayli yad'u li-rahil Lahhud al-yawm qabla al-ghad." *Al-Safir,* February 28, 2006.

Shamseddine, Muhammad Mahdi. *Dirasat wa-mawaqif fi al-fikr wa-al-siyasa wa-al-mujtama': Abhath fikriyya wa-islamimyya 'amma.* Beirut: Al-Mu'assasa al-Dawliyya li-al-Dirasat wa-al-Nashr, 1990.

Sharaf al-Din, Ja'far. "Al-Sayyid Ja'far Sharaf al-Din." In *Min daftar al-dhikrayat al-janubiyya,* part 2, edited by al-Majlis al-Thaqafi li-Lubnan al-Janubi, 11–78. Beirut: Dar al-Kitab al-Lubnani, 1984.

Sharara, Balqis. *Min al-iman ila hurriyyat al-fikr.* Damascus: Dar al-Mada, 2009.

Sharara, Waddah. *Dawlat Hizbullah: Lubnan mujtama'an islamiyyan.* Beirut: Dar al-Nahar, 1996.

Sharara, Musa al-Zayn. "Min dhikrayat al-sha'ir Musa al-Zayn Sharara." In *Min Daftar al-dhikrayat al-janubiyya,* edited by al-Majlis al-Thaqafi li-Lubnan al-Janubi, 55–79. Beirut: Dar al-Kitab al-Lubnani, 1981.

"Sheik Muhammad Husayn Fadlallah." *Al-Mashriq,* March 13, 1996.

Al-Shirazi, Muhammad al-Husayni al-Sayyid. *Fatima al-Zahra': Afdal uswat al-nisa.* Karbala': Dar al-'Alqami, 2008.

Shuman, Muhammad. "Qira'a fi fikr Charles Malik wa-al-Kaslik: Al-'Unsuriyya bayna zuhurat al-kiyan wa-al-intihar." *Al-Tariq,* July 1985, 101–25.

Al-Suri, Hassan Muhammad. "Hayat al-talib fi al-Najaf." *Al-Irfan* 25, no.3 (1934), 235–36.

Tajammu' al-'Ulama' al-Muslimin fi Lubnan. *Mu'tamar 'ulama' al-Islam: Inqadh al-Quds wa-nusrat al-sha'b al-filastini taklif shar'i wa-wajib jihadi.* Beirut: Tajammu' al-'Ulama' al-Muslimin fi Lubnan, 2003.

Talib, Adib. "Hizbullah: Dawlat wilayat al-faqih mu'ajjala." *Al-Hiwar al-Mutamaddin,* October 22, 2008.

Talib, Mirvat. "Nur al-mas'uliyya." *Madaris al-Mahdi, Bint Jubayl,* June 28, 2008.

Taqi al-Din, Sulayman. "Al-Janub al-lubnani bi-ri'ayat al-istiqlal." In *Safahat min tarikh Jabal 'Amil,* edited by al-Majlis al-Thaqafi li-Lubnan al-Janubi. Beirut: Dar al-Farabi, 1979.

Tehrani, Buzurg Agha. *Al-Dhari'a ila tasanif al-Shi'a.* Volume 18. Beirut: Dar al-Adwa', 1983.

Al-Thawr, 'Abd al-Shahid. "Al-Layla al-yatima fi al-dahr." In *Tajarib mawkibiyya fi sirat radud. Muntada al-Sahil al-Sharqi,* April 24, 2008.

The Lebanese Constitution. Translated by Gabriel M. Bustros. London: Bureau of Lebanese and Arab Documentation, 1973.

Traboulsi, Fawwaz. *A History of Modern Lebanon.* London: Pluto Press, 2007.

Al-'Udhari, Sa'id. "Baqat ward wa-qubulat li-al-shuyu'iyyin fi 'id tajammu'ihim: Min islami mutashaddid." *Al-Nur,* March 29, 2011.

Al-Wardi, 'Ali. *Lamahat ijtima'iyya min tarikh al-'Iraq al-hadith.* Part V. London: Al-Warrak, 2007.

"Ya alf sawm wa-sala 'ala al-Regie." *Lisan al-Hal,* May 23, 1930.

Ya'qub, Rabi'. "Hakadha yurabbi Hizbullah al-atfal 'ala thaqafat al-mawt." *Al-Naqid,* July 17, 2007.

Yusuf, 'Ali. "Kayfa naqi al-tifl min al-isaba bi-al-ittikaliyya." *Madaris al-Mahdi,* September 2008.

Yusuf, Hassan. "Muhammad Husayn Fadlallah." In *Mustaqbal al-usuliyya if al-'alam al-'arabi.* Beirut: Al-Markaz al-'Arab li-al-Ma'lumat, 1993.

———. "Al-Sayyid Hasan Nasrallah." *Ma'lumat Mustaqbal al-Usuliyya fi al-'Alam al-'Arabi,* May 1993, 107.

Al-Zayn, Ahmad 'Ali. "Rawafid: Ma'a al-Sayyid Muhammad Husayn Fadlallah. Parts 1 and 2." *Al-Arabiya,* July 9, 2004.

Al-Zayn, 'Ali. "Bawadir al-islah fi al-Najaf aw nahdat Kashif al-Ghita'." *Al-Irfan* 29, no. 2 (1939).

Al-Zayn, Jihad. "Min dhikrayat al-Shaykh 'Ali." In *Min daftar al-dhikrayat al-janubiyya,* edited by al-Majlis al-Thaqafi li-Lubnan al-Janubi, 24–37. Beirut: Dar al-Kitab al-Lubnani, 1981.

Al-Zayn, Nizar. Editorial. *Al-'Irfan,* nos. 9–10 (January–February 1971): 999–1000.

Persian Sources

Asadullahi, Mas'ud. *Junbish-i Hizbullah-i Lubnan: Ghuzashtah va-Hal.* Tehran: Pazhuhashkadah-yi Mutali'at-i Rahburdi, 2004.

———. *Az Muqavamat ta Piruzi: Tarikhchah-yi Hizbullah-i Lubnan, 1361–1379.* Tehran: Mu'assasah-yi Mutali'at va-Tahqiqat-i Andishah Sazan-i Nur, 2000

Mutahheri, Murtaza. "Muskhil-i Asasi dar Saziman-i Ruhaniyyat." *Howzeh*, nos.1–6 (1961): 13–21.

Ruhani, Hamid. *Nehzat-e Imam Khomeini*. Volume 2. Tehran: Intisharat-i Rah-i Imam, 1985.

Shariati, Ali. *Tashayyu'-i 'Alavi va Tashayyu'-i Safavi*. Tehran: Intisharat-i Chapakhsh, 1998.

Western Sources

Abboushi Dallal, Jenine. "Hizbullah's Virtual Civil Society." In *Internationalizing Cultural Studies: An Anthology*, edited by M. Ackbar Abbas, John Nguyet Erni, and Wimal Dissanayake, 232–36. Malden, MA: Blackwell, 2005.

Abisaab, Malek. "Contesting Space: Gendered Discourse and Labor among Lebanese Women." In *Geographies of Muslim Women*, edited by Ghazi Falah and Caroline Nagel, 249–74. New York: Guilford, 2005.

———. *Militant Women of a Fragile Nation*. Syracuse, NY: Syracuse University Press, 2010.

———. "Shi'ite Peasants and a New Nation in Colonial Lebanon: The *Intifada* (Uprising) of Bint Jubayl, 1936." *Comparative Studies of South Asia, Africa, and the Middle East* 29, no. 3 (November 2009): 483–501.

———. "Syrian–Lebanese Communism and the National Question, 1924–1968." Master's thesis, City College, City University of New York, 1992.

Abisaab, Jurdi Rula. "The *'Ulama* of Jabal 'Amil in Safavid Iran, 1501–1736: Marginality, Migration, and Social Change." *Iranian Studies* 27, nos. 1–4 (1994): 103–22.

———. "Shi'ite Beginnings and Scholastic Tradition in Jabal 'Amil in Lebanon." *Muslim World* 89, no. 1 (January 1999): 1–21.

———. *Converting Persia: Religion and Power in the Safavid Empire, 1501–1736*. London: I. B. Tauris, 2004.

———. *Encyclopaedia Iranica*, s.v. "Shi'ite 'ulama' of Jabal 'Amel," 1–7.

———. "The Cleric as Organic Intellectual: Revolutionary Shi'ism in the Lebanese *Hawzas*." In *Distant Relations: Iran and Lebanon in the Last 500 Years*, edited by Houchang E. Chehabi, 231–58. London: Center for Lebanese Studies and I. B. Tauris, 2006.

———. "From the Shi'ite *Hawza* to Marxism: 'Amili Interpretations of Anti-Colonial Modernism, 1920–1950." Paper presented at the Conference for Middle East Studies, Boston, 2006.

———. "Deconstructing the Modular and the Authentic: Husayn Muroeh's Early Islamic History." *Critique: Critical Middle Eastern Studies* 17, no. 3 (Fall 2008): 239–59.

———. "Lebanese Shi'ites and the Marja'iyya: Polemic in the Late Twentieth Century." *British Journal of Middle Eastern Studies* 36, no. 2 (August 2009): 215–39.

———. "The Shi'ite 'Ulama', the Madrasas, and Educational Reform in the Late Ottoman Period." *Ottoman Studies*, no. 36 (2010): 155–83.

Abou-El-Haj, Rifa'at. *Formation of the Modern State: The Ottoman Empire, Sixteenth to Eighteenth Centuries.* 2nd ed. Syracuse, NY: Syracuse University Press, 2005.

Abu Khalil, As'ad. "Against the Taboos of Islam: Anti-Conformist Tendencies in Contemporary Arab/Islamic Thought." In *Between the State and Islam*, edited by Charles E. Butterworth and I. William Zartman, 110–33. Cambridge: Cambridge University Press, 2001.

———. "Hizbullah in Lebanon: Islamisation of Leninist Organizational Principles." *Middle Eastern Studies* 27, no. 3 (July 1991): 390–403.

Ajami, Fouad. *The Vanished Imam: Musa al-Sadr and the Shia of Lebanon.* Ithaca, NY: Cornell University Press, 1986.

Akarli, Deniz Engin. *The Long Peace: Ottoman Lebanon, 1861–1920.* Berkeley: University of California Press, 1993.

Alagha, Joseph. "Hizbullah and Martyrdom." *Orient* 45, nos. 1–4 (2004): 54–67.

———. "Hizbullah's Conception of the Islamic State." In *Les mondes chiites et l'Iran*, edited by Sabrina Mervin, 87–112. Beirut: Karthala et IFPO, 2007.

Alexander, Jeffrey C. *The Civil Sphere.* Oxford: Oxford University Press, 2006.

'Ali, Yusuf Abdallah. *The Holy Qur'an: English Translation of the Meanings and Commentary.* Al-Madina al-Munawwara, Saudi Arabia: King Fahd Holy Qur'an Print Complex, 1990.

Allawi, A. Ali. *The Occupation of Iraq: Winning the War, Losing the Peace.* New Haven, CT: Yale University Press, 2007.

Amanat, Abbas. "Meadow of the Martyrs: Kashifi's Persianization of Shi'i Martyrdom in Late Timurid Herat." In *Culture and Memory in Medieval Islam: Essays in Honor of Wilfred Madelung*, edited by Farhad Daftari and Josef W. Meri, 250–75. London: I. B.Tauris, 2003.

Anderson, J. N. D. "A Draft Code of Personal Law for 'Iraq." *Bulletin of the School of Oriental and African Studies* 15, no. 1 (1953): 43–60.

Appadurai, Arjun. "Disjuncture and Difference in the Global Cultural Economy." In *The Globalization Reader*, edited by Frank J. Lechner and John Boli, chapter 13. Oxford: Blackwell, 2004.

"Arabs Boycott U.S. Goods Against American Mideast Policies." Associated Press, July 28, 2002.

Arjomand, Said Amir. *Authority and Political Culture in Shiism*. Albany: State University of New York Press, 1988.

———. "Authority in Shi'ism and Constitutional Developments in the Islamic Republic of Iran." In *The Twelver Shia in Modern Times,* edited by Rainer Brunner and Werner Ende, 301–32. Boston: Brill, 2001.

———. *The Shadow of God and the Hidden Imam: Religion, Political Order, and Societal Change in Shi'ite Iran from the Beginning to 1890*. Chicago: University of Chicago Press, 1984.

———. *The Turban for the Crown: The Islamic Revolution in Iran*. New York: Oxford University Press, 1988.

Asad, Talal. *Formations of the Secular: Christianity, Islam, and Modernity.* Palo Alto, CA: Stanford University Press, 2003.

———. *Genealogies of Religion: Discipline and Reasons of Power in Christianity and Islam*. Baltimore: John Hopkins University Press, 1993.

———. "The Idea of an Anthropology of Islam." In *The Social Philosophy of Ernest Gellner,* edited by John A. Hall and Ian Jarvie, 381–404. Amsterdam: Rodolpi, 1996.

Asfour, Y. Edmund. "Industrial Development in Lebanon." *Middle East Economic Papers* (1959): 1–16.

Aziz, M. Talib. "Baqr al-Sadr's Quest for the Marja'iyya." In *The Most Learned of the Shi'a: The Institution of Marja' Taqlid,* edited by Linda S. Walbridge, 140–48. New York: Oxford University Press, 2001.

———. "Fadlallah and the Remaking of the Marja'iyya." In *The Most Learned of the Shi'a: The Institution of Marja' Taqlid,* edited by Linda S. Walbridge, 205–15. New York: Oxford University Press, 2001.

———. "The Role of Muhammad Baqir al-Sadr in Shi'i Political Activism in Iraq from 1958-1980." *International Journal of Middle East Studies* 25, no.2 (1993): 207–22.

Badawi, Abdurrahman. "A Pioneer of Socialism in Islam: Abu Dharr al-Ghifari." *Minbar al-Islam* 2, no. 1 (January 1962): 49–51.

Badran, Tony. "Hizbullah Is Being Elusive on Wilayat al-Faqih." *Now Lebanon,* June 24 2009.

Bahl, Vinay. "Situating and Rethinking Subaltern Studies for Writing Working-Class History." In *History after the Three Worlds*, edited by Arif Dirlik, Vinay Bahl, and Peter Gran, 85–124. Lanham, MD: Rowman & Littlefield, 2000.

Barkey, Karen. *Bandits and Bureaucrats: The Ottoman Route to State Centralization*. Ithaca, NY: Cornell University Press, 1994.

Bashkin, Orit. *The Other Iraq: Pluralism and Culture in Hashimite Iraq*. Palo Alto, CA: Stanford University Press, 2009.

Batatu, Hanna. *The Old Social Classes and the Revolutionary Movements of Iraq: A Study of Iraq's Old Landed and Commercial Classes and of Its Communists, Ba'thists, and Free Officers*. Princeton, NJ: Princeton University Press, 1978.

———. "Shi'i Organizations in Iraq: Al-Da'wah al-Islamiyah and al-Mujahidin." In *Shi'ism and Social Protest*, edited by Juan Cole & Nikki Keddie, 179–200. New Haven, CT: Yale University Press, 1986.

Becherer, Richard. "A Matter of Life and Debt: The Untold Costs of Rafiq Hariri's New Beirut." *Journal of Architecture* 10, no. 1 (February 2005): 1–42.

Beinin, Joel. "Islamic Responses to the Capitalist Penetration of the Middle East." In *The Islamic Impulse*, edited by Barbara F. Sotowasser, 87–105. Washington, DC: Center for Contemporary Arab Studies, 1987.

Berger, Peter L., and Richard John Neuhaus. "To Empower People: From State to Civil Society." In *The Essential Civil Society Reader*, edited by Don E. Eberly, 143–82. Lanham, MD: Rowman & Littlefield, 2000.

Berman, Joseph Harold. *Faith and Order: The Reconciliation of Law and Religion*. Grand Rapids, MI: Eerdmans, 2000.

Bertucci, Guido, and Adriana Alberti. *Globalization and the Role of the State: Challenges and Perspectives*. United Nations World Public Sector Report 2001. New York: United Nations, 2001.

"Biography of His Eminence, the Secretary General, Sayyid Hassan Nasrallah." *Mawqi' al-Muqawama al-Islamiyya fi Lubnan*, accessed March 20, 2008.

Bishara, 'Azmi. "Israel at a Loss." *Al-Ahram Weekly On-line*, August 2006.

Böttcher, Annabelle. "Ayatollah Fadlallah und seine Wohltaetigkeits organisation al-Mabarrat." In *Islamstudien Ohne Ende, Festschrift für Werner Ende zum 65. Geburtstag, Abhandlungen fur die Kunde des Morgenlandes 54.1*, edited by Rainer Brunner, M. Gronka, J. P. Laut, and U. Rebstock, 41–47. Würzburg, Germany: Ergon, 2002.

———. "Sunni and Shi'i Networking in the Middle East." In *Shaping the Current Islamic Reformation*, edited by Barbara Allen Roberson, 41–62. London: Frank Cass, 2003.

Browers, Michaelle. *Democracy and Civil Society in Arab Political Thought: Transcultural Possibilities*. Syracuse, NY: Syracuse University Press, 2006.

Brumberg, Daniel. *Reinventing Khomeini: The Struggle for Reform in Iran*. Chicago: University of Chicago Press, 2001.

Brunner, Rainer. *Islamic Ecumenism in the 20th Century: Al-Azhar and Shiism Between Rapproachment and Restraint*. Leiden: Brill, 2004.

Buckley, Ron. "The Imam Ja'far al-Sadiq, Abu'l-Khattab, and the 'Abbasids." *Der Islam* 79, no. 1 (2002): 137–40.

Calhoun, Craig J. "Concluding Remarks." In *Habermas and the Public Sphere*, edited by Craig J. Calhoun, 462–80. Cambridge, MA: MIT Press, 1992.

———, ed. *Habermas and the Public Sphere*. Cambridge, MA: MIT Press, 1992.

———. "Introduction: Habermas and the Public Sphere." In *Habermas and the Public Sphere*, edited by Craig J. Calhoun, 1–48. Cambridge, MA: MIT Press, 1992.

Calhoun, Craig J., and Joseph Gerteis. *Classical Sociological Theory*. 2nd ed. Malden, MA: Blackwell, 2007.

Casanova, Jose. *Public Religions in the Modern World*. Chicago: University of Chicago Press, 1994.

———. "The Secular, Secularizations, Secularisms." In *Rethinking Secularism*, edited by Craig J. Calhoun, Mark Juergensmeyer, and Jonathan Van Antwerpen, 54–74. Oxford: Oxford University Press, 2011.

Chaib, Kinda. "Le Hezbollah libanais a travers ses images: La représentation du martyr." In *Les mondes chiites et l'Iran*, edited by Sabrina Mervin, 113–32. Paris: Karthala, 2007.

Chalabi, Tamara. *The Shi'is of Jabal 'Amil and the New Lebanon: Community and Nation-State, 1918-1943*. New York: Palgrave Macmillan, 2006.

Chehabi, Houchang. "The Anti-shah Opposition and Lebanon." In *Distant Relations: Iran and Lebanon in the Last 500 Years*, edited by Houchang Chehabi, 180–98. London: Centre for Lebanese Studies and I. B. Tauris, 2006.

———. "Iran and Lebanon after Khomeini." In *Distant Relations: Iran and Lebanon in the Last 500 Years*, edited by Houchang Chehabi, 287–308. London: I. B. Tauris, 2006.

———. "Iran and Lebanon in the Revolutionary Decade." In *Distant Relations: Iran and Lebanon in the Last 500 Years*, edited by Houchang Chehabi, 201–30. London: Centre for Lebanese Studies and I. B. Tauris, 2006.

———. *Iranian Politics and Religious Modernism: The Liberation Movement of Iran under the Shah and Khomeini*. London: Centre for Lebanese Studies and I. B. Tauris, 1990.

Chehabi, Houchang, ed. *Distant Relations: Iran and Lebanon in the Last 500 Years.* London: Centre for Lebanese Studies and I. B. Tauris, 2006.

Houchang Chehabi, and Majid Tafreshi. "Musa Sadr and Iran." In *Distant Relations: Iran and Lebanon in the Last 500 Years,* edited by Houchang Chehabi, 137–61. London: Centre for Lebanese Studies and I. B. Tauris, 2006.

Chiha, Michel. *Politique interieure.* Beirut: Editions du Trident, 1964.

Churchill, Charles. "Village Life of the Central Beqaʿ Valley of Lebanon." *Middle East Economic Papers* (1959): 1–48.

Cleveland, William. *A History of the Modern Middle East.* Boulder, CO: Westview Press, 2000.

Cole, Juan. *The Ayatollahs and Democracy in Iraq.* ISIM Papers. Leiden: Amsterdam University Press, 2005.

———. "Millennialism in Modern Iranian History." In *Imagining the End: Visions of Apocalypse from the Ancient Middle East to Modern America,* edited by Abbas Amanat and Magnus Thorkel Bernhardsson, 282–311. London: I. B. Tauris, 2002.

———. *Sacred Space and Holy War: The Politics and History of Shiite Islam.* London: I. B. Tauris, 2002.

Crone, Patricia. *God's Rule: Government and Islam.* New York: Columbia University Press, 2005.

Dabashi, Hamid. *Islamic Liberation Theology: Resisting the Empire.* London: Routledge, 2008.

———. "The Onslaught of Colonialism: An Appendix to 'The End of Islamic Ideology.'" *Social Research* 67, no. 2 (Summer 2000): 475–518.

———. *Theology of Discontent: The Ideological Foundations of the Islamic Revolution in Iran.* New York: New York University Press, 1993.

Daftary, Farhad. *The Ismaʿilis: Their History and Doctrines.* Cambridge: Cambridge University Press, 2007.

Davis, Eric. *Memories of State: Politics, History, and Collective Identity in Modern Iraq.* Berkeley: University of California Press, 2005.

Dawahare, D. Michael. *Civil Society and Lebanon: Toward a Hermeneutic Theory of the Public Sphere.* Parkland, FL: Brown Walker Press, 2000.

Deeb, Lara. "Deconstructing a 'Hizbullah Stronghold.'" *MIT Electronic Journal of Middle East Studies,* no. 6 (Summer 2006): 115–25.

———. *An Enchanted Modern: Gender and Public Piety in Shiʿi Lebanon.* Princeton, NJ: Princeton University Press, 2006.

Deleuze, Gilles. *Foucault.* Translated by Sean Hand. London: Athlone, 1988.

Douglas, Mary. *Purity and Danger: An Analysis of Concepts of Pollution and Taboo.* London: Routledge, 2002.

Early, Evelyn. "The 'Amiliyya Society of Beirut: A Case Study of an Emerging Urban Za'im." Master's thesis, American University of Beirut, 1971.

Eickelman, F. Dale, and Jon W. Anderson, eds. *New Media in the Muslim World: The Emerging Public Sphere.* Bloomington: Indiana University Press, 1999.

"The Electoral Program of Hizbullah, 1996." *Al-Mashriq*, June 20, 1997.

Eley, Jeff. "Nations, Publics, and Political Cultures: Placing Habermas in the Nineteenth Century." In *Habermas and the Public Sphere*, edited by Craig J. Calhoun, 289–339. Cambridge, MA: MIT Press, 1992.

Elias. "Hizbullah Fighting under the Leadership of Imam Khamene'i: Interview with Sayyid Hasan Nasrallah, Secretary General of Hizbullah in Lebanon." *Der Spiegel* (Hamburg), October 20, 1997.

Esposito, John L. "Islam and Civil Society." In *Modernizing Islam: Religion in the Public Sphere in Europe and the Middle East*, edited by John L. Esposito and François Burgat, 69–96. New Brunswick, NJ: Rutgers University Press, 2003.

Euben, Leslie Roxanne, and Muhammad Qasim Zaman, eds. *Princeton Readings in Islamist Thought.* Princeton, NJ: Princeton University Press, 2009.

Farouk-Sluglett, Marion, and Peter Sluglett. *Iraq since 1958: From Revolution to Dictatorship.* New York: Routledge, 1987.

Farsoun, Samih. "Student Protests and the Coming Crisis in Lebanon." *MERIP Reports*, no. 19 (1973): 3–14.

Firro, Kais. *Inventing Lebanon: Nationalism and the State under the Mandate.* London: I. B. Tauris, 2003.

———. "Lebanese Nationalism versus Arabism: From Bulus Nujaym to Michel Chiha." *Middle Eastern Studies* 40, no. 5 (September 2004): 1–27.

Fitzpatrick, Sheila. *Education and Social Mobility in the Soviet Union, 1921–1934.* Cambridge: Cambridge University Press, 2002.

Flores, Alexander. "The Arab CPs and the Palestinian Problem." *Khamsin*, no. 7 (1980): 21–40.

Flyvbjerg, Bent. "Habermas and Foucault: Thinkers for Civil Society?" *British Journal of Sociology* 49, no. 2 (June 1998): 210–33.

Foucault, Michel, and Paul Rabinow, ed. *The Foucault Reader.* New York: Random House, 1984.

Franzén, Johan. "Education and the Radicalization of Iraqi Politics: Britain, the Iraqi Communist Party, and the 'Russian Link,' 1941–49." *International Journal of Contemporary Iraqi Studies* 2, no. 1 (2008): 99–113.

Fraser, Nancy. "Rethinking the Public Sphere: A Contribution to the Critique of Actually Existing Democracy." In *Habermas and the Public Sphere*, edited by Craig J. Calhoun, 109–42. Cambridge, MA: MIT Press, 1992.

Fortna, C. Benjamin. *Imperial Classroom: Islam; the State, and Education in the Late Ottoman Empire*. Oxford: Oxford University Press, 2002.

Gabbay, Rony. *Communism and Agrarian Reform in Iraq*. London: Croom Helm, 1978.

Gaspar, Gaspar K. *A Political Economy of Lebanon, 1948–2002: The Limits of Laissez-Faire*. Leiden: Brill, 2004.

Gellner, Ernest. *Conditions of Liberty: Civil Society and Its Revivals*. London: Penguin Books, 1994.

———. "Islam and Marxism: Some Comparisons." In *Islam: Critical Concepts in Sociology*, edited by Bryan S. Turner, 24–30. London: Routledge, 2004.

———. *Muslim Society*. Cambridge: Cambridge University Press, 1983.

———. *Postmodernism, Reason, and Religion*. London: Routledge, 1992.

Gendzier, Irene. "Exporting Death as Democracy: An Essay on U.S. Foreign Policy in Lebanon." *MIT Electronic Journal of Middle East Studies* 6 (Summer 2006): 177–87.

Gilsenan, Michael. *Lords of the Lebanese Marches: Violence and Narrative in Arab Society*. London: I. B. Tauris, 1996.

Gonzalez-Quijano, Yves. "The Birth of a Media Ecosystem: Lebanon in the Internet Age." In *New Media in the Muslim World: The Emerging Public Sphere*, edited by Dale F. Eickelman and Jon W. Anderson, 61–79. Bloomington: Indiana University Press, 2003.

Gramsci, Antonio. *Prison Notebooks*. New York: Columbia University Press, 1992.

Gran, Peter. *Beyond Eurocentrism: A New View of Modern World History*. Syracuse, NY: Syracuse University Press, 1996.

———. "The Failure of Social Theory to Keep Up with Our Times: The Study of Women and Structural Adjustment Programs in the Middle East as an Example." Paper presented at the 34th annual conference of the Association of Muslim Social Scientist, Temple University, September 30, 2005.

———. "Islamic Marxism in Comparative History: The Case of Lebanon, Reflections on the Recent Work of Husayn Muruwah." In *The Islamic Impulse*, edited by Barbara Stowasser, 106–20. Washington, DC: Croom Helm and Georgetown University, 1987.

———. *Islamic Roots of Capitalism: Egypt 1760–1840*. Syracuse, NY: Syracuse University Press, 1998.

————. "Modern Middle East History beyond Oriental Despotism, World History beyond Hegel: An Agenda Article." In *New Frontiers in the Social History of the Middle East*, edited by Enid Hill, 162–98. Cairo Papers in Social Science 23, no. 2. Cairo: American University in Cairo Press, 2001.

————. *The Rise of the Rich: A New View of Modern World History*. Syracuse, NY: Syracuse University Press, 2009.

Habermas, Jürgen. *The Philosophical Discourse of Modernity: Twelve Lectures*. Translated by Frederick G. Lawrence. Cambridge, MA: MIT Press, 1990.

————. *The Structural Transformation of the Public Sphere: An Inquiry into a Category of Bourgeois Society*. Translated by Thomas Berger with the assistance of Frederick Lawrence. Boston: MIT Press, 1991.

Habib, Osama. "Fneish Wants to Spark Electric Revival." *Daily Star*, June 12, 2006.

Haddad, Yazbek Ynonne. *Contemporary Islam and the Challenge of History*. Albany: State University of New York Press, 1982.

Haj, Samira. *The Making of Iraq, 1900–1963: Capital, Power, and Ideology*. Albany, NY: State University of New York Press, 1997.

————. *Reconfiguring Islamic Tradition: Reform, Rationality, and Modernity*. Palo Alto, CA: Stanford University Press, 2009.

Hakim, George. "Industry." In *Economic Organization of Syria*, edited by Sa'id Himadeh, 117–50. Beirut: American Press, 1936.

Halawi, Majed. *A Lebanon Defied: Musa al-Sadr and the Shi'a Community*. Boulder, CO: Westview Press, 1992.

Hall, John A. *Powers and Liberties: The Causes and Consequences of the Rise of the West*. Harmondsworth, UK: Penguin, 1985.

Hallaq, Wael. *The Impossible State: Islam, Politics, and Modernity's Moral Predicament*. New York: Columbia University Press, 2012.

————. *An Introduction to Islamic Law*. Cambridge: Cambridge University Press, 2009.

————. *The Origins and Evolution of Islamic Law*. Cambridge: Cambridge University Press, 2005.

————. "What Is Shari'a?" In *Yearbook of Islamic and Middle Eastern Law, 2005–2006*, vol. 12. Leiden: Brill, 2007.

Halm, Heinz. *Shi'a Islam: From Religion to Revolution*. Princeton, NJ: Markus Wiener, 1997.

Hamzeh, Nizar Ahmad. *In the Path of Hizbullah*. Syracuse, NY: Syracuse University Press, 2004.

―――. "Lebanon's Hizballah: From Islamic Revolution to Parliamentary Accommodation." *Third World Quarterly* 14, no. 2 (1993): 321–27.

Harb, Mona. "Pious Entertainment in Beirut: Al-Saha Traditional Village." *ISIM Review*, no. 17 (Spring 2006): 10–11.

Harb, Mona, and Reinoud Leenders. "Know Thy Enemy: Hizbullah, 'Terrorism,' and the Politics of Perception." *Third World Quarterly* 26, no.1 (2005): 173–97.

Hardt, Michael, and Antonio Negri. *Empire*. Cambridge, MA: Harvard University Press, 2000.

Harik, Judith. *Hezbollah: The Changing Face of Terrorism*. London: I. B. Tauris, 2004.

Hartman, Michelle, and Alesandro Olsaretti. "'The First Boat and the First Oar'": Inventions of Lebanon in the Writings of Michel Chiha." *Radical History Review* 86, no. 1 (Spring 2003): 37–65.

Harvey, David. *The Condition of Postmodernity: An Inquiry into the Origins of Cultural Change*. Oxford: Blackwell, 1990.

Hefner, W. Robert. *Civil Islam: Muslims and Democratization in Civil Islam*. Princeton, NJ: Princeton University Press, 2000.

Hegel, Georg. *Philosophy of History*. Translated by J. Sibree. New York: Dover, 1956.

―――. *Philosophy of Right*. Translated by T. M. Knox. London: Oxford University Press, 1952.

Herbert, David. *Religion and Civil Society: Rethinking Public Religion in the Contemporary World*. Aldershot, UK: Ashgate, 2003.

Hersh, M. Seymour. "Watching Lebanon: Washington's Interests in Israel's War." *New Yorker*, August 21, 2006, 1–6.

"Hizbullah's Successful Prisoner Swap Promotes Armed Struggle." *Daily Star*, July 22, 2008.

Hobsbawm, J. Eric. *The Age of Empire, 1875–1914*. New York: Pantheon Books, 1987.

Hodgson, G. S. Marshall. "How Did the Early Shi'a Become Sectarian?" *Journal of the American Oriental Society* 75, no. 1 (January–March 1955): 11–13.

Hoogland, James Eric. *Twenty Years of Islamic Revolution: Political and Social Transition in Iran*. Syracuse, NY: Syracuse University Press, 2002.

El-Hosseini, Rola. "Women, Work, and Political Participation in Lebanese Shi'a Contemporary Thought: The Writings of Ayatollahs Fadlallah and Shams al-Din." *Comparative Studies of South Africa and the Middle East* 28, no. 2 (2008): 273–82.

Hourani, Albert. *Arabic Thought in the Liberal Age: 1798–1939.* New York: Cambridge University Press, 1983.

Hovespian, Nubar. *The War on Lebanon: A Reader.* Charles City, VA: Olive Branch Press, 2008.

Hudson, C. Michael. "Trying Again: Power-Sharing in Post–Civil War Lebanon." *International Negotiation* 2, no. 1 (1997): 103–22.

———. *The Precarious Republic: Political Modernization in Lebanon.* New York: Random House, 1968.

Human Rights Watch. "Israeli Cluster Munitions Hit Civilians in Lebanon." July 23, 2006.

Huntington, Samuel. *The Clash of Civilizations and Remaking of World Order.* New York: Simon and Schuster, 1997.

Inda, Jonathan Xavier, and Renato Rosaldo. *The Anthropology of Globalization.* Malden, MA: Blackwell, 2008.

International Finance Corporation, World Bank. *A Diagnostic Study on the Demand for Financial Services by Micro and Small Entrepreneurs.* Washington, DC: World Bank, July 2008.

Ismael, Y. Tareq. *The Rise and Fall of the Communist Party of Iraq.* Cambridge: Cambridge University Press, 2008.

Issawi, Charles. "Economic Development and Liberalism in Lebanon." *Middle East Journal* 18, no. 3 (Summer 1964): 279–92.

———. *The Fertile Crescent, 1800–1914: A Documentary Economic History.* Oxford: Oxford University Press, 1988.

Al-Jabbar, Faleh A. *The Shi'ite Movement in Iraq.* London: Saqi, 2003.

Jaber, Hala. *Hezbollah: Born with a Vengeance.* New York: Columbia University Press, 1997.

Jaber, Talal. "Le Discours Shi'ite sur le Pouvoir." *Peuples Méditerranéens* 78, no. 20, Revue trimestrielle (July–September 1982): 75–92.

Joseph, Suad. "Civic Myths, Citizenship, and Gender in Lebanon." In *Gender and Citizenship in the Middle East,* edited by Suad Joseph, 107–36. Syracuse, NY: Syracuse University Press, 2000.

———. "The Politicization of Religious Sects in Borj Hammoud, Lebanon." PhD dissertation, Columbia University, 1975.

"Junblat Accuses Hizbullah of Creating Parallel State." *Naharnet,* January 21, 2008.

Kamali, Masoud. "Civil Society and Islam: A Sociological Perspective." In *Islam: Critical Concepts in Sociology,* vol. 2. Edited by Bryan S. Turner. London: Routledge, 2004.

Karyergatian, Vahe. "Monopoly in the Lebanese Tobacco Industry." Master's thesis, American University of Beirut, 1965.

Kaufman, Asher. *Reviving Phoenicia: In Search of Identity in Lebanon.* London: I. B.Tauris, 2004.

Kelidar, A. R. "Aziz al-Haj: A Communist Radical." In *The Integration of Modern Iraq,* edited by Abbas Kelidar, 183–92. London: Croom Helm, 1979.

Al-Khafaji, Isam. *Tormented Births: Passages to Modernity in Europe and the Middle East.* London: I. B. Tauris, 2004.

Khalaf, Samir. *Civil and Uncivil Violence: A History of the Internalization of Communal Conflict.* New York: Columbia University Press, 2002.

———. *Lebanon's Predicament.* New York: Columbia University Press, 1987.

Khalidi, Tarif. "Shaykh Ahmad 'Arif al-Zayn and *al-'Irfan.*" In *Intellectual Life in the Arab East, 1890–1939,* edited by Marwan Buheiry, 110–24. Beirut: American University of Beirut Press, 1981.

Khalidi, Walid. *Conflict and Violence in Lebanon: Confrontation in the Middle East.* Cambridge, MA: Center for International Affairs, Harvard University, 1979.

Khalili, Laleh. *Heroes and Martyrs of Palestine: The Politics of National Commemoration.* Cambridge: Cambridge University Press, 2007.

———. "'Standing with My Brother': Hizbullah, Palestinians, and the Limits of Solidarity." *Comparative Studies in Society and History* 49, no. 2 (April 2007): 276–303.

Khomeini, Imam [Ruhollah]. *Islam and Revolution: Writings and Declarations of Imam Khomeini.* Translated and annotated by Hamid Algar. Berkeley: Mizan Press, 1981.

Khoury, S. Philip. "Continuity and Change in Syrian Political Life: The Nineteenth and Twentieth Centuries." *American Historical Review* 96, no. 5 (December 1991): 1374–95.

Khuri, I. Fuad. "The Changing Class Structure in Lebanon." *Middle East Journal* 23, no. 1 (Winter 1969): 29–44.

Kim, Ho. *Max Weber's Politics of Civil Society.* Cambridge: Cambridge University Press, 2004.

Kiwan, Fadia. "Consolidation ou recomposition de la société civile d'après-guerre." In *Liban, état et société: la reconstruction difficile,* edited by Ghassan El-Ezzi. Special issue of *Confluences Méditerranée,* no. 47 (Autumn 2003): 67–78.

Klaus, Dorothée. *Palestinian Refugees in Lebanon: Where to Belong?* Berlin: Schwarz, 2003.

Hans Kohn, *Nationalism and Imperialism in the Hither East.* London: George Routledge and Sons, 1932.

Kollock, Paige. "The Shiʻa Political Elite: Talking to Ziad Majed." *Now Lebanon,* January 30, 2011.

Kumar, Krishan. "Civil Society: An Inquiry into the Usefulness of a Historical Term." *British Journal of Sociology* 44, no. 3 (September 1993): 375–95.

Laurens, Henry. *La Question de Palestine, tome 1: 1922–1947.* Paris: Fayard, 1999.

Lawson, Todd. "Fatima's Religious Authority in an Early Work by the Bab." In *The Most Learned of the Shiʻa: The Institution of Marjaʻ al-Taqlid,* edited by Linda S. Walbridge, 94–127. New York: Oxford University Press, 2001.

"Lebanon's Mobile Phone Boycott." *Daily Star,* July 16, 2004.

Lenin, Il'ich Vladimir. *Religion.* Bristol, UK: Burleigh Press, 2007.

Litvak, Meir. *Shiʻi Scholars of Nineteenth Century Iraq: The ʻUlama of Najaf and Karbala.* Cambridge: Cambridge University Press, 2002.

Lobkowicz, Nikolaus. "Karl Marx's Attitude toward Religion." *Review of Politics* 26, no. 3 (July 1964): 319–52.

Lockman, Zachary. *Contending Visions of the Middle East: The History and Politics of Orientalism.* Cambridge: Cambridge University Press, 2004.

Longrigg, Hemsley Stephen. *Syria and Lebanon under French Mandate.* Oxford: Oxford University Press, 1958.

Louer, Laurence. *Transnational Shia Politics: Religious and Political Networks in the Gulf.* New York: Columbia University Press, 2008.

Löwy, Michael. *Redemption and Utopia: Jewish Libertarian Thought in Central Europe: A Study in Elective Affinity.* Translated by Hope Heaney. Palo Alto, CA: Stanford University Press, 1992.

Luizard, Jean-Pierre. "The Nature of the Confrontation Between the State and Marjaʻism: Grand Ayatollah Muhsin al-Hakim and the Baʻth." In *Ayatollahs, Sufis and Ideologues: State, Religion and Social Movements in Iraq,* edited by Faleh Abd al-Jabbar, 90–100. London: Saqi, 2002.

Madelung, Wilfred. "Authority in Twelver Shiism in the Absence of the Imam." In *La notion d'autorité au Moyen Age: Islam, Byzance, Occident,* edited by George Makdisi, D. Sourdel, and J. Sourdel-Thomme, 163–73. Paris: Presses Universitaires de France, 1982.

———. *The Succession to Muhammad.* Cambridge: Cambridge University Press, 1997.

Makdisi, George. *The Rise of Colleges: Institutions of Learning in Islam and the West.* Edinburgh: Edinburgh University Press, 1981.

———. "Scholasticism and Humanism in Classical Islam and the Christian West." *Journal of the American Oriental Society* 109, no. 2 (April–June 1989): 175–82.

Makdisi, Ussama. "After 1860: Debating Religion, Reform, and Nationalism in the Ottoman Empire." *International Journal of Middle Eastern Studies* 34, no. 4 (November 2002): 601–17.

———. *The Culture of Sectarianism: Community, History, and Violence in Nineteenth-Century Ottoman Lebanon.* Berkeley: University of California Press, 2000.

———. "Moving beyond Orientalist Fantasy, Sectarian Polemic, and Nationalist Denial." *International Journal of Middle Eastern Studies* 40, no. 4 (November 2008): 559–60.

———. "Reconsctructing the Nation-State: The Modernity of Sectarianism in Lebanon." *Middle East Report*, no. 200 (July–September 1996): 23–30.

Maktabi, Rania. "The Lebanese Census of 1932 Revisited: Who Are the Lebanese?" *British Journal of Middle Eastern Studies* 26, no. 2 (November 1999): 219–41.

Mallat, Chibli. "Muhammad Baqer as-Sadr." In Ali Rahnema, *Pioneers of Islamic Revival*, 251–72. London: Zed Books, 1988.

———. *The Renewal of Islamic Law: Muhammad Baqir as-Sadr, Najaf, and the Shi'i International.* Cambridge: Cambridge University Press, 1993.

———. "Shi'ism and Sunnism in Iraq: Revisiting the Codes." In *Islamic Family Law*, edited by Chibli Mallat and Jane Frances Connors, 71–92. Newcastle, UK: Athenaeum Press, 1990.

Marcinkowski, Ismail M., and Hamid Algar. *Religion and Politics in Iraq: Muslim Shia Clerics Between Quietism and Resistance.* Singapore: Pustaka Nasional, 2004.

Masri, Rania. "The Human Impact of the Environment in Lebanon." November 1995. http://almashriq.hiof.no/lebanon/300/360/363/363.7/humanimp2.html.

McCarthy, Thomas. "Practical Discourse: On the Relation of Morality to Politics." In *Habermas and the Public Sphere*, edited by Craig J. Calhoun, 51–72. Cambridge, MA: MIT Press, 1992.

Modarressi, Hossein. *Introduction to Shi'i Law.* London: Ithaca Press, 1994.

Moïsi, Dominique. "The Clash of Emotions." In *The Clash of Civilizations? The Debate*, edited by James F. Hoge Jr., 120–30. New York: Council on Foreign Relations, 2010.

Momen, Moojan. *Introduction to Shi'i Islam*. New Haven, CT: Yale University Press, 1985.

Moos, Olivier. "Lebanon: Hizbullah, a Progressive Islamic Party?—Interview with Joseph Alagha." *Religioscope*, May 17, 2007, 2–3.

Moosa, Matti. *The Maronites in History*. Syracuse, NY: Syracuse University Press, 1986.

Mouawad, Youssef. "Civil Society, God, and Cousins: The Case of the Middle East." In *A New Euro-Mediterranean Cultural Identity*, edited by Stefania Panebianco, 108–24. London: Frank Casss, 2003.

"Mufti al-Amin: Amal Gunmen Are Still Occupying My House and Offices." *Now Lebanon*, May 16, 2008.

Muhammad, Ayman. "Sectarian Tension: From Extremists to Moderates." *Conflicts Forum*, October 15, 2008.

Mundy Martha, and Richard Saumarez Smith, eds. *Governing Property, Making the Modern State: Law, Administration, and Production in Ottoman Syria*. London: I. B. Tauris, 2007.

Naef, Silvia. "La presse en tant que moteur du renouveau culturel et littéraire: La revue chiite libanaise al-'Irfan," *Études Asiatiques, revue de la société Suisse-Asie* L2 (1996): 385–97.

———. "Shi-i-Shuyu'i or How to Become a Communist in a Holy City." In *The Twelver Shia in Modern Times: Religious Culture & Political History*, edited by Rainer Burnner and Werner Ende, 255–67. Leiden: Brill, 2001.

Nakamura, Mitsuo, Sharon Siddique, and Omar Farouk Bajunid, eds. *Islam and Civil Society in Southeast Asia*. Tokyo: Sasakawa Peace Foundation, 2001.

Nakash, Yitzhak. *The Shi'is of Iraq*. Princeton, NJ: Princeton University Press, 1994.

Nasr, Salim. "Backdrop to Civil War: The Crisis of Lebanese Capitalism." *MERIP Reports*, no. 73 (December 1978): 3–13.

Nasr, Salim, and Diane James. "Roots of the Shi'i Movement." *MERIP Reports*, no. 133 (June 1985): 10–16.

Nasr, Vali Reza Seyyed. *The Shia Revival: How Conflicts within Islam Will Shape the Future*. New York: W. W. Norton, 2006.

Neilsen, Kai. "Reconceptualizing Civil Society for Now: Some Somewhat Gramscian Turnings." In *Toward a Global Civil Society*, edited by Michael Walzer, 41–68. Providence, RI: Berghahn, 1995.

Nisbet, Robert. "Idea of Progress: A Bibliographical Essay." *Journal of Literature of Liberty: A Review of Contemporary Liberal Thought* 2, no. 1. (January–March 1979): 7–37.

Noe, Nicholas, and Nicholas Blanford, eds. *Voice of Hezbollah: The Statements of Sayed Hassan Nasrallah*. Translated by Ellen Khouri. London: Verso, 2007.

Norton, Augustus Richard. *Amal and the Shiʿa: Struggle for the Soul of Lebanon*. Austin: University of Texas Press, 1987.

———. "Changing Actors and Leadership among the Shiites of Lebanon," *Annals of the American Academy of Political and Social Science* 482, no. 1 (November 1985): 109–21.

———, ed. *Civil Society in the Middle East*. Leiden: Brill, 2001.

———. *Hezbollah: A Short History*. Princeton, NJ: Princeton University Press, 2007.

———. "Hizbullah: From Radicalism to Pragmatism?" *Middle East Policy* 5, no. 4 (January 1998): 147–59.

———. "Making Enemies in South Lebanon: Harakat Amal, the IDF, and South Lebanon." *Middle East Insight* 3, no. 3 (1984): 13–20.

———. "The Shiites and the MNF." In *The Multinational Force in Beirut, 1982–1984*, edited by Anthony McDermott and Kill Skjelsbaek, 226–36. Gainesville: University Press of Florida, 1991.

Ohrstrom, Lysandra. "Some of Fneish's Reforms Left When He Stepped Down." *Daily Star*, March 12, 2007.

Pappe, Ilan. *Britain and the Arab–Israeli Conflict, 1948–51*. Basingstoke, UK: Macmillan, 1988.

———. *The Ethnic Cleansing of Palestine*. Oxford: Oneworld, 2006.

Pasha, Kamal Mustafa. "Globalization, Islam, and Resistance." In *The Globalization Reader*, edited by Frank J. Lechner and John Boli. Malden, MA: Blackwell, 2004.

Persen, William. "Lebanese Economic Development since 1950." *Middle East Journal* 12, no. 3 (Summer 1958): 277–94.

Picaudou, Nadine, ed. *Territoires palestinienes de mémoire*. Beirut: Institut français de Proche-Orient, 2006.

Al-Qazwini, Jawdat. "The School of Najaf." In *Ayatollahs, Sufis, and Ideologues: State, Religion, and Social Movements in Iraq*, edited by Falih Abd al-Jabbar, 245–81. London: Saqi Books, 2002.

Rafei, Raed. "Hezbollah Finds Friends Abroad." *Los Angeles Times*, August 30, 2008.

Ranstorp, Magnus. *Hizb'allah in Lebanon: The Politics of the Western Hostage Crisis*. New York: St. Martin's Press, 2002.

Rastegar, Kamran. *Literary Modernity between the Middle East and Europe: Textual Transactions in Nineteenth-Century Arabic, English, and Persian Literatures.* New York: Routledge, 2007.

Rees, John. *The Algebra of Revolution: The Dialectic and the Classical Marxist Tradition.* New York: Routledge, 1998.

Reich, Bernard. *Political Leaders of the Contemporary Middle East and North Africa: A Biographical Dictionary.* New York: Greenwood, 1990.

Richards, Allan, and John Waterbury. *A Political Economy of the Middle East: State, Class, and Economic Development.* Boulder, CO: Westview Press, 1990.

Al-Ruhaimi, Abdul-Halim. "The Da'wa Islamic Party: Origins, Actors, and Ideology." In *Ayatollahs, Sufis, and Ideologues: State, Religion, and Social Movements in Iraq,* edited by Falih Abd al-Jabbar, 149–61. London: Saqi Books, 2002.

Ryan, Mary P. "Gender and Public Access: Women's Politics in Nineteenth-Century America." In *Habermas and the Public Sphere,* edited by Craig J. Calhoun, 259–88. Cambridge, MA: MIT Press, 1992.

Saad-Ghorayeb, Amal. *Hizbu'llah: Politics and Religion.* Sterling, VA.: P l u t o Press, 2002.

Al-Sadr, Baqir Muhammad. "The General Framework of the Islamic Economy." In *Princeton Readings in Islamist Thought,* edited by Roxanne Leslie Euben and Muhammad Qasim Zaman, 181–206. Princeton, NJ: Princeton University Press, 2009.

———. *Lessons in Islamic Jurisprudence.* Translated by Roy P. Mottahedeh. Oxford: Oneworld, 2003.

Al-Safadi, Ayman. "Dawlat Hizbullah." *Al-'Arabiyya,* April 13, 2007.

Sahliyeh, F. Emile. *Religious Resurgence and Politics in the Contemporary World.* Albany: State University of New York Press, 1990.

Sajoo, Amyn, ed. *Civil Society in the Muslim World: Contemporary Perspectives.* London: I. B. Tauris, 2002.

Salucci, Ilario. *A People's History of Iraq: The Iraqi Communist Party, Workers' Movements, and the Left, 1924–2004.* Chicago: Haymarket Books, 2005.

Sampson, Philip. "The Rise of Postmodernity." In *Faith and Modernity,* edited by Philip Sampson, Vinay Samuel, and Chris Sugden, 29–57. Oxford: Regnum Books International, 1994.

Sankari, Jamal. *Fadlallah: The Making of a Radical Shi'ite Leader.* London: Saqi Books, 2005.

Segev, Tom. *One Palestine Complete: Jews and Arabs under the British Mandate.* New York: Henry Holt, 2000.

Shaery-Eisenlohr, Roschanack. *Shi'ite Lebanon: Transnational Religion and the Making of National Identities.* New York: Columbia University Press, 2008.

Shah-Kazemi, Reza. *Justice and Remembrance: Introducing the Spirituality of Imam 'Ali.* London: I. B. Tauris, 2007.

Shakir, M. H. *The Qur'an: Hardcover Arabic and English.* 9th ed. N.p.: Tahrike Tarsile Qur'an, 2002.

Shaoul, Jean. "Israel Used Chemical Weapons in Lebanon and Gaza." World Socialist Web Site, October 24, 2006.

Sharara, Waddah. *Transformation d'une manifestation religieuse dans un village du Liban Sud.* Beirut: Centre de recherche de L'Institut des sciences sociales de l'université libanaise, 1968.

Shuman, Batul. "Talawwuth al-hawa'." *Madaris al-Mahdi, al-Majadil,* February 5, 2008.

Al-Solh, Raghid. *Lebanon and Arabism: National Identity and State Formation.* London: Centre for Lebanese Studies in association with I. B.Tauris, 2004.

Somel, Akşin Selçuk. *The Modernization of Public Education in the Ottoman Empire, 1839–1908.* Leiden: Brill, 2001.

Suleiman, Michael. "The Lebanese Communist Party." *Middle Eastern Studies* 3, no. 2 (January 1967): 134–59.

Tavakoli-Targhi, Mohamad. "The Homeless Texts of Persianate Modernity." In *Iran: Between Tradition and Modernity,* edited by Ramin Jahanbegloo. Plymouth, UK: Lexington Books, 2004.

Taylor, Charles. "Western Secularity." In *Rethinking Secularism,* edited by Craig J. Calhoun, Mark Juergensmeyer, and Jonathan Van Antwerpen, 31–53. Oxford: Oxford University Press, 2011.

Thompson, Elizabeth. *Colonial Citizens: Republican Rights, Paternal Privileges, and Gender in French Syria and Lebanon.* New York: Columbia University Press, 2000.

Tibebu, Teshale. *Hegel and the Third World: The Making of Eurocentrism in World History.* Syracuse, NY: Syracuse University Press, 2011.

Tripp, Charles. *A History of Iraq.* Cambridge: Cambridge University Press, 2000.

———. *Islam and the Moral Economy: The Challenge to Capitalism.* Cambridge: Cambridge University Press, 2006.

Tueni, Ghassan. *Une Guerre pour les autres.* Paris: J. C. Lattès, 1985.

Turner, Bryan S., ed. *Islam: Critical Concepts in Sociology*. London: Routledge, 2004.

Varulkar, H. "Radicalization in Hizbullah's Positions Following the Gaza War: Hizbullah Must Be Independent of All State Institutions." *MEMRI*, March 11, 2009, 1–4.

Volk, Lucia. *Memorials and Martyrs in Modern Lebanon*. Bloomington: Indiana University Press, 2010.

Walbridge, John. "Muhammad-Baqir al-Sadr: The Search for New Foundations." In *The Most Learned of the Shi'a: The Institution of Marja' al-Taqlid*, edited by Linda Walbridge, 131–39. New York: Oxford University Press, 2001.

Walbridge, Linda, ed. *The Most Learned of the Shi'a: The Institution of Marja' al-Taqlid*. Oxford: Oxford University Press, 2001.

Wallerstein, Immanuel. "Eurocentrism and Its Avatars: The Dilemmas of Social Science." *New Left Review* 26, no. 1 (November–December 1997): 93–107.

Warn, Mats. "Staying the Course: The 'Lebanonization' of Hizbollah—the Integration of an Islamist Movement into a Pluralist Political System." Master's thesis, Stockholm University, 1999.

Watt, Montgomery W. *Muhammad: Prophet and Statesman*. Oxford: Oxford University Press, 1961.

Weiss, Max. *In the Shadow of Sectarianism: Law, Shi'ism, and the Making of Modern Lebanon*. Cambridge: Cambridge University Press, 2010.

Wiley, Joyce. "'Alima bint al-Huda, Women's Advocate." In *The Most Learned of the Shi'a: The Institution of Marja' al-Taqlid*, edited by Linda Walbridge, 149–60. Oxford: Oxford University Press, 2001.

Winter, Stefan. *The Shiites of Lebanon under Ottoman Rule, 1516–1788*. New York: Cambridge University Press, 2010.

Wrathal, A. Mark, ed. *Religion after Metaphysics*. Cambridge: Cambridge University Press, 2003.

Yusuf 'Ali, 'Abdullah. *The Holy Qur'an: Text, Translation, and Commentary*. New York: Tahrike Tarsile Qur'an, 1998.

Young, Michael. *The Ghosts of Martyrs Square: An Eyewitness Account of Lebanon's Life Struggle*. New York: Simon & Schuster, 2010.

Young, Terri de. *Placing the Poet: Badr Shakir al-Sayyab and Postcolonial Iraq*. Albany: State University of New York Press, 1998.

Zaatari, Zeina. "The Culture of Motherhood: An Avenue for Women's Civil Participation in South Lebanon." *Journal of Middle East Women's Studies* 2, no. 1 (Winter 2006): 33–64.

Zaret, David. "Religion, Science, and Printing in the Public Spheres of England." In *Habermas and the Public Sphere*, edited by Craig J. Calhoun, 212–35. Cambridge, MA: MIT Press, 1992.

Zubaida, Sami. "Is There a Muslim Society? Ernest Gellner's Sociology of Islam." In *Islam: Critical Concepts in Sociology*, edited by Bryan S. Turner, 31–69. London: Routledge, 2004.

———. *Law and Power in the Islamic World*. London: I. B. Tauris, 2005.

Index

Italic page numbers denote illustrations.